P9-DEH-646

MARRIAGE, FAMILY AND RESIDENCE

PAUL BOHANNAN received his B.Sc. and his D.Phil. from Oxford University, which he attended as a Rhodes Scholar. He has taught anthropology at Oxford University and Princeton University and is at present Professor of Anthropology at Northwestern University. Dr. Bohannan has done field research among the Tiv of central Nigeria and the Wanga of Kenya. He is the author of numerous monographs, articles and books, including two volumes in the American Museum Sourcebooks in Anthropology series (for which he is the General Editor): *Law and Warfare* and, with Fred Plog, *Beyond the Frontier*.

JOHN MIDDLETON received his D.Phil. from Oxford in 1953. He has taught anthropology at London, Capetown, and Northwestern universities, and is at present head of the Department of Anthropology at New York University. He has done field research in Uganda, Zanzibar, and Nigeria and has published on the Lugbara of Uganda and the Shirazi of Zanzibar. Dr. Middleton is also the editor of several books, including four other volumes in the American Museum Sourcebooks in Anthropology series: *Myth and Cosmos, Gods and Rituals, Magic, Witchcraft, and Curing,* and, with Ronald Cohen, *Comparative Political Systems*.

American Museum Sourcebooks in Anthropology, under the general editorship of Paul Bohannan, are published for The American Museum of Natural History by the Natural History Press. Directed by a joint editorial board made up of Dr. Bohannan and members of the staff of the Museum and the Natural History Press, this series is an extension of the Museum's scientific and educational activities, making available to the student and general reader inexpensive, up-to-date, and authoritative books in the field of anthropology. The Natural History Press is a division of Doubleday & Company, Inc., and has its editorial offices at The American Museum of Natural History, Central Park West at 79th Street, New York, New York 10024, and its business offices at 501 Franklin Avenue, Garden City, New York.

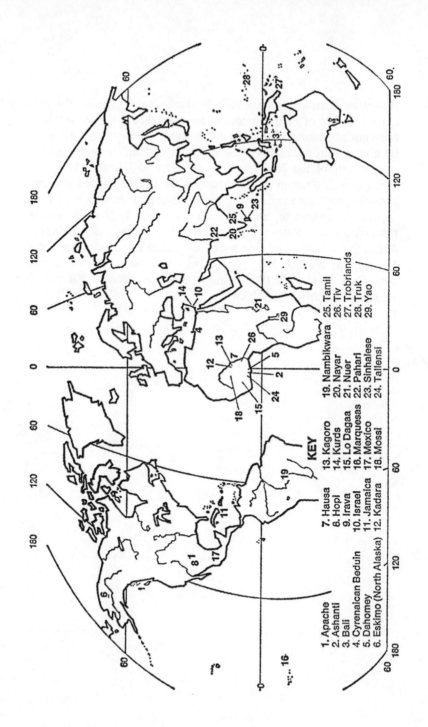

KEY

1. Apache
2. Ashanti
3. Bali
4. Cyrenaican Beduin
5. Dahomey
6. Eskimo (North Alaska)
7. Hausa
8. Hopi
9. Irava
10. Israel
11. Jamaica
12. Kadara
13. Kagoro
14. Kurds
15. Lo Dagaa
16. Marquesas
17. Mexico
18. Mossi
19. Nambikwara
20. Nayar
21. Nuer
22. Pahari
23. Sinhalese
24. Tallensi
25. Tamil
26. Tiv
27. Trobriands
28. Truk
29. Yao

MARRIAGE, FAMILY
AND RESIDENCE

EDITED BY PAUL BOHANNAN
AND JOHN MIDDLETON

AMERICAN MUSEUM SOURCEBOOKS IN ANTHROPOLOGY

PUBLISHED FOR

THE AMERICAN MUSEUM OF NATURAL HISTORY

THE NATURAL HISTORY PRESS

1968 · GARDEN CITY, NEW YORK

The illustrations for this book
were prepared by the Graphic Arts Division of
The American Museum of Natural History

Library of Congress Catalog Card Number 67–22462
Copyright © 1968 by Paul Bohannan and John Middleton
All Rights Reserved
Printed in the United States of America
First Edition

CONTENTS

PART IV THE FAMILY

PART V RESIDENCE AND HOUSEHOLD

PART VI SOME SPECIAL PROBLEMS

INTRODUCTION

HUMAN BEINGS, being mammals, spend an inordinate—but scarcely disproportionate—amount of time involved in institutions whose task is to make into an orderly and predictable entity the expression and control of sexuality, replacement of the population, succession to rights and offices, and education of the young. Murdock (1949: 2) has claimed that the nuclear family is universal in pursuit of these ends, and often other ends as well. Whether or not this universality is more than an epiphenomenon of the mammalian mode of reproduction is open to argument (for, it would seem, many peoples who "have" the nuclear family either fail to recognize it or consider it secondary to other family groupings). But what is not open to argument is that there is a wide variety of ways in which human beings can mate, reproduce, and train the young.

Everywhere, however, there are prohibitions and limits about who can properly mate. Incest regulation, in short, *is* universal, even though the particular kinsmen who are forbidden may vary, and even though the "origin" of incest prohibitions is shrouded in history, conjecture, and contradictory theories. In many societies there are also positive injunctions about whom one *should* marry, and there are widely varying degrees of conformity with such requirements.

The problem of "marriage", when seen cross-culturally, is a problem in discerning what rights in other people are garnered by individuals and by social groups, and what the environing social milieu of a married pair may be. Marriage may be exclusive for either partner or for both—but it may not be. The result is the various forms of marriage: monogamy, polygyny, and polyandry. The importance of these "forms" of marriage is ultimately to be found in the different structures of the family to which they lead. In some societies, arrangements are casual enough that all three forms are found.

A family is a biologically interrelated group of people involving links of descent and links of sexuality. Murdock has claimed that the family must also live together. We demur on the latter point, even though a family usually does, in most societies, form a residential unit. But we think that the form of the residential unit and the form of the family, and their relationships to one another, should be examined overtly rather than merely thrown together by definition.

Finally, the family has to live somewhere in space, and it is the arrangement of families in space—usually called "residence patterns" by anthropologists—that is one of its most important features.

The questions of kinship and descent have been, insofar as it is possible, transferred to another volume so as not to make this one unwieldy. The reasoning is this: "Descent" is, paradoxically enough, both the essence of kinship and the mode in which kinship can be superseded. Descent is the way in which the facts of generational kinship association are utilized not merely for household formation, but for a very much wider range of social control and social phenomena. Here we stick to household, family, and marriage.

We have found, rather to our consternation, that the selections we have made come from a very small number of original sources. At first we thought we ought to spread out and give more material that is less widely known. However, we finally came to the conclusion that we were interested in presenting case material on a subject rather than bringing to light little-known ethnographies. Our selections are well-known for obvious and right reasons. We would necessarily have reduced our range of geography as well as our "pay rate per page" to have chosen more esoteric material.

The arrangement of the book needs a few comments: We have included the most recent good article on incest, and an example of the way particular peoples see incest and distinguish it from exogamy. We have then skipped the whole matter of courtship and gone direct to marriage. We have selected articles that give a good dollop of ethnography at the same time that they question defining "marriage" cross-culturally.

We have included discussions of polyandry (but not polygyny which, interestingly enough, is not—as we write—as well documented and analyzed as is polyandry), and examples of parallel cousin marriage and cross-cousin marriage. We have included two articles on "secondary marriage" but nothing extensive on the difficult problems of concubinage or cicisbeism, per se.

We have treated "the family" as we did marriage, concentrating on articles that both question concepts and give facts. "Residence" has been treated in the same way. There are articles on ritual kinship and the association of family with the other institutions of society.

We have no doubt that our colleagues may argue with us about the selections. We would undoubtedly agree with some of their criticisms. We have consulted a number of people, including the contributors to this book. But we, of course, remain responsible. One-sided our selection undoubtedly is, but we think it is the kind of one-sidedness that any editor faces, not the grinding of axes or projection of our own points of view. We have tried to set before students and professionals a group of papers that are important for their analytical soundness. We cannot claim—nor could anybody else—to have covered the field. The field is very long and very wide, and, it would seem, very shallow.

PAUL BOHANNAN
JOHN MIDDLETON

Evanston, Illinois
1966

MARRIAGE, FAMILY AND RESIDENCE

PART I

INCEST AND EXOGAMY

1 THE INCEST TABOO AND
THE MATING PATTERNS OF ANIMALS

David F. Aberle, Urie Bronfenbrenner, Eckhard H. Hess,
Daniel R. Miller, David M. Schneider, and James N. Spuhler

WE HAVE NOTED a new wave of interest in the theoretical and empirical study of the incest taboo. This is manifested by Slater's (1959) paper and by three papers on the subject at the American Anthropological Association Annual Meetings in 1961: Margaret Mead, "A Re-Examination of the Problem of Incest," Peter J. Wilson, "Incest—A Case Study," and Melvin Ember, "The Incest Taboo and the Nuclear Family." We have felt moved by this activity to present the results of a work group, which met in the spring of 1956 at the Center for Advanced Study in the Behavioral Sciences at Stanford, to consider the problem of the origins of the incest taboo.

The group consisted of the authors and the late Alfred L. Kroeber. After several months of work, the seven members of the group presented a mutually acceptable theoretical formulation at a seminar for Fellows at the Center. We hoped to move on to a well-documented publication, but this has proved impossible.[1] We have been handicapped by our dispersion over several universities and have hitherto been hesitant to publish because we wished to assemble more materials on the limitations of inbreeding in animals and to construct various models of the population genetics of small, inbred groups. Although we have abandoned

Reprinted from *American Anthropologist*, 1963, Vol. 65, No. 2, pp. 253–65, by permission of the authors and the editor of *American Anthropologist*.

[1] Washburn's book (1961) has been consulted, but we have not tried to incorporate relevant new materials. Cohen's paper (1961) has not been read, although kindly made available to us by Cohen. Nor have we seen the papers read by others at the Symposium on Cross-Species Incest Behavior, held a few days after the first draft of the present paper had been completed.

hope of more ample publication, we believe that the current interest in theories of incest justifies the publication of a schematic statement of the approach we developed in 1956. A few minor changes or elaborations of the 1956 seminar are specifically noted.

The incest taboo in any society consists of a set of prohibitions, which outlaw heterosexual relationships between various categories of kinsmen. Almost always, it includes prohibitions on sexual relations between brother and sister, father and daughter, mother and son. Invariably, where any prohibitions are present, other, non-primary relatives are tabooed as well. There are rare cases where the taboos seem to have been abandoned. In the main, these involve very small groups in some way or other isolated from other populations to a degree which makes it impossible to maintain the taboo if the group is to reproduce at all. There are other cases where sexual relations between brother and sister or father and daughter are permitted or prescribed for special categories (e.g., chiefs, kings), or under special circumstances (e.g., ritual). It must be emphasized, however, that in the very societies where these sexual relations are permitted to some people, or under some circumstances, they are forbidden to the bulk of people and under most circumstances. Incest prohibitions are not always obeyed, but we will not attempt here to discuss rates, causes, or consequences of transgressions.

Most theories about the incest taboo attempt to account for its origin and persistence, but especially for the origin and persistence of the taboo on sexual relationships within the nuclear family. (Here and elsewhere, the phrase "sexual relationships within the nuclear family" will refer to sexual relationships between brother and sister, father and daughter, and mother and son. The phrase "familial incest taboo" will refer to the prohibition of these relationships.) It is hard to provide satisfactory support for any theory, which attempts to account for a universal phenomenon. (Thus far, almost no theory of the origin of the incest taboo, which has any currency, has attempted to utilize the exceptions to universality noted above to account for origins. For all practical purposes, virtually all theories treat the familial taboo as a universal in discussing origins. Fortune (1932a) is an exception.) With a little ingenuity, virtually any universal phenomenon can be explained by, or can be used to explain the existence of, any other universal phenomenon in the realm under discussion. There are no criteria save aesthetics and logical consistency for choosing among theories, since there is no possibility of demonstrating that A varies with B, if both A and B are universally and invariably present. Furthermore, most of the theories about the incest taboo provide a demonstration that in one or another sense it is adaptive, and thereby often confuse the question of origin and the question of persistence. It is not logically admissible to assert that a phenomenon has come to exist because it is adaptive: that men grew noses because they support spectacles. It can be said only that if something comes into existence, which has superior adaptive potential, it is likely to be perpetuated or to spread. The question of the cause of its origin, however, remains unsolved.

Our concern, then, was to account for the origin of the incest taboo, and to find a range of phenomena such that the familial incest taboo need not be treated as a universal. This range of phenomena was the mating behavior of humans and certain other animals. Before this mating behavior is discussed, it is necessary to outline some of the theories respecting the origin and persistence of the incest taboo.

(1) *The inbreeding theory.* This theory asserts that the mating of close kin produces bad results, such as abnormal, enfeebled, or insufficiently numerous offspring. The incest taboo is therefore adaptive because it limits inbreeding, and arose on that account [Westermarck (1894: 352–53; 1929: 36–37); Muller (1913) provides information on beliefs of this sort; Morgan (1907: 69) seems to view inbreeding as deleterious, but assumes a prior stage when inbreeding did occur—hence inbreeding was not for Morgan an intolerable state of affairs.]

(2) *The socialization theory.* This theory asserts that the regulation and control of erotic impulses is an indispensable element in socialization—that it serves to maintain the growing child's motivation to accept the roles that he is taught. These roles include extra-familial and society-wide roles as well as those in the nuclear family. Since societies must be larger than a single nuclear family to be viable, and since non-familial roles are different from family roles, these roles in the wider society must be learned by

the child. In order for this learning to occur, the socializing agent must control but not directly gratify the child's erotic impulses. Therefore it is necessary that these impulses be frustrated and directed outside the nuclear family. The incest taboo does this (Parsons 1954; Parsons and Bales 1955: 187–258).

(3) *The family theory.* This theory asserts that unregulated sexual competition is disruptive for any group, that the family is a crucial group, and that the incest taboo is needed to maintain the family intact. The theory asserts that the incest taboo originated because it served this function. Freud, one of the proponents of this theory, made a vigorous effort to imagine the series of events which could have led from promiscuity and unregulated, lethal competition, to the final promulgation of nuclear family taboos (Freud 1950; Malinowski 1927; Malinowski 1931: 630; Seligman 1929, 1950).

(4) *The social and cultural system theory.* This theory asserts that, left to their own devices, human beings would prefer to mate within the family, but that the advantages of a wider group for mutual aid, collective economic security, internal peace, offense and defense, and of a wider group for the sharing of cultural innovations, make family and supra-family exogamy highly adaptive as a device for joining families or larger kinship groups. These advantages would be marked in any kinship-based society but were crucial in early human history. This is so because the first ordered human group to emerge was the family, and the incest taboo and exogamy permitted a society built on existing materials: these devices linked families by bonds developed within the family—the ties of parents and children and of siblings. Because of the strong tendency to mate within the family, the familial incest taboos were necessary to insure exogamy (Tylor 1888: 267; Fortune 1932a; White 1949, 1959: 69–116; Murdock 1949: 284–313). The general theory of the social advantages of exogamy for a culture-bearing animal is to be found in all these writers; the theoretical sequence of development from anthropoid to human social organization is White's (1959); Murdock has stressed the importance of the spread of cultural innovations through marriage ties between families. Fortune has utilized lapses of the taboo among chiefs and kings to support his argument.

(5) *The indifference or revulsion theory.* According to this theory, the incest taboo is either a formal expression of the sexual indifference of kinsmen toward each other, or a formal expression of an instinctive horror of sexual relations among kinsmen. It is principally identified with Edward Westermarck (1894: 352–53, and 1929: 36–37).

(6) *The demographic theory.* This theory holds that for early man, the short life-span, small number of offspring to reach maturity, spacing of those offspring, and random sex ratio made intrafamilial inbreeding a virtual demographic impossibility. Hence very early man bred out by necessity. Later, when technological improvements made for larger families and longer life, and intrafamilial mating became possible, the already existing pattern of familial exogamy was given normative backing through the creation of the familial incest taboo. This taboo sustained a practice advantageous from the point of view of group cooperation. This theory, presented by Slater (1959), was not considered by the 1956 work group.

We omit various theories which center on the role of religious or mystical ideas in determining the specific prohibition on incest, such as those of Durkheim (1898) and Raglan (1933). We do not explicitly consider the numerous composite theories, most of which combine various elements from theories 1–4 to arrive at their conclusions.

We will now discuss various criticisms that have been, or might be directed at each of the six theories. The criticisms themselves are of three types. (1) The adaptive value claimed by the theory for the incest taboo may be rejected. (2) The adaptive value claimed by the theory for the incest taboo may be accepted, but the possibility that the adaptive quality gave rise to the taboo may be disputed. (3) The adaptive value claimed by the theory may be accepted, but the necessity to achieve this result through the incest taboo may be denied.

The inbreeding theory in its simplest form has been rejected for decades because it was thought to be wrong. In its pre-genetic form the inbreeding theory asserted that inbreeding caused a weakening or deterioration of the stock. The facts of genetics provided a simple corrective to this notion. It was found that inbreeding could not produce "deterioration" but could only bring to expression what was already present in the stock, by producing offspring homozygous for some recessive character. Therefore, it was argued, if deleterious recessives were present, they would appear with greater frequency as a result of inbreeding, but if advantageous recessives were present, they would also receive full expression. Thus the disadvantages of inbreeding were offset by the advantages.

This simple corrective, however, does not stand up in the face of new information from the field of population genetics (cf. Lerner 1958; Morton 1961; both of which appeared after the 1956 argument had been developed). First, it has become clear that the ratio of deleterious and lethal recessive genes to selectively advantageous genes is very high indeed. This results from the random character of mutation. Second, as we move from (biologically defined) second cousin matings to first cousin matings to parent-child or sibling matings, both the models of population genetics and the experimental and observational evidence from animals indicate that the reduction of heterozygocity increases rapidly, and hence that the percentage of individuals homozygous for lethal or deleterious recessive genes also rises sharply. The same is true, of course, for adaptive recessive forms. Provided that the species in question can stand the loss of many offspring, close inbreeding can provide a superior strain—superior either from the point of view of adaptation to the environment or from the point of view of a human being practicing the selective breeding of some plant or animal domesticate. But where births are widely spaced, where the animal produces few offspring at a time, or only one, and where the animal reaches reproductive maturity only slowly, the closely inbred population may not be able to stand either culling or natural selection. The abortions, still births, animals incapable of surviving to reproductive maturity, and the animals whose breeding period or capacity to rear their young is drastically shortened, through the inheritance of homozygous, disadvantageous recessive genes, may so reduce the total effective breeding population as to make its survival impossible, or as to result in its expulsion from its niche by an expanding, neighboring population. Close inbreeding of rats is possible over many generations; with chickens the process becomes more difficult; with cattle it seems to be impossible. Thus, in the perspective of population genetics, close inbreeding of an animal like man has definite biological disadvantages, and these disadvantages are far more evident as respects the mating of primary relatives than as respects other matings. Hence the biological advantages of the familial incest taboo cannot be ignored. (Ember, 1961, parallels this argument.)

It is difficult to see, however, how primitive man would come to understand the connection between familial inbreeding and low net reproductive rate or the production of monstrosities. We will return to this point.

It is often argued, however, that since many simple societies regard the marriage of first cross-cousins as highly desirable, the incest taboo by no means eliminates fairly close inbreeding. In this connection we must stress the fact that the familial incest taboo is virtually universal, and that familial inbreeding shows far more effects from the point of view of population genetics than cousin inbreeding.

The socialization theory is difficult to deal with. Fundamentally, it rests on psychoanalytic hypotheses of fixation and regression, which have not yet been fully demonstrated. For this reason we will not attempt to discuss it further here.

The family theory has certain empirical difficulties. It rests on the supposed acute conflict that would arise out of sexual rivalries between father and son over mother and sister, between mother and daughter over father and brother, between brothers over sisters, and sisters over brothers. Yet father and son, mother and daughter, brother and brother, sister and sister do in fact share sexual partners in a number of societies. With polyandry, father and son sometimes share the same wife (but not the son's mother), or brothers share the same wife (but not their sister). With polygyny, mother and daughter sometimes share the same husband (but not the daughter's father), or sisters share the same husband (but not their brother); there are a large number of instances of institutionalized sharing of sexual favors outside the marital bond, as well.

These objections to the family theory do not lead to the conclusion that the family could tolerate *unregulated* intra-familial sexual relations. There is ample evidence that sexual competition is disruptive. But there would seem to be two solutions to the problem of maintaining order within the family, rather than one. The first solution is, of course, the interdiction of sexual relations except for the parents: the familial incest taboo. The second, however, is the institutionalization of sexual access in the family. This would define the time, place, and rate of access of each member of the family to every other. This institutionalization could not be a complete solution for all families. In some families there would be no male offspring, and in others no female. Cohabitation with the parent of opposite sex would temporarily solve this problem, but since children normally outlive their parents, the solution would be only temporary. Nevertheless, it would be possible to adopt this sort of institutionalization as the primary pattern, with secondary alternatives available. Thus, societies with other preferential, or even prescribed mating patterns, must ordinarily afford alternatives to these patterns, or redefine the groups suitable for prescribed alliances over time.

The family theory has one distinctive advantage. It is easy to see how human groups might evolve rules to deal with immediate and obvious potential sources of disruption of social life. If indeed jealousy threatened the integrity of the family, it is possible to conceive of the development of norms to cope with this. And the incest prohibitions of any society constitute a set of conscious norms.

The social and cultural system theory, especially in its evolutionary form, as stated by White, does not raise serious empirical difficulties. It is clear that the advantages postulated by White exist, and that, given a tendency to choose the most easily available mates, a complete prohibition on familial sexual relations is the simplest device for forcing ties between families. His theory seems to assert that because this shift was advantageous, it came into being. Yet, like the family theory, this theory requires a movement in opposition to certain strong trends. It requires the elimination of some younger members from the family, in spite of emotional attachments, and entrusting these members to groups where stable relationships do not yet exist. It also requires that primitive men understand the advantages of the exchange—or else must assume that familial exogamy and the familial taboo arose as a chance "mutation" and survived because of their adaptive character.

The indifference theory has both logical and empirical difficulties. It is hard to see why what is naturally repugnant should be tabooed, and the evidence for sexual attraction among kinsmen is quite adequate for rejecting the theory. We mention it only for the sake of completeness.

The demographic theory makes certain assumptions about the life-span, breeding period, etc., of very early man. If these assumptions are correct, most of the rest of what is said in this presentation is irrelevant and unnecessary. But if any of its assumptions about age of maturity or spacing of births or length of breeding period can subsequently be shown to be wrong, this theory would also face difficulties. It serves to remind us of the number of implicit or explicit assumptions about the time and conditions of the emergence of the incest taboo which are made in the case of each theory. Slater assumes a cooperative group and normal breeding population larger than the family; White and our work group assume a situation where family cooperative relationships have become reasonably firm, whereas inter-family relationships are fluctuating and unstable. Either approach, and various others, make assumptions about the biology and social life of our ancestors which cannot be fully validated at present. More primatological and archeological data may still make it possible to choose more carefully among these assumptions.

Thus far, for all of these theories except the demographic and the socialization theories, there are either empirical objections as regards their validity, or logical difficulties in understanding how the function that the taboo supposedly fulfills would have led to institutionalization of the taboo, or both. It should be noted that the empirical objections do not apply to the inbreeding theory or to the social and cultural system theory: in each case it seems fair to say that the advantages postulated would have resulted from the familial taboo, and that, for primitive man, it is hard to see what other device might have been an effective alternative.

In order to broaden the range of phenomena to be considered, let us now turn to the realm of animal behavior. We will here restrict the term "animal" to birds and non-human mammals. There is a wide range of behavior as regards inbreeding among animals. At one end of the spectrum there is no restriction on matings except opportunity. At the other end, there is no intra-familial mating whatever, except for the parental pair. (An animal family will be defined as a relatively stable grouping of two generations of animals, of both sexes, including at least one sexual partnership, and smaller than a band of animals.) The most spectacular limitation on familial inbreeding is found in the case of the Canada Goose and the Graylag Goose. The behavior of the Canada Goose will be described here, based on observations by Eckhard H. Hess.

The young geese hatch in the spring. The following spring, they are not sexually mature, but are driven away from the family group while the parents rear the new brood. When the new brood is a few months old, the young from the previous year's brood rejoin the family group. During the next spring, the parents again drive off the older broods while they rear the current brood, and the older broods again join the family group a few months later. Hence, quite a large family develops. In the third year, the goslings from the first brood are sexually mature. They mate with individuals from other families. They will not mate with siblings or with the opposite-sex parent. The newly formed pairs may join either family of orientation, making one of the families even larger, or they may start their own family groups. Thus, in the Canada Goose, parents and children tend to remain in the same larger group after the young mature. These ties are very stable. Indeed, mating tends to be for life.

Experimental work on the Canada Goose indicates that this fastidious behavior is the result of sexual imprinting. It is necessary to emphasize that the reaction persists without external sanctions. The luckless breeder who takes a male and a female from the same brood to raise geese is doomed to disappointment: the pair will not mate even if no other partners are available. If, however, two members of the same brood are separated before hatching occurs and are subsequently re-introduced to each other, having been raised in different families, they may become mates.

There is no evidence to suggest that asexual imprinting occurs among mammals. There, the principal mechanism limiting inbreeding in animal groups with families—where there is such a mechanism—seems to take the form of competition between the parent and its same-sex child, when this child approaches or reaches sexual maturity. The older animal's superior size and strength normally result in the expulsion of the young animal from the family, so that it is forced to mate elsewhere. In the course of time, an older animal becomes enfeebled and may be overcome, so that some intra-familial mating will occur, but on a statistical basis this mechanism of intergenerational competition does ensure a large amount of outbreeding. It is particularly effective where most births are single births, so that two siblings of opposite sex rarely become sexually mature at the same time. The beaver seems to expel its sexually mature young and this may be true of the gibbon.

Among animals with apparent complete promiscuity may be mentioned the rat, the spider monkey, and the macaque. (By promiscuity we refer to patterns which result in the animal's mating indifferently with siblings, parents, or others. Since there are more "others," promiscuity involves a preponderance of outbreeding, as regards primary relatives. Promiscuity need not imply truly random mating. Size, strength, age, etc., always result in some departure from randomness, if only in the ordering of the sequence of copulatory partnerships.)

Sexual behavior among animals, as has been said, varies from complete promiscuity to complete elimination of familial inbreeding. Under what circumstances is elimination of familial inbreeding likely to occur? It would seem that, on a cross-species basis, restriction of inbreeding, whether by competition or by asexual imprinting, is found among the larger, longer-lived, slower-maturing, and more intelligent animals. On a cross-species basis, these are also relatively late evolutionary products. Those species which limit inbreeding are among those which form families, although not all species that form families limit inbreeding. It would appear that a certain level of intelligence and length of life are necessary for animals to form stable attachments—that otherwise they will breed with kin or non-kin indifferently. When stable attachments are combined with familial groupings, however, they give rise to the potentiality for close inbreeding. Thus, there seems to be an empirical tendency for barriers against close inbreeding to be found where close inbreeding would otherwise be most likely to occur. Finally, it should be mentioned that among birds, asexual imprinting is particularly common in species which have both stable families and larger than familial groupings—a feature which we have not tried to account for.[2]

We will now bring the animal and human data into juxtaposition and define the range of mating behavior which we will attempt to explain. Some animals have no barriers which prevent parent-child, brother-sister matings. Some animals have barriers which reduce or prevent such matings. Humans drastically limit such matings through the familial incest taboo. Thus human beings share with some animals a limitation on familial inbreeding, even though the mechanism of limitation differs from those of all animal species. Only humans have any limitations on mate choice beyond the nuclear family: in no human society is the incest taboo limited to the nuclear family, whatever its range of variation may be.[3]

Let us first consider these facts in the light of the genetic theory. It has been suggested above that close inbreeding might not be deleterious to animals, which mature quickly and have numerous offspring. It is in such cases that promiscuity is most likely, and promiscuity itself tends to reduce inbreeding, on a purely statistical basis. So even here, close inbreeding is unlikely. Where intensive inbreeding is most likely to occur, barriers are common. The more intelligent, slower-maturing animals living in family groups, where stable attachments are likely, and human beings, who also live in family groups where stable attachments are likely, manifest patterns which limit familial inbreeding: asexual imprinting, intergenerational competition, and the familial incest taboo. We suggest that with the emergence of culture, if not before, relatively stable family groupings in the human evolutionary line required *some* limitation on familial inbreeding. From this inference, alone, however, one cannot predict the familial incest taboo.

----

[2] The socialization theory would profit from the examination of animal cases where the young learn a fairly large part of their response repertory from their parents.
[3] Here and at other points we must except those rare cases where the familial taboo has been partially or wholly abrogated for the sake of the propagation of the group.

Asexual imprinting would be an equally effective mechanism—but it does not seem to occur in man, the apes, the monkeys, or even in more remote mammalian species. It is plausible to assume that this adaptive device was simply not available—not a part of the genetic equipment of man's ancestors or relatives. Intergenerational competition, however, would seem, at first blush, to be a feasible alternative. Competing with others to get and to keep mates is a widespread mammalian pattern, though not a universal one. Nothing is required to bend it in the service of limiting inbreeding except that it be directed to maturing members of the family as well as to outsiders—and this does not represent a change in pattern, but merely the preservation of the mechanism as family life develops.

If, for any reason, a gap develops between the point at which the young animal is sexually mature and the point at which it is capable of fending for itself, expulsion becomes an unsuitable mechanism. There is such a gap in all known human groups—or at least in no known human group does the onset of sexual maturity coincide with *full* assumption of adult economic and social responsibilities. Even where marriage occurs at a very early age —indeed, especially where it does—the youthful marital partner, or pair, remains under the direction of senior members of the kingroup. In early human or protohuman society, a gap of even a year between sexual maturity and the capacity to operate independently would create problems for a family unit, which used intergenerational competition and expulsion to limit inbreeding. If expulsion continued, the young would be exposed to dangers —unless they could find acceptance in another group, which would presuppose no intergenerational competition in the other group. If expulsion were abandoned, the family unit would be exposed both to an increase of the impetus toward inbreeding and to unregulated sexual competition within the familial unit. A gap between sexual maturity and full capacity could occur either through changes of maturational pattern or through the development of culture and the consequent need for time to transmit cultural information, information about the local scene, etc., or both. The incest taboo is a cultural phenomenon, and we must therefore assume that it emerged concomitantly with, or subsequent to, the beginnings of culture. We cannot, however, be certain whether the gap between sexual maturity and full performance was a matter of culture, physical maturation, or both.[4]

What we seek is a situation which will result in the normative definition of the nuclear incest taboo. If, as can safely be assumed, unregulated sexuality is incompatible with a stable family unit, and if expulsion of the sexually maturing human animal is not possible, then the problem of maintaining order within the family posed by sexual competition would have to be solved. As has been said, two solutions are possible: institutionalized sexual access within the family, or the familial incest taboo. Either solves the competitive problem. Either is within the scope of a human animal with language and limited culture. The problem of order within the nuclear family would also be observable as a pressing problem, on a day-to-day basis, and the sources of the problem in sexual competition would be equally evident. Either mechanism might be adopted: regulation of sex, or its elimination from the family. But whereas either mechanism would solve the problem of order, only one mechanism, the familial taboo, would solve the genetic problem. Hence that group, or those groups of human beings which adopted a taboo on intra-familial mating would have an advantage both over those groups which could not solve the problem of order and over those groups which solved the problem by institutionalized intra-familial sexual activity, thereby encouraging close inbreeding. Hence, over time, only the familial incest taboo could survive, because of its superior selective advantages.

We suggest, then, that man, along with certain other animals, is particularly vulnerable to deleterious effects arising out of close and continuous inbreeding, and that he shares with these animals the characteristic of having a mechanism which limits or prevents inbreeding within the family. We suggest that this problem may have been the underlying cause for the development of the familial incest taboo, since man shares a limitation on familial inbreeding with other animals, which are not cultural, which socialize their young far less elaborately than do humans, which do not have to educate them for role systems in a wider cultural order,

---

[4] The maturation argument has been elaborated here more fully than in the 1956 presentation—stimulated in part by Mead (1961).

and which do not have to cope with the problem of ordering the relationships of a number of potential sexual competitors in the same family. This suggestion of a common core shared by the various devices of animals and humans, which limit familial inbreeding, has the advantage of theoretical parsimony. It is also open to partial test, since there are a large number of studies of animals which could be carried out to demonstrate whether the variation we suggest on the basis of somewhat piecemeal evidence in fact occurs. But the human device, the familial incest taboo, is unique to humans, and is both required by, and made possible by culture. The incest taboo requires symbols, but it becomes significant only when expulsion from the family is impossible: a state of affairs largely, though perhaps not wholly dependent on the existence of a corpus of cultural tradition which must be fully transmitted for adequate functioning as an adult to occur.

The familial taboo has, of course, the *de facto* result of linking families, as well as of solving the problem of order within the family and the genetic problem. The stable attachments between individuals long associated in family units which make intrafamilial mating so potent a possibility also create ties of interest and sentiment between members of an original family of procreation as they disperse. The advantages of ties between families have been clearly pointed out by Tylor, White, Fortune, and others: an enlarged circle of cooperation, sharing, offense, and defense. These advantages, in turn, generate the last phenomenon to be accounted for: the fact that in no animal group are there restrictions on inbreeding except for the family unit, whereas in no human group are incest taboos limited to the nuclear family. Once the familial taboo is in existence, extensions of the taboo to other categories of kin become a simple evolutionary step. Whether this step is made by stimulus generalization, planning, aesthetic reactions, or whatever, its adaptive value is such as to perpetuate the extensions, which increase the circle of cooperation still further.

Extensions of the incest taboo beyond the family sometimes involve permitted, preferential, or theoretically prescribed matings between first cousins. Hence, the extensions may involve no further genetic advantage. Once again, we must point out that the results of familial inbreeding are genetically far more deleterious than those of first cousin matings.

Among animals, in the absence of symbolling, it is still conceivable that further restrictions on inbreeding might occur—e.g., through severe intergenerational sexual competition within a band, or through asexual imprinting such that the young would accept no members of the local group as mates. Such instances are, however, unknown. The genetic advantages of such a step would be considerably less than those of preventing familial inbreeding, and in the absence of culture the social advantages would also appear to be slight. This is so because cooperation in animals is limited in scope.

We might briefly query why a mechanism particularly suitable for maintaining the social and biological integrity of kinship-based societies is maintained not only in these societies but in complex societies as well. First, the problem of order within the family remains important, and the familial taboo, though not the only possible device for solving this problem, is the existing and well-institutionalized device. Second, for the bulk of pre-industrial complex societies, the functions of the incest taboo in its extended form remain important at the community level. There, the regulation of affairs is not impersonal and legal. On the contrary, the world remains divided into kinsmen, consanguine allies, and neutral or hostile groups. The nexus of social life and cooperation continues to be based on kinship to a significant degree, until societies with well-developed market-economies appear. In just these societies, the scope of the incest taboo narrows, until in our own society its legal definition is often limited to primary relatives, secondary relatives, and the spouses of certain primary and secondary relatives. It is in such societies that participation on a relatively impersonal basis in a social system of considerable scope becomes significant, and it may be that under these circumstances the significance of the familial incest taboo in socializing individuals toward participation in this larger orbit increases. It is probable that if the nuclear family were to be dissolved, and to be supplanted by collective, nonkinship forms of life, the incest taboo would dissolve with it, provided that these new forms made close inbreeding statistically a rare phenomenon.[5]

In sum, we propose that the adoption of the familial incest taboo was adaptive primarily because of the genetic results of close inbreeding, and that man's familial taboo is to be considered part of the class of devices that limit familial inbreeding among intelligent, slow-maturing animals, which bear few offspring at a time, and which live in family units. The selection of the taboo, however, we hypothesize, occurred through efforts to solve the problem of sexual competition within the family in a cultural animal with an organized family life. Among the available mechanisms, the incest taboo solved this problem and the genetic problem. Other alternatives solved only one of these problems. Hence it had high selective value. We suggest that it might not have come into being as a response to needs for cooperation between families, but that, once it existed, it did promote this cooperation, which had an adaptive function of little significance for animals. Finally, the familial taboo could be extended, by a simple evolutionary step, to a wider group of kinsmen, with great selective advantages. To date, some combination of the various advantages imputed to the nuclear and more extended incest taboos has resulted in their perpetuation, even in postindustrial societies organized as states. The taboo in some form or other is likely to survive so long as the family remains a significant part of the social order.

---

[5] This argument includes material on the future of the incest taboo, which was not a part of the 1956 presentation.

2 A COMPARATIVE APPROACH TO INCEST AND ADULTERY[1]

Jack Goody

IN A RECENT ARTICLE entitled "Changing Emphases in Social Structure" (1955) Murdock maintains that sciences first go through a classificatory stage and subsequently arrive at a second phase in which an attempt is made to analyse the "dynamic processes which give rise to the phenomena thus classified" (361). As far as anthropology is concerned, "the initial classificatory task has by now been substantially accomplished in the field of social structure" (361).

This thesis, which has been propounded on other occasions by other writers, seems to me not only to take a naïve view of scientific discovery, but definitely to mislead those from neighbouring fields of study into thinking that anthropological terms necessarily have some primary referent which is accepted by the large majority of anthropologists. That is by no means the case. In the first place, there is often a considerable measure of overt disagreement. Secondly, even where apparent agreement is found, the ambiguity of the terms themselves may conceal a number of different usages.

Partly this derives from the fact that the continuous analysis in depth of different societies calls for more precise conceptual discriminations than were previously required. And partly too it is related to the fact that the terms often employed by anthro-

Republished from *The British Journal of Sociology*, Volume 7, No. 4, pp. 286–305, with permission of the author and of the editor of *The British Journal of Sociology*.
[1] An earlier version of this paper was read to the Graduate Seminar of the Department of Social Relations, Harvard, in March, 1956.

pologists are those which we use as members of a particular
society to refer to our own institutions. Such concepts may turn
out to be quite inappropriate for the purpose of cross-cultural
analysis. The English "family" is an obvious case in point. From
the sociological point of view, the term has at least four analytically separable meanings. A statement of the kind, "the family
is a universal institution among all human societies", is meaningless without further elaboration.

In sum, these concepts cannot be regarded as having been
defined once and for all time, leaving anthropologists now free to
get on with other types of activity. A refinement of concepts is
a product of onward going research; it proceeds hand in hand
with it. The depth analysis of societies through long periods of
residence by trained anthropologists is a necessary concomitant
of the sharpening of concepts for cross-cultural studies.

The particular concept in which I am interested here is that of
"incest". I want also to mention the related ones of adultery and
fornication, as I shall later be concerned with them as categories
of heterosexual offence. The everyday meanings given by the
Concise Oxford Dictionary are as follows:

1   Incest: sexual commerce of near kindred.
2   Adultery: voluntary sexual intercourse of married person with
      one of the opposite sex, married (double adultery) or not
      (single adultery).
3   Fornication: voluntary sexual intercourse between man (some-
      times restricted to unmarried man) and unmarried woman.

These particular definitions are by no means standardized. For
instance, the *Encyclopædia Britannica* (11th Edition) and *Web-
ster's Dictionary* both define incest as "sexual intercourse between
persons so related by kindred and affinity that marriage cannot
take place between them", a formula which assumes an identical
range in prohibitions on heterosexual intercourse and prohibitions on marriage.

It is these everyday usages which have formed the basis of the
anthropological concepts. Malinowski, for example, appeared to
treat the incest taboo, the prohibition on sexual intercourse, and
exogamy, the prohibition on marriage, as being but two sides of
a coin.

Murdock, on the other hand, adheres more closely to the *Concise Oxford Dictionary* when he defines incest and adultery:

> When it (heterosexual intercourse) takes place outside of marriage between two persons of whom at least one is married to another person, it is called *adultery*. If its participants are related to one another by a real, assumed, or artificial bond of kinship which is culturally regarded as a bar to sex relations, it is classed as *incest* (1949: 261).

Radcliffe-Brown, while retaining the criteria of kinship, offers a more restricted definition of incest. He writes, "Incest is properly speaking the sin or crime of sexual intimacy between immediate relatives within the family, father and daughter, mother and son, brother and sister" (1950: 69).

Such extensive controversies have raged around the "incest taboo" that it may perhaps appear impertinent to raise the question as to whether all these writers are in fact discussing the same range of phenomena or looking for explanations of the same set of prohibitions. But when we put the definitions of Murdock and Radcliffe-Brown side by side it is obvious that such doubts are not altogether misplaced. It is clear for instance that in terms of Radcliffe-Brown's definition, Murdock's "second factual conclusion" . . . "that incest taboos do not apply universally to any relative of opposite sex outside of the nuclear family" (1949: 285) is tautologous. Equally, on the basis of Murdock's formula it is difficult to decide whether sexual intimacy with the father's wives other than one's own mother would constitute incest or adultery, particularly in societies like the Tiv or Bedouin where kinship is universal. The difference between the two definitions is this, that though both apparently see the regulations as "grounded in the constitution of the nuclear family" (1949: 284), Radcliffe-Brown attempts to limit the application of the term to the elementary family itself, while Murdock prefers to include all kin-based prohibitions, seeing these as "extensions" of the primary taboo. Murdock's emphasis is in line with Malinowski's stress upon the elementary family and with his dogma of "extension of sentiments". Both definitions are clearly based upon the institutions of our own society, where prohibitions on intercourse, like prohibitions on marriage, are bilaterally organized within limited ranges of kin. But are these necessarily adequate for the analysis of non-European societies?

In order to answer this question, let us examine the evidence from two societies characterized by unilineal descent, one by matrilineal, the other patrilineal descent. I have selected for this purpose the Ashanti and Tallensi of the Gold Coast, for which the main sources on incest are Rattray (1929) and Fortes (1936, 1949b) respectively. These societies were chosen partly because of the high standard of the reports and partly because of my own familiarity with the area. The Trobriand and the Nuer material will be used as a check upon the results obtained from an analysis of the examples from the Gold Coast. In each case I want to examine both the explicit verbal categories of the actors themselves and the classifications implicit in the system of sanctions. These will be compared with the concepts employed by the observers.[2]

THE MATRILINEAL CASE

In his treatment of sexual offences among the Ashanti, Rattray distinguished what he calls sins or tribal offences (*oman akyi-wadie*) from household offences (*efiesem*). The former demanded the intervention of the central authority and the execution of the guilty party, although in some instances compensation was allowed. The latter "were settled by the persons directly concerned or were decided by argument before any Elder, without reference to the 'house-father', who stood entirely aloof" (1929: 287). The offences falling under these two categories were discussed separately. I have listed them together in the table below.

From this table it can be seen that among the Ashanti sexual offences can be categorized in two ways, firstly, according to the different names used by the Ashanti themselves, and, secondly,

---

[2] In the course of this paper I have reconsidered some of the data presented by my teachers, Professor Meyer Fortes and Professor Evans-Pritchard. What may appear as a criticism is in fact a compliment to their work. In the first place, their monographs on the Tallensi and the Nuer remain the most outstanding analyses of the social systems of non-European societies which have been written, and it is because of this fact that I am able to offer such a reinterpretation. In the second place, I am trying to carry their analysis a stage further within the framework of the general approach which they have done so much to develop.

Table 1. Heterosexual Offences among the Ashanti[3]

	Offence		Sanction
	Ashanti name	*Definition*	
Tribal:			
A i	*mogyadie* "eating up of one's own blood"	SI* with female member of matriclan (*abusua*)	Death for both parties
A ii	*atwebenefie* (1) "vagina near to the dwelling-house"	SI with female of patriclan (*ntoro*) sub-group	Death or expulsion from matriclan
A iii	*baratwe*	SI with "unclean" woman	Death
A iv	*di obi yere* (1) "eat a man's wife"	(*a*) SI with chief's wife	"
		(*b*) *ahahantwe* (1), SI with unwilling married woman in the bush	"
Household:			
B i	*di obi yere* (2)	*ahahantwe* (2), SI in bush with:	
		(*a*) unmarried woman	Ridicule
		(*b*) married woman	Adultery payment plus sheep
		(*c*) own wife	Ridicule
B ii	" " "	SI of chief with subject's wife	Special adultery payment
B iii	" " "	SI by master with wife of a slave	" "
B iv	*atwebenefie* (2)	SI with wives of matriclan	" "
		SI with wives of patriclan sub-group	" "
		SI with wives of military company	" "
		SI with wives of guild	" "

| | *Offence* | | *Sanction* |
Ashanti name		*Definition*	
		SI with affines (wife's mother, wife's sister)	" "
Household:			
C	*di obi yere* (3)	Residual—SI with any married woman not falling in any of the above categories	Ordinary adultery payment

according to the different sanctions employed. I shall consider first the classification according to the nature of the sanctions. This reveals three classes of offence. In the first class falls *mogyadie*, intercourse with a woman of the same clan, punishable by death; this includes intercourse with full siblings and maternal half-siblings and with the mother; it excludes intercourse of father with daughter. But there is another type of offence, which though not given the same name, is also punish-

---

[8] In constructing this table I have followed Rattray's presentation of the offences except in the last category of section B (*atwebenefie* 2). Here is his list for this category (1929: 320):

Adultery with i   a brother's wife
            ii   a son's wife
           iii   wife's mother
           iv   an uncle's wife
            v   wife of anyone of same *fekuo* (company)
           vi   wife of anyone of same trade or guild
          vii   wife of one's own slave
         viii   father's wife, other than the adulterer's own mother
          ix   wife's sister, married or single.

In all these instances, the punishment is an adultery payment less or more than the standard amount. In addition, an animal has in some cases to be provided for a sacrifice; if a man has committed an offence with his wife's mother he then has to appease his wife with a gift. I have assumed that in i, ii, iv, viii, Rattray was referring to classificatory kin and have therefore reinterpreted the prohibitions in the way shown in the table. It should be added that the wives of fellow company and guild members are called "wife". Apart from affines, this particular category of "vaginas too near" refers to classificatory wives, wives of group members.

* Sexual intercourse. In treating household offences, Rattray explains that "adultery" may include various forms of "intimacy" besides actual intercourse. Since it was not always possible to distinguish from his account where this distinction was relevant, I have included these under the heading of intercourse.

able by death; this is *atwebenefie* (1), intercourse with a member of the same patrilineal sub-group, which of course includes that between father and daughter. Terminologically this constitutes a different category, but in respect of the nature of the sanction it must be associated with *mogyadie*. Both are cases of intercourse with members of the same descent group. The terminological distinction indicates that it is intercourse within the matriclan which is the major prohibition here while that within the patrilineal sub-group is subsidiary. This is consistent with the nature of double clanship among the Ashanti.

The second class of offence consists basically of intercourse not with members of the same descent group but with the wives of fellow members, as well as with other classificatory wives. It also includes some prohibitions on intercourse with affines which might tend to confuse the social position of the wife herself. The punishment for this class of offence varies. It is never death, but consists of some variant of the adultery payment.

The third class of sexual offence is with wives of other men, and the sanction here is the simple adultery payment.

The threefold typology on the basis of sanctions is an indication of the weight placed by the society on these various offences. The first class brings together offences relating to the structure of descent groups, both matrilineal and patrilineal (A i & A ii), offences relating to the hierarchical organization (A iv *a*) and "ritual" offences relating to the cult of the Earth (A iv *b*) and to the fertility of women (A iii).

When we look at the terms used by the Ashanti themselves, we find there is another threefold typology, if we exclude the category *baratwe*, which represents a different method of classifying these offences. Intercourse within the matriclan is sharply differentiated terminologically from intercourse within the patriclan, the latter falling into the same category as intercourse with the *wives* of members of the matriclan and of other social groups. In this way it is assimilated to what I wish to call group-wife offences to distinguish them from intra-group offences. This is clearly related to the overwhelmingly greater importance of the matriclans in the social system. The third category is residual in that it consists essentially in sexual intercourse with people other than the members or wives of members of the descent groups, and of a few other quasi-kin groups such as guilds and military

companies. Thus the concepts of the Ashanti themselves concerning heterosexual offences closely reflect the system of social
groups. Intercourse with a daughter falls into a different category
from intercourse with a sister, although for us both would be
classified as "incest".

Now let us turn to Rattray's own use of the terms "incest" and
"adultery" to see how he meets this situation. "Incest" he uses
simply to translate *mogyadie*, "eating of one's own blood", that
is, sexual intercourse with a matriclanswoman. He applies the
term to none of the other offences, even those also punishable
by death. The term "adultery" he uses to translate all the household offences, "eating a man's wife" (*di obi yere*, 2 and 3) and
atwebenefie (2)—"a vagina near to the dwelling-house". He also
uses it to translate those offences called *di obi yere* (1) which
fall under tribal jurisdiction and are therefore punishable by
death. This consists of two offences only, intercourse with a
chief's wife, and the worst type of sexual sin against the Earth,
the rape of a married woman in the bush. His difficulty arises
with category A ii, that is, *atwebenefie* (1). In his original list
of offences, he translates this neutrally as "sexual intercourse
with certain individuals other than those related by 'blood' "
(304)—i.e. females of the same matriclan. On the following page
he writes:

> *Atwe-bene-fie* means literally (having sexual intercourse with) "a
> vagina that is near to the dwelling-house", and the offence, as the
> title implies, consisted in committing adultery with the wives of cer-
> tain persons with whom the existing *ménage* necessarily compelled
> close social intercourse or constant physical proximity . . . (305)

The term "adultery" has now replaced the neutral circumlocu-
tion previously used. However when we examine the list of
atwebenefie offences we find that those included under "tribal
sins" (i.e. *atwebenefie* (1)) are not defined by the affinal relationship to ego. The women are forbidden not because they are
someone's wives but because they are female members of the
same patrilineal sub-group. For such an offence adultery seems a
misleading translation.

The point at issue is this. In English usage the term "adultery"
is defined in relation to the marital status of one or both partici-

pants and is in effect residual to the category "incest". The term "incest" is defined bilaterally, in keeping with other aspects of the social system. Heterosexual offences among the Ashanti do not fall into these categories, and in trying to translate these simply by the English words "incest" and "adultery" Rattray was faced with an impossible task. The English concept "incest" refers to heterosexual intercourse with persons within a particular range of kin, whether they fall within that range by birth or by marriage. When a male ego marries, the immediate female kin of his wife are assimilated to his own kinship chart by becoming sisters- or mothers-in-law. Intercourse with affines is defined as incestuous, and placed in the same conceptual category as intercourse with consanguineous kin.

Thus, whereas the Ashanti differentiate between intra-group offences and group-wife offences, the European system does not have to do this because at marriage the spouses are assimilated, for many social purposes, into each others' natal groups. There is no distinction, in the context of heterosexual offences, between group-member and group-spouse.

This interpretation is strikingly confirmed in another matrilineal case, that of the Trobriands. Malinowski discusses incest in considerable detail in his book *The Sexual Life of Savages* (1932). First let us ask what Malinowski means by incest. "Incest within the family and breach of exogamy", he says, is the meaning of the Trobriand word *suvasova* (389). As the family is bilateral, the term *suvasova* should therefore cover the intercourse of a man with his mother, his sister, or his daughter.

When we look at the Trobriand concepts themselves we find that this is not the meaning of the word *suvasova*. Malinowski himself makes this apparent in another context, although he continues to assume an equivalence.

> It must be clearly understood that, although father to daughter incest is regarded as bad, it is not described by the word *suvasova* (clan exogamy or incest), nor does any disease follow upon it; and, as we know, the whole ideology underlying this taboo is different from that of *suvasova* (447).

Suvasova corresponds precisely to the Ashanti concept *mogyadie*. It is the name for what I have called intra-group offences (intercourse or marriage), and has to be distinguished from

intercourse with wives of members of the matriclan, such as
brother's wife, which to judge from the example Malinowski
gives (98) is not heavily sanctioned. The category *suvasova*
includes intercourse with the mother, the daughter and the sister,
the latter being considered the most heinous, possibly because
this was felt to be the most likely. The worst heterosexual offences
in the Trobriands as among the Ashanti, in each case distinguished terminologically, are those committed with members of
the same matriclan. Malinowski repeatedly insists that it is the
brother-sister prohibition which is the basis of the "incest" taboo
in Trobriand society.

THE PATRILINEAL CASE

Let us now consider a patrilineal case, the Tallensi. According
to Fortes (1949b) the Tallensi have no word for incest. There is
a term *poyamboon* which might be translated literally "matters
concerning women". Fortes himself translates this as "adultery",
but on the basis of my own experience among the LoDagaa I
would suggest that it covers a wider range of heterosexual offences than is usually indicated by this term.

If the Tallensi have no specific word for incest, what range of
phenomena does Fortes include under this term and how does
he differentiate this from other types of offence? Looking at his
analysis, we find that incest consists in sexual relations within
the "expanded family", that is, the family group based upon the
inner lineage (1949b: 111). Thus, in the absence of an indigenous concept, Fortes has introduced what is essentially a bilateral
classification, one that includes in the same category offences
with a paternal aunt, a sister or a daughter (intra-group offences)
as well as offences with the wife of a father, brother or a son
(group-wife offences). But though he calls both of these offences
"incest" he emphasizes that they are differently thought of by
the Tallensi. For the first category of offences is merely "disreputable", while the latter is viewed with the horror usually
taken as being characteristic of incest. Outside the inner (or
medial) lineage this dichotomy becomes even more obvious, for
a lover relationship with a female lineage member is in fact permitted, while intercourse with the *wife* of a lineage or even a

clan member is still considered a wrong. Fortes claims that this latter offence is not incest, but "the most reprehensible form of adultery. It does not bear the same moral stigma as the corresponding form of incest, nor does it carry religious penalties for the adulterer" (1949b: 116). For Fortes, therefore, incest consists in sexual intercourse with female members of the inner lineage and with the wives of its male members, while adultery consists in intercourse with the wives of male members outside that range as well as with wives of non-clansmen.

There is then no Tallensi term for heterosexual offences other than one for "matters concerning women". Fortes uses the English terms "incest" and "adultery" to divide up this category. The way in which he does so is bilaterally oriented. "Incest" is the offence of sexual intercourse within the "expanded family", "adultery" the offence of sexual intercourse with any married woman outside it.

An alternative method of treating this problem is to infer the implicit classification of offences among the Tallensi from the nature of their reaction to any breach. This in effect is what Fortes does when he insists that "incest" with a sister or daughter falls in a different category of sexual acts than "incest" with a wife of the lineage (1949b: 114). This standardized procedure for the investigation of moral, ritual or legal norms gives the following threefold division:

i. sexual intercourse with a member of the same patriclan (up to the inner lineage only).
ii. sexual intercourse with the wife of a member of the same patriclan.
iii. sexual intercourse with the wife of a non-clansman.

I suggest that this classification has more inherent probability for three reasons. Firstly, it appears to fit better with the Tallensi emphasis on unilineal descent. Secondly, it corresponds to the classification I found among the LoDagaa of the same general area who are culturally similar to the Tallensi in very many ways. Thirdly, it is analogous to the classification which we have found among the Ashanti. Thus in both the matrilineal and patrilineal cases prohibitions on sexual intercourse are grouped together depending upon whether they were:

    i.   with a member of the same descent group (intra-group sexual prohibition).

   ii.   with the wife of a member (group-wife prohibition).

  iii.   with another married woman (extra-group prohibition).

I suggest that a similar typology will be found in most societies characterized by unilineal descent, but has been obscured in anthropological reports because of the ethnocentric bias of the observers towards bilateral classifications. It is only possible to rectify this in the case of the Tallensi and Ashanti because of the excellence of the reporting and the fact that the authors have provided us with the terms used by the actors themselves. If we accept these three basic categories for heterosexual prohibitions and offences in societies characterized by unilineal descent groups, it would be reasonable to refer to the last as adultery, or more specifically non-group adultery. But what about the other two types of offence? Which of these should be called "incest"?

THE CLASSIFICATION OF HETEROSEXUAL OFFENCES

The whole lengthy discussion of incest has turned on the supposition that it is a type of illicit sexual intercourse which is characterized by a particular horror. In the Western European system it is true that the whole range of offences included under the category incest is so regarded. But in many other societies, this is not so. Even within the minimal domestic units, heterosexual offences may be differently classified both terminologically and with regard to the organized sanctions with which they are met. Furthermore, they are also distinguished by diffuse sanctions, by the reactions which they arouse in the other members of the community. Among the Tallensi, offences between brother and sister (intra-group offences) are merely "disreputable", while group-wife offences are met with "horror". On the other hand, and this is a point of fundamental theoretical interest, among the Ashanti the reverse is the case. It is the intra-group offences which are dealt with by death, while the group-wife offences are treated as a heightened form of extra-clan adultery. I would claim that it is a mistake in either of these societies to class both these types of

offences together as "incest", because they are treated in such
markedly different ways in terms of the sanctions employed,
and, among the Ashanti, in terms of the actor categories themselves. Equally it would be difficult to classify either the first or
the second types as incest on the basis of the internal reaction
to them, as this varies so markedly in the two societies. I suggest
that the word incest be retained for the category of offences inside the group and that it be divorced from the criteria of "horror". The group-spouse category should be associated with adultery rather than incest, for at the core of the prohibition lies the
fact that the woman is *married* into the group; the taboo depends
upon her married status. If she were not married, intercourse
with her would be neither incest nor adultery but rather fornication, an act which may not be negatively sanctioned at all. For
the group-wife category I therefore suggest the somewhat clumsy
phrase, "group-wife adultery". Let me now schematize the threefold categorization of offences which we found among the Ashanti
and the Tallensi. The terminology I suggest seems to me more
appropriate for the cross-cultural analysis of heterosexual acts
outside marriage (see table below).

There are three points about this table which require explanation. Firstly, it is constructed from the point of view of an ego
of either sex, whereas previously I have often taken the male
ego's vantage point, in speaking, for example, of offences with
the wife of a group member rather than the spouse of a group

Offences that are	*Offences with*	
	Unmarried person	*Married person*
Intra-group	Incest	Incestuous adultery
Extra-group	Fornication	i. Spouse of group (group-spouse adultery)
		ii. Other married person (non-group adultery)

member. In certain respects it would have been preferable to
have retained the earlier standpoint. For this was not merely a
reflection of my own sex role; it corresponds to ethnographic
reality. Although in European law adultery is defined as sexual
intercourse where one of the partners is married, in most other

societies it is only considered adultery when the woman is married. This is the case in Roman law. The reason for this is that in general marriage confers relatively exclusive rights on a man over the sexual services of a woman. It is most unusual to find that the woman acquires similar rights over the male, even in matrilineal societies. However it seemed preferable to construct the table to take account of this case, rare as it is.

Secondly it should be pointed out that in addition to the prohibitions on sexual intercourse which can be discussed in terms of the structure of descent or kin groups, there are also those attached to specific kinship positions. For instance, in English law, it is incestuous adultery to sleep with one's wife's sister. This is also true of the Nuer and of many other African societies. As Evans-Pritchard points out in this connection, these prohibitions are to be seen as preventing a confusion of kinship statuses, a disruption of the solidarity of the sororal group.

Thirdly, a further variable has been introduced into this table, namely that of marital status. I have already explained why this is essential in considering extra-group offences. But it may also be relevant in the case of intercourse with a fellow-member of the group. For instance, the LoDagaa, of the Northern Territories of the Gold Coast, among whom I worked, and who are in many ways very similar to the Tallensi, regarded intercourse with a clanswoman before her marriage, that is, before her sexuality had been alienated to a member of another clan, as being of very minor importance. But intercourse with the same woman after her marriage, what I have called "incestuous adultery", is more severely treated.

For the comprehensive analysis of heterosexual offences, it is essential to introduce yet a further variable, not shown in the table, that of generation. Social relationships with a member of the same or alternate generation are usually characterized by relative equality and those between adjacent generations by super- or sub-ordination. This fact is likely to affect the severity with which the offence is treated. It will tend to be more severely treated where the relationship is characterized by authority, and especially where the male offender is of junior generation, for example, in the event of intercourse of a man with his father's wife.

THE INCIDENCE OF HORROR

By breaking down the categories of incest and adultery in this manner, it is possible to offer not only a more adequate analysis of heterosexual offences in any one particular society, but also to begin to examine these offences on a cross-cultural basis. I have already called attention to the different incidence of "horror" among the Tallensi and the Ashanti. In the former case it was offences with clan wives which were considered most heinous, whereas among the latter it was with the clan females themselves. The category heavily sanctioned among the Ashanti was relatively lightly treated among the Tallensi and vice versa. Why should the Tallensi represent the "mirror image" of the Ashanti in this respect?

I suggest the following is the explanation of this remarkable reversal. The Tallensi are patrilineal; their classification of offences resembles that of many other patrilineal peoples. The category "wives" is of fundamental importance to the descent group because it is through them that the continuity of the clan is obtained. Hence illegal intercourse with the wife of another member of the group is treated most severely.

The Ashanti are matrilineal. Social reproduction, as distinct from physiological reproduction, is obtained not through wives but through "sisters", the female members of the clan.[4] Hence it is interference with *their* sexuality that constitutes the most heinous heterosexual offence. An interesting aspect of this explanation is that it accounts for the differential treatment of father-daughter and mother-son offences. In neither the patrilineal Tallensi nor in matrilineal Ashanti does the father-daughter relationship fall into the most heinous category, while in both societies the mother-son relationship does. In the Tallensi the mother is the closest *wife* of a clansman of *senior* generation, while in the Ashanti she is the closest *female clan member* of *senior* generation. This I suggest forms a more satisfactory ex-

---

[4] This formulation was suggested to me in another context by Professor Max Gluckman who told me that it originated with Radcliffe-Brown.

planation of the different treatment of these offences than the
usual "biological" one.

To put this difference in another way, in patrilineal societies
the rights over a woman which are transferred at marriage include rights to her reproductive capacities as well as rights to
her sexual services, whereas in matrilineal societies, it is only
the latter which are transferred. Indeed among the Ashanti, a
male only acquires exclusive sexual rights by the payment of a
special sum, known as the *tiri-nsa*, which is not intrinsic to the
"marriage" itself.

The rights over the sexual services of women are customarily
vested in one man, except in the rare cases of polyandrous systems. But the degree of this exclusiveness varies. For example,
the LoDagaa, like the Tallensi, regard intercourse with the wife
of a patriclansman as being the worst form of heterosexual offence. Yet the junior of a pair of male twins, if unmarried, is said
to have access to the wife of his elder brother. In this case, the
social identification of the siblings is such that it over-rules the
individualization of rights to the sexual services of the wife.
There is always an incipient contradiction in patrilineal societies
centring around the fact that while rights to the sexual services of
women are in general acquired by individuals, rights to their
procreative capacities are to some extent vested in the clan as a
whole. An offspring of a particular union is an offspring of the
entire clan. This contradiction is differently resolved in various
societies. In Brahmin groups, for example, rights over women
are so highly individualized that a widowed woman may not
marry again. Among the Tallensi a man's exclusive rights in a
woman cease at his death, and by the institution of widow inheritance are taken over by another member of the same patriclan. Fraternal polyandry, or polycoity, represents the extreme
case of corporate rights over the sexual services of women, at
the opposite pole as it were to the individualization of Brahmin
society. The problem of plural access is different from, but not
unrelated to, that of plural marriage.

The Nuer are an interesting case in this connection, both because of the nature of the material and because of the theoretical position adopted by Evans-Pritchard. Both Evans-Pritchard
(1949b, 1951) and Howells (1954) speak of the Nuer as having

a word for incest, namely *rual*. Evans-Pritchard explains that this term covers offences with clanswomen as well as other kins-women falling within the range of prohibited degrees of marriage, and further that the prohibition on sexual relationships derives from the prohibition on marriage. But he also adds that the same term is used to designate offences with women who are married to kinsmen. Evans-Pritchard brings this within the framework of his explanation of the incest taboo as derived from the rule of exogamy by asserting that such women are "brought within the circle of the incest taboo not so much as wives of kinsmen but as mothers of kinsmen" (1951: 44–45). This contention seems somewhat strained. Women married to kinsmen surely fall into the forbidden category by virtue of their marriage and their *potential* child-bearing capacity. The Nuer certainly regard the presence of children as increasing the dangers of incest, but there is no indication in the literature that they look with any approval upon intercourse with the wife of a kinsman who has not yet given birth to children, except in one or two rather special cases (Evans-Pritchard, 1949b: 97).

Evans-Pritchard then uses incest to translate the Nuer word *rual* and maintains that the Nuer include in this category sexual relations with women falling within the range of prohibited de-grees as well as with women married to such kin. If this were the whole situation, then the Nuer would have very similar categories of heterosexual offences to those which exist in our own society. But this does not appear to be altogether the case, for he also writes that "sexual relations with the wives of half-brothers, paternal uncles, and patrilineal cousins of every degree are re-garded as being either incestuous peccadillos or not incestuous at all. The wife of a 'bull' is, in a general social sense, the wife of all the 'bulls' . . . She is our wife" (1951: 45). It would appear from this statement that the term *rual* is not generally used for intercourse with the wives of agnates, other than the father, a full brother or a son. "There is no incest", the Nuer say, "among bulls" (1949b: 92).

Howell's account confirms this. He includes intercourse with women married to kinsmen in his discussion of adultery rather than under the rules of incest and exogamy, and concludes with the following remark . . . "the act is therefore tantamount to incest (*rual*)" (1954: 164). His use of "tantamount" again appears to indicate that the Nuer make a verbal distinction between intercourse with kinswomen ("intra-group offences") which is *rual* and intercourse with the wives of kinsfolk which is "tantamount to *rual*". It is probable that Howell here means agnates rather than the entire range of kinsfolk, for Evans-Pritchard is quite definite that it is only intercourse with "bulls" that could fall outside the category *rual*, while intercourse with the wives of other kinsfolk is included. The failure to be clear on this matter is yet another example of the way in which reports have been skewed by terminology which reflects the institutions of the society to which the anthropologist belongs rather than those of the society he is analysing. It must be admitted however that in so far as the Nuer classify offences with kinsfolk and the wives of kinsfolk in the same category, their concepts present a closer, albeit deceptive, approximation to our own than is the case with the other societies we have examined.

Let me now turn from the way in which the Nuer classify heterosexual offences terminologically to the sanctions with which a breach of the prohibition is met. The punishment of intercourse with women falling within the prohibited degrees of marriage is left to supernatural forces . . .

> there is no question of compensation, and the spiritual contamination which is considered to follow incest (*rual*) and which is manifested in physical disorders (*nueer*), sometimes resulting in death, falls equally on both parties and even upon their relatives (Howell, 1954: 82–83).

The effectiveness of these sanctions varies with the genealogical distance between the two persons involved, for Howell later states that "there is no great condemnation of extra-marital intercourse with distant clanswomen" (147).

The statement concerning intercourse with distant clanswomen strongly recalls the Tallensi situation. On the other hand, intercourse within the closer ranges of kin seems more heavily condemned among the Nuer. This is not easy to assess, as both authorities at times omit to state whether their remarks refer to a breach of the prohibition on sexual intercourse or a breach of the rule of exogamy. *Rual* appears to mean both these offences. Indeed it is possibly because of this identification that Evans-

Pritchard, like Malinowski, regards incest as being linked so firmly with exogamy.

I now want to deal with the question of intercourse with the wives of kinsmen, or what I have previously referred to as group-wife offences. In a passage quoted above, Evans-Pritchard speaks of intercourse with the wives of agnatic kinsmen as being "incestuous peccadillos or not incestuous at all" (1951: 45). It is clear that, if we accept the implication that such offences are excluded from the category *rual*, some differentiation in treatment is to be expected. The interesting feature of the Nuer case is that, according to Evans-Pritchard, group-wife offences are relatively lightly treated, a situation quite different from the normative system of the other patrilineal case we have examined, namely the Tallensi. Before discussing a possible explanation of this phenomena, it is necessary to turn to the other authority on the Nuer.

Howell gives some additional information on intercourse with the wives of kinsmen, a subject which, significantly, he treats under the heading adultery rather than incest. I quote in full his main paragraph on this question:

ADULTERY WITH THE WIVES OF KINSMEN

The full rate of compensation is usually demanded unless the husband and the adulterer are on exceptionally good terms in other respects, or their relationship in the kinship structure is sufficiently close to modify feelings of moral indignation on the part of the husband. Although the wives of kinsmen are brought within the sphere of kinship by the process of marriage, and to have relations with the wife of a kinsman is in a sense tantamount to a breach of the rules of exogamy, this is modified by the feeling that a wife, acquired by the transfer of cattle in which other kinsmen have limited rights, is theoretically the wife of all of them. Yet it is not considered correct that two kinsmen should have sexual relations with the same woman at the same period. There is no real conflict in these two concepts, but the attitude behind the payment of *yang kule* includes an idea that sexual relations with the legal wife of another man create an impurity, and that there is greater impurity if two men of the same kinship group have sexual relations with the same woman. It is felt that the wife of a kinsman is in some degree also a kinswoman, especially as a potential mother of kinsmen in the next generation. The act is therefore tantamount to incest (*rual*) (1954: 163–64).

It is difficult to compare the statements of the two authorities, for Howell speaks of the "wives of close kinsmen" without indicating whether or not these kinsmen are agnates, while Evans-Pritchard is concerned specifically with these latter. But identity should perhaps be assumed from Howell's use of the phrase "kinship group". In any case the whole tenor of his remarks suggests that Evans-Pritchard's assessment of intercourse with the wives of close kinsmen as "incestuous peccadillos" requires some modification. For although the greater part of the adultery payment may be waived, Howell specifically declares that "adultery is an offence which brings greater spiritual dangers when the husband and the adulterer are kinsmen". From this remark it would seem that Evans-Pritchard has perhaps neglected the spiritual dangers which intercourse with the wives of agnates involves.

Howell accounts for increased spiritual danger as well as the reduced compensation in cases of adultery with a group wife in terms of the conflict between the rule of exogamy and the corporate aspects of marital rights in women. He seems here to be falling into the error, also made by Evans-Pritchard, of confusing intra-group prohibitions (which have a direct relationship with prohibitions on marriage) and group-wife prohibitions (which clearly do not). And this confusion, deriving from Western European institutions, makes for some difficulty in interpreting the Nuer data.

Evans-Pritchard uses a similar explanation to account for the comparative leniency with which offences with the wives of agnates are dealt. This he contends can be easily understood by reference to "the importance attached to children by the Nuer". As it stands this explanation is inadequate, in that it could "explain" intercourse not only with the wives of agnates, but also with any married women whatsoever. What Evans-Pritchard means is not the importance attached to children in themselves but the importance attached to children of the lineage, in other words to the continuity of the descent group. This relates to the argument I presented earlier. If we accept Evans-Pritchard's account of intercourse with agnates as a peccadillo, this is clearly a very different situation from the Tallensi one. Another variable is present. This is the extent of the corporate rights over the woman's sexual services. In any society with unilineal descent

groups, there must be an incipient conflict between the individualized and corporate aspects of these rights. The Nuer, as distinct
from the Brahmin and the Tallensi, tend to extend the corporate
aspect to include rights over the woman's sexual services as well
as her procreative capacity.

This interpretation receives support from the Nuer version of
the common African prohibition on two members of a descent
group having intercourse with the same woman. Among the Tallensi and the LoDagaa, this prohibition falls most severely on
full siblings. Among the Nuer, however, the corporate character
of rights over women receives greater emphasis and the situation
is reversed; "it is wrong for two kinsmen to court the same girl,
unless they are members of the same lineage" (Evans-Pritchard,
1951: 45; my italics).

To sum up the Nuer evidence, two points emerge, despite
some inconsistencies in the available data. Firstly, there does
exist a somewhat similar differentiation of heterosexual offences
to the threefold classification which were found in the other
descent societies. Whether or not there is any discrimination at
the verbal level is not altogether clear, but there appears to be
a valid distinction in terms of sanctions brought into play. The
three categories are intercourse with the wife of a non-kinsman
(simple adultery), intercourse with the wife of a clansman (or
rather "bull"), and intercourse with kinswomen and with the
wives of kinsmen other than "bulls". The reference group is not
merely ego's own patrilineal descent group; it also includes, as
far as the last category is concerned, the mother's patriclan and
other kin. But at the core of this range of kin lies the descent
group. Secondly, although the evidence regarding the "horror"
reaction is not unambiguous, it would seem that intercourse with
the wives of patriclansmen is not regarded as severely as among
the Tallensi or the LoDagaa. This does not I think invalidate the
hypothesis that the differential incidence of the horror reaction
to intercourse with group members and with group wives among
the Tallensi and the Ashanti is related to the nature of the linear-
ity of the major descent groups. What the Nuer material does is
to bring out a further variable, namely the degree to which rights
over women are vested in the descent group. Put in another way,
this factor is the extent to which a distinction is made between

rights over the reproductive powers of women and the rights over their sexual services. For where this distinction is emphasized, there appears to be greater individualization of the rights over sexual services.

EXPLANATIONS OF INCEST

Once the distinction between intra-group and group-wife sexual offences has been understood, the problems of the "explanation" of incest, and of the relationship between incest and exogamy, can be seen in a new light. Explanations of incest fall into three categories. Firstly, there are those framed in terms of the internal relations of the group. These are associated with writers who have concentrated their attention on sexual prohibitions within the elementary family: Freud, Radcliffe-Brown, Malinowski, Brenda Seligman, Murdock, Parsons, and others. Secondly there are those framed in terms of the external relations of the group, which are associated principally with Tylor, Fortune, and Lévi-Strauss. In the third category fall the biological, psychological-genetic variety. With this latter I am not concerned here, although I am aware that they find their way into the formulations of some of the writers mentioned above. I take the two sociological hypotheses as my starting point not because I automatically assume that they will serve as complete explanations, but because for heuristic purposes it seems to me desirable to see how far one can get with these before employing theories which from the sociologist's standpoint are residual.

The two sociological theories are normally viewed as alternatives and a considerable literature has accrued as to their relative merits. Brenda Seligman has recently summarized this discussion, herself coming down on the side of internal relations. Her argument is worth presenting not only because it gives some idea of how the discussion has developed but also because it deals fairly with both points of view. She writes:

> Dr. R. W. Fortune . . . considers that the barrier itself is adopted not because of its internal value to the family, but because the external value of the marriage alliance is essential to social structure (1950: 313).

She distinguishes two types of incest. "One is the union of parent and child, the other is of siblings of opposite sex" (306). And she maintains that while the marriage alliance might account for the brother-sister taboo, it cannot possibly explain the parent-child prohibition. Therefore, she concludes, it is the internal value of the arrangement which is the most important aspect of incest. "With the prohibition of incest within the elementary family, the foundation of social structure is laid" (307). Thus she succeeds in categorizing heterosexual offences on generation lines and perceives that different explanations might be appropriate to each. But she fails to dichotomize either in terms of group members and group wives, or in terms of the structure of unilineal descent groups. The reason for this appears to be her commitment to the Malinowskian stress on the elementary family. If this is seen as the primary unit in relation to which the incest taboo functions, then the only possible breakdown of incest is by generation. The point elaborated in this paper is that, in the analysis of descent societies, a further breakdown is necessary, and exists within the actor frame of reference either in the terms used or in the sanctions employed. But the breakdown is made according to whether the prohibition is on intercourse with a group member or with a group wife; and the groups in question are in general based upon unilineal descent. It is from this point of view that explanations of incest and exogamy must be considered.

Incest and exogamy are usually analysed as related prohibitions, the one on intercourse, the other on marriage. For example, Evans-Pritchard in his study of the Nuer maintains that the former is derived from the latter. Malinowski sometimes speaks of incest and exogamy as if they were entirely complementary. This point of view arises from a failure to make the distinction discussed above. For while the rule prohibiting marriage inside the group (exogamy) may be associated with the prohibition on intercourse within the group (intra-group prohibition), it cannot possibly be related, in any direct manner, to the prohibition on intercourse with the wives of the group, for these women must of necessity fall within the general category of permitted spouse. They cannot possibly be excluded by any marriage rule.

Exogamy, then, can only be related to the prohibition on intra-group intercourse. But as Fortes has shown, there need be no complete overlap even here. The Tallensi allow sexual intercourse with distant clansmen where they do not allow marriage. The reason is clear. Marriage affects the alignment of relationships between groups; it has to be publicly validated by overt transactions, and it provides a precedent for similar arrangements in the future. Sexual intercourse in itself does none of this, and therefore when carried on in semi-secrecy requires no realignment of social groups. And indeed, as Fortes has also shown, under certain conditions there may be advantages for the individuals concerned if the lover is forbidden as a spouse for then these relationships are necessarily of limited duration. Within groups of more restricted span, however, intercourse between members can render other social relationships difficult. This is especially true where the relationship is characterized by super-subordination, as for example between members of adjacent generations.

Although there is no inevitable overlap between the prohibition of intra-group intercourse and the prohibition of intra-group marriage, there is nevertheless a strong tendency for such an overlap to occur. Exogamy is frequently phrased in terms of kinship . . . "We cannot marry our 'sisters'." So is the intra-group sexual taboo . . . "We cannot sleep with our 'sisters'." It is true that the classificatory reference of the term "sister" may not be the same in the two cases. This is so with the Tallensi. In the first instance "sister" refers to clan females as a whole, in the second, to those belonging to the inner or medial lineage. But the principle of structural congruence acts in favour of the same referent in both cases. And indeed the prohibition on temporary sexual relations and the prohibitions on semi-permanent sexual relations are patently not unrelated.

If therefore the rule of exogamy is to be related to the external value of the marriage alliance, as Fortune and others have suggested, I think correctly, then the intra-group prohibition on intercourse cannot be dissociated from it. The rejection of temporary sexuality within the group is in part a reflection of the rejection of permanent sexuality, and the latter is related to the importance of establishing inter-group relationships by the exchange of rights in women.

Let us now turn to the prohibition on intercourse with those who have married members of the descent group. This is spoken of by Seligman, Fortes, and many others as incest. Yet clearly the explanations of Fortune, Lévi-Strauss and others concerning marriage alliances have no bearing at all upon this phenomenon, because it is not intercourse with the women as such which is forbidden, but intercourse with them as wives of group members. Rights over their sexual services have been pre-empted by other males with whom one has prior relationships. These women are not necessarily consanguineal kin at all, with the exception of ego's mother; they are affines. Moreover, when the specific relationship with the member of the descent group ceases, then they may be legitimate sexual partners. In many cases one is in fact obliged to marry them when their husband dies, because of one's relationship with the dead man. Now this type of prohibition has nothing directly to do with marriage alliances, but rather with the other explanation which has been put forward, namely, the necessity of preserving the structure, not merely of the "family", for there would then be no need for a rule of any extensive application, but rather of the descent group. For where rights of sexual access are individualized, conflict over females may be a cause of internecine dispute, and this prohibition renders such disputes less likely. It is indeed closely related to the taboo, found among the Tallensi, and among many other African peoples, against clansmen having sexual relationships with one woman during the same period.

CONCLUSIONS

The current sociological explanations of incest are not, then, alternatives. Explanations in terms of external relations are relevant to the prohibitions on intra-group intercourse, while those in terms of internal relations are primarily relevant to the group-wife prohibition, although they also bear upon the intra-group taboo. Exogamy can be related to the former, but not to the latter.

This paper has attempted to establish a typology of heterosexual prohibitions to facilitate both cross-cultural studies and the depth analysis of particular societies. The typology depends in the first place upon a distinction between women who are considered to belong to the group and women who are married to its male members. In the societies with which the discussion has been mainly concerned, the reference group is the unilineal descent group rather than the elementary family. It is impossible to relate the concepts "incest" and "exogamy" when one term is held to refer to a bilateral group, the family, and the other to a unilineal one, the clan or lineage. It is impossible to account for the different sanctions placed upon these acts among the patrilineal Tallensi and the matrilineal Ashanti unless one introduces the system of descent as a variable. For the "grisly horror of incest" is not a universal characteristic of all heterosexual offences with kinswomen and the wives of kinsmen. The reactions to a breach vary within and between societies. This is a fact which psychologists venturing into the cross-cultural field have often forgotten. Indeed, so concerned have they been with their own findings that they have tended, even more than anthropologists, to impose the categories derived from their own institutions upon the other societies with which they have been concerned. This is noticeable even in the type cases which psychologists have taken from classical Greek mythology. The unilineal nature of early Greek society makes it probable that their system of classification was closer to the patrilineal societies of Africa than the bilateral ones of modern Europe.

Like anthropologists, sociologists and psychologists dealing with our own society have patently failed to realize the ethnocentric nature of their categories. They have tended to treat "incest" as an isolate instead of examining the system of prohibitions as a whole in relation to the social structure. Thus there is a quite disproportionate amount of literature devoted to "incest" as compared to "adultery", yet from the standpoint of social problems the latter would seem to deserve the greater attention. But the lure of the exotic has overcome the attraction of the mundane.

The study of "incest" in any society must be related not merely to the analysis of marriage prohibitions or preferences, but also to "adultery", so that it can be seen within the total constellation of sexual offences within that society. And this can only be done by accepting a breakdown of the monolithic category "incest" into concepts more closely related to the structure of the society in question.

PART II
MARRIAGE

INTRODUCTION TO THE SECTION ON MARRIAGE

The arrangement in this section needs comment, for the first three articles are reprinted here in an order exactly the reverse of chronological order. This has the disadvantage that some of the references in the articles are to those that appear in later articles. However, it is our impression that the articles as they have been arranged give a view of increasing complexity of institutional arrangements, and understanding the complication of these arrangements is more important than mere chronological ease of referencing.

Editors

3 THE NAYARS AND THE DEFINITION OF MARRIAGE[1]

E. Kathleen Gough

THE PROBLEM OF A SATISFACTORY DEFINITION of marriage has vexed anthropologists for decades and has been raised, but not solved, several times in recent years. Over time it became clear that cohabitation, ritual recognition, definition of sexual rights, or stipulation of domestic services each had too limited a distribution to serve as a criterion for all the unions anthropologists intuitively felt compelled to call 'marriage'. For good reason therefore the *Notes and Queries* definition of 1951 makes no reference to any of these: 'Marriage is a union between a man and a woman such that children born to the woman are recognized legitimate offspring of both parents.'

Admirably concise though it is, this definition, too, raises problems in a number of societies. The Nuer institution of woman-marriage-to-a-woman would be a case in point. Here, both parties to the union are women yet, as Evans-Pritchard (1951: 108–9) has shown, the legal provisions of the union are strictly comparable to those of simple legal marriage between a man and a woman. Few, therefore, would question Evans-Pritchard's logic in calling this union a marriage.

The *Notes and Queries* definition contains two criteria: that

Reprinted from the *Journal of the Royal Anthropological Institute*, Vol. 89, 1959, pp. 23–34, by permission of the author and of the Royal Anthropological Institute.

[1] The fieldwork on which this paper is based was carried out in three villages of Kerala between September 1947 and July 1949 with the aid of a William Wyse Studentship from Trinity College, Cambridge. Writing it has formed part of a project financed by the American Social Science Research Council.

marriage is a union between one man and one woman, and that
it establishes the legitimacy of children. Nuer woman-marriage
does not conform to the first criterion but it does to the second.
At this point the problem therefore becomes: is a definition
feasible which would insist only on the second criterion, that of
legitimizing children?

In Europe[2] Dr Edmund Leach initiated the most recent chapter in this discussion (Leach 1955), and rather than review its
whole history it is pertinent for me to take up the argument
where he and others have left it. In effect, Dr Leach answered
'no' to the question posed above. He argued not only against
the vagueness of the phrase 'legitimate offspring' but also against
any use of potential legal paternity as a universal criterion of
marriage. He concluded, in fact, that no definition could be
found which would apply to all the institutions, which ethnographers commonly refer to as marriage. Instead he named ten
classes of rights,[3] which frequently occur in connection with
what we loosely term marriage, added that 'one might perhaps
considerably extend this list', and seemed to conclude that since
no single one of these rights is invariably established by marriage

---

[2] In America Miss Alisa S. Lourié, Douglass College, Rutgers University,
has recently worked on this problem, and I have been stimulated by correspondence with her and by reading an unpublished paper of hers, *Concepts
in Family Sociology*. In this paper Miss Lourié formulates a definition of
marriage, which is narrower than mine, but when her work is published
readers will see that I was helped towards my definition by her analysis. I
have also profited much from discussions with my husband, David F. Aberle.

[3] A. To establish the legal father of a woman's children.
B. To establish the legal mother of a man's children.
C. To give the husband a monopoly in the wife's sexuality.
D. To give the wife a monopoly in the husband's sexuality.
E. To give the husband partial or monopolistic rights to the wife's domes-
tic and other labour services.
F. To give the wife partial or monopolistic rights to the husband's labour
services.
G. To give the husband partial or total rights over property belonging or
potentially accruing to the wife.
H. To give the wife partial or total rights over property belonging or po-
tentially accruing to the husband.
I. To establish a joint fund of property—a partnership—for the benefit of
the children of the marriage.
J. To establish a socially significant 'relationship of affinity' between
the husband and his wife's brothers. (Leach 1955, p. 183.)

in every known society, we ought to feel free to call 'marriage' any institution which fulfils any one or more of the selected criteria.

There is, surely, a quite simple logical flaw in this argument. For it would mean in effect that every ethnographer might extend at will Dr Leach's list of marital rights, and in short define marriage in any way he pleased. This may be legitimate in describing a single society. But I would argue that for purposes of cross-cultural comparison, we do need a single, parsimonious definition, simply in order to isolate the phenomenon we wish to study.

In support of his argument against using the legitimizing of children as a universal criterion of marriage, Dr Leach cited the Nayar case. On the basis of two of my papers on the Nayars (Gough 1952a, 1955a), he stated that the Nayars traditionally had 'no marriage in the strict (i.e., *Notes and Queries*) sense of the term but only a "relationship of perpetual affinity" between linked lineages (Gough 1955a). The woman's children, however they might be begotten, were simply recruits to the woman's own matrilineage.' He stated further, 'The notion of fatherhood is lacking. The child uses a term of address meaning "lord" or "leader" towards *all* its mother's lovers, but the use of this term does not carry with it any connotation of paternity, either legal or biological. On the other hand the notion of affinity is present, as evidenced by the fact that a woman must observe pollution at her ritual husband's death (Gough 1955a).' Later Dr Leach concludes that 'among the matrilineal matrilocal Nayar, as we have seen, right J (to establish a socially significant "relationship of affinity" between the husband and his wife's brothers) is the only marriage characteristic that is present at all' (Leach 1955, p. 183).

This paper has two objectives. It will begin by analyzing traditional Nayar marital institutions and thereby showing that in fact the notion of fatherhood is not lacking and that marriage does serve to establish the legitimacy of children. My analysis will, I hope, not only dispose of a misinterpretation on Dr Leach's part, but will in general clarify what has always proved a crucial but difficult borderline case for theorists of kinship. The paper will conclude with a new definition of marriage which will again make the status of children born to various types of union critical for decisions as to which of these unions constitute marriage. The ultimate aim is not, of course, to redefine marriage in a dogmatic way to suit a particular case, for definitions are tools of classification and not aims of research. The aim is to show that there *is* a common element not only in the institutions anthropologists have confidently labelled 'marriage' by the *Notes and Queries* definition, but also in some unusual cases to which that definition does not apply. Whether we call the element 'marriage' does not much matter provided it is made explicit, but it would probably be convenient to do so.

This account will refer to Nayars in the former kingdoms of Calicut, Walluvanad, and Cochin in the centre of the Malabar Coast or Kerala. In the northernmost kingdoms (Kolattunad, Kottayam) and probably also in the southernmost kingdom of Travancore, Nayar residence appears to have been avunculocal even before the period of British rule, marriage was optionally polygynous but not polyandrous, and individual men appear to have had definite rights in, and obligations to their children. Full information is not available for these northernmost and southernmost kingdoms in the pre-British period. But it seems probable that in the northern kingdoms at least, even the *Notes and Queries* definition of marriage was applicable to the Nayars. It was certainly applicable in the latter half of the nineteenth century for which I have accounts from informants.

My account of marriage in the central kingdoms is a reconstruction of a state of affairs which appears to have been general before 1792 when the British assumed government of the Coast. As I have shown elsewhere (Gough 1952a), Nayar kinship was slowly modified in the nineteenth century and more rapidly in the twentieth. But in remote villages the traditional institutions persisted until towards the end of the nineteenth century and were remembered by a few of my older informants. Their reports are not contradicted and are substantially corroborated by writings of Arab and European travellers of the fifteenth to eighteenth centuries.

In this account I shall use the terms 'marriage', 'husband' and 'wife' without definition. My reasons for doing so will appear later.

In each of the three central kingdoms the Nayar caste was

divided into a number of ranked subdivisions characterized by different political functions. Chief of these were (a) the royal lineage, (b) the lineages of chiefs of districts, (c) the lineages of Nayar village headmen and (d) several sub-castes of commoner Nayars. Each of these last either served one of the categories (a) to (c) or else served patrilineal landlord families of Nambudiri Brahmans. I shall deal first with the commoner Nayars of category (d).

There were present in each village some four to seven exogamous matrilineages of a single sub-caste of commoner Nayars. These owed allegiance to the family of the head of the village, which might be a patrilineal Nambudiri family, a Nayar village headman's matrilineage, a branch of the lineage of the chief of the district, or a branch of the royal lineage. The commoners held land on a hereditary feudal-type tenure from the headman's lineage and, in turn, had authority over the village's lower castes of cultivators, artisans, and agricultural serfs. Each retainer lineage tended to comprise some four to eight property-owning units, which I call property-groups. The property-group formed a segment of the total lineage and was usually composed of a group of brothers and sisters together with the children and daughters' children of the sisters. The members owned or leased property in common, lived in one house, and were under the legal guardianship of the oldest male (*kāranavan*) of the group. Both the property-group and the lineage were called *taravād*.

Nayar men trained as professional soldiers in village gymnasia, and for part of each year they tended to be absent from the village in wars against neighbouring kingdoms or for military exercises at the capitals. Only the *kāranavan*, the women and the children of the property-group, remained permanently in their ancestral homes.

The Nayars of one village or of two adjacent villages formed a neighbourhood group (*kara* or *tara*) of some six to ten lineages. Each lineage was linked by hereditary ties of ceremonial co-operation with two or three other lineages of the neighbourhood. These linkages were reciprocal but not exclusive, so that a chain of relationships linked all the lineages of the neighbourhood. The lineages linked to one's own were called *enangar*; the total neighbourhood group, the *enangu*. At least one man and one

woman of each linked lineage must be invited to the house of a
property-group for the life-crisis rites of its members. Its linked
lineages were also concerned if some member of a lineage committed a breach of the religious law of the caste. It was their duty
at once to break off relations with the offending lineage and to
call a neighbourhood assembly to judge and punish the offence.
Its linked lineages thus represented the neighbourhood group as
a whole to the offending lineage and were special guardians of
its morality. Sometimes in small neighbourhoods the commoner
Nayar lineages were all *enangar* to each other, but in larger
neighbourhoods this was not feasible, for the heads of property-
groups would have had too many ceremonial obligations to fulfil.

The linked lineages played their most important role at the
pre-puberty marriage rites (*tālikettukalyānam*) of girls (Gough
1955b). At a convenient time every few years, a lineage held
a grand ceremony at which all its girls who had not attained
puberty, aged about seven to twelve, were on one day ritually
married by men drawn from their linked lineages. The ritual
bridegrooms were selected in advance on the advice of the village
astrologer at a meeting of the neighbourhood assembly. On the
day fixed they came in procession to the oldest ancestral house of
the host lineage. There, after various ceremonies, each tied a gold
ornament (*tāli*) round the neck of his ritual bride. The girls had
for three days previously been secluded in an inner room of the
house and caused to observe taboos as if they had menstruated.
After the *tāli*-tying each couple was secluded in private for three
days. I was told that traditionally, if the girl was nearing puberty,
sexual relations might take place. This custom began to be
omitted in the late nineteenth century, but from some of the
literature it appears to have been essential in the sixteenth and
seventeenth centuries. At the end of the period of seclusion each
couple was purified from the pollution of cohabitation by a ritual
bath. In Calicut and Walluvanad each couple in public then tore
in two the loin-cloth previously worn by the girl during the 'cohabitation' period, as a token of separation. This rite appears
to have been omitted in Cochin. In all three kingdoms, however,
the ritual husbands left the house after the four days of ceremonies and had no further obligations to their brides. A bride,
in turn, had only one further obligation to her ritual husband:

at his death, she and all her children, by whatever biological father, must observe death-pollution for him. Death-pollution was otherwise observed only for matrilineal kin. In Cochin, even if their mother's ritual husband never visited his wife again, her children must refer to him by the kinship term *appan*. Children in the lower, patrilineal castes of this area used this word to refer to the legal father, who was presumed also to be the biological father. In Walluvanad and Calicut I did not hear of this verbal usage and do not know by what term, if any, Nayar children referred to their mother's ritual husband.

The pre-puberty *tāli*-rite was essential for a girl. If she menstruated before it had been performed, she should in theory be expelled from her lineage and caste. In fact, however, my informants told me that in such a case the girl's family would conceal the fact of her maturity until after the rite had been performed. But it was a grave sin to do so and one which would never be publicly admitted.

The *tāli*-rite marked various changes in the social position of a girl. First, it brought her to social maturity. She was now thought to be at least ritually endowed with sexual and procreative functions and was thenceforward accorded the status of a woman. After the rite people addressed her in public by the respectful title *amma* meaning 'mother', and she might take part in the rites of adult women. Second, after the *tāli*-rite a girl must observe all the rules of etiquette associated with incest prohibitions in relation to men of her lineage. She might not touch them, might not sit in their presence, might not speak first to them and might not be alone in a room with one of them. Third, after the *tāli*-rite and as soon as she became old enough (i.e., shortly before or after puberty), a girl received as visiting husbands a number of men of her sub-caste from outside her lineage, usually but not necessarily from her neighbourhood. In addition she might be visited by any Nayar of the higher sub-castes of village headmen, chiefs or royalty, or by a Nambudiri Brahman. All of these relationships were called *sambandham*. Among commoner Nayar women, however, the great majority of unions were with men of commoner sub-caste.

Relations between any Nayar women and a man of *lower* Nayar sub-caste, or between any Nayar woman and a man of one of the lower, non-Nayar castes, were strictly prohibited. If a woman was found guilty of such a relationship her lineage's *enangar* carried the matter to the neighbourhood assembly. This temporarily excommunicated the woman's property-group until justice had been done. In the nineteenth century and early this century the property-group was re-accepted into caste only after its *kāranavan* had dismissed the woman from her household and caste, never to return. In pre-British times a woman so dismissed became the property of the king or chief and might be sold into slavery with foreign traders. Alternatively, however, the men of her property-group had the right, sometimes exercised, to kill both the woman and her lover and thus preserve the good name of their lineage.

After the ritual marriage, the bridegroom need have no further contact with his ritual wife. If both parties were willing, however, he might enter into a sexual relationship with his ritual bride about the time of her puberty. But he had no priority over other men of the neighbourhood group. There is some uncertainty as to the number of visiting husbands a woman might have at one time. Writers of the sixteenth and seventeenth centuries report that a woman usually had some three to eight regular husbands but might receive other men of her own or a higher caste at will. Hamilton in 1727 stated that a woman might have as husbands 'twelve but no more at one time' (Hamilton 1727 I: 310). As late as 1807 Buchanan reported that Nayar women vied with each other as to the number of lovers they could obtain (Buchanan 1807 I: 411). A few of my older informants could remember women who had had three or four current husbands, although plural unions were being frowned upon and had almost died out by the end of the last century. There appears to have been no limit to the number of wives of appropriate sub-caste whom a Nayar might visit concurrently. It seems, therefore, that a woman customarily had a small but not a fixed number of husbands from within her neighbourhood, that relationships with these men might be of long standing, but that the woman was also free to receive casual visitors of appropriate sub-caste who passed through her neighbourhood in the course of military operations.

A husband visited his wife after supper at night and left before breakfast next morning. He placed his weapons at the door of his wife's room and if others came later they were free to sleep on the verandah of the woman's house. Either party to a union might terminate it at any time without formality. A passing guest recompensed a woman with a small cash gift at each visit. But a more regular husband from within the neighbourhood had certain customary obligations. At the start of the union it was common although not essential for him to present the woman with a cloth of the kind worn as a skirt. Later he was expected to make small personal gifts to her at the three main festivals of the year. These gifts included a loin-cloth, betel-leaves and areca-nuts for chewing, hair-oil and bathing-oil, and certain vegetables. Failure on the part of a husband to make such a gift was a tacit sign that he had ended the relationship. Most important, however, when a woman became pregnant it was essential for one or more men of appropriate sub-caste to acknowledge probable paternity. This they did by providing a fee of a cloth and some vegetables to the low-caste midwife who attended the woman in childbirth. If no man of suitable caste would consent to make this gift, it was assumed that the woman had had relations with a man of lower caste or with a Christian or a Muslim. She must then be either expelled from her lineage and caste or killed by her matrilineal kinsmen. I am uncertain of the precise fate of the child in such a case, but there is no doubt at all that he could not be accepted as a member of his lineage and caste. I do not know whether he was killed or became a slave; almost certainly, he must have shared the fate of his mother. Even as late as 1949, over a hundred and fifty years after the establishment of British rule, a Nayar girl who became pregnant before the modern marriage ceremony was regarded as acting within the canons of traditional religious law if she could simply find a Nayar of suitable sub-caste to pay her delivery expenses. But if no Nayar would consent to this she ran the danger of total ostracism, with her child, by the village community. I heard of several cases in which such a girl was driven from her home by her *kāranvan* at the command of the sub-caste assembly. Her natal kinsmen then performed funeral rites for her as if she had died. In each case the girl took refuge in a town before or shortly after her child was born.

Although he made regular gifts to her at festivals, in no sense of the term did a man maintain his wife. Her food and regular clothing she obtained from her matrilineal group. The gifts of a woman's husbands were personal luxuries which pertained to her role as a sexual partner—extra clothing, articles of toilet, betel, and areca-nut the giving of which is associated with courtship, and the expenses of the actual delivery, not, be it noted, of the maintenance of either mother or child. The gifts continued to be made at festivals only while the relationship lasted. No man had obligations to a wife of the past.

In these circumstances the exact biological fatherhood of a child was often uncertain, although, of course, paternity was presumed to lie with the man or among the men who had paid the delivery expenses. But even when biological paternity was known with reasonable certainty, the genitor had no economic, social, legal, or ritual rights in nor obligations to, his children after he had once paid the fees of their births. Their guardianship, care and discipline were entirely the concern of their matrilineal kinsfolk headed by their *kāranavan*. All the children of a woman called all her current husbands by the Sanskrit word *acchan* meaning 'lord'. They did not extend kinship terms at all to the matrilineal kin of these men. Neither the wife nor her children observed pollution at the death of a visiting husband who was not also the ritual husband of the wife.

In most matrilineal systems with settled agriculture and localized matrilineal groups, durable links are provided between these groups by the interpersonal relationships of marriage, affinity, and fatherhood. The husbands, affines, fathers, and patrilateral kin of members of the matrilineal group have customary obligations to and rights in them which over time serve to mitigate conflicts between the separate matrilineal groups. The Nayars had no such durable institutionalized interpersonal links. This does not mean that men did not sometimes form strong emotional attachments to particular wives and their children. My information indicates that they did. I know for example that if a man showed particular fondness for a wife, his wife's matrilineal kin were likely to suspect the husband's matrilineal kin of hiring sorcerers against them. For the husband's matrilineal kin would be likely to fear that the husband might secretly convey to his wife gifts and cash which belonged rightfully to his matrilineal kin. This suspicion was especially rife if the husband was a *kāranavan* who controlled extensive property. Informal emotional attachments did therefore exist between individuals of different lineages. But what I wish to indicate is that among the Nayars, these interpersonal affinal and patrilateral links were not invested with customary legal, economic, or ceremonial functions of a kind which would periodically bring members of different lineages together in mandatory forms of co-operation. Four special kinship terms did apparently exist for use in relation to affines acquired through the *sambandham* relationship, although, as I have said, there were no patrilateral terms for kin other than the mother's husbands. All men and women currently engaged in *sambandham* unions with members of ego's property group, and all members of the property-groups of these individuals, were collectively referred to as *bandhukkal* ('joined ones'). A current wife of ego's mother's brother was addressed and referred to as *ammāyi*, and a wife of the elder brother as *jyeshtati amma* (lit. 'elder-sister-mother'). Finally, the own brother and the *sambandham* husband of a woman employed the reciprocal term *aliyan* to refer to each other but used no term of address. All the current *bandhukkal* of a property-group were invited to household feasts, but as individual affines they had no ceremonial or economic obligations and were not obliged to attend. As representatives of *enangar* lineages, however, some of these same individuals might be obliged to attend feasts and to fulfil ceremonial obligations as *enangar*. But as particular affines they had no obligations. In place therefore, of institutionalized interpersonal patrilateral and affinal links, the Nayars had the hereditary institution of linked lineages. Whether or not, at a particular time, sexual relationships existed between individuals of linked lineages, the linked lineages must fulfil their obligations at household ceremonies and give neighbourly help in such emergencies as birth and death. In the patrilineal and double unilineal castes of Kerala precisely the same obligations are fulfilled by the matrilateral kin and affines of individual members of the patrilineal group. The linked lineages of the Nayars must therefore, I think, be regarded as having a relationship of 'perpetual affinity', which carried the more formal functions of affinity and persisted through the making and breaking of individual sexual ties.

In view of these facts, it is convenient to mention here that Dr Leach's statement that Nayar marriage served 'to establish a socially significant relationship between the husband and his wife's brothers' is not, strictly speaking, correct. The *sambandham* union did not establish 'a socially significant relationship' between brothers-in-law, for in spite of the reciprocal kinship term these persons had no institutionalized obligations to one another by virtue of the particular *sambandham* tie. Further, the *tāli*-rite did not *establish* a relationship between the ritual husband and the brothers of his ritual bride. The ceremony set up no special obligations between these persons; it was merely that their lineages were, hereditarily, *enangar*, both before and after any particular *tāli*-rite. What the rite did *establish* was a ritual relationship between the *tāli*-tier and his ritual bride, and, as I shall try to show later, a relationship of group-marriage between the bride and all men of her sub-caste outside her lineage. But a particular *tāli*-rite in no way modified the hereditary relationships between male *enangar*. It is for this reason that I call the *enangar* relationship one of 'perpetual affinity' *between lineages*, which, though it carried the ceremonial functions of affinity, persisted irrespective of particular *sambandhams* and *tāli*-rites.

The Nayars of this area were thus highly unusual. For they had a kinship system in which the elementary family of father, mother and children was not institutionalized as a legal, productive, distributive, residential, socializing or consumption unit. Until recent years, some writers have thought that at least as a unit for some degree of co-operation in economic production and distribution, the elementary family was universal. This view has been put forward most forcibly by Murdock (Murdock 1949, chapter I). Radcliffe-Brown, however, was one of the earliest anthropologists to observe that if the written accounts of the Nayars were accurate, the elementary family was not institutionalized among them.[4] My research corroborates his findings.

I turn briefly to marital institutions among the higher Nayar

---

[4] Radcliffe-Brown expressed this view most recently and fully in his Introduction to *African Systems of Kinship and Marriage* (1950, pp. 73 seq.).

sub-castes of village headmen, district chiefs, and royalty. At various times during the pre-British period these lineages were accorded political office and set themselves up as of higher ritual rank than the commoner Nayars. The ritual ranking between these major aristocratic subdivisions was fairly stable, but the mutual ranking of lineages within each subdivision was in dispute. Most village headmen acknowledged the ritual superiority of district chiefs, and most chiefs, of the royal lineage. But some village headmen disputed among themselves for ritual precedence and so did many chiefs. As a result, each of these aristocratic lineages tended to set itself up as a separate sub-caste, acknowledging ritual superiors and inferiors but acknowledging no peers. In the course of time, moreover, following the vicissitudes of political fortune, such lineages could rise or fall in the ritual hierarchy. It was in these lineages therefore that hypergamous unions became most highly institutionalized, for most of these lineages refused to exchange spouses on equal terms. Instead, most of them married all their women upwards and all their men downwards. Women of village headmen's lineages entered *sambandham* unions with chiefly, royal, or Nambudiri Brahman men. Men of these lineages had unions with commoner Nayar women. Chiefly women had unions with royals or Nambudiris; chiefly men, with the women of village headmen's or commoner Nayar lineages. Royal women for the most part had unions with Nambudiri Brahmans of the highest rank. A few, especially in Calicut, however, had unions with men of older and ritually higher ranking royal lineages which had through conquest become politically subordinate to their own. Among Nambudiri Brahmans, only eldest sons were permitted to marry Nambudiri women and beget children for their own families. Younger sons of Nambudiri households might have *sambandham* unions with Nayar women of any sub-caste.

In all these hypergamous unions the visiting husband owed the same periodic gifts to his wife as in the case of equal unions between persons of the same commoner sub-caste. The husband in a hypergamous union was also held responsible for payment of delivery expenses at the birth of a child to his wife. Hypergamous unions differed from 'equal' unions in that in the former, the husband, being of higher ritual rank, might not eat in the house of his wife. The husband was also prohibited from touching

his wife, her children, or her other kinsfolk during the daytime
while he was in a state of ritual purity. Finally, although children
called their mother's higher caste husband by the term *acchan* plus
the caste title, Nayars as a whole were not permitted to use affinal
terms towards the Nambudiri husbands of their womenfolk, nor
did Nambudiris address or refer to their Nayar wives' brothers as
affines. Nayars insist, however, that a *sambandham* union with a
Nambudiri Brahman was of the same character as a *sambandham*
union with a Nayar of equal sub-caste. It seems that from the legal
point of view we must also judge it to be so, since the Brahman
husband, like the Nayar, was responsible for payments at the
birth of a child to his Nayar wife. During my fieldwork, the three
Nambudiri Brahmans whom I was able to question closely on this
subject told me that from *their* point of view, only marriage to a
Nambudiri woman with Vedic rites could be regarded as true marriage, and that *sambandham* unions with Nayar women were a kind
of concubinage. There seems to me no reason why we should not
regard these latter unions as concubinage from the point of view of
the Brahmans and (since they fulfilled the conditions of Nayar
marriage) marriage from the point of view of the Nayars. This
seems to me, in fact, the only possible interpretation, since the
Brahmans are patrilineal and the child of a Brahman-Nayar union
is not legitimized into the Brahman caste. The contrast from the
Brahman point of view appears most sharply in the case of an eldest
son, who may marry one or more Nambudiri women with Vedic
rites and may also have liaisons with one or more Nayar women.
The Brahman wife's children are, of course, fully legitimized into
the Brahman caste from birth. But the Nayar wife and her children traditionally had no rights of patrilineal descent or inheritance whatsoever, might not enter the kitchen of the Brahman
house and might not touch its inhabitants.

Consistently with the difference in direction of *sambandham*
unions, the *enangar* institution in these aristocratic Nayar lineages differed somewhat from that in the commoner sub-castes. In
general, an aristocratic Nayar lineage had as *enangar* two or more
lineages of a sub-caste higher than itself from which its women
were wont to draw husbands in the *sambandham* relationship.
The linked lineage relationship was in these cases not reciprocal.
A chiefly lineage might act as *enangar* for the lineages of one or

two village headmen, but had as its own *enangar* one or two chiefly or royal lineages of higher rank than itself. Nambudiri Brahman lineages acted as *enangar* for the highest ranks of chiefs and royalty. In this case too the aristocratic Nayar lineage had, of course, no reciprocal ritual obligations towards the Brahman families with which it was linked. The functions of these aristocratic *enangar* were, as far as I can detect, the same as in the case of commoner Nayars. In particular, men of the higher-ranking *enangar* lineages tied the *tāli* at the pre-puberty marriage of aristocratic girls—appropriately, for it was from these and other such higher-ranking lineages that the girls would later draw visiting husbands. Plural unions were customary in these aristocratic lineages as among commoner Nayars. Obviously, however, the choice of husbands became more and more restricted as one ascended the scale of ranked sub-castes, and at the top of the Nayar hierarchy it was restricted to Nambudiri Brahmans.

I turn now to my interpretation of Nayar marital institutions. To accomplish this it is necessary to classify the rights and obligations obtaining between 'spouses' and between 'fathers' and their 'children'. These fall into two categories: those of the *tāli*-rite and those of the *sambandham* union. In relations between spouses of the *tāli*-rite, the important rights are those of the woman. The ritual husband had, it is true, apparently at one time the right to deflower his bride. But the accounts of many writers indicate that this right was not eagerly sought, that in fact it was viewed with repugnance, and performed with reluctance. The ritual husband also had the right that his ritual wife should mourn his death. But we may assume that this right had more significance for the wife than for the husband, for it was not attended by offerings to the departed spirit. These could be performed only by matrilineal kin. The ritual bride's rights were complementary to her husband's, but for her they were of supreme importance. She had, first, the right to *have* a ritual husband of her own or a superior sub-caste before she attained maturity. Her life depended on this, for if she was not ritually married before puberty she was liable to excommunication and might possibly be put to death. She held this claim against her sub-caste as a whole exclusive of her lineage, or (in the case of aristocratic lineages) against a higher sub-caste. This group must, through the institution of the linked lineages, provide her with a ritual husband of correct rank and thus bring her to maturity in honour instead of in shame. It was the duty of her lineage kinsmen to see to it that some representative from their linked lineages fulfilled this right. The ritual wife's second right was that of observing pollution at the death of her ritual husband. I interpret this as a mark of proof that she had once been married in the correct manner and that this ritual relationship had retained significance for *her* throughout her ritual husband's life.

The *tāli*-tier had no rights in his ritual wife's children except that they should observe pollution at his death. From the child's point of view, however, his mother's ritual husband must have been a figure of great symbolic significance. For a child whose mother had no ritual husband could not acquire membership in his caste and lineage at all. The birth of a child before his mother's *tāli*-rite was absolutely forbidden and, in the nature of the case, can scarcely ever have happened. If it did occur, mother and child must certainly have been expelled and were most probably killed. The child's observance of pollution for his mother's ritual husband —like the use of the kinship term *appan* in Cochin—was a formal recognition that, for ritual purposes, he had been 'fathered' by a man of appropriate caste.

Turning to the *sambandham* union, it seems clear that the husband had no exclusive rights in his wife. He had only, in common with other men, sexual privileges which the wife might withdraw at any time. Again it is the wife's rights which are important. The wife had the right to gifts from her husband at festivals, gifts of little economic value but of high prestige value, for they established her as a woman well-favoured by men. But most significant was the woman's right to have her delivery expenses paid by one or more husbands of appropriate caste, that is, to have it openly acknowledged that her child had as biological father a man of required ritual rank. Her matrilineal kinsmen could if necessary press for the fulfillment of this right in a public assembly of the neighbourhood: in cases of doubtful paternity any man who had been currently visiting the woman could be forced by the assembly to pay her delivery expenses. But if no man of appropriate rank could be cited as potential father, woman and child were expelled from their lineage and caste.

The *sambandham* father had no rights in his wife's children. Here again, however, the child had one right in his possible biological fathers: that one or more of them should pay the expenses associated with his birth, and thus entitle him to enter the world as a member of his lineage and caste.

It is clear therefore that although the elementary family of one father, one mother, and their children was not institutionalized as a legal, residential, or economic unit, and although individual men had no significant rights in their particular wives or children, the Nayars did institutionalize the concepts of marriage and of paternity, and gave ritual and legal recognition to both. It is here that I must contradict Dr Leach's interpretation of the situation, for it is not true that 'the notion of fatherhood is lacking' nor is it true that 'a woman's children, however they might be begotten, were simply recruits to the woman's matrilineage' (Leach 1955: 183). For unless his mother was ritually married by a man of appropriate caste and, unless his biological paternity was vouched for by one or more men[5] of appropriate caste, a child could never enter his caste or lineage at all. As I pointed out in both the papers quoted by Dr Leach, the Nayars were aware of the physiological function of the male in procreation and attached significance to it, for they expected a child to look like his genitor. Like all the higher Hindu castes of India, they based their belief in the moral rightness of the caste system in part upon a racist ideology which involved the inheritance of physical, intellectual, and moral qualities by a child from both of its natural parents, and which held that the higher castes were, by virtue of their heredity, superior to the lower castes. It was ostensibly for this reason that the Nayars forbade with horror sexual contacts between a Nayar woman and a man of lower caste, and that they expelled or put to death women guilty of such contacts. This racist ideology also provided a motive for hypergamous unions, for Nayars of aristocratic lineages boasted of the superior qualities they derived from royal and Brahmanical fatherhood.

---

[5] I do not know whether the Nayars believed it possible for two or more men to contribute to the formation of one embryo. I think it possible that they did, for I found this belief among villagers of the Tamil country. Among these castes it formed part of a belief that several acts of intercourse are necessary to 'feed' the embryo and assist it to grow.

Moreover, although individual men had no significant customary rights in their wives and children, marriage and paternity were
probably significant factors in political integration. For hypergamous unions bound together the higher sub-castes of the political and religious hierarchies. Multiple sexual ties, as well as the
enangar relationship, linked office-bearing lineages to each other
and to their retainers in a complicated manner. And Nayar men
phrased their loyalty to higher-ranking military leaders, rulers,
and Brahmans in terms of a debt owed to benevolent paternal
figures whose forebears had collectively fathered them and whose
blood they were proud to share. The generalized concept of fatherhood thus commanded the Nayar soldier's allegiance to his
wider caste unit, to the rulers of his village, chiefdom, and kingdom, and to his religious authorities. It was associated with tender
loyalty and with fortitude in war.

I cannot entirely blame Dr Leach for underestimating the significance of Nayar paternity on the basis of his reading of my
earlier papers. For in those papers I was concerned to emphasize
the lack of rights of individual men in their spouses and children.
It is true that in 1952 I wrote: 'Marriage . . . was the slenderest
of ties, while as a social concept fatherhood scarcely existed'
(Gough 1952a: 73). I had not then realized the fundamental necessity to a Nayar of having both a ritual and a biological father
of appropriate caste. Moreover I myself confused the issue by
referring to the *sambandham* partners as 'husbands' and 'wives'
in my first paper (Gough 1952a) and as 'lovers' and 'mistresses'
in my second (Gough 1955a). For it was not until some time after I read Dr Leach's paper that I decided to classify Nayar unions unequivocally as marriage and arrived at a definition of
marriage which would include the Nayar case. In my own defence
I must, however, note that in my paper of 1955 I mentioned that
children must observe death pollution for their mother's ritual
husband, and that in Cochin they used the kinship term *appan*
for this ritual father. In both papers quoted by Dr Leach, finally,
I noted that sexual relations were forbidden between a Nayar
woman and a man of lower caste or sub-caste, and that the current *sambandham* husbands of a woman must pay her delivery
expenses.

I regard Nayar unions as a form of marriage for two reasons.

One is that although plural unions were customary, mating was not promiscuous. Sexual relations were forbidden between members of the same lineage on pain of death. It was also forbidden for two men of the same property-group wittingly to have relations with one woman, or for two women of the same property-group to have relations with one man. (This rule of course automatically excluded relations between a man and his biological daughter.) Further, relations were absolutely prohibited between a Nayar woman and a man of lower sub-caste or caste. These prohibitions are directly connected with my second and more important reason for regarding these unions as marriage, namely, that the concept of legally established paternity *was* of fundamental significance in establishing a child as a member of his lineage and caste.

Granted that Nayar unions constituted a form of marriage, we must I think, classify them as a clear case of group-marriage. This was the interpretation to which I inclined in 1952 (Gough 1952a: 73) and it is, I now think, the only interpretation which makes sense of the descriptive material I have presented. The *tāli*-rite, as I see it, initiated for each individual Nayar girl a state of marriage to a collectivity of men of appropriate caste. First, the rite ceremonially endowed the girl with sexual and procreative functions. (The mock menstrual seclusion before the rite is relevant to this, as is the actual defloration.) Second, the woman's natal kinsmen surrendered the newly acquired rights in her sexuality, though not in her procreative functions, to a male representative from outside her lineage. This appears in that rules of etiquette associated with incest prohibitions came into force from this date. Third, rights in the woman's sexuality were received by her *enangan* as representative of the men of his sub-caste as a whole. This appears in that the individual *enangan,* as a special sexual partner, was dismissed at the end of the ceremonies and might approach the woman again only as one among a series of equal husbands. In the commoner sub-castes the *enangan* was of the same sub-caste as the woman, and through him as representative sexual rights in the woman were conferred on all men of her sub-caste as a collectivity. They were also in fact extended to any man of higher sub-caste who might favour her with his attentions. In aristocratic lineages the ritual husband was of a sub-caste higher than the woman's, and through him, as representative, sexual rights in the woman were conferred upon all men of higher sub-caste as a collectivity. Fourth, the *tāli*-rite, by providing the woman with a ritual husband who (in my view) symbolized all the men of his sub-caste with whom the woman might later have relationships, also provided her children with a ritual father who symbolized the correctness of their paternity. The children acknowledged their debt to him by mourning at his death.

The later *sambandham* unions, by this interpretation, involved the claiming of sexual privileges by men all of whom were potential husbands by virtue of their membership in a sub-caste. The husbands had, however, no individually exclusive rights and could be dismissed at the woman's wish. Their duties as members of their caste were to provide the woman and her lineage with children and to acknowledge their potential biological paternity through birth-payments which legitimized the woman's child.

THE DEFINITION OF MARRIAGE

I have called the Nayar unions marriage because they involved the concept of legal paternity. It is clear, however, that such a form of group-marriage will not fit the *Notes and Queries* definition of 'a union between *a* man and *a* woman such that children born to the woman are recognized legitimate offspring of both parents' (my italics). For legitimacy in the case of the Nayar child required both a ritual father and a 'legalized genitor' of appropriate rank, and indeed a child might have more than one 'legal genitor' if two or more men had jointly paid the expenses of his birth.

As a tentative move toward a new definition, which will have cross-cultural validity and will fit the Nayar and several other unusual cases, I suggest the following: 'Marriage is a relationship established between a woman and one or more other persons, which provides that a child born to the woman under circumstances not prohibited by the rules of the relationship, is accorded full birth-status rights common to normal members of his society or social stratum.'

A few footnotes to this definition may help to vindicate its inevitably clumsy phraseology. 'One or more persons' (in place of 'a man') will bring into the definition both group-marriage of the Nayar type and also true fraternal polyandry.[6] It also brings within the definition such unusual types as woman-marriage-to-a-woman. 'Under circumstances not prohibited by the rules of the relationship' would bring into the definition various problematic cases. It is possible for example that there are patrilineal societies in which a husband may legally repudiate a child illicitly begotten upon his wife by another man, without divorcing the wife herself. In this case the previous establishment of the marriage would *not* ensure full birth-status rights to the child, for the rules of the marriage relationship would have been broken through the circumstances which led to his birth. 'Full birth-status rights common to all normal members . . .' is a compressed reference to all the social relationships, property-rights, etc. which a child acquires at birth by virtue of his legitimacy, whether through the father or through the mother. For patrilineal societies the phrase 'full birth-status rights' will include the rights which a child acquires in his *pater* as a person and in his *pater*'s group. It will include, that is to say, the legitimization of fatherhood, or more precisely, of 'father-sonhood'. The phrase is, however, broader than any concept of specific rights in a particular father. It will therefore take care of a case like the Nayar in which all rights are acquired *through* the mother but in which a relationship must be established between the mother and one or more other persons in order for these matrilineal rights to be ratified. Such a process may be called the legitimization of motherhood, or more precisely of 'mother-sonhood'. Moreover 'full birth-status rights' is, I think, not only broader but more precise than 'recognized legitimate offspring', to the vagueness of which Dr Leach took exception. The inclusion of 'society or social stratum' makes allowances for class or caste systems in which birth-status rights vary between strata. The case of the Nayars, who are a matrilineal

---

[6] I agree with Dr Leach that the Iravas of Central Kerala had true fraternal polyandry. My own enquiries produced evidence supporting Aiyappan's view that the brothers shared equally both sexual rights in the woman and also legal paternity of the children, in the same manner in which they were co-owners of the ancestral property. The eldest living brother at any given time was simply the legal representative of this corporation.

caste in a predominantly patrilineal society, is an obvious example
of this.

It should also perhaps be pointed out that this definition does
not state that full birth-status rights cannot be acquired by a child
except through the marriage of its mother, but only that marriage
provides for the acquisition of these rights. The definition does
not therefore exclude societies like the Nuer in which a man may
legitimize the child of an unmarried woman upon payment of a
legitimization fee, without becoming married to the mother
(Evans-Pritchard 1951: 21, 26).

Prince Peter has objected to the *Notes and Queries* definition
and, by implication, to any definition which would make the legitimization of children through the mother's relationship to another
party the distinctive characteristic of marriage (1956: 46). His
reason for objecting is that in some societies like the Toda, 'marriage and legitimacy of the children can be looked upon as two
different and separate concepts, and it may be necessary to go
through a ceremony of legitimization of the offspring (the Toda
pursütpimi ceremony) in order to establish who is the legal father, because marriage rites are insufficient in themselves to do
this.'

However, it seems from Rivers' account that precisely what distinguishes the Toda institution which Prince Peter translates as
'marriage' (*mokh-vatt*) from that which he translates as 'concubinage' (*mokhthoditi*) (1957: 35), is that a 'husband' holds
the right to legitimize some or all of his 'wife's' children by the
pursütpimi ceremony, whereas a lover in the *mokhthoditi* union,
being of a different endogamous group from the woman, does not
hold this right (Rivers 1906: 526). A husband acquires the right
to perform the *pursütpimi* ceremony, it seems, by virtue of arranged marriage to an infant or through payment of cattle to a
former husband or to a group of former husbands of the wife.
The Toda marriage union at its inception does therefore provide
that a child born to the woman (under circumstances not prohibited by the rules of the relationship) *must be* legitimized before
his birth; the *pursütpimi* ceremony confirms his legitimacy by at-
taching him to a particular father and giving him rights in the
father's patrilineal group. In the Toda case again therefore the
concept of legal paternity is *the* distinguishing characteristic of

marriage, even though the individual husband, because of polyandry, may be permitted to legitimize only some and not all of the children born to his wife. The Toda case, therefore fits my definition,[7] whether we regard the *pursütpimi* ceremony as the final one of a sequence of marriage rites, or as a legitimizing act which, under circumstances not prohibited by the rules of the relationship, one or another of the woman's husbands is legally obliged to fulfil.

I do not argue that all societies must necessarily be found to have marriage by my definition. There may yet turn out to be whole societies—or more probably whole social strata—in which children acquire no birth-status rights except through their mother, by the simple fact of birth. It is possible for example that some slave populations do not have marriage in this sense of the term. What I do wish to suggest, however, is that for most if not all the societies for which we now have information, including the Nayar, marriage as I have defined it is a significant relationship, distinguished by the people themselves from all other kinds of relationships. My definition should therefore enable us to isolate marriage as a cross-cultural phenomenon, and from there to proceed to the more exciting task: that of investigating the differential circumstances under which marriage becomes invested with various other kinds of rights and obligations. Some of the most important of these Dr Leach has already listed for us.

---

[7] I agree with Dr Fischer that Prince Peter's definition of marriage is a tautology and so of no assistance (1956, 92). All that Prince Peter's second note shows (1957, 35) is that several peoples of his acquaintance have different terms for different kinds of relationships between men and women. But unless we approach these with some guiding concepts of our own in mind, we cannot decide which of them to translate as 'marriage' and which as 'concubinage.'

4 POLYANDRY, INHERITANCE AND THE DEFINITION OF MARRIAGE[1]

E. R. Leach

ALTHOUGH POLYANDRY HAS BEEN an important topic of anthropological discussion for almost a century the definition of the concept remains strikingly unsatisfactory. This is sufficiently indicated by the fact that Fischer (1952) maintains that adelphic polyandry, regarded as a form of polygamy, is non-existent, while H.R.H. Prince Peter of Greece and Denmark (1955a), ignoring Fischer, continues to discuss adelphic polyandry as a species of polygamy.

At first sight the issue seems a simple one with the logic all on Fischer's side. The *Notes and Queries* (1951) definition of marriage is: 'Marriage is a union between a man and a woman such that children born to the woman are recognized legitimate offspring of both partners.' Now certainly, in many cases of polyandry, the legal status of the children is similar to that described by Cæsar for the ancient Britons (Fischer 1952: 114): 'Wives are shared between groups of ten or twelve men, especially between brothers and between fathers and sons; but the offspring of these unions are counted as the children of those to whom the maid was conducted first.' This clearly is not a condition of polygamy; the children have only one legal father and the woman has only one legal husband. The other 'husbands' have tolerated sexual access to the woman, but she is not married to them in

Reprinted from *Man*, Volume 54, 1955, pp. 182–86 with permission of the author and of the Royal Anthropological Institute.
[1] This paper is based in part upon fieldwork carried out in Ceylon in 1954 with the aid of a Leverhulme Research Award and a grant from the Wenner-Gren Foundation.

terms of the *Notes and Queries* definition. The situation is one
of plural mating, or, as Fischer would call it, 'polykoity.'

More specifically, Fischer argues that we should reserve the
concept of polygamy for situations in which the polygamous
spouse goes through a succession of marriage rites with different
partners. In adelphic polyandry 'the woman does not contract
different successive marriages. There is no reason for this, since
the social position of her children is guaranteed completely by
the fact that she is married' (Fischer 1952: 114).

Fischer agrees that an institution of polyandrous polygamy is a
possibility. For example, a woman might be mated to several men
in such a way that each of them in turn assumed the role of social
father in respect to her successive children. This very approximately seems to be the state of affairs among the Todas, and
Fischer concedes that it 'approaches very closely to that of polygamy.' The institution of secondary marriage as described by Smith
(1953) is also polyandrous polygamy in Fischer's sense. In both
these cases every child has one, and only one, clearly defined social father.

But is it really so certain that the role of social father cannot
be vested simultaneously in several different individuals? Is it not
possible that in some societies social fatherhood is not an attribute of individuals at all but of a collective corporation which may
include several brothers or even fathers and sons?

When Radcliffe-Brown (1941) argued that adelphic polyandry
is to be 'interpreted in the light of the structural principle of the
solidarity of the sibling group,' he presumably had in mind that
social fatherhood might sometimes be vested in a collective corporation of this kind, and Prince Peter sought to demonstrate that
this is in fact the case. Does this mean that the notion of group
marriage is once again respectable?

There is certainly one well-attested case of 'corporate polyandry' of this kind, namely that of the Iravas (Aiyappan 1945:
98–103). Although Aiyappan states that on the occasion of a
marriage 'the common practice is for the eldest brother alone to
go to the bride's house to fetch her,' it is plain, from the further
details that he gives, that the eldest brother is here acting as
representative of the group of brothers considered as a corporation. Even so, it is not entirely clear what rights this corporation

possesses. It is Aiyappan's thesis that *all* marital rights are completely merged in the corporation—that the sexual rights of the individual husbands and the property rights of the individual children are alike indistinguishable. Nevertheless one would welcome more detailed evidence on these points.

There is another way of looking at the problem. Instead of arguing pedantically about whether adelphic polyandry does or does not constitute plural marriage, let us consider whether a definition of marriage solely in terms of legitimacy (*Notes and Queries* 111; Fischer 108) is altogether adequate. There are other definitions of marriage with respectable backing, *e.g.* 'a physical, legal, and moral union between a man and a woman in complete community of life for the establishment of a family' (Ranasinha 1950: 192). Is the *Notes and Queries* definition any less question-begging than this? What, for example, does the phrase 'legitimate offspring' really connote?

Prince Peter, in the lecture under discussion, seemed to assume that, of the various forms of heterosexual mating recognized and tolerated in any society, there is always one which may properly be described as 'marriage' in the anthropological sense. Yet if we adhere rigidly to our *Notes and Queries* definition this is not the case.

Thus traditionally among the matrilineal Nayar of South India (Gough 1952a and 1955a) a woman had a ritual husband in her *enangar* lineage and also various 'recognized lovers' (*sambandham*), who lacked ritual status; but all of these men were excluded from any legal rights in respect to the woman's children. There was here then no marriage in the strict sense of the term but only a 'relationship of perpetual affinity' between linked lineages (Gough 1955a). The woman's children, however they might be begotten, were simply recruits to the woman's own matrilineage.

Yet as Gough has shown, even in this system, certain *elements* of a normal marriage institution are present.

The notion of fatherhood is lacking. The child uses a term of address meaning 'lord' or 'leader' towards *all* its mother's lovers, but the use of this term does not carry with it any connotation of paternity, either legal or biological. On the other hand the notion of affinity is present, as evidenced by the fact that a woman must observe pollution at her ritual husband's death (Gough 1955a).

Both Gough (1952a) and Prince Peter have described the Nayar as having a system of polyandrous marriage. I do not wish to insist that this is a misnomer, but we need to be clear that *if* we agree that the Nayar practise polyandrous marriage then we are using the term 'marriage' in a sense different from that employed by Fischer and by *Notes and Queries*.

My personal view is that the *Notes and Queries* definition of marriage is too limited and that it is desirable to include under the category 'marriage' several distinguishable subtypes of institution.

The institutions commonly classed as marriage are concerned with the allocation of a number of distinguishable classes of rights. In particular a marriage may serve:

1. To establish the legal father of a woman's children.
2. To establish the legal mother of a man's children.
3. To give the husband a monopoly in the wife's sexuality.[2]
4. To give the wife a monopoly in the husband's sexuality.
5. To give the husband partial or monopolistic rights to the wife's domestic and other labour services.
6. To give the wife partial or monopolistic rights to the husband's labour services.
7. To give the husband partial or total rights over property belonging or potentially accruing to the wife.
8. To give the wife partial or total rights over property belonging or potentially accruing to the husband.
9. To establish a joint fund of property—a partnership—for the benefit of the children of the marriage.
10. To establish a socially significant 'relationship of affinity' between the husband and his wife's brothers.

One might perhaps considerably extend this list, but the point I would make is that in no single society can marriage serve to establish all these types of right simultaneously; nor is there any one of these rights, which is invariably established by marriage, in every known society. We need to recognize, then, that the institutions commonly described as marriage do not all have the same legal and social concomitants.

---

[2] I use the term "monopoly" advisedly. I consider that this right 3 is to be regarded as a monopoly control over the disposal of the wife's sexuality rather than an exclusive right to the use thereof. In discussing adelphic polyandry this distinction is important.

If we attempt a typology of marriage on these lines it is at once obvious that the nature of the marriage institution is partially correlated with principles of descent and rules of residence. Thus in a society structured into patrilineal patrilocal lineages we commonly find that right 1 is far and away the most important element, whereas among the matrilineal matrilocal Nayar, as we have seen, right 10 is the only marriage characteristic that is present at all. Or again, in the matrilineal virilocal structure of the Trobriands, right 7 assumes prior, though not altogether unique, importance (Malinowski 1932, with reference to *urigubu* payments).

Although the early writers on polyandry (*e.g.* McLennan 1865) supposed that it was an institution closely associated with matriliny, Prince Peter has pointed out that the best-established cases of adelphic polyandry occur in societies which express patrilineal ideals. This was true of the Kandyan Sinhalese (D'Oyly 1929); it is true of the patrilineal Iravas of Madras (Aiyappan 1945) and of the Tibetans (Bell, 1928: 88). But it is also the case that the patriliny in these societies is of an ambiguous and rather uncertain type. The position in each case is that while the people concerned profess a preference for patrilocal marriage and the inheritance of landed property through males only, matrilocal marriage and inheritance through females is not at all uncommon (Aiyappan 1945; Li An-Che 1947; D'Oyly 1929: 110). Moreover, although women who marry patrilocally surrender their claims on their own ancestral land, they receive a dowry of movable goods in lieu.

This aspect of polyandry, namely that it is intimately associated with an institution of dowry, has previously received inadequate attention. In patrilineal systems of the more extreme type *all* significant property rights are vested in males so that, from the inheritance point of view, marriage does no more than establish the rights of a woman's sons in her husband's property (right 1 above). Fission of the patrimonial inheritance group does of course occur, and when it occurs it is very likely that individual marriages will be cited (retrospectively) as a justification for such a split; the model given by Fortes (1945: 199) is typical in this respect. Yet, in such cases, marriage, as such, does not create an independent partible estate.

But when property in land and saleable valuables is vested in women as well as in men, a very different state of affairs prevails; for each marriage then establishes a distinct parcel of property rights and the children of any one marriage have, of necessity, a different total inheritance potential from the children of any other marriage.

Systems of inheritance in which both men and women have property endowment are very general in Southern India, Ceylon and throughout South-East Asia. Such systems are found in association with patrilineal, matrilineal, and cognatic descent structures. The general pattern is that the nuclear family, as a unit, possesses three categories of property, namely the entailed inheritance of the father, the entailed inheritance of the mother, and the 'acquired property'—that is, the property owned jointly by the parents by virtue of their operations as a business partnership during the period of the marriage. The children of the marriage are heirs to all three categories of property, but the categories are not merged.

Now it is quite obvious that an inheritance principle whereby women as well as men can be endowed with property conflicts with the ideal that landed property should be maintained intact in the hands of the male heirs. Yet it is a fact that there are many societies which manage to maintain both principles simultaneously. There are a variety of customary behaviours which can best be understood if they are regarded as partial solutions to the dilemma that arises from maintaining these contradictory ideals.

Let us be clear what the dilemma is. On the one hand there is the ideal that the patrimonial inheritance ought to be maintained intact. Full brothers and the sons of full brothers *ought* to remain together in the ancestral home and work the ancestral land. On the other hand, since the wives of these men, when they join the household, bring with them property which will be inherited by their own children but not by their husbands' nephews and nieces, each new marriage creates a separate block of property interests, which is in conflict with the ideal of maintaining the economic solidarity of male siblings.

One way out of the difficulty was that adopted in the Jaffna Tamil code of Thesawalamai (Tambiah 1954: 36): the sons inherited the hereditary property of their father, and the acquired property of both spouses was inherited by the sons and the un-dowered daughters. The dowries to the daughters were given out of the mother's dowry. Systems of double unilineal descent, such as that described by Forde for the Yakö, operate in a somewhat comparable way (Forde 1950: 306), though the distinction here is between property passed to men through men (the patrilineal inheritance of land rights) and property passed to men through women (the matrilineal inheritance of movables).

The Moslem preference for patrilineage endogamy likewise re-solves the conflict between female rights of inheritance and a patrilineal principle of descent. A declared preference for recipro-cal or patrilateral cross-cousin marriage may sometimes have similar implications. Indeed, marriage preferences of this latter type seem to be more or less confined to societies in which a sub-stantial proportion of the inheritance rights are transmitted through women.

Adelphic polyandry, I would suggest, is to be understood as yet another variation on the same theme. If two brothers share one wife so that the only heirs of the brothers are the children born of that wife, then, from an economic point of view, the marriage will tend to cement the solidarity of the sibling pair rather than tear it apart, whereas, if the two brothers have separate wives, their children will have separate economic interests, and main-tenance of the patrimonial inheritance in one piece is likely to prove impossible. If the ethnographical evidence is to be believed, polyandrous institutions, where they occur, are deemed highly virtuous and tend to eliminate rather than heighten sexual jeal-ousies (Aiyappan 1937).

In the lecture under discussion, Prince Peter referred repeat-edly to contemporary polyandry among the Kandyan Sinhalese. It seems important that we should be clear what the word 'poly-andry' means in this case. Sinhalese law does not recognize the existence of polyandrous marriage and it is not possible for any individual to maintain in a law court that he or she is 'the rec-ognized legitimate offspring' of two different fathers, nor can a woman bear 'legitimate offspring' to two different husbands with-out an intermediate registration of divorce. Thus, strictly speak-ing, polyandry in Ceylon is not a variety of marriage, if marriage be narrowly defined. On the other hand it is certainly the case that there are parts of Ceylon where two brothers often share a common domestic household with one 'wife', these arrangements being permanent, amicable and socially respectable.[3]

Polyandrous households of this type contrast rather strikingly with the more normal pattern in which two or more brothers live together in a single compound each with his separate 'wife.' This latter situation is characterized by marked restraint between the brothers and even complete avoidance between a man and his 'sister-in-law.'

The 'wives' in such cases may or may not be married according to Sinhalese law. In a high proportion of cases they are not so married. In law the children of these unions are then illegitimate. The children, however, have birth certificates and these certificates give the name not only of the mother but also of the acknowledged father, a circumstance which provides the child with a potential claim to a share of the heritable property of each of its parents.[4] The child therefore, although not the *legiti-*

---

[3] It is difficult to accept Prince Peter's claim that in the Ratnapura District of Ceylon polyandry is so common as to be the norm. The *Census* (Ceylon Government 1946, Vol. I, Part 2) includes figures for 'customary marriages' as well as 'registered marriages.' The Census enumerators were required to enter as 'married' anyone who 'claimed to be married according to custom or repute' and there seems no reason why they should have excluded 'polyandrous husbands.' However, in all districts, the overall total of 'married' males is roughly equal to the overall total of 'married' females, which does not suggest that the frequency of polyandry can be numerically significant. For Ceylon as a whole the *Census* gave 389,846 women as 'married by custom' and 843,493 as 'legally married by registration.' While this is evidence that the strict definition of legitimate marriage is unrealistic, it does not follow that the anthropologist must accept the Census enumerators' notions of what constitutes customary marriage.

[4] *The Report of the Kandyan Law Commission* (Ceylon Government 1935, paragraphs 199–210) recommends that all children born of non-registered marriages shall be deemed illegitimate and shall be excluded from any share in the entailed property of the father. The *Report* recognizes that this conflicts with the customary law of the pre-British period which did not restrict entailed (*paraveni*) property to the offspring of formal marriages. Ranasinha (1950, Vol. I, Part 1, p. 192) ignores this *Report* and asserts that the highest authorities have held that 'registration was not essential to the validity of a marriage in Ceylon, and the marriage relation could be presumed on adequate evidence of cohabitation and repute.' Certainly in many parts of Ceylon today the children of non-registered 'marriages' are treated as having full inheritance rights in their father's property, but whether this right could now be sustained in a Court of Law I am uncertain.

mate offspring of both its parents, is nevertheless a *legitimate heir* of both its parents. If then the principle of legitimacy be here defined in terms of property rights rather than descent it seems quite proper that Sinhalese customary unions should be regarded as marriages.

Is it then possible in this case to have a polyandrous *marriage*? Legally, no. Since a birth certificate certainly cannot show more than one father, no child possesses the basis for establishing a legal claim to the property of a polyandrous corporation. All the same, it seems probable that in polyandrous households the children do ordinarily inherit jointly the undivided property of the two fathers and that Sinhalese custom recognizes their right to do so. Provided that we are not too pedantic about what we mean by 'legitimate' it does appear that we are dealing here with something that an anthropologist can properly call polyandrous marriage. Even so the issue is by no means clear-cut.

Aiyappan (1945: 103), in commenting on the refusal of an English judge to admit the possibility of a woman being simultaneously married to two brothers, treats the issue as being simply one of a conflict between English law and customary Irava law. But so far as the Sinhalese are concerned the issue is not so simple.

The classical formulation of the former Sinhalese law regarding polyandry appears in Sawers' *Digest* (D'Oyly 1929: 129):

> Polygamy as well as polyandry is allowed without limitation as to the number of wives or husbands—but the wife cannot take a second associated husband without the consent of the first—though the husband can take a second wife into the same house as his first wife without her consent. The wife, however, has the power of refusing to admit a second associated husband at the request of her first husband, even should he be the brother of the first. And should the proposed second associated husband not be a brother of the first, the consent of the wife's family to the double connection is required.

It is clear that two separate rights are here distinguished. First, there is the right in the wife's sexuality which marriage serves to vest partly, but not completely, in the person of the first husband. The sexual rights of the other husbands are exercised, not by virtue of the marriage, but through the individual consent of the first husband and the joint wife. On the other hand, the ritual of patrilocal marriage—the essence of which is that a man conducts his bride from her father's house to his own (Ceylon Government 1935, paragraph 168)—serves to establish a relation of affinity between the wife's family as a whole and the husband's family as a whole. The wife's family have no interest in what sexual arrangements pertain unless it is proposed to extend the rights of sexual access beyond the limits of the husband's sibling group.

It is notable that, in this formulation of Sawers, the rights of the children are not mentioned; the ritual procedures of Sinhalese marriage are not concerned with the rights of the potential children. The marriage rite disposes of the woman's sexuality to her first husband; it also has the effect of making a public pronouncement that the woman has been properly endowed so that she has no further claims on her parental property. The status of children arises from quite a different source.

In Sinhalese customary law it was (and is[5]) the rule that if a man and a woman are publicly known to have cohabited together and the woman bears a child, then the woman has a claim on the man for the support of the child (D'Oyly 1929: 84). In ordinary rural practice, all of a man's acknowledged children are equally his heirs whether or not he has at any time gone through a ritual of marriage with the children's mother. Likewise all of a woman's children have equal claims on her inheritance.

My conclusion is that in the Sinhalese case, and very probably in other analogous cases, we are dealing with two different institutions both of which resemble marriage as ordinarily understood, but which need to be carefully distinguished. Neither institution corresponds precisely to the ideal type of marriage as defined in *Notes and Queries*.

On the one hand we have a formal and legal arrangement, by which, so far as Ceylon is concerned, a woman can only be married to one man at a time. 'Marriage' in this sense establishes a relationship of affinity between the family of the bride and the family of the first husband, and it gives the disposal of the bride's sexuality to the first husband, subject to the bride's personal con-

---

[5] See footnote 4, page 80.

sent. On the other hand we have another institution of 'marriage,' which is entered into quite informally but which nevertheless, by virtue of its public recognition, serves to provide the children with claims upon the patrimonial property of the men with whom the woman cohabits and publicly resides. This second form of 'marriage,' although it establishes the inheritance rights of the children, does not establish their permanent status as members of a corporate descent group, and Sinhalese children, as they grow up, have wide choice as to where they finally align themselves for the purposes of affiliation.

If we accept this second institution as a form of 'marriage,' then polyandry in Ceylon is a form of polygamy. If we confine the term 'marriage' to the first institution, polyandry in Ceylon is a form of polykoity. These niceties of definition are worth making because it is important that anthropologists should distinguish the various classes of right that are involved in marriage institutions.

Of greater importance is my hypothesis that adelphic polyandry is consistently associated with systems in which women as well as men are the bearers of property rights. Polyandry exists in Ceylon because, in a society where both men and women inherit property, polyandrous arrangements serve, both in theory and practice, to reduce the potential hostility between sibling brothers.

5 DAHOMEAN MARRIAGE:
A REVALUATION

Laura Bohannan

WE ARE FORTUNATE in possessing enough good ethnographic material on Dahomey to attempt a reassessment in the light of later theoretical developments of the very interesting types of marriage reported there.

Analysis shows that three criteria are involved in the thirteen 'types' of marriage as given by Herskovits's Dahomean informants (Herskovits 1938: i, 301–2): (1) the method of arranging the marriage, including courtship and payment of the bride-wealth; (2) the status of the children; and (3) the relationship between man and wife—a constant which is, however, influenced by the distribution of rights and duties in regard to the children. The nature of the social groups concerned in the configuration of rights and duties connected with marriage is a point of great importance, which does not appear in connexion with Herskovits's analysis of marriage; he divides these 'types' into a matrilineal and a patrilineal class on the basis of the status of the children. The starting point of the following analysis is the transfer or non-transfer of *puissance*, or jural authority, through marriage—a criterion emphasized by Le Hérissé (1911).[1]

MARRIAGE WITH TRANSFER OF JURAL AUTHORITY

There are, in the 'types' of marriage accompanied by a transfer of jural authority over the woman and her potential children, one

Reprinted from *Africa*, Vol. 19, No. 4, 1949, pp. 273–87, with permission of the author and the International African Institute.
[1] I shall translate *puissance* as 'jural authority' rather than *potestas* to avoid confusion with the implications of the latter term in Roman Law.

variable—the preliminaries to marriage, courtship, and the method of paying bride-wealth—and three constants: the nature of the marital relationship, the nature of the corporate groups involved, i.e., lineages,[2] and the status of the children. The marriage is marked by the payment of the bride-wealth, which is in two portions: gifts and services usually directed towards the parents of the girl, which may or may not be given, and the ritual 'payment' made to the head of the girl's lineage, which must be given if the marriage is to be accompanied by a transfer of jural authority over the woman and her children (Le Hérissé 1911: 203–8; Herskovits 1938: i, 303–8).

In 'money with woman' marriage (Herskovits 1938: i, 303–9; 335–37), the man selected as fiancé by the girl's father, accompanied by members of his lineage, calls on the girl's family. The customary gifts and services, the ritual payment, and the notification of the ancestors follow. Finally, the man and two men and two women of his lineage call for his wife. After a display of gifts from the bride, her parents, and the groom, an old woman of the girl's lineage blesses her in the name of her ancestors. The bride spends the first night at her husband's house with his mother or with his first wife. Though she may be rejected if, on the following evening, she should prove not to have been a virgin, generally she is forced instead to give the name of her seducer, who will be fined for adultery. The next morning the husband publicly and ceremonially gives his new wife the name by which she will thenceforth be known.[3]

Another 'type', 'child ask ask', differs only in that it is the future husband who initiates courtship. If the girl should already be betrothed and her father favours the second suitor, it is the latter who repays the original fiancé.[4]

A third 'type', 'woman give back woman' (Herskovits 1938: i, 310–11), brings out a very important aspect of the mechanism

---

[2] I shall refer to Herskovits's term 'sib' as 'lineage', and to the 'extended family' and the 'compound' as segments of the lineage. For definitions: Herskovits 1938: i, 137 ff., Evans-Pritchard, E. E. 1940: 6–7.
[3] In Dahomey a name, generally allusive, is given at the assumption of every new status (Herskovits 1938: i, 263).
[4] If such repayment is necessary, the marriage becomes one of the 'woman give back woman' type (Herskovits 1938: i, 311–13).

of the transfer of jural authority. If the betrothed girl elopes with another man, she and her seducer are brought by her parents before the chief.[5] The chief requires the original fiancé to calculate the amount he expended in gifts and services. By repaying this sum, the seducer acquires jural authority over the girl and obtains her as his wife, for the lineage (here that of the original fiancé), which has acquired jural authority over a woman can retransfer it (here to the seducer's lineage). The seducer cannot make the payments to the girl's own lineage, which no longer holds the rights to be transferred. The girl's lineage retains only the apparently inalienable right to exercise the ritual power of her own ancestors over her. This right is exercised as a coercive measure in inter-lineage disputes. Thus in such a crisis, the head of the fiancé's lineage could recall in the name of their founding ancestor all the daughters of his lineage who had married men of the eloping girl's lineage. The girl's lineage could similarly recall all the daughters of that lineage who had married men of the seducer's lineage, and by that means attempt to ensure that the seducer is forthcoming with the girl, and if possible, with the bride-wealth.[6]

In exchange marriage ('wife by exchange', 'give us we give you') two men each take an eligible sister or daughter of the other as wife. The usual services are omitted, as they would cancel each other out, but in both cases the ritual payments are made and the ancestors are notified (Herskovits 1938: 313): both women are under the jural authority of their husbands' lineages. If one of them should leave her husband, 'this man will divorce his sister or daughter from the other in retaliation'—a 'retaliation' common whenever relations between lineages are strained.[7]

---

[5] The village or quarter chief, who serves in this case primarily as witness (Herskovits 1938: i, 7–16 and *passim*).

[6] If he does not do so, the girl may be expelled from her lineage, especially if the original marriage had been arranged to ease tense relations between the two lineages and the consequences of her elopement were serious (Herskovits 1938: i, 311).

[7] Despite Herskovits's use of the term 'divorce', there is under such circumstances no permanent dissolution of the marriage and the return of the bride-wealth is not an issue. This is implicit in Herskovits 1938: i, 311.

Exchange marriage may accompany cross-cousin marriage—especially when palm-trees are at stake. By the rules of inheritance for this very valuable portion of Dahomean wealth, the palm-trees planted by a man are on his death held in trust as 'lineage' property by his two oldest sons. On their death, the trees are divided equally between their surviving siblings. The trees inherited by a sister may be given by her to one of her daughters. To avoid the loss of these trees, this daughter is married to one of her mother's brother's sons. The son of this cross-cousin marriage will inherit the palm-trees; he is also the grandson of the man who planted them. However, the same problem will arise in the next generation, if the girl given in exchange should become heir to any palm-trees. Although it is difficult to see why exchange marriage should be the preferred system in this connexion,[8] exchange marriage might be favoured to strengthen the marriage ties between two lineages. Cross-cousin marriage also, though nowhere singled out as a 'type', seems a favoured form of Dahomean marriage both because of its economic advantages and the stated desire to bring a woman's children's children back into the lineage (Herskovits 1938: i, 313).

If the father provides the bride-wealth ('father my wife'),[9] the son may not set up an independent household until the debt is repaid (Herskovits 1938: i, 138–42). In any case, the wife is under the direct jural authority of her husband only when he is at least the head of a minimal lineage.

If a man's best friend provides the bride-wealth, the resulting complex of events is called 'stomach empty' marriage (Herskovits 1938: i, 313–16). Throughout, the husband has jural authority and responsibility and the friend, a financial obligation: thus on the birth of a child, the husband consults the diviner and performs the sacrifice; the friend provides the necessary materials. The debt is cancelled when the husband gives his friend (as in exchange marriage) a daughter as wife. If there are only sons, or if the daughter dies before she is of marriageable age,[10]

---

[8] Herskovits associates the two explicitly (1938: i, 93).

[9] Cf. the bride's blessing (Herskovits 1938: i, 307).

[10] In no other case is the bride-wealth returnable if the girl dies before consummation of the marriage (Le Hérissé 1911: 207). Here, however, it is a matter of a heritable debt.

the heir of the husband, as soon as possible, gives a girl from his compound to the heir of the best friend. The obligation is then cancelled. If that girl eloped, the mechanism of recalling wives described above was brought into play by the two lineages concerned. If the seducer refused to give her up, his lineage threatened to take away his wives, his fields, and his property. The girl was not to be given either to her original fiancé or to her seducer[11] but to some man not affiliated with any of the three lineages involved. The friend's son was given the most eligible girl in his fiancée's lineage as wife; he had to accept her and notify the head of his lineage of the fact. Shortly thereafter, the wives recalled to their natal lineages were allowed to return to their husbands.

The jural and ritual aspects of the resulting marriage are unaffected (1) whether the girl's father initiated the proposal ('money with woman'), or the proposal first came from the suitor ('child ask ask'); (2) whether the suitor, his father ('father my wife'), or his best friend ('stomach empty') paid the bride-wealth; (3) whether the bride-wealth was repaid by a second suitor to the first ('woman give back woman')—the adjustments necessary under such circumstances are initiated by the action of the lineage units, and not by the three individuals most directly concerned; (4) or whether only the ritual payments are made in the case of a simple exchange of women ('give us we give you' or 'wife by exchange') or a marriage with the daughter or son's daughter, which repays financial aid for the mother's bride-wealth.[12]

Whenever the ritual payments marking the transfer of jural authority have been made, the same constellation of rights and duties results:

1. There is a differential distribution of ritual authority over the wife. She remains under the power of her own ancestors:

---

[11] Both offenders might be expelled from their lineages and cut off from their ancestors to become wanderers in Dahomey. The breach of obligation here is much more serious than in an ordinary elopement (Herskovits 1938: i, 314).

[12] A creditor might claim a female pawn as wife if she were not redeemed in a reasonable time; the debt cancelled the bride-wealth (Herskovits 1938: i, 83). The ritual payments are not mentioned.

therefore the head of her natal lineage may recall her in their name. However, as wife and mother, she falls under the ritual as well as the jural authority of her husband's lineage: she must observe the prohibitions of his lineage for pregnant women (Herskovits 1938: i, 162); it is to his ancestors that she must confess her adultery (Herskovits 1933: 28). Although she will be an ancestress of her husband's lineage, by whom she must be buried, her own ancestors are those of her natal lineage: she is buried just outside the walls of her husband's compound (Le Hérissé 1911: 205; Herskovits 1938: i, 335).

2. The wife must be provided with food and a house. What she earns or inherits herself is her personal property; she may become independently wealthy.

3. The wife may not be divorced for barrenness (Herskovits 1938: i, 337). The ritual 'payment' merely sealed the transfer of jural authority over her children when and if born; it did not guarantee her fertility.

4. The husband is the father of his wife's children. An impotent man tries to arrange that his wife shall have children by a member of his lineage, preferably one of his own brothers (Le Hérissé 1911: 208; Herskovits 1938: i, 342). If, in case of adultery, the husband demands the return of the bride-wealth, he forfeits all rights over mother and child. Otherwise, all her children are considered children of the husband, 'auquel l'enfant adultérin appartenait au même titre que les siens propres' (Le Hérissé 1911: 77).

5. The children have jural and ritual status in the lineage, which has jural authority over the mother at the time of their birth—in all these cases the lineage of the *pater* (Radcliffe-Brown: 1930–31; Evans-Pritchard: 1945). They are full heirs to the *pater* and to any lineage office for which they possess the requisite age and capabilities.

6. If the wife gave grounds for divorce, the bride-wealth was returnable. If the husband offended the wife's lineage, she had to return but her children remained under the jural authority of the husband's lineage.[13] If the wife was personally dissatisfied

---

[13] Such offences are: (1) grave injuries to her parents; (2) sexual relations of her husband with her sister or with a wife under the jural authority of her

with her husband, the head of his lineage had the right to give her to another member of the lineage as wife (Le Hérissé 1911: 204–5).

7. A widow is inherited by a member of her husband's lineage, a brother or a son by another marriage.[14]

It is clear from this description that jural authority over a woman ultimately vests in the husband's lineage; on the dissolution of her marriage, as a result of the death or personal default of her husband, she still remains under the jural authority of his lineage. Of the various rights held in her, the rights over the children she may bear are the most sedulously guarded: these are retained even if she should insist on living with a man of another lineage in the case of her husband's death or impotence (Le Hérissé 1911: 204). Because of this transfer of jural rights over a woman's potential children, a child in Dahomey falls under the same jural authority as did its mother at the time of its birth. The child has rights to the titles, lands, properties, and occupations, which may vest in the lineage, by virtue of his status by birth in the lineage, i.e., by virtue of the fact that he is under the jural authority of that lineage. Nowhere, in a true lineage system, do two lineages have identical jural rights in one person; a man has jural rights only in that lineage which has jural rights in him. In Dahomey the transfer of these jural rights and duties as to a woman's children from one lineage to another may accompany her marriage and is marked by the ritual 'payments'. Except in her roles as wife and mother, however, a woman remains under the ritual authority of the ancestors of her natal lineage. This right is exercised when a woman's lineage wishes to bring pressure to bear on her husband's lineage. Also, the fact that a woman's lineage may, if offended by the husband or his lineage, sue for her divorce in court, is another means of bringing pressure: such a divorce case may be used as a threat to speed

---

father, brother, or father's brother; (3) failure of her husband to participate in certain funeral ceremonies of her close relatives. Her lineage could then initiate divorce (Herskovits 1938: i, 346).

[14] The inheritance of widows, 'dead man woman' marriage, appears in the class of marriages in which the children stay with the mother (Herskovits 1938: i, 302). It is more correct to say that the dead husband's lineage retains jural authority over his widow and children.

the collection of an outstanding debt (Herskovits 1938: i, 349).
Hence the importance of maintaining marriage ties between lineages, as by exchange marriage. In addition, then, to sealing a
marriage between two individuals, with all that this implies in
regard to sexual, domestic, and economic rights and duties, the
full payment of the bride-wealth, with the ritual portion as the
critical element, is also a mechanism for the transfer of jural
authority over a woman and the children she may bear from one
lineage to another; and, secondly, owing to the differential distribution of rights in the woman, the marriage is also an important
mechanism for the regulation of inter-lineage relations.

MARRIAGE WITHOUT TRANSFER OF JURAL AUTHORITY

A consideration of two 'types' of marriage ('child stay father
house' and 'prince child child') in which no transfer of jural authority over the children a woman may bear takes place, necessitates the division of the concept of 'jural authority' into rights
over a woman as wife, the granting of which constitutes marriage,
and rights over a woman as to her children.[15] This distinction is
clearly articulated in Dahomean ritual and both illuminates and
is confirmed by many aspects of Dahomean custom and social
organization.

'Child stay father house' marriage occurs when a lineage, faced
by a shortage of male heirs, seeks to increase its strength. The
head of the lineage segment tells one of his daughters or brother's
daughters to choose a husband. This man is presented to the
household and the couple is blessed in the name of the girl's
ancestors. The man furnishes all the bride-wealth, with one exception: he is expressly forbidden to give the ritual payments
which would bring 'spiritual sanction from the ancestral founder
for the children to belong to the father's sib'.[16] The husband

---

[15] For the general importance of analysing the rights which together define a
person's jural position, I am indebted to Radcliffe-Brown 1935.

[16] (Herskovits 1938: i, 346.) Since the corollary of this statement—where
the ritual payments are not given, the children do not 'belong to the father's
sib'—is supported by other evidence, I have used this assumption. However,
Herskovits also states exactly the opposite (i, 156, 302): there can be little
doubt that a child is in some special relation to the lineages of both parents,
irrespective of which lineage has jural authority over him.

builds his wife a house in her father's compound; he contributes to the support of his wife and children. There exists between husband and wife a well-articulated and socially defined body of sexual, domestic, and economic, i.e. marital, rights and duties.

The mother's lineage is under a moral, but not legal, obligation to abandon its original rights over some of the children in favour of their father.[17] A son thus sent to his father cannot inherit from that father, whose heirs are those sons over whom he has jural authority by virtue of having given the ritual payments for their mother. A daughter sent to her father may be married with transfer of jural authority over herself and her children, whereas the daughters retained by the mother's lineage must marry as did their mother (Herskovits 1938: i, 324). It is difficult to explain this variation in the daughters' marriages in terms of receipt of bride-wealth.

To assume that the reason for this variation lies in the possibility of giving the bride-wealth to the girl's father and his ancestors in one case, and its impossibility in the other, is to ignore the statement that 'spiritual sanction for the children to belong to the father's sib' is *not* given and that therefore the father's lineage could not receive the ritual payments, which must be presented to those ancestors who can spiritually sanction the transfer of jural authority. The marriage of a daughter retained by her mother's family must be regarded as a preferred type (discussed later) rather than a ritual dilemma. The children do not *ipso facto* have full status in their father's lineage; he has control of the daughters sent to him by virtue of a later transfer of rights over those individual children and not by default of such rights being vested in the mother's lineage. One must assume that the children not sent to the father have full jural and ritual status in the mother's lineage. Since the mother was specifically retained to provide her lineage with male heirs, one assumes that her sons are eligible to headship of that lineage segment at least. An important part of that office consists in the ritual duties connected with ancestor worship; the performance of these duties usually indicates full jural and ritual status in the lineage. It would rather

---

[17] (Herskovits 1938: i, 323.) Of five or six children, two are sent to the father; of four, only one goes to the father (Le Hérissé 1911: 210).

seem to be the sons sent to the father who suffer jural disa-
bilities.[18]

'Child stay father house' marriage shows a differential distribution of authority over a woman and her children. It has become
evident that the full bride-wealth marks the transfer of ritual and
jural authority over a woman as wife and mother: that is, there
are transferred rights in a woman as wife, *uxor*, and as mother,
genetrix, i.e., rights in her children once born are held by virtue
of holding rights *in genetricem*.[19] In the first class of marriages
discussed, these rights were transferred concomitantly to the husband, with the husband's lineage holding the over-right of retransfer on the death or default of the active holder. Thus on the
husband's death, rights *in uxorem* are transferred to another individual, whereas rights *in genetricem* are retained by the lineage,
in which they ultimately vest. In 'child stay father house' marriage
and in the marriage of women of the royal lineage ('prince child
child') rights in a woman as wife, *uxor*, are transferred; rights in
her as *genetrix* are retained. The transfer of rights *in uxorem*
is 'paid for'; the marriage is celebrated and is a socially recognized institution. The transfer of rights *in uxorem* constitutes
marriage. Divorce is necessary to break the arrangement, though
always somewhat easier where rights *in genetricem* are not also
involved.

Rights *in genetricem* are held in the woman in reference to the
children she may bear. If the husband made the ritual payments,
he holds rights *in genetricem* in his wife, whether or not she is
barren. Rights *in genetricem* in the mother give original jural and
ritual authority over her children, once born. But rights in a child
once born may be retained or transferred—a child may be pawned,

---

[18] (Herskovits 1938: i, 345.) Dahomean marriage prohibitions corroborate
this view: a man may not marry the daughter of a brother by a wife whom
he may inherit, i.e. one for whom the ritual payments have been made; conversely, if he may not inherit his brother's widow, i.e. if she does not fall
under the jural authority of her dead husband's lineage, he may marry her
daughter. Marriage prohibitions and widow inheritance are compatible with
the distribution of jural authority and jural status. (However, in the royal
lineage half-brother and sister may marry.) (Le Hérissé 1911: 211–12.)
[19] I have coined the phrases 'rights *in uxorem*' and 'rights *in genetricem*'
both for convenience and to indicate that I am discussing both rights which
may be held in the woman.

adopted, or married out—without prejudice to the rights held in its mother or its siblings.

In 'child stay father house' marriage, rights *in uxorem* were transferred to the husband; rights *in genetricem* in that same woman were not transferred, but were specifically retained by the original holder, here the head of the woman's lineage segment. The holder of rights *in genetricem* has original jural authority over the children, which can later be transferred without prejudice to the rights *in genetricem* in their mother or siblings. The children sent to the father thus remain under the jural and ritual authority of the mother's lineage and have jural status in the father's lineage only if the mother's lineage formally renounces its rights over them.[20] Thus a Dahomean child has jural and ritual rights and status in that lineage which held rights *in genetricem* in the mother at the time of its birth. This may or may not be the lineage of its socially recognized father,[21] i.e., the man who held rights *in uxorem* in the mother. Furthermore, whether or not these rights are held concomitantly in Dahomey is apparently determined by the operation of economic and political factors.

The royal lineage never transfers rights in a woman as *genetrix*, either acquired as in a wife, by payment of the ritual portions of the bride-wealth, or original as in the case of daughters of that lineage. Rights *in uxorem* are freely given, often for political purposes. In fact, the royal marriages represent special adaptations

---

[20] 'Les enfants nés d'union libre ou de toute autre union qui les place sous la puissance maternelle ne peuvent hériter de leur père, à moins que la famille de leur mère n'ait formellement renoncé à ses droits sur eux' (Le Hérissé 1911: 252).

[21] In Evans-Pritchard's discussion of Nuer marriage *pater* refers either to cases in which both rights *in uxorem* and rights *in genetricem* are held concomitantly, or to the holder of rights *in genetricem* where they are not held concomitantly (Evans-Pritchard 1940). In Dahomey rights *in genetricem* may be vested in an office, title or estate as well as a lineage; it is difficult to reify these as *pater*. In Ashanti marriage as discussed by M. Fortes (1950), the term *pater* refers to the socially recognized father, the mother's husband. In Dahomey also the socially recognized father of the child is the mother's husband, i.e., the man who held rights *in uxorem* in the mother at the time of the child's birth. The distribution of rights *in genetricem* does not affect this status.

of marriage within a patrilineal descent system to other principles of the social structure.

Marriage with acquisition of rights *in genetricem* cannot occur between members of the same lineage: the ritual payments must be displayed to the ancestors of the two lineages. If a man or a woman of the royal lineage wishes to hold rights *in genetricem* in a wife, that wife must come from one of the commoner lineages. Since the heir to an office or title, which runs in the male line from eldest son to eldest son, barring personal incompetents, must be the son of a woman whose husband held rights *in genetricem* in her, the kingship thus goes to the son of the King and a commoner wife. Since rights *in genetricem* are not transferred when a woman of the royal lineage is involved, the children of a princess have full jural and ritual status only in the royal lineage.[22] However, women of the royal lineage were married off by the King to political favourites, e.g., chiefs, officials, and soldiers ('prince child child'). The formal transfer of rights *in uxorem* and the retention of rights *in genetricem* are ritually expressed in the formula pronounced to the husband at the wedding: 'You did not give the gifts that are customarily required of husbands. You did not perform the *xɔŋgbô* [the ritual payments]. Therefore know that you have no rights over this girl. She is your wife and you are her husband, but the children born of your mating will be members of the royal family. Yours is not the right to ask of a diviner the name of the ancestral soul from which the soul of your children derives, for their souls are of the royal ancestors. You must not take her to your *tɔhwíyŏ* [lineage founding ancestor] to tell him you have made this marriage, for your *tɔhwíyŏ* has no rights over this girl. . . .' (Herskovits 1938: i, 1, 330–31).

Such a formula is, probably, applicable in all cases in which the ritual payments are not made, and hence the children, being under the ritual authority of the mother's ancestors, are fully eligible for lineage office with its ritual duties connected with ancestor

---

[22] The Dahomeans give a political explanation: if the child of a princess were to become a commoner, that child, as a commoner, would be eligible for high political office and yet possibly have connexions with other than the ruling branch of the royal lineage, which might make him disloyal (Le Hérissé 1911: 30–32).

worship.[23] One cannot speak here of conflicting theories of descent. In a matrilineal system jural authority over a woman's children cannot be acquired by entering into any kind of marital arrangement with her; there is no provision for the transfer of rights *in genetricem* by marriage. In a patrilineal society the transfer of jural authority and rights *in genetricem* through marriage is apparently preferred; we are told, for example, that 'Tallensi express contempt for the Gɔrisi, who, it is notorious, often constrain a daughter to "sit at home and bear children" to augment her father's family' (Fortes 1949b: 110), a custom allied to Dahomean 'child stay father house' marriage. In Dahomey the variation corresponds to political and economic variables.

JURAL AUTHORITY

That the transfer or non-transfer of rights *in genetricem* in Dahomey is determined not only by the functioning of the lineage and its segments, but by economic and political factors which may be concentrated in an office, title, or estate is seen even more clearly in the remaining forms of Dahomean marriage and offers another basis for classification.

The political element is prominent in 'cloth with woman' marriage, a 'type' concerning the marriage of women who were attached to a political office (rather than to the officeholder as an individual).[24] Although these women were free, as were all persons born on Dahomean soil, they were probably slaves, pawns or 'wives of the law'[25] in origin. The data on 'cloth with woman'

---

[23] In his discussion of kinship groups Herskovits couples 'prince child child' marriage with 'child stay father house' as regards the position of the children (in this connexion compare the differential marriage of the daughters) (1938: i, 156). He does not do so elsewhere (1938: i, 302, 346).

[24] Le Hérissé points out that they were neither slaves nor relatives of the officeholder (1911: 211). Herskovits's statement that they were young women sent from the countryside to the King's palace as attendants on the princesses (1938: i, 325–26) probably refers to the daughters of such women, who would be returned to the holder of rights *in genetricem* in their mother.

[25] If the head of a 'family' committed a serious crime, his lands were confiscated and his wives and children were given to the 'law' in the person of the King or certain of his chiefs. The position of the women, who were usually married out again, seems similar to that of pawns, except that they were apparently kinless (Le Hérissé 1911: 78–79).

marriage show that the right to give a woman in marriage, i.e., to transfer rights over her as wife, and in some cases, to recall those rights and dissolve the marriage, vests in the holder of original rights *in genetricem* in the mother—whether it was a lineage which acquired those rights in the mother through marriage or whether the status of the original mother was that of pawn or slave. Thus by 'cloth with woman' marriage the officeholder could reward a favourite by giving him a wife, often with substantial gifts, and at the same time benefit from the services which the husband was bound to render. The officeholder had to consent to divorce and could even force a divorce if, for example, the husband's services were not considered adequate (Herskovits 1938: i, 326). Secondly, the right to give in marriage is but part of the original jural authority held in a woman's children by the holder of rights *in genetricem* in her. Herskovits says specifically that the officeholder had all the rights that a Dahomean man 'in ordinary life' held over his children (1938: i, 325). These rights might be retained—the daughters returned to the officeholder and later married as their mothers had been—or waived. Generally the sons were left with the father.[26]

It is, therefore, important to consider in connexion with marriage the distribution of rights *in genetricem* and *in uxorem*, for the person in whom these rights are held often serves as a link between the parties in whom the rights are vested. Thus in the cases of marriage first discussed, a differential distribution of rights in the woman served as a mechanism for the regulation of inter-lineage relationships. In the present case, the distribution of rights indicates the political relationship of patron and client. The husbands perform economic services for the officeholder and swell the ranks of his clients and followers; they also benefit by the possession of a wife and any gifts given with her. Such a marriage is not the grant of a slave and her descendants. Its analogies are rather with the custom, found elsewhere in Africa, of giving the use, and sometimes, as a favour, a certain portion

---

[26] The father could retain the sons only at the express wish of the officeholder (Le Hérissé 1911: 211). If the officeholder relinquished these rights formally, the sons apparently had (as in 'child stay father house' marriage) full status in their father's home (1911: 223).

of the increase of a herd to the tender of the cattle, who, by his acceptance, enters into a relation of clientship.

The most complex instance of Dahomean marriage is that institution, which Herskovits terms 'woman marriage' when he refers to the woman who institutes the proceedings by taking a 'wife' and 'giving the goat to the buck' when he refers to the relationship of that 'wife' with the father of her children (Herskovits 1937). Herskovits connects this practice both with barrenness on the part of the female husband and with the existence of wealthy, economically independent women. A barren wife may marry a woman, never of her own family, whom she gives to her husband and whose children are known as 'her own' (Herskovits 1938: i, 342). In this case 'woman marriage' gives a barren wife children; it is not connected with the founding of a separate compound. However, as Herskovits notes specifically, when 'woman marriage' is associated with the founding of a compound, it is directly connected with women of wealth, who, having acquired land and palm-trees, must acquire people to work these lands and palm-trees,[27] i.e., she founds a compound and marries wives whose children she and her heirs will control. There can be little doubt that the necessary corollary of the foundation of such a compound lies not in a woman's barrenness, but in her jural and economic position.

The female 'husband' chooses a man to live with her 'wife'— possibly, if the 'husband' is married, from men of her husband's lineage (Herskovits 1938: i, 320), or the matter may be arranged with her 'wife's' family.[28] The children's father is socially recognized as such. The 'female husband' has transferred to him rights *in uxorem* and as the active holder of these rights he is the true husband of the woman: it is to this relationship that the Dahomean phrase 'giving the goat to the buck' refers, and from this viewpoint that they call the marriage one 'in which the mother

---

[27] (Herskovits 1938: i, 319.) A man, who is married or head of a lineage segment, has through his jural authority over his children and members of his lineage, a source of labour, which a woman lacks.

[28] Once the 'wife' has children, she may not easily 'divorce' their father, 'particularly when both her own family and the woman who has "married" her insist that she remain with him' (Herskovits 1938: 346).

has control over the children'.[29] In fact, it is the holder of rights *in genetricem* in the mother, the 'female husband', who has control of the children.

The woman founding such a compound takes as many wives as she can afford: as in 'cloth with woman' marriage, she retransfers rights *in uxorem* in them, but retains rights *in genetricem*, so that she and her heirs may control their children. On the founder's death, she becomes the main object of the ancestor cult of the descendants, for as the head of a compound, she had her 'Fate' (Herskovits 1938: i, 53). In the first generation, the eldest son takes charge of the women of the compound; the eldest daughter controls the men. 'These children must intermarry, and since they are the offspring of mothers and fathers of different sibs, this violates no rule of incest;'[30] that is, no kinship link is assumed merely because the 'female husband' retained rights *in genetricem* in the mothers. After the first generation, the eldest daughter of the eldest daughter inherits both the founder's name and the headship of the compound. Such heads continue to marry wives: rights *in genetricem* in them and their female descendants are never transferred on their marriage. Whether these heirs are the founder's uterine daughters or the daughters of her 'wives' is not explicitly stated. Neither view is necessarily supported by the fact that the founder becomes an important ancestor and has her 'Fate': irrespective of the inheritance of the compound headship, she remains its founder. However, as the children of her 'wives' are not 'kin', they apparently do not consider her their 'pater' any more than in the case of 'cloth with woman' marriage the office-holder who retained rights *in genetricem* in the mother was considered the 'pater' of the children. It would seem, then, that in Dahomey it is not necessary to manufacture kinship ties to explain the possession of jural authority over children by virtue of retention of rights *in genetricem* in the mother: the rights may

---

[29] Herskovits notes, 'every Dahomean with whom the matter of marriage types was discussed placed this form ('giving the goat to the buck') in the second category rather than the one in which strictly and legally speaking it ('woman marriage') should belong' (1938: i, 337). That is, the Dahomeans consider the active holder of rights *in uxorem* as the woman's husband. (Cf. Le Hérissé 1911: 210.)

[30] (Herskovits 1938: i, 321.) Apparently in non-lineage compounds marriage prohibitions are not coterminous with the distribution of jural authority.

be attached to an office or title, and presumably also to an estate. To assume that the heirs are the eldest son and daughter of one of the founder's 'wives' rather than her own children is to assume that the founder creates an autonomous compound which is of no benefit to those who would otherwise be her heirs; whereas, if the uterine children inherit, then it can be seen that an 'estate' has been created which will benefit the founder's daughter and her daughter's daughters *ad infinitum*.[31]

If in any generation there should be no daughters, the oldest son becomes head of the compound and assumes the name of the female founder; from that time the compound is inherited in the male line. If he has wives in whom he holds rights *in genetricem* but with whom he does not cohabit, he must give their daughters to his sons as wives; he may himself, however, marry these daughters if he wishes, since their fathers were 'always brought from outside the group'.[32]

As regards the relationship of such a compound to the lineage system, it is noteworthy that great precautions are taken to prevent the fission of the compound: members are not allowed to move outside, if it can be avoided; intermarriage is favoured. It is to remain a compact, self-contained unit subject to pressures from without rather than to the internal tensions leading to the growth and fission characteristic of the normal compound housing a lineage segment. Also, if the hypothesis is correct that such a compound is a heritable estate in a direct female descent line, then the position of the head within the lineage of her birth is of interest. The available data, however, warrant no more than the suggestion of some problems. Unless the founder were a member of the royal lineage, or rights *in genetricem* were not transferred

---

[31] A barren woman might, of course, found a compound, but I believe that in such a case further inquiry would reveal that the compound would be inherited by the woman's sisters or brothers, as is the case with other property. The population of the compound seems rather an asset attached to it than the beneficiary of its foundation.

[32] (Herskovits 1938: i, 321.) Herskovits states that: (1) the daughters may not marry a man outside the family; (2) their husbands are always brought from outside the group; (3) their husbands are chosen from the lineage of the compound head's husband, or (4) if the head is a man, his sons marry within the compound, (5) the population of the compound intermarries (1938: i, 319–46).

at her marriage, the successive daughters and their wealth would pass out of the lineage—a situation which could only partially be remedied by repeated cross-cousin marriage.[33] Even so, the founder and her descendants would form a direct descent line with certain privileges within the lineage. The possibilities of conflict between such a direct descent line and other collateral branches of the lineage are greater in the case of a male heir who, being a man, would be eligible for lineage office.[34] Such a man would also be in the position of marrying wives as compound head and as potential ancestor of a lineage segment, with the result that two sons might have very different status. Given the variations in the distribution of rights *in uxorem* and *in genetricem* and the fact of favoured polygyny, a man might frequently be the *pater* of two children, but have jural authority only over one. But in none of these cases have both been under jural authority held by the same man in two capacities: it is doubtful whether such fine distinctions could work in practice.[35] The various marriage regulations, which come into effect on the accession of a male heir, might be interpreted as an attempt to mitigate this conflict.

In short, 'woman marriage' enables a woman with wealth in land and palm-trees to found a compound, acquire control of people—everywhere an essential to native wealth—and to establish an estate held in trust for the next heir by the person who inherits the founder's name. Control of people is acquired through marriage: rights *in uxorem* are retransferred ('giving the goat to the buck'); rights *in genetricem* are retained by the founder and her heirs *in perpetuum* in these 'wives' and their descendants. These rights, like the land and palm-trees, are a part of the property attached to the founder's name and inherited with it.

'Child father threshold over' marriage is also associated with the establishment of a compound headed by a woman who has control of the property attached to the compound and of the

---

[33] Cf. instance in connexion with palm-trees, *supra* (Herskovits 1938: i, 274–75).

[34] Cf. Le Hérissé 1911: 210–12, 370, for overt manifestations of such conflict. Also *vide infra*, p. 103.

[35] Le Hérissé records a comparable confusion as to the status of the son of a free man and a female slave (1911: 54 ff.).

children born to her and to members of her compound and is also inherited in the direct female line. In this case, however, the head is in and of the group. The founder builds a compound and arranges her daughter's marriage;[36] this daughter is bound by solemn oath to rear children for her ancestors.[37]

Herskovits, without further comment, refers to this also as 'cousin marriage'. Now if the daughter's daughter of the founder marries her father's brother's son, apparently no advantages result. If she marries her mother's brother's son, she is marrying a person who falls under the same jural authority; such a marriage is said to be prohibited (Le Hérissé 1911: 211–12). Furthermore, since rights *in genetricem* may not be transferred at the marriage of this daughter, her children cannot inherit from their father; no economic advantages would then result. However, a reason for frequent 'cousin' marriage is indicated by a consideration of the structure of similar descent groups marked by the inheritance of 'titles'. A man always assumes a new name on taking political office. His eldest son will not necessarily succeed to that office; he will, however, inherit the name his father took on entering office, a stool, certain honours, and various lands, slaves, and palm-trees. This name, which I call a 'title' to differentiate it from the similarly inherited name of a founding ancestress, together with the honours and economic assets attached to it, goes from eldest son to eldest son. Often such an heir will retain rights *in genetricem* in his daughters when they marry, so that his group will grow rapidly (Le Hérissé 1911: 37, 200).

In the inheritance of names and of titles there is a direct line of descent from oldest child to oldest child of the same sex as the original holder, whereas lineage headship passes through all the collateral lines of the lineage segment under consideration and goes to the oldest male among them: the lineage headship may fall to a title-holder, but the title cannot pass to the other

---

36 The girl is not a pawn nor a 'wife' (Herskovits 1938: i, 324). It is difficult to see how the mother would be in such a position unless she were either disinherited from her lineage or *de facto* independent through spatial separation. As a 'friend custody' wife (*vide infra*, p. 105) her husband might have given her enough to build a compound.

37 (Herskovits 1938: i, 347.) Note that when rights *in genetricem* are not transferred, neither is ritual power over a woman as mother.

collateral lines of the lineage. The heir to a name or title retains rights *in genetricem* in the daughters and thus assures control of their descendants; the sons, however, can acquire rights *in genetricem* in their own wives and their sons tend to form collateral lines within the lineage system. Just as the collateral lines in the 'title' descent line remain outside the inheritance of the title honours but within the lineage system, so it is likely that in the case of a compound founded by a woman, the lines descending from the head's brothers would tend to separate and form a compound on the lineage system. For a woman in Dahomey cannot found a lineage: she may found a descent group, and the children of all her daughters will fall under the jural authority of the head of that group. But although the son himself, and therefore the children whom he controls, are under the jural authority of his mother, after the death of that mother and son, the son's descendants will have a male ancestor to whom they may establish a shrine and thus found an autonomous compound operating within the lineage system.

'Cousin' marriage cannot be satisfactorily explained on the basis of economic interest, owing to the operation of the rules of inheritance; nor, owing to marriage prohibitions, is it likely to occur with actual rather than classificatory cross-cousins. If, however, it is taken as an attempt to tie the male line back into the compound after it has separated, or, conversely, on the part of that male line to retain a connexion with the compound, it is in accordance with other principles observed in Dahomey: the attachment of rights and properties either to a lineage segment or to a name or title; the exclusion of collateral branches from the inheritance of such names or titles; the resort to marriage as a bond between groups and, conversely, the retention of rights *in genetricem* in order to obtain control over people. Thus the fact noted by Herskovits that daughters must marry as did their mothers, whereas sons are free to acquire wives with rights *in genetricem*, is not an arbitrary distribution of 'types' of marriage or a simple difficulty of bride-wealth payment, but the adjustment of jural rights in accordance with the operation of the lineage system opposed to the operation of special descent lines of heirs to titles or names with the properties and personnel attached to them.

'FRIEND CUSTODY'

It is not clear from the data whether all situations described as 'friend custody' are regarded as 'marriage' by the Dahomeans (Herskovits 1938: i, 318–35). The term may refer to the interval between elopement and marriage, to the status of a woman living in her husband's compound with the knowledge of her parents (in such a case her natal lineage apparently accepts her children if she returns), or to a woman expelled from her lineage who is quite literally a 'free' woman. The children of a 'friend custody' wife may not inherit from their father, nor is she inherited by her husband's heirs; she may leave her husband when she wishes, apparently without formal divorce. However, a man devoted to such a wife may give her much wealth before his death in order to assure her future and that of her children.[38] 'Friend custody' is a disruptive event resented by those who held rights in the woman who ran off and flouted the vested interests of the lineage, estate or title-holder. In fact, the woman has asserted her status as a 'free woman'. Its increasing frequency is, according to Herskovits, due to the weakened jural authority of parents over children and to the ever-increasing tendency towards 'individualism' and independence under French rule.

SUMMARY AND CONCLUSIONS

The data on Dahomean marriage, when analysed as to the rights and duties of the contracting parties, have led to a necessary distinction between rights in a woman as wife—rights *in uxorem*—and rights in a woman as to the children she may bear, rights *in genetricem*. The fact that these rights are usually held concomitantly in Dahomey justifies a consideration of their distribution when they are not so coupled, as being of equal influence on the form and functions of the marriage—functions which are sociologically of a wider scope than the regulation of inter-

---

[38] This is probably the origin of many female compounds of the 'child father threshold over' type; the daughters of 'friend custody' wives are generally married without transfer of rights *in genetricem* (Herskovits 1938: i, 318).

personal relations between man and woman. It has been shown
that in all the thirteen 'types' of marriage listed by Herskovits,
with the possible exception of some instances of 'friend custody',
rights *in uxorem* are recognized and that where they are recognized the status of the husband is regulated *vis-à-vis* his wife;
he is also the socially recognized father of her children. Rights
in genetricem may be vested (*a*) in the wife's or in the husband's
lineage, (*b*) in an office, 'title', or 'name', and these rights give
original jural authority over the woman's children—rights which
may later be transferred without prejudice to the rights held in
the mother and other children.

The differential distribution of rights in a given person, in these
cases the woman (and her children), acts as a structural link
between the persons or corporate groups concerned; marriage is
a mechanism for the regulation of inter-lineage relations where
there is a differential distribution of rights in the couple. Where
the rights *in genetricem* do not vest ultimately in the husband's
lineage, the husband's status is regulated *vis-à-vis* the person,
'office' or lineage in which these rights are vested.[39] The distribution of these rights varies not at random but with the needs
and nature of the social units concerned. The differential distribution of these rights has in some cases been explicable in
terms of the lineage system and inter-lineage relations, in others,
of the tendency to perpetuate individual prerogatives by the formation of direct descent lines, and in still others the differential
distribution of rights has served as a social link of a political or
economic nature, without the assumption of kinship ties. It has
also been seen that such recent tendencies as greater freedom
from kinship controls are reflected in the marriage system, e.g.
'friend custody'.

In Dahomey the transferability of rights *in genetricem* ceases
if that right becomes attached to an office, title, or name—as all
'property', i.e. rights in and over things and persons, is attached
inalienably to such offices, titles, or names and held in trust by
the holder for the next heir. The data suggest that once a lineage
retains an original right *in genetricem* over a woman born into

---

[39] Even when they vest in his own lineage, the power of that lineage to de-
prive him of his wives (*supra*, p. 96) is important.

the lineage, it ceases to become transferable in her descendants. This would suggest that although 'patriliny' is correctly identifiable with the possibility of transferring rights *in genetricem* through marriage, other factors than 'matriliny' are connected with its non-transference. It is to be noted that the usual definitions of 'matriliny' and 'patriliny' consist in a distinction between the transferability and non-transferability of rights *in genetricem*, but that the variation in Dahomey is not to be ascribed to conflicting theories of descent but to the operation of economic and political factors as well as to the growth and inter-relations of kinship units. It is noteworthy that although rights *in genetricem* are to be acquired by marriage, the purpose of acquiring such rights is not necessarily the acquisition of a woman as wife; in 'woman marriage' rights in a woman as wife are held separately from rights *in genetricem*. Furthermore, the possession of original jural authority over children does not *ipso facto* postulate a kinship relationship with those children either through the father or through the mother (e.g. 'woman marriage', 'cloth with woman'); it merely implies possession of rights *in genetricem* in the mother —within or without the field of kinship.

6 SECONDARY MARRIAGE AMONG KADARA AND KAGORO

M. G. Smith

KADARA

ACCORDING TO OFFICIAL SOURCES, the Kadara are a tribe of approximately 22,000 souls located mainly in the Kajuru and Kacia districts of Zaria Province, but with some elements in Minna Division, Niger Province. The Kadara of Kajuru district distinguish themselves from a different linguistic group in the same district whom they call Ajure. Ajure number approximately 6000 and, like Kadara, appear to speak a semi-Bantu language, but Kadara of different areas sometimes speak widely different dialects; it is thus possible that Ajure are not a distinct ethnic group.

Kadara tribal territory in Zaria Province is large, probably 1500 square miles, with a low population density, approximately 15 per square mile. Traditionally settlement was in compact village sites among the rocky outcrops of the area. Sometimes the villages were walled, as the Kadara were subject to attacks and slave raids from their Hausa overlords of Zaria during the last century, in the course of which several settlements were dispersed.

Kadara are sedentary grain-farmers with a keen interest in hunting, very little in rearing livestock, no indigenous clothing or blacksmith crafts, and even today they trade with Hausa and Fulani mainly by barter. Apart from farm work and hunting the

Extracted from 'Secondary Marriage in Northern Nigeria,' *Africa*, Vol. 23, No. 4, 1953, pp. 298–323, with permission of the author and of the International African Institute.

principal handicrafts are pot-making by women and straw-work carried on by males. Internal exchange still proceeds mainly within the context of kinship and affinity, each unit of domestic economy (*engau*) being ideally, and to a large extent in practice, self-sufficient.

Kadara trace descent patrilineally and live in compact lineage groups most usually referred to as *ute*. Often, however, as a consequence of dispersion in past wars, *ute* settled in two or more villages recognize common agnatic kinship, the more inclusive and dispersed unit being also referred to as *ute*. Though the maximum genealogical depth seems to be three generations removed from fully adult males, and despite the frequent local derivation of names for localized *ute* sections, Kadara of various village areas state that sections of an *ute* dispersed in different communities are aware of their common lineage ties and honour the associated obligations.

Within any community, however, the most significant unit is not the individual patrilineage, but a group of such lineages sharing a common locality. This more inclusive group, which Kadara may also refer to as their *ute* but which is more correctly described by their term *ategburu*, is often given the administrative status of a ward, the component lineages providing further divisions of more manageable size, each under its own representative in ward matters. It would, however, be a mistake to regard the *ategburu* as merely a territorial unit. Though its composition and functions give it prominence in this respect, Kadara regard it as mainly an association of distinct patrilineages for the proper conduct of the major rituals. Briefly, the principal events of the Kadara ritual cycle are held at the start of the farming season, after the maize harvest in August, and after the main harvest of guineacorn (*sorghum vulgare*) in December when the dry season begins. These occasions mark stages in the annual cycles of funeral rites, which include an initiation ritual every eighth year at which young males over seven years old are isolated in the bush for three months, those not previously circumcized being operated on at this time, when a new age-set (*ufro*) is also formed. Age-mates within each *ategburu* form a separate division of the age-set of the total community, and these divisions were frequently assigned different tasks in war and in the community hunting battues (*kalagu*), which are sometimes restricted to ward members.

As they say themselves, 'Kadara never rest from ritual', the most striking feature of which is the number and variety of spirit-representations involved. These spirit-representations fall into two classes—the visible representations, which are masked dancers, and the audible representations, involving the use of the bull-roarer, certain drums of unusual design in this area, holed gourds covered by cobweb, bone flutes, etc.

Few localized patrilineages have anything like the complete apparatus or status necessary for all required ritual, and as it seems that certain of the more important objects, such as the bull-roarers and *ibini* drums just mentioned, may not be manu-factured *ad hoc*, lineages lacking the ritual requirements asso-ciate with more fortunate groups in the ritual association known as *ategburu*. Exclusion of all women and uninitiated males from participation in the ritual or knowledge of the spirit-representation (*ohuma*), by emphasizing the secrecy of the rites, lends an urgency and seriousness to their performance which, however, would not obtain if the male performers and partici-pants, who are all aware of the element of human manipulation involved, did not strongly regard these formalized traditional practices as necessary for individual and social well-being. Kadara combine an interesting form of ancestor-worship with beliefs in reincarnation.

Kadara have no tribal chief, and are at present organized for administrative purposes in units known as village areas, each under a village-area chief. Usually the village area consists of two or more villages, the village-area chief being drawn from the most important settlement of the group, which is usually also the most ancient, as the modern village areas are based to a large extent on traditional territorial groupings. Thus, for in-stance, Kufana village area contains the following villages: Ku-fana, Danbagudu, Rafin Kunu, Dutsen Gaya, and Kiamara. Of these Kufana is the oldest and the largest settlement, the other villages having been established by emigration from Kufana. The different settlements of Kufana village area contain sections of several common *ute*, initiate their age-sets together, and in pre-British days, as now, recognized the supervisory powers of the chief of Kufana village in cases of dispute between members of different villages in that group. A group of villages united in these ways forms a separate community; within the community, and thus within each of its constituent villages also, secondary marriage is forbidden. That is to say, a man cannot take the wife of any other member of his community in secondary marriage.

Sexual relations and marriages are forbidden between all members of the same *ute* (patrilineage), and between a man (or a woman) and a member of the localized patrilineage from which his (or her) mother came. But persons from two unrelated patrilineages within an *ategburu* frequently marry. Kadara regard it as incest when men of the same *ute* seduce one another's wives, and the offence is also very serious between a man and the wife of a member of an unrelated *ute* (patrilineage) of the same *ategburu*. Repeated offences of this kind give rise to expulsion from the *ute*, *ategburu*, and usually from the community also.

Kadara practise three types of marriage: marriage by betrothal, widow-inheritance, and a form which will be referred to here as secondary marriage. All forms are called *uballe* (marriage), are virilocal, and have the same status. The notion of cross-cousin marriage is abhorred.

Infant betrothals are usually arranged for their children under customary law (*okara*) by men living in the same community and are symbolized by an exchange of beer. When the girl is three to six years old, the annual farm-service on the bride's father's farms commences. Farm-service increases from two man-days' work in the first year to twelve man-days' work in the tenth year, at which the bridegroom may demand his bride. Whether the marriage is solemnized then or not, the farm-service must be completed by another consecutive two years of twenty to twenty-four man-days' work each. During each year of farm-service small gifts of salt are made to the bride's mother. At the tenth year substantial gifts of rice or *acca* (*digitaria exilis*), guineacorn, and a native mattress of palm-branches is added to this. A large spurred hoe and five baskets of threshed guineacorn must also be given to the bride's father before the bride moves to live with her betrothed. The bride is sent to her father's sister for a few days, and is then taken to her husband's home. The apron of cowrie-shells and other ornaments of maidenhood are removed, she is stained with the oil and red ochre worn by married women, and performs the binding rite of marriage by feeding her husband and his friend with porridge from a spoon on the night of her arrival in his compound. This is the only time when the spouses eat together.

Kadara set no value on premarital chastity. It is fairly common for unmarried girls to be impregnated or to give birth to children by youths other than their betrothed. Offspring of such premarital pregnancies are members of the patrilineage of the girl's betrothed and are welcomed as proofs of the bride's fertility.

When his wife bears her first child in his compound, the husband sends five large pots of beer to her father. Two of these are returned. These gifts of beer are repeated triennially as long as the wife resides with her husband until the third child is born, when they cease. Should the bride refuse to consummate the marriage with her betrothed, she is asked to select a husband from within the localized patrilineage. If she refuses, her father is asked to take her back and provide a more amenable substitute, her sister, real or classificatory.

Three modes of widow-inheritance obtain. A man may inherit the wife of his elder brother, real or classificatory, or the wife of his paternal grandfather, or the wife of his maternal grandfather. Of these, widow-inheritance by a junior sibling of the deceased is the preferred and most frequent type. In effect inheritance of the paternal grandfather's widow was limited to cases where no junior siblings survived the deceased. A man's lineage often oppose his inheritance of the maternal grandfather's widow on grounds that the mother's father's lineage will claim any issue of the marriage. In such cases, if a chosen heir still wishes to marry his maternal grandfather's widow, he may go to live with his mother's lineage. Extra-lineage widow-inheritance of this type thus conforms to the levirate. Within the patrilineage, children borne by inherited widows are attributed to the genitor rather than to the deceased. Widow-inheritance of the first two types is confined to members of the deceased's lineage (*ute*), and of the third type to members of the deceased's daughter's lineage.

Secondary marriages take place when a married woman deserts her husband and goes to live with another man. Before the desertion the woman's lover obtains her father's permission privately and makes a token gift of beer and money or goods. On leaving her husband's home, the woman goes to the compound of a man in her lover's village who is linked to her father by ties of kinship, and has the role of 'foster-father'. There she remains for three days. She is then accompanied by an elder sister of her foster-father to her new husband's home, and the rite of marriage previously described is solemnized. In a feast, which publicly announces the marriage, the new husband makes small gifts to his own lineage and to the bride's foster-father. Two years later the second husband sends six large pots of beer to the foster-father. The foster-father keeps three and takes the rest to the girl's true father, who holds a drink with members of his lineage. Triennial gifts to the bride's father and gifts after the birth of children are the same as in primary marriage.

When a woman departs in this way, her original husband complains to her father, who pretends ignorance of her whereabouts, but sends out her younger siblings in a mock search. When the woman's next marriage has been solemnized, her original husband is informed of her whereabouts and her father undertakes to establish whether or not the woman was pregnant at her departure by sending some of her younger siblings to visit her at each of her three succeeding menstrual periods. The deserted husband meanwhile employs various magical techniques to secure his wife's return.

Secondary marriage is forbidden between a man and the wife of any member of his community or of any section of his *ute*, wheresoever located. The community, it will be recalled, has been defined as a group of villages, which carried out the ritual of initiation and age-set formation together, and recognized a common chief. Within such a unit, which now usually forms a single administrative village area, it was forbidden to contract secondary marriage, but recently this rule has been broken on several occasions within the Kufana village area. Such behaviour, which is regarded as highly immoral, will be discussed in some detail later.

Primary marriages involving betrothal take place between members of different lineages within the same community; secondary marriages take place between members of different communities; widow-inheritance of any type only involves men and the wives of their deceased senior kinsmen, generally within the community. Though the women and their inheritors are thus linked only by ties of affinity, and not by kinship, sexual relations between them are prohibited as incestuous until the inheritance actually takes place.

Two groups of communities within Kajuru district are distinguished by the observance of different procedures for the formation of secondary marriages. Each group, which is composed of villages located near to one another, contains Kadara and Ajure. Although secondary marriages occur between members of these two different groups of communities, they are said to be infrequent. Intermarriage of either primary or secondary type with neighbouring tribes such as Ikulu and Gwari was denied.

The union of a runaway wife with another man, as described above, is marriage (*uballe*), not concubinage; it takes place with the bride's father's consent, is established ritually, and gives rise to claims and duties which are identical with those of marriages preceded by betrothal. Thus, certain payments of beer are due to the woman's father at stated times and after the birth of any children in each case. Following the death of a woman's father, her primary and secondary husbands are required to bring a goat apiece to sacrifice at the deceased's tomb during his second funeral rites. In all types of marriage, with the exception of inheritance of the maternal grandfather's widow, noted above, the domestic relations of spouses and their reciprocal obligations and duties are identical.

But although unions formed by women who have deserted their first husbands are recognized as marriage, they in no way abrogate or annul the woman's previous marriage. The deserted husband and runaway wife still describe and address one another as 'my wife' (*ashimi*) and 'my husband' (*akimi*). The woman's two husbands refer to one another by the term which co-wives apply to each other. The woman may, with the knowledge and consent of her cohabiting husband, return to visit her deserted husband for a longer or shorter period of time, during which she fully resumes her previous role, cooking for her husband, farming at his direction, sleeping with him, etc. Such a 'visit', known as *abusan*, is not a remarriage but simply a reunion of persons already married to one another, and is not marked by any cere-

monial exchange or behaviour. Furthermore, a woman is obliged
to take part in the funeral rites of her deceased husband and be
inherited as his lineage directs; this obligation to marry the heir
of her deceased husband holds for a woman with respect to both
her primary and her secondary marriages. Thus while she lives
with one husband a woman is widowed by the death of another,
and returns to discharge the obligation of being inherited, which
is an essential part of the funeral ritual. This holds for each of
her husbands in turn. Patently, widowhood presupposes wife-
hood at the time of the husband's decease, hence a wife's desertion and remarriage do not terminate the pre-existing marriage.
That is to say, there is no indigenous recognition of divorce. Only
the cohabitation ceases when the wife deserts. The marriage and
the relationships centred upon it persist. A new cohabitation may
be formed should the woman return either on a formal visit
(*abusan*), or without her other spouse's consent, or after the
husband's death to be inherited by a lineage successor. This distinction between a cohabitation of spouses and the institution of
marriage, within and through which alone such cohabitations are
possible for the Kadara, is implicit in their practice. Thus, since
marriage is virilocal and men of the same community are forbidden to seduce one another's wives, a woman can participate
in only one cohabitation at a time, though she may be a party to
two or more legal marriages. Among Kadara, members of either
sex are permitted a plurality of spouses, but whereas men may
simultaneously enjoy a plurality of cohabitations as well as marriages, women may only participate in one cohabitation at any
one time, though remaining parties to a plurality of marriages.
Given the absence of divorce, the practice of virilocal marriage,
and the rule that members of the community within which marriages by betrothal are arranged may not contract secondary
marriages with one another, the preceding distinctions and practice are both logical and necessary; they represent an institutionalized adjustment of the competing claims of exogamous
patrilineages for the fertility of which women are the bearers,
such that the individual issue may only accrue to the genitor's
patrilineage, while each lineage retains decisive control over the
disposal of its daughters' fertility.

KAGORO

Comparable institutions exist among the Kagoro, of whom the majority (*c.* 10,000) are located in the independent district of Kagoro in the south-east corner of Zaria Province at the foot of the Jos Plateau. The tribal territory of *c.* 70 square miles has a population density of approximately 140 per square mile, but the Kagoro Rock, a huge massif several square miles in extent rising about 2000 feet above the surrounding country, has remained unoccupied and uncultivated since the last Kagoro were compelled by the British to settle at the northern base of the Rock in 1925. Undoubtedly the Kagoro are greatly indebted to their rock for the independence which they retained despite frequent attacks in the last century from the Muslim Hausa-Fulani kingdoms of Zaria and Jema'a, the latter twelve miles to the south-west.

Culturally and linguistically, Kagoro have little in common with Kadara, [who] differ markedly in physical type, material culture, and social organization. The closest similarity between the two groups is found in economy, which is based on sedentary grain-farming, the main Kagoro cereals being eleusine millet and *acca* (*digitaria exilis*). The present Kagoro settlement pattern is dispersed. Livestock consists of goats, dogs, and chickens. Like the Kadara, Kagoro traditionally lacked metal-work and cloth-making, while internal trade was desultory and principally by barter. Moreover, owing partly to their successful resistance of Hausa attacks, Kagoro retained their acephalous political system up to the time of their contact with the British.

At present, as in the past, the principal political units of Kagoro are territorial communities, which nowadays have administrative status as village areas under chiefs within the Independent District and Tribe administered by the newly created tribal chief as District Head. Internally, the communities break down into localized patrilineages (*kwai*), which are grouped into two moieties known as Ankwai and Kpashan. The Kpashan moiety contains the descendants of immigrants from various nearby tribes who joined the original Kagoro at different times during the nineteenth century, and were accepted on grounds of cultural and

linguistic similarity by the Ankwai, but were prohibited from
participating directly in the major rituals known as *Ci*. Distinctions were originally drawn between earlier immigrant groups
known as Munzaram and later, more numerous, arrivals called
Kpashan. These have lapsed for reasons to be made clear later,
and the immigrants now form a single moiety referred to indifferently as Kpashan or Munzaram.

Important social differences persist between the two moieties.
Thus, members of Kpashan moiety may not intermarry, whereas
Ankwai may and do. Moiety solidarity lapsed during the frequent
inter-community fighting with bows and arrows, or disputes over
land boundaries, hunting, women, etc. Intra-community disputes
were settled by fights with clubs and stones and were limited
strictly to the lineages of the parties concerned.

The tribal territory is divided into three *bin* (ritual areas)
under the ritual supervision of the clan-heads and chief priests
(*tenci*) of the three most senior Ankwai clans, Zafan, Mingio,
and Atswan. The *Niebin* (pl. *tiebin*) or chief priest of each area
had rights to portions of the larger beasts hunted there, was
responsible for rituals which terminated extra-tribal fighting in
which his area was engaged, administered certain oaths in most
serious disputes, and so forth. The three *Tiebin* each have different ritual tasks necessary for the well-being of the tribe as a
whole, and when tribal disasters threatened, as in smallpox epidemics or locust infestations, acted together to convene the males
of the tribe at a special place in the centre of the tribal territory
known as the *teyanpen*, where rites of purification were performed.

The widest politically effective group of agnatic kin is called a
kwai. Translation of this term is difficult by reason of the fact
that whereas several *kwai* are linked by ties of ascribed agnatic
kinship to other units of similar order in different communities,
a good many are not, and the former may be collectively referred
to as a *kwai*. Thus the term may denote a body of patrilineal
kinsmen, localized in one community only, or a segment of a
more inclusive patrilineage settled in two or more communities,
or a dispersed clan. In its political sense the term *kwai* always
denotes the most inclusive independent politically effective unit
based on agnatic kinship, that is, a patrilineal group localized in

one community. Such a localized patrilineage is the widest unit mobilized in the fights which take place within a community. Disputes between lineages of different communities are *ipso facto* inter-community disputes. Land, housesites, economic trees, livestock, and other possessions are inherited and succession to lineage-office takes place within the localized patrilineage. Localized lineages hold corporate rights to certain property such as hunting areas, and also to certain ritual tasks and prerogatives. The minor rituals of the *Obwai*, a spirit-representation in certain formal respects recalling those current among the Kadara, are also conducted independently by localized patrilineages (*kwai*). Initiation of circumcized twelve-year-old boys of the *kwai* into the *Obwai* cult is held each year at the *Tu obwai* (*Obwai* hut), the initiation ceremony lasting one day only, during which the initiates are sworn to secrecy after being instructed that the *Obwai* is a masquerade serviceable only to discipline the wives of lineage-members, as women believe and fear it. There are no age-sets among the Kagoro.

Within any localized patrilineage (*kwai*) segments are differentiated in terms of agnatic descent traced to a depth of six or seven generations with fair consistency. Where the genealogy extends beyond that depth telescoping appears and the intermediate links are often given in different orders at different times before the eponymous ancestor of the group (if one exists) is reached. Not all *kwai* have eponymous ancestors.

Among Kpashan particularly, careful inquiry frequently shows that some *kwai* contain two or more unrelated agnatic descent groups, though the *kwai* may have a common name, such as Kalahu, not found in any of the separate genealogies. Whether the *kwai* is conceived as genealogically homogeneous or not, the order of units internally differentiated remains the same. Major segments of a *kwai* are known as *tusa* or *uli*, and are themselves segmented into units known as *ufam*, which in turn contain less clearly articulated divisions known as *kyambwak*. At each level of segmentation different ritual and social behaviours characterize and differentiate the units concerned.

Kagoro marriage-types, like those of the Kadara, can be classified according to their modes of formation, as primary marriage by betrothal, widow-inheritance, and secondary marriage. All forms have equal social recognition and legal status. All marriage is virilocal. With only one exception, explicable in particular historical terms, all *kwai* are exogamous units. *Kwai* localized in different communities who share a common name and traditions of common agnatic descent also practise mutual exogamy (*bin*). Thus the Mingio in the several communities of Fadan Kagoro, Kpak, Agbam, Chanje, and Malagum do not intermarry, nor may they take one another's wives in secondary marriage, though inheritance of widows is practised. But among the Kagoro exogamy has two forms: that which prohibits both primary and secondary marriage within the unit concerned, and that which prohibits primary marriage only. As will be shown later, Kpashan moiety provides instances of this second type. Data from Kagoro suggest that further refinement of the concept of exogamy may be both useful and necessary.

Primary marriage (*tin ebiuk*) is preceded by betrothal arranged during the infancy or early childhood of the spouses by their parents through intermediaries. Stages in the betrothal are marked by gifts, usually from the bridegroom's kin to that of the bride. Farm-service is not among the obligatory payments, which include one metal bracelet, one spurred hoe, benniseed, beans, chickens, two goats, and ten pots of beer of particular types, etc. Acceptance of the bracelet symbolizes acceptance of the betrothal offer, and thereafter the betrothed couple may not speak to one another in public and are not allowed to meet in private, though the boy pays formal visits, known as *luo*, to the girl in her parents' compound, at which formal courtship takes place indirectly and the groom gets to know the bride's kin. After the bride has passed puberty she is cicatrized and preparations for the marriage go forward.

Primary marriage is celebrated throughout the tribe in the late dry season by the communities in sequence, beginning with the Zafan clan at Kadarko, which dispatches its brides at a certain day and with a ritual known as *tuk pirrung*. The only exceptions to this rule occur in the cases of unmarried girls who are pregnant. It is a stringent rule among Kagoro that no woman must ever give birth in her parents' home or lineage; hence a pregnant girl is bundled off to her betrothed without ceremony soon after her condition is discovered. Such cases are said to be rare, for Kagoro place a high value on virginity at marriage, and regard

their neighbours the Atakar who, like the Kadara, regard premarital pregnancies or births with favour as proof of the bride's
fertility, with undisguised contempt.

Primary marriage is most usually arranged between members
of different *kwai* in the same community. It does not involve full
ritual incorporation of the bride in her husband's lineage. She is
required to be present at certain annual rites of her lineage, for
instance, during the annual four-day *Obwai* ritual, and has certain other obligations, such as helping her brothers at harvest,
which necessitate seasonal visits. After postnatal bleeding has
ceased, mothers pay a visit of several months to their parents'
home, known as *swat-uli*, which ends after the seasonal rite
known as *abeyen* in the late dry season.

Among the Kagoro a special bond is created between a woman
and her brother whose marriage payments include items received
on her behalf. After their father's decease, the linked brother
(*atiengya*) acts as the protector and guardian of his sister
(*anap*); he has authority in the arrangement of her subsequent
marriages and in disputes related thereto, and is the special
angat (mother's brother) of her children. The *atiengya* receives
marriage-payments made subsequently for his sister, and then
makes final gifts of household equipment to her, known as
giyakuluo and *diuli*. Apart from his personal influence, the
atiengya controls certain ritual mechanisms such as the *Obwai*,
and various oaths, which provide him with means to discipline
his sister and guide her in certain directions. The only form of
kinship marriage practised by Kagoro derives from this *atiengya*
relation, and is diagrammatized below.

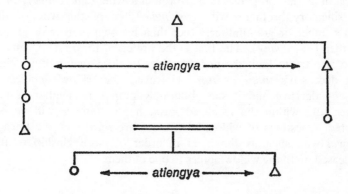

Such a marriage is favoured and proposed by elderly women when their daughters' sons and their *atiengya* are alive together, and although kinship is traced through persons of both sexes in this case, is probably linked with the submerged line of uterine descent and kinship known as *dra*, which will not be discussed here. This form of marriage, called *tabawak ingwarak ufa* (hold hands, embrace stomach) is the closest form of kinship marriage permitted among the Kagoro, and also the only form, as *dra* in the following generation does not give rise to preferred marriage.

When his wife's child is about four years old, the husband must make a payment to his wife's father or *atiengya*, which is known as *drangwan*. *Drangwan* consists of one spurred hoe and two goats, or two hoes and one goat, or three of either, and is obligatory for each of the first two of every three children which a man's wife bears to him. Non-payment of *drangwan* leads to the removal of the child by its mother's *atiengya*, and usually to the mother's desertion as well. Such a child is incorporated in his mother's lineage as a son of her *atiengya* with full enjoyment of lineage rights. Until recently *drangwan* was a universal Kagoro practice, and clearly denotes that husbands do not hold rights *in genetricem* over their wives, but only claims which, once admitted, must be converted into rights by payment of *drangwan* to effect the transfer from the lineage of the mother to that of the father of the first and second of every three children born to her. If *drangwan* was not paid by a certain time, the claims lapsed. Until recently this rule held in all types of marriage.

Kagoro practise several forms of widow-inheritance: inheritance of a full or paternal half-brother's wife (*sak ebiuk*), of a classificatory brother's wife (*ashinguo*), or of the wife of the heir's father or grandfather, other than his own mother or grandmother (*sak ayang*). The first is the preferred form among males, who also try to limit the possible heirs to close agnatic kin within the deceased's *ufam* or *tusa*. However, the widow's choice is usually decisive and if she obdurately prefers a member of another *tusa* within the localized *kwai*, her preference will be accepted. Questions of widow-inheritance are settled by the lineage *Obwai* who suggests the heirs in order of close kinship to the deceased, until the widow agrees to one of them.

In certain cases widow-inheritance occurs between differently localized sections recognizing ties of patrilineal kinship, but these instances are exceptional, and the widest unit of widow-inheritance is normally the localized patrilineage (*kwai*). Widow-inheritance is not a new marriage, but a continuation of the former marriage within a new ritually sanctioned union. Attribution of the heir's issue by the inherited widow to the deceased is frequent though not invariable. The critical factor differentiating between leviratic and non-leviratic widow-inheritance seems to be linked with the order of segment within which the successive lineage husbands of the woman are included. That is to say, whether and by whom children of the new union are claimed as belonging to the heir or to the deceased may depend on the position of the two husbands and their relation to the speaker within the segmentary genealogical structure of the lineage. Widow-inheritance invokes two structural principles: the principle of the substitutability of lineage males, and the principle that marriage is a public relation, i.e. a relation between the lineages of the spouses, which terminates only with the woman's death. As among the Kadara, a man's death widows all his wives equally, wherever they may be, and imposes the obligation of return to the deceased's lineage to undergo the rite of widow-inheritance. Hence termination of a union by the wife's cohabitation with another spouse in no way implies termination of the marriage, which is a public relation between the lineages of the spouses concerned within which their union takes place, recognizing the substitutability of lineage males in the event of the husband's death, with reciprocal obligations of the woman to cohabit with her husband's heir.

Absence of divorce in the indigenous Kagoro system is further established by consideration of the procedures employed against husbands who sought to dismiss unwanted wives. Such a husband could either order his wife to leave, or force her departure by hanging a certain shrub called *nesham* over the doorway of the woman's hut. Whatever the provocation, such actions gave rise to severe fines known as *tinbang*, levied by the community clan-heads under the priest of *Ci* at the community meeting-place where matters of urgent public concern were discussed, but in no way terminated the marriage. The husband removed the ban, paid the fine, apologized to his wife's *atiengya*, and the wife was reinstated. The frequency of such actions was severely limited by their ineffectiveness.

Soon after a woman's first marriage has been solemnized, new betrothals are contracted on her behalf and with her consent by her father or *atiengya*, through intermediaries. Courtship follows the *luo* pattern referred to above, at her father's compound on her frequent visits. The woman refers to her betrothed by the reciprocal term *asak* (the one who waits), and her husband refers to him by the reciprocal term *nendwang* (thing of trouble). Betrothal payments made to a woman's *atiengya* on behalf of this type of secondary marriage (*tswo ebiuk*) are standardized at present as follows: one goat, one spurred hoe, 10s. to 30s. currency (formerly paid in cowries or by equivalent values in kind), one dog and two pots of beer, the pots being of a special type. The marriage could not take place until all these payments had been completed. In the rare event of the woman's refusal to fulfil her obligations over a sufficiently long period after the payments had been completed, repayment could be claimed from her *atiengya*; such a step usually had the effect of securing cohabitation, and was really an indirect request to the *atiengya* to use the ritual techniques at his disposal to secure the betrothed's desire. By kidnapping the woman's child the betrothed was usually able to secure fulfilment of the contract without any assistance from the *atiengya*. Under this convention, a woman immediately removes herself to her *asak*'s home when she wakes in the morning and finds her child missing. As the child in question may have been weaned, the woman's behaviour on such occasions appears to have a conventional rather than a biological motivation. *Asak* visits his betrothed in her husband's home at night stealthily, at first to solicit early marriage, and later to kidnap her child as she sleeps. If the husband discovers the lover, etiquette demands that he should treat him with every mark of kindness and hospitality on these occasions. To do otherwise is highly disrespectful to his wife and her *atiengya*, who are fully entitled and expected to arrange these further betrothals. Finally, when the woman deserts her husband for another spouse, she goes to her *atiengya*'s home and is conducted to the new husband's compound by their kinsfolk who acted as intermediaries in arranging the betrothal. Paternity disputes are the most frequent and bitter expressions of tension on such occasions. Traditionally the woman is responsible to her *atiengya* in this matter, and is required to show proofs of menstruation at each of the three succeeding monthly periods following her change of residence. In unresolved cases, where his decision was disputed, or when violence was resorted to by either husband, the *atiengya* had authority to retain the child as his own. Usually satisfactory evidence determining paternity could be obtained either during the woman's labour or afterwards by compelling her to swear a formal oath. Concealment or perjury is held to cause the mother's death.

A wife's departure does not abrogate marriage to her former husband. The parties still refer to one another as *etuok* (husband) and *ebiuk* (wife). The departed wife is obliged to help her husband with the harvest and certain other tasks when required, and must be present in the compound when her son is initiated into the *Obwai* cult or circumcized. Frequently, however, the woman returns voluntarily either with the intent of permanent cohabitation—in which case she informs her *atiengya* but not the husband she will be leaving—or on a visit, in which case her *atiengya* and both husbands are informed. These visits are normally for agreed periods, lasting from six months to a year, and are said to be of two types. *Dinwan* is the visit women make to absent husbands by whom they have had children. *Yankwainta* is the visit of a wife to an absent husband to whom she has borne no children. There seems to be no other distinction. Both visits take place with the cohabiting husband's foreknowledge and consent, and in both cases the woman fully resumes the role of wife on arrival in her former home. She cooks for her spouse, sleeps with him, works on his farm, fetches wood and water, etc. As before, proofs of non-pregnancy are presented by the woman to her *atiengya* for three months after the change of residence.

Another type of secondary marriage known as *kwak ebiuk* was not preceded by betrothal, but effected by forcible capture of the woman. Unmarried girls were not subject either to *kwak* or *tswo* as they lacked the status of *ebiuk* (wife), a difference of condition visibly expressed in difference of dress. Kagoro distinguish several types of *kwak* according to the amount of force used to effect the capture and various similar criteria, but all forms of *kwak*, intra-tribal and otherwise, gave rise to sharp fighting between the communities of the parties concerned, who were mobilized by the blowing of a horn as soon as the outrage was discovered. Such intra-tribal fights were halted as soon as possible by the *tienci* of the communities concerned employing ritual measures. Thereafter the offended party awaited a chance of retaliatory *kwak*, while the offender sought to legitimize his claim *post facto* by retrospective betrothal payments to the woman's *atiengya*, acceptance of which constituted the ground for further claims to her subsequent offspring, which must themselves be ratified by payment of *drangwan*.

An even more anomalous procedure, of which only two instances were recorded, arose when a woman went to live with a man not betrothed to her without his foreknowledge or her *atiengya*'s. Such unions gave rise to scornful comment, and are not regarded as marriage. In one case the betrothal payments were made retrospectively and the union was to some extent regularized. In the other, the man has retained the woman and his children by her without making payments for betrothal or *drangwan*.

Independently formed unions, such as *kwak* and this last type, are viewed with disfavour by Kagoro because by their occurrence they may, and usually do, effect permanent changes in the social relations of the lineages of the parties concerned. They are deviations with irreversible generalized consequences, ritually marked by fighting and feud. It is now necessary to particularize the interlineage marriage relations, which are thus affected.

Intermarriage and intermarrying lineages are reciprocally *niendi*, 'wife-abduction' and lineages in such a relation are reciprocally *nendwang*. Exogamy has two possible forms—that in which neither intermarriage nor 'wife-abduction' is permissible to the units concerned (*bin*); and that in which intermarriage is forbidden, but not wife-abduction. Exogamy of the Kpashan moiety is an example of the last type. Exogamy of such clans as Mungwop, Kpaguwak, Mingio, sections of which are localized in different communities, is an example of the first type. Kagoro refer to this

first type of exogamy as *bin* and to the second type as *nendwang*.
Within the tribe, *bin*, *niendi*, and *nendwang* are mutually exclusive
forms of relation. *Niendi* (intermarriage) abrogates *bin* irreversibly. *Nendwang* (wife-abduction) irreversibly abrogates *niendi*.
All husbands of the same woman are *niendi* of her lineage (*kwai*)
and *nendwang* to one another.

Secondary marriage is prohibited between lineages localized in
the same community, hence Kpashan lineages of any one community are *bin*—i.e. they may not marry one another's daughters
or wives. Primary marriages are usually arranged within the community. Since there are no *nendwang* within a community, the
greatest possible number of marriages a woman may simultaneously contract within the tribe is the number of communities less
one. That is to say, two men in the same community may not be
married to the same woman simultaneously.

It will not be clear that systematic application of the rule of
alternative and mutually exclusive types of marriage relation provides the pivotal principle of Kagoro social structure. An historic
demonstration of this is ready to hand. As mentioned above, earlier and later immigrant groups were originally distinguished as
Munzaram and Kpashan respectively, but they are now members
of the same moiety. Immigrants were forbidden to form secondary
marriages with the wives of Ankwai, probably so that fighting and
hostility on this score should not mobilize the moieties as opposed
units. Given this essential safeguard, and the principle that immigrants must not intermarry, there is no possibility of a tri-section
system such as the original distinction between Munzaram and
Kpashan implied. This analysis is also in agreement with the
findings of a census of the marriage and other relations of all
lineages of *tusa* and super-ordinate orders in all the communities,
which contain only Kagoro—namely, Fadan Kagoro, Kpak, Kukum,
Agbam, Safio, Chanje, and Kadarko. The only characteristic common to all units which Kagoro recognize as *kwai* revealed by this
inquiry is the unity and uniqueness of the sets of marriage relations of which each *kwai* is a nexus. That is to say a *kwai* can be
defined as a localized group of agnatic kin whose relations involving marriage with all other *kwai* are both uniform and unique.
Groups which share an identical pattern of marriage relations are
not separate *kwai* but segments of the same *kwai*. Groups of

common agnatic descent, which have differentiated their marriage relations, are not segments of the same *kwai*; although they practise mutual exogamy they are independent *kwai*, even when they are found to be localized in the same community. The validity of this induction is established by the fact that the list of *kwai* and *tusa* was given by the Kagoro, and their interrelations were catalogued, before any such formulation suggested itself to anyone. Instances attesting certain aspects of its significance must be left for another publication, but it may be worth pointing out here that neither of the two criteria, which Kagoro quote as constituting *kwai*, namely localization and community of agnatic descent, holds universally. It has already been mentioned that the Mingio of Agbam are distinguished from the Mingio of Fadan Kagoro as separate *kwai*. So are the Katuk, Katuwak, Kangai, Kusali, Kunduwak, and Zukpon *kwai* of Kukum, though all these recognize common agnatic descent. Contrariwise, such *kwai* as Kalahu contain unrelated patrilineages. Moreover, when the compounds of Fadan Kagoro were mapped and their lineage affiliations determined, the dispersal of lineage members throughout the community was revealed.

One last important point must be mentioned. Once a woman has cohabited with her betrothed under the indigenous system, he can make no claim for refund of any part of the betrothal payments. That is to say, in Kagoro law a husband has neither permanent nor prescriptive rights *in uxorem*. He has a claim against his betrothed as wife, which is fulfilled when they cohabit. During cohabitation he enjoys rights over his wife *in rem* and *in personam*, most of which lapse on her departure. Thus several men may simultaneously have claims *in uxorem* against the same woman, but only the one with whom she cohabits enjoys rights in her during that period. An alternative formulation requires distinctions to be drawn between the various types of right which a husband has over his wife. On desertion some lapse, such as rights to performance of her domestic duties, right of sexual access, etc. Others do not, such as the right to require assistance at harvest and her presence at her son's circumcision. Other rights are not held by the husband but by his lineage as a corporate group—e.g., the right to inherit the woman after her husband's death. In still other cases, such as the affiliation of her children and attribution of paternity, neither the husband nor his lineage has a true right at all, but only a claim which must be ratified by further procedures. Patently, if a husband has no prescriptive rights *in genetricem* over his wife, it would be unusual if he had such rights *in uxorem*.

COMPARISON

It is now possible to define secondary marriage tentatively as marriage of a wife during the lifetime of her primary husband, which neither follows nor precedes divorce or annulment of pre-existing marriages. Data from the two societies studied suggest that different types of the same institution defined in such general terms may occur in different groups, so that it may be more correct and useful to think of types of secondary marriage rather than of an identical institution with a particular distributional field. Comparison of the Kadara and Kagoro further suggests certain factors, which may be linked with various forms of the institution, some of which will now be discussed in particular terms.

There is an important difference in the form of betrothal payments for primary marriage in the two societies, and among the Kadara the character of payments for secondary marriage also differs markedly from payments for primary marriage, which consist mainly of farm-service. At a different level there are significant differences in the range of secondary marriage practised by either group, and the degree of structural elaboration of the associated relations. Among the Northern Kadara and Ajure, as previously noted, two different groups of communities are distinguished as units within which secondary marriages usually occur. Each group contains villages of Kadara and Ajure but recognizes different procedures for the formation of secondary marriage. Within the Kagoro tribe relations of primary and secondary marriage are also mutually exclusive, but beyond the tribal boundaries they often hold simultaneously. Thus a Kagoro may make primary and secondary marriages with women of the same kinship unit of other tribes, such as Atakar, Kaje, etc. Among Kagoro lineages are distinguished by differences of their marriage-relations, and the two moieties enjoy different conditions of marriage, so that the formal interlineage relations of *niendi* and *nendwang* have a central position in the social structure.

Both the Kadara and the Kagoro have developed similar means for resolving disputed pregnancies and paternity, though on the data available certain differences of procedure are apparent here also, and intra-tribally the Kagoro practise a more elaborate and effective form of settlement. Among both groups all wives recognize the obligation to return and be inherited by another spouse chosen by the lineage of the former husband after his death; and among both groups the practice of visits by absconded wives to their deserted husbands obtains, though here also the Kagoro seem to have elaborated this aspect more prominently.

In any comparative study of this type, such similarities and differences raise questions of the distinction between and inter-relations of cultural and structural factors, but no formal discussion of these problems will be attempted here, though it must be noted that an exhaustive comparative study of any institution as practised by different societies would require a general theory of such relations. It will be useful to examine the changes in secondary marriage amongst the Kagoro and Kadara, which have occurred under British rule; in this way the present analysis may be tested and refined.

7 SPOUSE-EXCHANGE AMONG THE
NORTH ALASKAN ESKIMO

Robert F. Spencer

THE LAND AND THE PEOPLE

IN NORTHWESTERN NORTH AMERICA, between the Brooks Range and the Arctic Ocean, lie some seventy-odd thousand square miles of tundra. In this area of tundra, a desert of cold, are to be found two configurations of aboriginal Eskimo culture, a situation which throws the caribou hunters of the inland regions sharply into contrast with the whalers of the coastal slope.

In the truest sense, the Alaskan Arctic plain is a desert. Rain and snowfall are very slight, averaging no more than 5 to 7 inches per year. It has been suggested that this limited precipitation is the primary factor in hindering the spread of glaciers northward. The principal basis for seasonal differentiation lies not in rainfall, but in the differing intensity of temperature and in the length of daylight. The brief summer season is marked by a thaw and, for a 2-month period, by 24-hour sunshine. The transition from 24 hours of sunlight in late July to the fall equinox is most rapid, and, again, the shift from the equinox to the winter solstice involves the change in a short period from 12 hours of daylight to total darkness. At Point Barrow, for example, at 71° 23′ N., 72 days of winter darkness, beginning November 15, are the rule. Temperature changes cannot be regarded as extreme. In summer, the averages hover somewhat above freezing, although highs of 60° or 65° F. may be reached for short periods. From this, there

Abridged from *The North Alaskan Eskimo*, Bureau of American Ethnology Bulletin No. 71. Reprinted with the permission of the author and the Bureau of American Ethnology.

is a gradual shift to the winter temperatures. These are not so extreme as might be imagined, particularly along the coast where 30° F. below zero may be regarded as essentially average.

Throughout this great area live the scattered groups of Eskimo. These represent a people settled over centuries but not the first groups in the region. Since Alaska formed the land bridge by which man entered the New World from Asia, there is widespread evidence of human antiquity, of the Paleo-Indian, the precursors of the pre-Columbian Indian tribes of North and South America.

But in addition to these and many other ancient remains, there is the tremendous richness of the prehistory of the Eskimo themselves. While not so remote in time, the Eskimo cultures of the past pose a good many as yet unsolved problems. The Eskimo cultures of the past are never simple, and the various suggestions as to their origin are being clarified slowly as new data come to light.

The general pattern of geographic settlement must be kept in mind in order properly to designate the peoples of the region. The terms nuunamiut (nuunataɣmiut) and tareumiut are of course derivative of native designations for the two ecological groupings. These terms are descriptive of a way of life and cannot be regarded as tribal designations. As is well known, aboriginal Eskimo society consisted of aggregates of individuals that formed bands or villages. Membership and residence in either depended pretty much on the choice of the individual; the size of the group could expand or contract depending on local circumstances.

FAMILY AND KINSHIP

In virtually every respect the aboriginal family structure carries through into the present. However much the inroads of modern living have disrupted other aspects of the cultures of the north Alaskan slope, the system of mutual aid, of social control, and of reciprocal obligation inherent in the family remains paramount.

People who lived together in one house, who worked together, who might move together for inland hunting or trade, and who called each other by kinship terms were ketuuneraareic, a localized family grouping. In practice, this consisted of as many as chose to live together. It might be parents and children, or it might consist of two brothers and their children. A wife's relative or relatives might also be present in the group. There was no prevailing attitude toward residence, this being arranged in a wholly practical way. Thus, if it were felt expedient, the man, on marriage, might choose to live in his wife's grouping. Or the reverse was true. As nearly as one can judge, there was a fairly even split as to residence, with perhaps some tendency toward a patrilocal and virilocal arrangement. Dependence was placed on needs of the moment. If a family were poor, which might mean that they had only daughters and no active provider, uxorilocal residence was called for. If a son were the only provider to aged parents, residence was patrilocal. Or a married couple simply built a new house in a community, although here again, residence near the family grouping of either the wife or the husband might be a factor. Informal though such an arrangement might be, there was nevertheless a consideration to be met. If a husband had a recognized place in a crew, whether for caribou hunting or whaling, the matter of residence had to be carefully weighed; he would be reluctant to abandon a remunerative connection with a crew or karigi. The nuclear family consideration is thus technically superseded by the demands of the wider circle of kinship. The question may then justly be asked: what is the ultimate function of the nuclear family? This was a residence unit and an economic unit. In the matter of day-to-day living, in the preparation of food, the making of clothing, and in the procurement of food through hunting, here being a reflection of the well-defined sexual division of labor, it was the nuclear family which came to the fore. In broader aspects, however, such as in mutual interdependence and aid, in assistance in times of stress, and perhaps most important, in the general pattern of basic individual security, it was the wider circle of kin which began to function.

THE EXTENDED FAMILY

The extended family was iilyagiic. These were, for the individual, kin on both the maternal and paternal side. In the final analysis, this was for the individual a circle based wholly on actual relationship. It was not otherwise a formalized institution.

MARRIAGE

The family groupings to which the individual belonged were
ideally exogamous. It is evident that a goal in marriage was to extend as far as possible the bonds of mutual aid and cooperation.
For this reason, marriage between cousins was not desirable and
similarly, there was no levirate or sororate. Cousin marriage is
reported as occurring in a few instances; here, however, even the
second collateral degree was held improper, such marriages occurring only between relatives of the third collateral degree. But
even such marriages were frowned on. It was felt that marriage
between blood kin, however remote the tie, produced inferior offspring, individuals who were "not quite human." This seems to
be an aboriginal concept and not derived from Euro-American
contact. One informant was asked if her own children could marry
the children of her brother's daughter, the respective children
designating each other by "cousin" terms. She remarked that this
"wouldn't look good" and indicated that she felt very strongly
against such a union. Indeed, the only circumstances which would
justify such a marriage arose when a person found himself alone,
lacking the benefits of the nuclear family. Then he might marry a
cousin, albeit a distant one, in order to reaffirm family ties.

The feeling was carried further in that the adopted child was
subject to the same restrictions in regard to the family of his
adoption. Not only were his blood kin prohibited but the adoptive
kin as well. Recently a case arose where a family had adopted
a boy and girl. They married and their behavior was considered
highly scandalous. "It looked terribly bad."

The various towns of the maritime peoples tended toward endogamy. Here again, however, there was no rigid regulation. The
nuunamiut, subject essentially to the same regulations of marriage, might tend to endogamy in the extended band. Here, however, the regulations of kinship exogamy on all sides might
necessitate going fairly far afield for a wife. It might generally be
said that a man married into a family with which he was acquainted.
To take a wife from an unknown group was simply to court trouble in that one could never be sure of the industry of the woman,

of the reputation of her family, or of any number of possible involvements.

A problem of some interest emerges in respect to the contacts between the nuunamiut and the tareumiut. These, as has been seen, were principally of a trading nature, a mutual interdependence based on the exchange of certain commodities. That there were sexual unions between members of the two groups goes without saying, in view of the exchanges of wives which took place between partners at the great trading sessions. Marriage between the two groups was, however, rare. It occurred sometimes but was, in general, exceptional. And, again, such marriages did not take place unless there was a thorough acquaintance of long standing. A man of the ikpikpaŋmiut, for example, came regularly to piγiniq to trade. While there, he married a woman named tupineraaluq and took her back to the inland country with him. Everyone, it is said, felt sorry for her. She was obliged to adjust to the inland life and to learn new skills. Moreover, she would have to move about all the time. She adjusted well to the inland life, however, and came with her husband back to piγiniq every summer, and visited her family at this time. There are a few other instances of such marriages between the two ecological groups, but it is to be emphasized that such unions were not sought. Each group had its own sets of skills, its own type of adjustment. The result was to keep contacts on the trading level but not to effect any greater degree of intimacy through marriages. As between the two groups there would thus be the relationship of the qataŋun (qataŋuutigiit) but not of actual kinship.

A man did not marry sisters in the accepted polygynous unions, nor could he marry a mother and daughter. There was also the strong feeling that a man could not marry the sister of a deceased wife, nor a woman her dead husband's brother. Two brothers were likewise forbidden to marry two sisters. There is one instance of such marriage recalled today, the case involving marriage between a man and woman whose respective sister and brother also married. This "only happened once" and "it was a terrible thing." In another case, quite recently in Barrow, a woman married the brother of her deceased husband. This was "not right."

No one had ever heard of an incestuous relationship between brother and sister. In only one instance was there recalled an incest situation. A family had adopted a daughter. When the wife died, the daughter remained with her adoptive father as his wife. People said of this man, "He should be ashamed" and of the girl that "she had no pride." While no group action could be taken in such a case, the guilty parties could be made to feel the full force of adverse public opinion. When the girl's adoptive father died, she was claimed by another family in marriage. It is thus clear that there was no lasting stigma in such cases.

Marriage in these cultures was of course essential. The unmarried man was virtually helpless since he then lacked the work which a woman could provide. It would appear that marriages were more or less permanent, since a couple learned to adjust to each other's ways and a strong bond of affection might arise. But while the state of marriage operated largely in economic terms, and was permanent on this basis, it was defined sexually. As will be seen, when a man and woman had had sexual relations, a state of marriage was considered to have existed between them. The result was to call forth certain kinds of attitudes and behavior reflecting a cooperative situation into which not only the principals concerned, but others as well, might be drawn. The criterion of a permanent marriage was of course coresidence. Divorce was simply the breaking of the residence tie.

But there was a vague sense of marital arrangement, particularly in the case of young people entering marriage for the first time. Parents, especially the women, made the arrangement directly and informally. Such arrangements were frequently made between families in the same community whose members felt that they could agree. A "good" marriage resulted in peaceful relations between the families involved.

When an agreement was made, the parents of the girl made a gift to the boy—a knife, a harpoon, a parka—while he in turn came to their house to work for them. Such bride service was of short duration, although somewhat formalized, since the boy might merely catch a seal and give it to his prospective parents-in-law. The marriage might be consummated at any time during these proceedings. And once consummated, it was viewed as marriage. There was no demand for chastity or virginity.

There was room in the society for romantic love. A love match was considered a good risk. Romantic affairs often went on after marriage and there was a definite ideal of female beauty. Men went after beautiful women, so it is said. A woman of beauty might succeed in playing one suitor off against the other. Her family often warned her not to do this, since she then might be seized by an older and stronger man and take a place as a second wife. Indeed, this not infrequently occurred. When a man desired a woman, he might simply seize her, take her to his house, and rely on his kin to see that she neither escaped nor was rescued by her own family. Both single girls and married women were taken in this way. Seizing a woman and keeping her as a wife was nusukaaktuat, "grabbing off a wife." If a single girl was taken, her kin usually let the matter go and permitted her to remain with the abductor. If the abductor were undesirable from the family's point of view, they might complain but there was usually no action. In fact, a family might abet an abductor. If a girl refused to marry, especially a man of the family's choice, they arranged for a kidnaping. Or, if she were abducted, it was said, "This is what she has been wanting."

But such abductions went well beyond marriage since married women were also seized. Sometimes it was merely a matter of rape and no permanent alliance was contemplated. Some men had reputations as "women chasers," although women might likewise attempt to attract men. If anything, the woman was blamed more than the man. It was felt that a busy, modest woman "wouldn't get into trouble." A man who wished sexual relations with a woman solicited them by seizing her belt. She might then agree to a clandestine meeting. Jealousy was frequent and many men felt that they had to "watch their wives." Because sexual rights were in a sense property rights and linked with male status, a cuckolded husband might feel some revenge necessary. His retaliation against his wife's seducer was to rape his wife or to attempt to arrange a meeting with her. A husband and his wife's seducer stood as nuliinuaroak to each other, the sense being that they shared a woman.

The term aŋutawkun, also aŋutawkattigiit, etymologically like that for parallel cousin, was employed in two specific ways. It referred to men, partners, who had exchanged wives. It also designated the men who had been married to the same woman at different times. Conceptually, this might be a significant relationship, especially since the woman's children by both men would be half-siblings. The men so involved might thus share an interest in the children and in each other. If partners, they would in any case have a common interest and tie.

If a man desired to keep a married woman as his own mate, he generally informed his kin of his intentions. They either agreed to support him or tried to dissuade him. If they did assist him in capturing the wife of another, the woman was simply dragged off and kept in the house or the band of the captor. The abduction of a wife was not a cause of a feud. But the husband could enlist the aid of his kin in getting the woman back and her own kindred could also offer their help. If the ensuing dispute resulted in bloodshed, as was not unlikely, a feud then resulted. A wife was free to return to her husband if she escaped her captor. But it seemingly frequently occurred that the abduction took place with the woman's connivance. If so, and if the husband from whom she was taken knew or suspected it, he might make no effort to recover her. The decision was his to make.

DIVORCE

The precontact cultures did not insist on marriage as a permanent union. Indeed, marriage may be defined only in terms of its economic involvements. In one sense, any sexual union or liaison constituted marriage inasmuch as there were recognized status shifts which arose as a result of sexual relations. More specifically, however, marriage, as a recognized institution, might be said to result when a couple shared the same house and worked together toward the upkeep of the house, each contributing a share of labor to its maintenance. Children, of course, created a basis for stability.

But since marriage must be defined so loosely, divorce likewise cannot be regarded as a formalized mechanism. The pattern in general was that if the couple agreed, shared its labor, had offspring, became recognized as sharing a common social role, the two were married. The same status was accorded to individuals with more than one mate. If, therefore, there was any discord, if a wife were abducted, if either partner chose to leave, divorce was recognized. If a couple disagreed or if a man mistreated his wife, relatives of either partner might urge divorce as a logical course of action. Divorce was not an item of gossip but rather a usual means of solving a problem. In the precontact cultures, it would appear that virtually everyone had been married and was divorced at least once. Here again, however, it becomes difficult to offer an exact definition. Sexual relations did not constitute marriage in the exact social sense but there were other involvements arising from sex. A person may have "played the field" before settling down to a more permanent marital union. Once a couple became used to each other's ways, it was unlikely that divorce would occur.

Since there was no formalized property involvement in marriage, divorce did not entail any redistribution of property. Each partner took his own personal possessions, such as clothing, tools, boats, dogs, or whatever. The matter of the house itself was decided by whatever arrangement had originally been made as to residence. If the couple had built its own house, and several children had arrived, divorce was in any case unlikely. An offended partner who left forfeited rights to a house. This matter can be somewhat complex when it is considered that a husband might leave, move to another place, take another wife, and so settle down elsewhere. His first wife might thus be left with house and property. She, in turn, might marry again. The couple is thus presumably divorced, even though it has made no formal decision on the matter. On the other hand, the husband might then return to take up with his abandoned wife again. He might also retain a wife in another place. By this token, divorce becomes difficult of definition.

If there was a formal disagreement, however, an actual makaruak, the offended partner might leave. He or she often did so on the advice of relatives. In such a case, custody of children was left to the most expedient solution. Children might be given a choice of parent; they might be divided between the separating couple; they might be given out to others in adoption. There was clearly no hard and fast rule.

WIFE LENDING AND WIFE EXCHANGE

It is clear that the marriage bond, while essential to the successful functioning of the culture, was not conceptually a permanent one. It frequently occurred that a man went to trade or on a prolonged hunting expedition and left his wife behind. If he had many relatives about, he could safely leave the woman with them. But if he had few, he might impose on a partner or neighbor, asking him to take the woman in charge. This situation was known as aleupaaktuat. A friend, partner, or neighbor had sexual rights to the woman, a relative of the husband did not. If a man thus went to trade, leaving his wife in a friend's care, he generally had some commission to discharge for the man in return.

Between partners, especially those of long standing and proven friendship, there could be wife exchange on a temporary basis. This was also true of "friends," often as between those who had established a joking relationship. Hospitality might involve wife lending, since such hospitality would be extended in any case only to individuals occupying a special status in relation to a host. Wife exchange on a temporary basis took place only between men who occupied a status of formally defined friendship or partnership. Aside from partners and joking partners, there was no institutionalized friendship. Informal good relations, however, as between men in a whaling crew, in the same karigi, might call wife exchange into being. Men who exchanged wives were aŋutawkattigiit. The two men involved agreed to exchange their wives and did not consult the women involved. A woman was told, "Go over and stay with so and so." The exchange lasted for a few days, the women then returning to their husbands. The return of a woman after an exchange was called allupaareik. The woman was taken to the house of a man to whom she was lent. Among the maritime people sexual relations took place in the suuvik.

The Eskimo of the area deny that such exchanges were economic and insist that they were purely sexual. In wife exchange, the cooperative tie between the men and women involved was enforced. The respective children stood to each other as qataŋuutigiit and, as will be seen, were likewise drawn into a situation of cooperation. Wife exchange was thus always arranged and had no implications of rape or abduction such as were described in the previous section. It was in a sense an exchange of property rights and led to the exchange of other forms of property, hence again to mutual aid. Rape or wife abduction, on the other hand, was wilful violation of property right and it was for this reason that the various mechanisms described might arise.

A wife was lent, as noted, when a man was obliged to be gone from the community for some time. The man to whom he lent his wife might request the same assistance at a later time. When a man's partner visited, assuming he came alone, his host might offer him sexual rights to the wife. If partners came together with their wives, they frequently exchanged wives on a temporary basis. It was felt to be advantageous to do so, since it strengthened the bond of partnership and extended the system of mutual aid to the children of the respective couples.

Sexual trading, wife lending, or wife exchange, was called simmixsuat. The point that it was a sexual matter and not an economic one should be emphasized. It has been said that such exchange might arise of work specializations which each woman commanded. This does not seem to be the case, since in the cooperative situation of community living, work was freely exchanged without reference to sexual privilege.

Women who were exchanged were known as aytpareik. It apparently happened not infrequently that the exchange might be permanent. This would arise out of a matter of preference. Several such instances are recalled.

QATAŋUUTIGIIT[1]

It would be erroneous to assume that the sexual freedom inherent in the cultures of the area was wholly random and uncontrolled. Sexual relations carried with them a degree of responsibility and served to create a series of reciprocal obligations not only between the principals concerned but also between the kin of those involved. Even casual sexual affairs had certain consequences, as,

---

[1] A paper describing this rather unusual social institution was read at the 1953 meetings of the American Anthropological Association, Tucson, Ariz., December 29, 1953.

for example, in the case of the girl who was "free." Here the failure to exert a degree of control over the situation was disturbing to her kin. Because sexual relations were regarded as rights, and because defined obligations arose from sexual activity, it is clear that a well-defined pattern of behavior arose in connection with sexual affairs and that the involvements of the individual were channeled and predictable. Perhaps in no case is this more precisely defined than in the development of the qataŋuutigiit (dual) relationship.

As one considers the balance between social forms and economic life, it is apparent that the North Alaskan Eskimo sought in every way possible to extend the patterns of economic cooperation. Not only is the kin and household unit founded in cooperation but marriage itself was a device which served to extend the forms of cooperation between otherwise unrelated family groupings. The strong feelings against the levirate, sororate, or cousin marriage may be explained on this basis. But there were also ways of developing lasting relationships between nonkin. An obvious way lay in the ties of crew and karigi, another in partnerships and in joking partnerships, both of which came as close to an idea of blood brotherhood as was possible without some formalistic declaration. And it is further evident that sexual relations provided a clinching point, serving to cement the ties of friendship and mutual aid. Wife exchange was thus not wholly lustful; it had a definite function in the society as a means of extending a cooperative relationship. When sexual relations took place, and when of such intercourse children were engendered, the offspring of the various unions came to occupy a special cooperative relationship to each other. They stood to each other as qataŋuutigiit (sing. qataŋun).

This relationship arose between nonrelatives on the basis of previous sexual relationships. It came about under the following circumstances:

    1   If two persons, divorced or widowed, married, each having offspring from the previous marriage, their respective offspring became qataŋuutigiit to each other.
    2   When wives were exchanged, the respective children of the two couples who then had engaged in an exchange stood in this relationship.

3 This provides the basic point of definition. From the point of view of Ego, the children of any person with whom his father or mother had previously had sexual relations were his qataŋuutigiit.

The qataŋuutigiit (pl. qataŋuutigiic) were thus not blood relatives. Under most circumstances, they could marry. This would be forbidden in the first instance listed above, where a man and woman marry, each having children. This was then an adoptive situation, the children called each other by sibling terms, and were forbidden to marry. They might extend the relationship here, designating it as nukaxrareik—half-siblings—a term not otherwise used.

Basically, this was a cooperative situation. A child was told that when he went to some other place where there were no kin, he should seek out such and such a person who would aid him. "He is your qataŋun." An individual could, in traveling, always seek out the children of his father's partners, assuming that in the partnership wives had been exchanged, and demand of them assistance and support. It was freely given. It is worth mentioning that here was a basis for forming new partnerships and it is in this respect that partnerships tended to follow along family lines, the two families involved retaining the relationship.

Some examples may serve to point up the importance of the relationship:

1. When taaluq traveled down the coast, he stopped at Kotzebue camping near two houses some distance from town. He was invited into one of the houses where a woman was living. She asked him who his father was and where he came from. He told her. She said, "My children are like your brothers." Then he remembered that his father had told him that he had been married to this woman. After that, in his journeys up and down the coast, he always stopped at that house. The woman's daughters would repair his clothes and chew his boots. He had intercourse with them.

2. A man from Barrow went down to Noatak. The people there were very suspicious of him and tried to kill him. They shut him up in the karigi and gave him no food and prevented his coming out. He had a qataŋun there, however, who got food to him and finally set him free. In escaping from Noatak, the man was lent a sled by his qataŋun. The latter urged him not to return to Noatak but said that if he did so, he would always be given help. The rescuer's mother had once had sexual relations with the father of the man from Barrow.

3.   A stranger came to utkeaaɣvik from kuvuk (Kobuk). He was accorded the usual treatment reserved for strangers, the men coming out and pummeling him, tearing his clothes, and crying, "hii, hii." His qataŋuutigiit recognized him and pulled him away from the others, bringing him home and caring for him.

As a result of the development of this relationship, it became necessary to recall the former sexual partners, to keep the tie with them alive, and to inform one's children of their where-abouts. The result was a quasi-kinship. While the family loyalties came first, it nevertheless followed that one attempted to give assistance to one's qataŋuutigiit whenever possible. It was an important relationship in other ways, as, for example, in termi-nating a blood feud. If a sexual arrangement could be worked out between a man and woman in the two feuding factions, the respective children then became qataŋuutigiit to each other and the now existing cooperative relationship forbade further bloodshed.

At present, there is still a strong sense for the relationship. Many who still recognize qataŋuutigiit call them by sibling terms and are close friends with them. As one woman remarks today, however, "You are just talking about your parents' sins when you have this." This statement would indicate, perhaps, that the coordinated patterns of mutual aid are falling away.

PART III
MARRIAGE FORMS

8 PAHARI POLYANDRY:
A COMPARISON[1]

Gerald D. Berreman

POLYANDRY HAS LONG BEEN a popular subject for speculation and occasionally for research by anthropologists. Recently efforts to explain the origin and functioning of this rather unusual institution have been supplemented by attempts to define it (Fischer 1952; Leach 1955; Gough 1959; Prince Peter 1955a). It can be most simply defined as that form of marriage in which a woman has more than one husband at a time.[2] In fraternal polyandry, which is by far the most common kind, a group of brothers, real or classificatory, are collectively the husbands of a woman (or women).

This kind of polyandry has been reported from many parts of the world (Westermarck 1922: 107 ff.), but its best-documented and most prevalent occurrence is in Tibet, described by Prince Peter (1955c: 176) as "the largest and most flourishing polyandrous community in the world today," and in India. Mandelbaum (1938: 581 f.) notes that "in South India polyandry is of

Republished from *American Anthropologist*, Vol. 64, 1962, pp. 60–75, with permission of the author and of the editor of *American Anthropologist*.
[1] This paper was read in abbreviated form before the Fourth Annual Meeting of the Kroeber Anthropological Society, May 21, 1960, at Berkeley. The research was carried out in India during 1957–58 under a Ford Foundation Foreign Area Training Fellowship and is reported in full in: Berreman 1959. I would like to thank David Mandelbaum for his helpful comments on the manuscript.
[2] Following the recent definition of marriage put forth by Gough (1959: 32), a husband may be defined as a person who is in a relationship to a woman such that a child born to her under circumstances not prohibited by the rules of the relationship is or may be publicly acknowledged to be that person's child and is accorded full birth-status rights common to normal members of the society or social stratum into which it is born.

especially frequent occurrence. Six polyandrous tribes have been reported for Cochin; the Nayars of Travancore and the Irava of British Malabar have this form of marriage; while the Todas are the classic example of a polyandrous people in the textbooks of anthropology." The Singhalese are known to practice polyandry to some extent (Leach 1955). In North India the Jats of the northern Punjab, and especially those who are Sikhs, have been repeatedly reported to practice polyandry (Briffault 1959: 137; Kirkpatrick 1878: 86; Prince Peter 1948: 215). The most consistent practitioners of polyandry in India today are probably the residents of certain sub-Himalayan hill areas in Himachal Pradesh, the northern Punjab, and northwestern Uttar Pradesh. It is the polyandry of this relatively little-known region which I propose to discuss in this paper.

Non-Tibetan, Indo-Aryan-speaking Hindus inhabit the lower ranges of the Himalayas from southeastern Kashmir across northernmost India and through Nepal. These people are collectively termed *Paharis* ("of the mountains"). They constitute a distinct culture area bordered by the peoples of Tibet to the north and by those of the Indo-Gangetic plains to the south. With the latter peoples they share historical origins as well as linguistic and cultural affinites (Berreman 1960). Among Paharis, polyandry has been reported in several districts (cf. Das-Gupta 1921) and has been studied in some detail in Jaunsar Bawar, a subdivision of Dehra Dun district in northwestern Uttar Pradesh (Majumdar 1944; Saksena 1955). All of the Pahari areas in which it occurs are in the western Himalayan hills and are inhabited by people who share the Western dialect of the Pahari language (Grierson 1916: 101). There are no reliable reports of Pahari polyandry east of Jaunsar Bawar and its immediate vicinity, i.e., in the Central or Eastern Pahari-speaking areas.[3]

This paper is based on a study carried out among Central Pahari-speaking people in Garhwal, a hill area adjacent to, and

---

[3] Polyandry has been reported in the Rawai and Jaunpur sub-districts of Tehri-Garhwal, immediately adjacent to Jaunsar Bawar (Kapadia 1955: 63). Those portions wherein polyandry is found are doubtless the western border areas, which fall into the Western Pahari sub-culture area, or on its peripheries.

east of, Jaunsar Bawar.[4] The people of Garhwal, though they have not previously been studied, have frequently been cited as nonpolyandrous by those who have written on polyandry in Jaunsar Bawar. One goal of the research, which led to this paper was to study marriage in its total cultural context among the nonpolyandrous people of Garhwal in order to compare that system with the polyandrous system of neighboring Jaunsar Bawar as reported in the literature. The general hypothesis with which the investigation began and which this paper will discuss was that economic, demographic, or social-structural differences would be found which would correlate with the occurrence of polyandry in Jaunsar Bawar and its absence in nearby Garhwal. Further, some of the features found in Jaunsar Bawar would correspond to those reported by people who have studied polyandrous societies in other parts of the world.

The peoples of Jaunsar Bawar and Garhwal live under virtually identical physical conditions and their populations and cultures are very similar, having derived from a common source (Berreman 1960). Conditions for a comparative study with polyandry as the dependent variable therefore seemed ideal. In both areas the economy of the majority high-caste population is primarily agricultural, with a secondary dependence on animal husbandry, while the low-status artisan castes live by their craft specialities. Land is valuable but not as scarce as in most of North India. All property is owned jointly by male members of the patrilineal, patrilocal extended family. If property is divided among brothers, they usually receive equal shares. Normally, however, brothers continue to hold the patrimony in common and division occurs in the next generation, among patrilateral parallel cousins. The eldest active male dominates in the joint

---

[4] By Garhwal, I mean the districts of Tehri-Garhwal, Garhwal, and the hill sections of eastern Dehra Dun district (other Central Pahari districts are Almora and parts of Naini Tal). The research reported here was in a hill area of western Garhwal, overlapping Tehri-Garhwal and Dehra Dun districts (Berreman 1960). The area can legitimately be lumped with Garhwal because its residents are culturally of Garhwal. Their ancestors came from interior Tehri-Garhwal, they consider themselves to be Garhwalis and are so considered by others. Generalizations in this paper about Garhwali marriage and family relationships are valid for western Garhwal and only inferentially for the rest of Garhwal.

family but cannot compel younger men to remain within it. Marriage takes place within the caste group and outside the clan and mother's clan. It involves a payment of bride-price, which must be returned if the marriage is dissolved unless the husband is clearly at fault. Where dowry is used it is exceptional and evidently of recent origin, having diffused from the plains. Levirate is the rule upon a husband's death and payment must be made to his family if his wife wishes to go elsewhere. These are general features of Pahari culture as I know it and as it is reported in the literature.

POLYANDRY IN JAUNSAR BAWAR

In Jaunsar Bawar fraternal polyandry has been described as "the common form of marriage." Indeed, it does seem to be the preferred, but not the exclusive, form. Monogamy, polygyny, and fraternal polyandry, including a combination of polyandry and polygyny approximating fraternal "group marriage," appear in the same villages and even in the same lineages (Majumdar 1944: 167 f.). Nonfraternal polyandry is not reported. In the one village for which figures are available, Majumdar (1955b: 165) reports that of 57 families, 39 percent are polyandrous with more husbands than wives, 10 percent are polyandrous with an equal number of husbands and wives, 12 percent are polygynous, and 39 percent are monogamous.[5]

---

[5] Note that a plurality of husbands constitutes polyandry and the number of wives is considered irrelevant in the definition implicit here. Most discussions of the advantages of polyandry imply either that only one wife is involved or at least that husbands outnumber wives.

The incidence of polyandry reported by Majumdar for this village is high if, as seems probable, he is referring to conjugal family units. If *all* sets of adult real brothers currently living in the Garhwal village I studied had formed fraternally polyandrous conjugal families, then 43 percent of all conjugal families in that village would have been polyandrous. This is comparable to the proportion of polyandrous families reported by Majumdar. Fraternal polyandry would therefore seem to be the preferred pattern of marriage in Majumdar's village, with an incidence about as high as possible. Monogamy probably occurs most often among men with no brothers. Plural wives are probably secured in either case primarily to remedy a shortage of labor or heirs in the family, as they are in Garhwal.

In this society a polyandrous union occurs when a woman goes through a marriage ceremony with the eldest of a group of brothers. This man represents the group of brothers, all of whom thereupon become the woman's husbands. Subsequent wives may be taken, especially if the first one is sterile or if the age differential of the brothers is great. If so, the wives are individually married in a ceremony with the eldest brother and are shared by all, unless one or more brothers wish to break away from the joint family. No brother can remain a member of the joint family and claim exclusive rights to a wife. The eldest brother dominates with respect to the wife or wives, but he has no exclusive sexual or reproductive rights. A woman considers all of the brothers to be her husbands. Children recognize the group of brothers as their fathers; they call all of them "father" and inherit from all as a group without regard to paternity or maternity within the polyandrous family (Majumdar 1944: 178; 1953: 179). In cases of division of the family, paternity may be assigned by lot, by mother's designation, or by order of birth (Majumdar 1944: 144 f.). This is "true" fraternal polyandry similar to that reported among the Iravas of Central Kerala by Aiyappan (cf., Aiyappan 1935: 114 ff.; Leach 1955: 182; Gough 1959: 34).

MONANDRY IN GARHWAL

Majumdar (1944: 168) has pointed out that "the Garhwalis do not observe polyandry but the Jaunsaris do." While people of Jaunsar Bawar acknowledge their polyandry quite readily and defend this custom, the idea of polyandry is rejected by Garhwal residents. I neither found nor heard of any case of polyandry in the area of my work. Of a total of 300 marital unions for which I accumulated complete information in one Garhwal village, 85 percent were monogamous and 15 percent were polygynous. There every family is careful to secure a wife for each of its sons, and each son normally goes through the marriage ceremony with his own bride.[6]

---

[6] I witnessed one Garhwal marriage in which an elder brother substituted for the groom. This arrangement was devised to avoid the consequences of incompatibility in the horoscopes of the intended bride and groom rather than to effect a polyandrous union. The intended husband took over after

Although there are strong negative feelings about polyandry in this region, sexual relationships within the family are not greatly different from those among fraternally polyandrous families of Jaunsar Bawar. The situation is very similar to that among the Kota as reported by Mandelbaum (1938). Brothers have the right of sexual access to one another's wives. Despite these rights of fraternal ciscisbeism, every man has his own wife and each child its own father. There is never ambiguity on this point. Brothers share their wives' sexuality but not their reproductivity. As long as a wife fulfills her sexual obligations to her husband and does not indicate a preference for another, she is normally available to all of her husband's brothers, but her children are the children of her husband only.

In assessing the hypothesis with which this study began I will look briefly at some of the factors which have been advanced in the literature as causal for, predisposing toward, or correlated with polyandry and consider them with reference to the societies being described here.

FACTORS ASSOCIATED WITH POLYANDRY

Economic factors

Contemporary discussions frequently emphasize economic factors in accounting for polyandry.

E. R. Leach (1955: 183 ff.) believes that polyandry ". . . is intimately associated with an institution of dowry rights," and has hypothesized that ". . . adelphic polyandry is consistently associated with systems in which women as well as men are the bearers of property rights." In such systems, as distinguished from those in which property is exclusively in the hands of males, each marriage "establishes a distinct parcel of property rights."

---

the ceremonies. One might speculate upon a polyandrous precedent for this device but I could find no evidence to support such a speculation. More probably this incident reflects the general equivalence of brothers in Pahari culture. David Mandelbaum has pointed out that it illustrates not only the ritual and social equivalence of brothers, but also their personal non-equivalence in relation to the supernatural. Nothing could be more personal than the horoscope and in that respect the brothers were significantly not equivalent.

> If two brothers share one wife so that the only heirs of the brothers are the children born of that wife, then, from an economic point of view, the marriage will tend to cement the solidarity of the sibling pair rather than tear it apart, whereas, if two brothers have separate wives, their children will have separate economic interests, and maintenance of the patrimonial inheritance in one piece is likely to prove impossible (Leach 1955: 184).

Polyandry thereby also serves "to reduce potential hostility between sibling brothers." Without polyandry there would be a tendency for children of brothers to break up the joint family in order that each group of siblings might pursue its own economic interests.

The Pahari evidence contradicts this hypothesis. Dowry is not part of the traditional Pahari marriage transaction which is, in fact, dependent upon bride-price for validity (Joshi 1929: 50 f.). Moreover, and more importantly, a woman has no property of her own except in most unusual circumstances and she forfeits even her jewelry if she divorces her husband. Children remain with their father or his family when a marriage dissolves. Therefore, in the Himalayan hills, children of brothers who share a wife have no different economic interests as a result of that fact than do children of brothers each of whom has his own wife.[7]

A widely cited economic advantage of fraternal polyandry is that it keeps family property, especially lands, intact in a patrilineal, patrilocal group (Westermarck 1922: 185 f.). It accomplishes this by restricting the number of heirs and by keeping them together around a common wife. This virtue of polyandry is cited for Ceylon (Prince Peter 1955b), Tibet (Prince Peter 1955c), and the Himalayan hill area (Saksena 1955: 33; Stulp-

---

[7] Majumdar (1944: 173 ff.) and Kapadia (1955: 73, 83) have argued rather unconvincingly that high-caste Paharis were once matrilineal or heavily influenced by matrilineal people, evidently in the belief that this is more compatible with polyandry than is a purely patrilineal tradition. This is in line with the belief of McLennan and others that polyandry is associated with matrilineality. Leach (1955: 183), who hypothesizes that inheritance of property through females as well as through males is consistently associated with polyandry, implies that only patrilineality of "an ambiguous and rather uncertain type," and not "patrilineal systems of the more extreme type," can be associated with polyandry. Although Pahari patrilineality is not extreme, it is so with regard to inheritance of property. Leach's hypothesis is not supported by my research nor by the evidence presented by Majumdar or Kapadia.

nagel 1878: 133).[8] It is an advantage that is claimed by Jaunsar
Bawar people themselves (Majumdar 1944: 168). Where this
economic function is served by polyandry it is attributed to the
desire to keep intact the property of the wealthy, to the necessity
to keep the property of the very poor from dropping below the
subsistence level, or to both (cf. Prince Peter 1955b: 169; Stulpnagel 1878: 133 ff.).

If fraternal polyandry were practiced consistently, there would
be no patrilateral parallel cousins, and it is they who generally
divide land in the Himalayan hills. If the number of wives were
appreciably less than in nonpolyandrous societies this would
reduce, absolutely, the number of offspring and hence heirs.
Either or both of these would theoretically tend to reduce fragmentation of property, especially if, as will be discussed below,
polyandry were to reduce the frictions which lead to break-up
of joint families.

The over-all effect of polyandry for family property retention in
Jaunsar Bawar is tempered by the fact that not all marriages are
polyandrous; of those that are, many involve a plurality of wives.
While in the Jaunsar Bawar village cited above 49 percent of the
families are polyandrous, 61 percent have as many (or more)
wives as husbands and hence no reduction in the number of
heirs. Occasional polygyny or monogamy among brothers in a
lineage might wipe out the advantage, for property retention, of
generations of polyandry. On the other hand, in the nonpolyandrous Garhwal village three of 16 land allotments have remained
intact in the joint families to which they were assigned nearly 150
years ago. Unfortunately, land fragmentation figures for Jaunsar
Bawar are not available to compare with those of the Garhwal
village. My guess is that they would not show significant
differences.

---

[8] An exception, according to Prince Peter (1955b: 171 f.), are the Todas. He
asserts that they share no property in the family. However, Rivers (1906:
558 ff.) describes the house as specifically belonging to a group of brothers
who share a wife, and he mentions that although buffaloes are largely individual property, "in practice, owing to the fact that brothers usually live
together, a herd of buffaloes is treated as the property of a family of brothers,
but whenever the occasion arises there are definite rules for the division of
the buffaloes among them." Such rules are undoubtedly to be found in all
polyandrous societies, as they are among the Paharis.

Polyandry has often been attributed to economic hardship which necessitates cooperative work among brothers for survival (Kapadia 1955: 71; Majumdar 1944: 168). The expense of obtaining and/or maintaining a wife and of supporting a family has been cited as an important factor in contributing to polyandry in several contexts. Stulpnagel (1878: 133) and Kapadia (1955: 71) mention the difficulty of raising a sufficient bride-price and the consequent necessity for several brothers to combine to purchase a single wife. Majumdar (1955a: 95) notes the similar difficulty of providing the costly jewelry which a Pahari woman requires.

Bride-price marriage, though it is the rule in Jaunsar Bawar as elsewhere in the Himalayan hills, is not a likely motivation for polyandry since the amount is proportional to the wealth of those involved. Moreover, permanent unions may be established without payment at all. In the nonpolyandrous areas men do not often go unwed because of bride-price. Precisely the same points are applicable with regard to the bride's jewelry.

Heath (1955) has suggested that polyandry is related to ". . . sex specialization in which the woman makes only an insignificant contribution to subsistence." This explanation could not be farther from the facts found in the Himalayan hills, including Jaunsar Bawar.[9] There women contribute as heavily as do men to subsistence, and a wife is an economic asset (Majumdar 1944: 171). In the Garhwal village which I studied, need for additional field labor was cited as a reason for securing *an additional wife* in eight of twelve current cases of polygyny. As one villager remarked, "Here two wives are better than one because they do much of the work. In your country and on the plains the husband has to support his wife so a second wife is a hardship and a luxury." In polygynous families the agricultural and pastoral labor is divided among wives just as in polyandrous families it is divided among husbands, except that in both cases

---

[9] The Tibetan evidence, too, contradicts this as a general explanation of polyandry. Carrasco (1959: 35, 68) describes the important and productive economic role of women in Tibetan society. It also seems doubtful, according to his data (Carrasco 1959: 36 f.), that Tibetan women are invested with property rights frequently enough to support Leach's hypothesis concerning the relationship between such rights and polyandry.

plowing is reserved for men and certain household tasks for women. Saksena (1955: 33) notes that in the difficult economic circumstances of Jaunsar Bawar it often takes several men to support a single wife and family: "In order to make life success- ful a system of life in keeping with the demand for joint labour within a village had to be evolved. The wide practice of polyandry seems to be the outcome of this demand." However, polyandry is only one means of enlarging the work force of the family. In Garhwal (and in many families of Jaunsar Bawar) the same end is achieved by polygyny, by adoption of sons, by hiring agricultural servants, or preferably by having several sons.

An advantage of polyandry may be that it tends to keep the ratio of working adults to children high in the family, just as it keeps the number of heirs low. In the polyandrous village men- tioned above, this would apparently not be true for the 61 percent of all families who have one or more wives per husband. How- ever, in that village about 20.5 percent of the population is ten years of age or under, while in the nonpolyandrous Garhwal village which I studied, about 28 percent of the population is in this age bracket. This sample is far too small to yield significant conclusions, but it does not contradict the contention that there are fewer children in polyandrous communities than in nonpoly- androus ones—an advantage in an economically hard-pressed area.

It must be noted in respect to all of the economic arguments for polyandry, that polyandrous Jaunsar Bawar is no more hard- pressed than nonpolyandrous Garhwal, and that Paharis in gen- eral are economically more secure than many people of North India, despite their reputation for poverty (Berreman 1959: 102).

Social factors

Security of wife and family in the prolonged absence of the husband has been noted as an advantage of polyandry among such martial peoples as the Jats of the northern Punjab and the Nayars of South India (Prince Peter 1948: 223; 1955b: 169; Westermarck 1922: 193). Likewise, it has been cited as an advantage to Paharis who travel considerable distances to tend lands and cattle and are therefore absent from their homes for extended periods (Kapadia 1955: 72). Brothers can arrange to protect a common wife in such circumstances where an individual could not. This advantage accrues equally in formal polyandry and in wife-sharing. In Garhwal a man may be sent to accompany his brother's wife on a trip or while she works in the forest or even to live with her in the absence of her husband to insure that she will have no liaisons with men outside the family.

A more fundamental social function of polyandry, and one of the benefits most widely acclaimed by both observers and practitioners of polyandry, is the maintenance of intrafamilial amity, i.e., it reduces quarrels among brothers (Aiyappan 1937; Carrasco 1959: 36; Leach 1955: 185; Prince Peter 1948: 224; 1955a: 181; 1955b: 170; Saksena 1955: 33). In India, joint family dissolution is frequently attributed to friction among wives who enlist the support of their respective husbands, with resultant fraternal strife.[10] Polyandry is said to minimize fraternal conflict by eliminating this source, though jealousy over the common wife or wives is also reported (Mukherji 1950). As was indicated above, Leach attributes decreased friction in fraternally polyandrous families to the identity of economic interests among their members. Reduction of friction might be achieved in part by the simple reduction in number of heirs, which polyandry theoretically accomplishes, and the consequently decreased number of potential disputants in the family. Unfortunately, no data such as frequency of joint family dissolution are available with which to test this alleged advantage of fraternal polyandry.

Socio-economic factors

Radcliffe-Brown defined the unity of the sibling group as "its unity in relation to a person outside it and connected with it by a specific relation to one of its members," and he said that "it is in the light of this structural principle that we must interpret . . . adelphic polyandry. . . ." (Radcliffe-Brown 1941: 7 f.).

---

[10] This explanation undoubtedly contains a large element of rationalization. It serves to preserve an ideal of fraternal amity in the face of a good deal of actual fraternal strife by blaming it on wives who are essentially outsiders in the family and who most often come from alien villages.

Prince Peter (1955a: 181) has suggested that "the economic function" of polyandry "intensifies the unity and solidarity of the sibling group."

The missionary Stulpnagel (1878: 135) commented that in the Himalayan hills "polyandry is . . . in reality nothing more than a mere custom of community of wives among brothers who have a community of other goods." Majumdar (1944: 172) has made the same point with regard to property and polyandry in both Tibet and the Himalayan hills where he has described marriage as a "group contract." This corresponds closely to the explanation for fraternal wife-sharing among the Kotas given by Mandelbaum (1938: 575 ff.), who describes it as one manifestation of a general principle of "equivalence of brothers" which shows itself in the sharing of labor and property, and which is maintained because (and as long as) it is economically worth while. Leach refers to similar "corporate polyandry" among the Iravas of Central Kerala as described by Aiyappan (Leach 1955: 182).

In Jaunsar Bawar and Garhwal, a group of brothers has the kind of unity to which Radcliffe-Brown referred. It is expressed prominently in economic matters, but also in ritual and social relations. The unity is especially apparent in the relationship between a group of brothers and their wife or wives. Marriage in these areas is in a sense a group transaction in which the family pays collectively for a woman and acquires her economic, sexual, and reproductive services. All three kinds of services are shared by a group of brothers in Jaunsar Bawar. In Garhwal, the first two services are shared by the brothers while the third, reproductive capacity, is granted to one brother exclusively during his lifetime and is passed to another on his death by the practice of levirate. Kapadia (1955: 66) has discussed in some detail the Pahari woman as the "property" of her husband(s) and the implications of this concept.

The economic arrangement helps explain the community of interest in the wife, but it leaves unexplained the difference in marriage pattern between Jaunsar Bawar and Garhwal, and it leaves unanswered the question of why groups in other parts of India with a similar community of property among brothers do not tolerate either fraternal polyandry or wife sharing.

Psychological factors

Psychological functions of polyandry have been little discussed in the literature and I have no new data on this subject. Prince Peter's suggestion (1955a: 181) that polyandry satisfies repressed incestuous desires seems tenuous at best.

Traditional factors

Most people attribute their customs to tradition. In India, polyandry is widely attributed to specific traditions, notably those embodied in the religious epic, *Mahabharata*, which tells of the exploits of the five Pandava brothers and their common wife Draupadi. Almost every group that practices fraternal polyandry in India attributes the practice to that precedent, and usually to an intimate association between themselves and the deities of that epic (cf. Kapadia 1955: 52 f., 75, 92 f.; Prince Peter 1948: 223). Paharis are well known as devotees of the Pandavas who roamed these very hills in their legendary travels. This tradition in the Himalayan hills has led to such statements as that of Munshi (1955: i) who says that Jaunsar Bawar culture represents "a fossil of the age of the *Mahabharata*."

The historical origins of polyandry in the Himalayan hills have been speculated upon at some length by Saksena. Mayne is quoted as having suggested that polyandry was adopted by the Indo-Aryan invaders of India from the aborigines or neighboring polyandrous people, and Majumdar seems to share this view (Saksena 1955: 30). Among neighboring people most often cited as possibly influential are the polyandrous Tibetans with whom Paharis have long been in occasional contact. Saksena holds the widespread view that polyandry in this area is a remnant of the culture of early Indo-Europeans who came to India via the Himalayan hills. Support for this opinion is found by its proponents, not only in the polyandry of the *Mahabharata*, but in other Hindu classics and ancient records wherein polyandry and other traits characteristic of the hills, such as animal sacrifice, meat-eating, freedom of women, widow remarriage, and lack of caste rigidity are mentioned without disfavor (cf. Briffault 1959: 138 f.). Saksena summarizes his view in the following words:

. . . A polyandrous belt can be traced extending from Jaunsar-Bawar through Kangra Valley to Hindu Kush and even beyond. This led Briffault to remark, "The practice of polyandrous marriage is among the Indo-Aryans of the Panjab associated with other survivals of a more archaic and tribal order of society, which are culturally identical with the usages of the polyandrous people of Hindu-Kush, whence the invaders came to India" (Saksena 1955: 30).

It is, therefore, evident that polyandry was an institution not unknown to the early Aryan settlers in the Western Himalayas from where it gradually spread southwards, and is even now the accepted form of marriage among the Rajputs and Brahmans of Jaunsar Bawar. To quote Briffault again: "The highland regions of the Himalayas are but a residual cultural island which preserves social customs that had once a far more extensive distribution. The institutions which are found there were once common throughout the greater part of Central Asia" (Saksena 1955: 32).

Thus, it is possible that polyandry was an acceptable form among the ancestors of the Central Asian invaders who are presumed by many to be ancestral to present-day high-caste Paharis. It is also possible that it was adopted by Paharis, or some groups of them, from aborigines (often thought to be the ancestors of low-caste Paharis) whom they presumably met and culturally absorbed in this area. It may have been adopted as a result of contacts with the polyandrous Tibetans. It could well have been a regional development, probably in the western Himalayan hills. Its precise origins have been obscured by time and are not now a fruitful subject for inquiry. More promising is the subject of the present functioning of polyandry and its economic and social structural implications among those who practice it.

Demographic factors

In most discussions of polyandry, the possible influence of the sex ratio has been mentioned (Aiyappan 1935: 118; Majumdar 1944: 168; Prince Peter 1955b: 173 f.; Westermarck 1922: 158 ff.), along with explanations to account for any disparity of the sexes found in association with it (e.g., Rivers 1906: 520 f.). Heath (1955) has suggested that polyandry is generally related to a shortage of women. The consensus of most modern writers is typified by Kapadia (1955: 70) when he states that "sex disparity is likely to perpetuate, though it does not necessarily give rise to, a polyandrous pattern."

Data on this subject from the Himalayan hills are suggestive but inconclusive. While North India shows a general surplus of males over females, polyandrous Jaunsar Bawar has an unusually great shortage of females: 789 per 1000 males as compared to the Uttar Pradesh state ratio of 922.[11] Adjacent nonpolyandrous Garhwal has a striking and very unusual (for India) surplus of females: a ratio of 1110 in one district and 1149 in the other. These contrasting sex ratios extend back as long as census figures have been available. The two small sub-districts of Garhwal (both adjacent to Jaunsar Bawar) for which polyandry has been reported are the only parts of Garhwal in which there is a relative shortage of women, with ratios of 942 and 965.

Thus, in the areas of immediate interest here there is a gross correlation between polyandry and a shortage of women and, conversely, between monandry and a surplus of women. From the point of view of explanation, the significant fact is that in the Himalayas there is not an equal distribution of the sexes among both polyandrous and monandrous groups as those who reject the sex ratio as an explanation would expect. Neither is there a simple shortage of women in the polyandrous areas in contrast to an equal distribution in the monandrous areas, as those who consider polyandry to be an adaptation to an unusual sex ratio might expect. Instead there is an unusual and unequal sex ratio among *both* the polyandrous and monandrous groups, with the inequality in each case apparently favoring the marriage system of that group. Under these conditions one system cannot be considered *prima facie* to be "natural" and the other deviant.

Figures for larger regions are more ambiguous. The entire Western Himalayan area, throughout which polyandry has a scattered distribution, shows a consistent though (for North India) not an unusual surplus of males, while the Central Himalayan region, where no polyandry has been reported, shows a more nearly equal distribution of the sexes. The latter may be a

---

[11] Sex ratios given here are figured as they are in the Census of India, i.e., number of females per 1000 males. This is the reciprocal of the usual ratio given in the United States Census.

All figures are for rural areas, i.e., excluding towns of over 5000 population in most cases, and are drawn from various volumes of the 1951 Census of India.

relatively recent trend, however, as the proportion of women has increased quite steadily from a ratio of 955 in 1901 to a ratio of 1019 in 1951.[12]

CONCLUSIONS

In describing and attempting to account for differences in the marriage rules of Jaunsar Bawar and Garhwal, a most important feature has been overlooked by previous commentators: that within the family, sexual and interpersonal connotations of the two systems are very similar, as described above. In view of this fact and of the nonuniversality of polyandry even where it is practiced, the systems are not as different in their functioning as might be expected. Polyandry and monandry in the Himalayan hills appear not to be polar types of marriage systems as has been implied in the literature and as was supposed at the initiation of this research. They are, in fact, relatively minor variations on a central theme, namely: that a wife brings common benefits to a group of brothers who have acquired her by common payment and who share other rights and property in common. The brothers are equivalent, and show their unity as a group, relative to the wife. In one case her reproductive capacity (i.e., the "title" to her offspring) is shared; in the other it is not. In both groups any one of a family of brothers may be the biological father of a particular offspring. In Jaunsar Bawar the role of social father is shared; in Garhwal it is exclusive. That is the main difference between polyandry and monandry in this area. It represents a significant difference in values but a less drastic difference in the functioning of the systems than had been anticipated.

In view of the over-all similarity of Pahari cultures, contrasts between polyandrous Jaunsar Bawar and monandrous Garhwal have not appeared as clearly as was expected when the research

---

[12] In nonpolyandrous and almost entirely non-Pahari Dehra Dun district adjacent to both Jaunsar Bawar and Garhwal, the shortage of women (ratio of 759) is even greater than in Jaunsar Bawar, and in nonpolyandrous Naini Tal to the east the sex ratio is only 728. These two areas border on the hills, but their populations are largely derived from the plains. Dehra Dun, at least, has been relatively recently settled and the sex ratio is affected by the presence of tea plantations and other innovations atypical of the hill areas.

began. However, some conclusions pertaining to the original hypothesis can be stated:

Features of polyandrous societies reported in other parts of the world correspond only partially with those found in Jaunsar Bawar. The Pahari case contradicts the hypotheses that virtual economic uselessness of women, and dowry or property rights held by women, are universal correlates of polyandry.

As evidenced by a comparison of marriage and family relations in Jaunsar Bawar and Garhwal, fraternal polyandry may be advantageous but is not inevitable when there is a shortage of women and when a low proportion of children in the family is economically advantageous.

"Equivalence of brothers" in economic matters and in relation to the sexuality of their wives may be advantageous when, in a patrilocal society, husbands leave their wives for extended periods, but there is no evidence to show the superiority of polyandry over wife-sharing in such circumstances.

It seems logical, but could not be demonstrated by this comparative study, that fraternal polyandry would be advantageous when cost of obtaining or maintaining a wife is high, and also when in a patrilineal society property upon which livelihood or wealth depends is unusually scarce and limited. The latter is an advantage frequently cited by people of South Asia who are fraternally polyandrous.

No evidence was adduced with regard to the psychological implications of polyandry nor the value of polyandry as a means toward intra-family cooperation and consensus. The latter is, however, widely held to be an adjunct of polyandry and is a necessary one if the economic advantages of unity of family property in such societies are to be fully realized.

Characterization of polyandry as an extension of the principle of equivalence of brothers, especially in economic matters, is valid for Jaunsar Bawar as well as for other Himalayan hill areas and probably for Tibet. It does not, however, characterize formal polyandry in contrast to fraternal wife sharing. This is evidenced by its applicability to the Garhwal Paharis and to the South Indian Kotas, neither of whom

allow a woman a plurality of husbands or endow a child
with more than one social father. Both polyandrous and
nonpolyandrous Paharis share a favorable attitude toward
the sharing of wives and property among brothers. This
equivalence of brothers may be a predisposing but not sufficient precondition for formal polyandry. Certainly this attitude characterizes most fraternally polyandrous people in
South Asia.

The question of why Jaunsar Bawar people are polyandrous
and Garhwal people are not has not been answered. The answer
undoubtedly lies in a combination of cultural-historical factors,
including the advantages which one system may have relative to
the other in a particular context (cf. Cooper 1941: 55). Without
going too deeply into conjectural history, some possibilities may
be considered.

Pahari culture functions satisfactorily under either polyandry
or monandry. Whatever the history of polyandrous and monandrous institutions of Pahari marriage, they likely proved differen-
tially advantageous among their practitioners or potential practitioners. Each would presumably have persisted most among those
groups to which it proved most advantageous or least disadvantageous. Advantages could take the form of the approval of neighbors, economic well-being, social integration, etc.

Accurate historical data on the origins and contacts of Himalayan peoples are lacking, and according to my evidence the
distribution of polyandry as contrasted with wife-sharing in this
region cannot be explained in terms of associated economic or
social structural features. It is therefore not unreasonable to
seek a partial explanation in the one apparently significant difference which does appear between polyandrous and monandrous
groups of the area: the sex ratio. The sex ratio could have been
a potent factor in the acquisition and/or retention of one system
or the other. For example, when external pressure for abandon-
ment of polyandry grew as a result of increasing administrative,
religious, and social contacts with people of the plains of India,
polyandry persisted most in Jaunsar Bawar, the area in which
the sex ratio favored it to the greatest extent.

Of the several advantages which can be cited for polyandry or monandry, a crucial one could have been the social and economic advantage which derives from insuring the availability of family life for every adult. These are societies in which it is difficult as well as almost unheard of to subsist without a family. The sex ratio might tip the scale toward polyandry or monandry on the basis of this advantage.

The weakness in this argument is that it depends on a disparity in the sexes as an antecedent condition, and this cannot be demonstrated. Some observers claim that male Garhwal residents emigrate in great numbers to work as servants on the plains. It is extremely doubtful that this occurs frequently enough to account for the sex ratio, but no data are available with which to verify or disprove the suggestion.[13] The same can be said of military service as a possible explanation. Some claim that selling of Jaunsar Bawar women to plains people has resulted in the shortage of women there, but this, too, doubtless occurs too infrequently to account for the sex ratio. Moreover, in Jaunsar Bawar, the ratio of the sexes among children is as uneven as that of adults. This suggests as "causes" of the paucity of females, female infanticide, for which there is no evidence; or neglect of female children, which is less unlikely (cf. Majumdar 1944: 171). Rivers (1906: 520 f.) was among the first to point out that such practices can as satisfactorily be attributed to the effects of polyandry as they can be described as its causes.

To explain the origin or distribution of polyandry and monandry in the area would therefore require data, which are not available: culture history and census data from earlier eras. The futility of seeking causes without knowledge of the attendant conditions is well known.

Why there is polyandry in Jaunsar Bawar and not in Garhwal is therefore not a question that is likely to be answerable now, or that in this context is very relevant. A comparable question would be that of why Jaunsar Bawar people speak Western Pahari while Garhwal residents speak Central Pahari. These are relatively minor differences; the culminations of culture history, contacts, and of drift from a common base. They have resulted

---

[13] In the immediate area of my research there was neither a surplus of women nor a significant amount of out-migration by men.

from many choices over considerable periods of time. The choices
have taken place within the cultural context of economic and
social equivalence of brothers and of the contractual nature of
marriage wherein a bride is "purchased" by the family into which
she marries. Both of these conditions are compatible with fraternal polyandry. The choices which have led to regional differences
in marriage patterns have been made in response to conditions
(limitations and opportunities) within and without the groups
involved directed in over-all patterns, perhaps, by certain advantages which followed from them. But the particular conditions
which influenced them are now largely unknown. According to
this research there are in the Himalayan hills no simple functional correlates of polyandry as contrasted to monandrous wife-
sharing except in so far as the sex ratio is so correlated. The
important correlations are those of specific cultural content:
polyandry is one feature of an over-all cultural pattern of the
Western Himalayas, which contrasts in a number of details with
the over-all pattern of the Central (and probably the Eastern)
Himalayas, one feature of which is the absence of formal polyandry. The present distribution of these patterns is apparently
the result of regional divergence from a common and relatively
homogeneous culture; a divergence made possible in part by
relative regional isolation.[14] The same processes which resulted
in divergence of such features as language, dress, and worship
facilitated the present distribution of marriage regulations (Berreman 1960). Therefore, regional variation in marriage regulations
is no more fundamental nor surprising than other cultural dif-

---

[14] This divergence may have been of polyandry from a monandrous base
in the Western Pahari area, or of monandry from a polyandrous base in the
Central and Eastern Pahari areas. The change need not have been a difficult
or disorganizing one in view of the over-all similarity of the cultures involved
and the apparent compatibility of both polyandry and monandry in these
cultures.

Gough (1952a: 86) records a case of significant structural change without
discontinuity in South India: "the Nayar system has, over a period of two
hundred years, changed from a very extreme form of matriliny into a 'bilateral' system with only a weak tendency to matriliny; but the latter system
developed imperceptibly out of the former."

Prince Peter (1955c: 183) notes that in Ladakh, Muslim converts dropped
polyandry almost overnight, apparently without seriously affecting other aspects of their culture.

ferences in these hills and is to be understood as being of approximately the same order.

Observers feel compelled to question and explain polyandry wherever it occurs because it is unusual. One might equally fruitfully question the occurrence of polygyny. The factors leading to one are probably no more consistent and compelling than those that lead to the other. Polyandry, like polygyny, is evidently not a sufficiently unitary phenomenon to be explained in the same terms everywhere.[15] It may have certain advantages or functionally related correlates in some areas and not in others. That they are not universal does not mean, of course, that they are not significant.

There may be conditions which correlate with fraternal polyandry on a widespread cross-cultural scale. However, these probably take the form of effects of the functioning of polyandry, or prerequisites for polyandry, rather than specific causes which inevitably lead to polyandry.

---

[15] The following parallel comment by Westermarck (1922: 206) was discovered by the author after this article was in press: "To explain in full why certain factors in some cases give rise to polyandry and in other cases not is as impossible as it often is to say exactly why one people is monogamous and another people polygynous."

9 THE SOCIAL USE OF KINSHIP TERMS AMONG BRAZILIAN INDIANS

Claude Lévi-Strauss

THE KINSHIP SYSTEM of the Nambikuara Indians of the Western Matto Grosso is one of the most simple in Brazil. At the same time it is typical of a sociological pattern, cross-cousin marriage, which according to our present information seems to have been very common throughout South America. The object of this article is to compare the familial organization of the Nambikuara with that of other tribes described in the older literature and to show that a certain kinship tie, the brother-in-law relationship, once possessed a meaning among many South American tribes far transcending a simple expression of relationship. This significance, still observable in Nambikuara culture, is both sexual and politico-social; and, owing to its complexity, the brother-in-law relationship may perhaps be regarded as an actual institution. Since the sixteenth century travellers and sociologists have failed to devote sufficient attention to the phenomenon, probably because it could readily be interpreted as a development of the imported Iberian *compadre* relationship. In our opinion, on the contrary, the brother-in-law relationship, together with its remarkable implications, constitutes an indigenous aboriginal institution based on the pattern of native culture. Nevertheless, it presents a striking example of convergence in which the native and Latin-Mediterranean institutions show numerous apparent similarities overlying important structural differences.

Reprinted from *American Anthropologist*, Vol. 45, 1943, pp. 398–409, with permission of the author and the editor of *American Anthropologist*.

The Nambikuara Indians are settled on the upper courses of the feeders of the Tapajoz River, between the eleventh and the fifteenth parallels. Their territory consists of a semi-desert savanna, which contrasts with the narrow gallery forests along the main waterways. The fertile soil of these forests allows the natives to cultivate a few gardens in the rainy season, but during most of the year the Nambikuara subsist mainly by hunting and gathering wild food. Compared to the majority of Brazilian tribes, their cultural level is low. As they were discovered only in 1907, and as they had practically no contact with white civilization between the year of the Rondon-Roosevelt Expedition in 1914 and the time of our own fieldwork in 1938–39, their familial and social organization may be considered still intact.

The Nambikuara kinship system may be summarized as follows: All the father's brothers are classified together with the father and are called "father," and all the mother's sisters are classified with the mother and are called "mother." The father's sisters and the mother's brothers are classified together with the spouse's parents and the parents' parents in a single category, which denotes simultaneously the cross-aunts and cross-uncles, the mother-in-law and father-in-law, and the grandparents. Passing to Ego's generation, the parallel cousins, both the children of the father's brothers and of the mother's sisters, are merged with siblings and are called "brother" and "sister." Turning to the children of the father's sisters and of the mother's brothers, a man calls all his female cross-cousins (to one of whom he is or will be married) "wife," and all his male cross-cousins "brother-in-law;" conversely, a woman calls all her male cross-cousins (among whom her actual or potential husband is numbered) "husband," and all her female cross-cousins "sister-in-law." No terminological difference is made between actual and potential spouses. The members of the next younger generation are similarly divided into "sons" and "daughters" (Ego's own children and parallel nephews and nieces) and "sons-in-law" and "daughters-in-law" (Ego's cross-nephews and nieces), since these are or may be the spouses of his children.

The system is somewhat complicated by secondary distinctions made between elder and younger siblings and by the fact that another kind of marriage—between a maternal uncle and his niece—is also practised. This new pattern usually appears in the polygynous unions which, in the prevailingly monogamous Nambikuara society, are the privilege of the chief. This point needs some elaboration. Nambikuara polygyny results from the fact that, subsequent to a first marriage having all the characteristics of the common (i.e., the cross-cousin) form, a man may contract one or more unions of somewhat different nature. Actually, the position of his new wives is not the same as that of his original one, and, although constituting real marriages, the later unions are nevertheless psychologically and economically different from the first. The atmosphere in which they evolve is less conjugal and more like a kind of amorous friendship. The younger wives cooperate more extensively in the numerous tasks imposed on their husband because of his special social obligations. Furthermore, the activities of these women do not conform as closely as those of the first wife to the general pattern of the sexual division of labor. Finally, they are younger and are classified, in relation to the earlier wife, as "daughters" or "nieces." Such "oblique" unions (that is, between members of different generations) may also take place in monogamous marriages, but less frequently. Although their occurrence among the Nambikuara is an important point in our demonstration, the consequent modifications of the kinship system are not essential for the purposes of this article and we may therefore omit further mention of them. Our present observations will be limited to the special implications of the brother-in-law relationship, which is expressed through the reciprocal terms *asúkosu* (Eastern dialect), *tarútẹ* (Central and Western dialect) or *iópạ* (Northern dialect).

It must be emphasized immediately that this useful translation of the native term is not in any way accurate. While the *asúkosu* is a man's male cross-cousin and also his potential brother-in-law, since the persons calling each other *asúkosu* (or *tarútẹ* or *iópạ*) call each other's sisters "wife," it is only in particular instances that one or more of the individuals involved is, in fact, the wife's brother or the sister's husband or both. The meaning of the term *asúkosu* is consequently much wider than "brother-in-law" as we understand it, including as it does approximately half the masculine members of a man's generation; the rest, of course, receive the name "brother" (consanguineous or classificatory). It should be noted that in the Nambikuara kinship system men alone have brothers-in-law and, conversely, women alone have sisters-in-law.

Only in the case of brothers-in-law are the Nambikuara conscious of a link between a special type of behavior and the position occupied by a kinsman in the relationship system. Generally speaking, there are no rules of avoidance or of privileged familiarity between particular kinds of relatives. The relations with the spouse's parents do not differ substantially from those with the parallel uncle and aunt and, although it is true that relations between consanguineous or classificatory siblings are rather reserved, the natives are unable to define this diffuse behavior. As a matter of fact, while siblings and parallel cousins do not avoid each other, they do not joke or even talk together unless there is a special reason for doing so. Sisters-in-law, on the contrary, comport themselves very freely. They laugh and joke together and render each other small services, such as rubbing each other's back with urucu paste. And, more especially, exceptional relations are revealed when one passes to the brothers-in-law.

We have already mentioned the partial polygyny which exists in the group. The chief or shaman periodically withdraws several of the youngest and prettiest women from the regular cycle of marriages; consequently, young men often find it difficult to marry, at least during adolescence, since no potential spouse is available. The resulting problem is solved in Nambikuara society by homosexual relations, which receive the rather poetical name *tamíndigę ki'ándigę*—"sham love." Relations of this kind are frequent among young men and are more publicly displayed than heterosexual ones. Unlike most adults, the partners do not seek the isolation of the bush, but settle close to the camp fire in front of their amused neighbors. Although the source of occasional jokes, such relations are considered childish and no one pays much attention to them. We did not discover whether the partners aim at achieving complete sexual gratification or whether they limit themselves to such sentimental effusions and erotic behavior as most frequently characterize the relations between spouses. In any event, the point is that homosexual relations occur only between *male cross-cousins.*

We never learned whether or not the same relations continue to exist between adult cross-cousins; it does not seem likely. Nevertheless, the freedom and demonstrativeness displayed by brothers-in-law toward one another are not characteristic of the relations between brothers or between the members of any other class of relatives. One often sees among the Nambikuara (who, in fact, like to indulge in expressions of affection) two or three men, married and sometimes the fathers of several children, walking together at dusk and tenderly embracing each other; always

tarúte̦ ialásie̦te̦

(these are) brothers-in-law embracing (each other).

Certain games, too, such as the "scratch game" (in which the opponents try to scratch each other especially in the face), are commonly played by brothers-in-law.

But the close relationship between "cross-cousins actually or potentially allied through a sister's marriage"—the more accurate translation of the aboriginal term for brother-in-law—may extend far beyond the family tie. Actually, it is sometimes used to establish between individuals not belonging to the same kin group new links of a special nature, the function of which is to amalgamate into a single familial unit several formerly unrelated groups. This is brought out clearly in the following case.

During the past twenty years, several epidemics nearly destroyed the central, northern and western divisions of the Nambikuara. Several groups were decimated to such an extent that they could no longer successfully maintain a socially autonomous existence. In the hope of reconstituting functioning units, some of these, therefore, attempted to join forces. In the course of our fieldwork we met and worked with such a merged group made up of seventeen individuals using the northern dialect (*Sabáne̦* group) and thirty-four using the central dialect (*Tarúnde̦* group). Each of the originally distinct groups, however, lived under the guidance of its own chief, although both leaders closely cooperated. It is probable that the demographic crisis did not by itself account for this situation, since the people of the second group formed merely a fraction of a more numerous unit from which it had split off for reasons unknown to us. However, from several events which occurred during our stay with them, we deduced that the break had been caused by political dissention, the details of which remained obscure to us. In any event, these groups now travelled and lived together although two separate but contiguous camps were maintained in which the families formed distinct circles, each around its own fire. The most amazing feature of this curious organization was that the two groups did not speak the same language and were able to understand one another only through interpreters; fortunately, one or two individuals belonging to each group had sufficient knowledge of the other dialect to act as intermediaries. Even the two chiefs could not communicate directly. The problem of whether these dialects belong to the same linguistic stock need not be raised here; but the Northern group undoubtedly must be classified with the Nambikuara cultural family because of the similarities of material culture and of the life pattern, and chiefly because of the psychological attitude of the people, who very evidently believed in their close affinity to the Central group.

A more fundamental problem raised by the union of the two groups, namely, the nature of the relations to be established between their respective members, was solved by the common statement that all the male members of the Sabáne̦ group were to be acknowledged as the "brothers-in-law" (*tarúte̦*) of the male adults of the Tarúnde̦ group, and, conversely, that the latter were to be acknowledged as "brothers-in-law" (*iópa̦*) by the former. Consequently, all the "wives" belonging to one group became the "sisters" of the "husbands" of the other, and the "sisters-in-law" of the latters' wives; and all children of both sexes in one group became the potential spouses of the children in the other. As a result, these two groups will be welded into a single consanguineous unit within two generations.

The conscious and systematic nature of this solution cannot be doubted. When asked for their kinship relation to any male adult of the allied group, the male informants, irrespective of the group to which they themselves belonged, never gave a different answer, but always emphasized that the question was meaningless since all the Sabáne̦ men were their *tarúte̦,* or all Tarúnde̦ men their *iópą*. On the other hand, no one seemed to have a clear idea of the exact relationship between the women, the children, or the adults and the children of the two groups. Occasionally the correct theoretical relationship could be deduced; more frequently only the group name was given in reply to our queries: She is calling the other one "Sabánę"—or "Tarúndę." Thus it may be assumed that the system was conceived of and applied according to (and exclusively according to) the *tarútę* (or *iópą*) relationship. This inference is rather important because, of course, the same result could have been achieved by other means.

If the sole aim of the system had been to ensure inter-marriage, it could have been brought about equally well in two other ways; perhaps we should say that two different interpretations might have been made of the same phenomenon. In the first place, the women might have been regarded as "sisters-in-law"; or, in the second place, all the men of one group and all the women of the other might have entered a brother-sister relationship. In both cases the result would have been the same as in the accepted interpretation, in which, indeed, these relationships are implied though not expressed. Nevertheless, the solution itself was actually based on the relationship between the male and his allied collaterals, the consequences of which must now be examined.

Two of the three possible interpretations implied the consideration of women; only one was purely masculine, and it is the latter which was adopted by the natives. The reason for the choice is obvious since the problem to be solved was a purely political one, concerning the chieftainship, which is exercised by men, rather than the normal mechanism of filiation, the pattern of which seems to be matrilineal. In a simple system of cross-cousin marriage, such as that of the Nambikuara, the brother-in-law may be either the matrilateral or the patrilateral cross-cousin; nevertheless, the chosen interpretation stresses the male side in Nambikuara society, or, let us say, it shows a strong tendency in this direction. At the same time we can see in such a solution a specifically social structure beginning to superimpose itself on the formerly simple familial units.

We do not intend in any way to base a theory of the origin of dual organizations on these restricted observations, the character of which is mainly anecdotal. However, this is a case where "the characteristic features of the sib organization are in some measure prefigured among sibless tribes" (Lowie 1919: 28). As a matter of fact, in order to fulfil the main requirements of a system of exogamic moieties, it would be sufficient for the new unit, once fixed, to retain the recollection of its dual origin by preserving the habit of not mingling the camp fires.

Moreover, the extension of the "brother-in-law" relationship provides an instance of the increasingly superior position of the men within the group, since it is through the men that group alliances are brought about, just as wars are waged by men.

The preceding observations have a further value, since with their help we may be able to interpret sociological information found in the older literature on South America, especially that dealing with the Tupi of the Brazilian coast.

There are striking similarities between several features of the Nambikuara kinship system and what may be inferred about the ancient familial organization of the coastal Tupi. When describing small details of Nambikuara daily life, one is often tempted to quote Jean de Léry (1880) or Yves d'Evreux (1864), so accurately do their words apply to certain live features of Nambikuara society, notwithstanding the fact that they were written four centuries before this culture became known. As a matter of fact, several metaphysical themes are common to both cultures and, indeed, certain names in the Nambikuara religious vocabulary have a conspicuously Tupi origin. The most important similarities, however, are those involving the kinship systems. In both cultures the same three principles of familial organization are stressed and are apparently similarly expressed: First the dichotomy of the parents' brothers and sisters between parallel uncles and aunts, called "fathers" and "mothers," and cross-uncles and aunts, called "fathers-in-law" and "mothers-in-law"; secondly, the marriage of cross-cousins with the correlative assimilation of parallel cousins to "brothers" and "sisters"; and, finally, the avuncular marriage, which, among the ancient Tupi, seems to have taken the form of a preferential union between the mother's brother and the sister's daughter.

An excellent text by Anchieta gives evidence of the occurrence of the first principle, as well as showing signs of the existence of the other two:

> In questions of relationship they never use the word *ete* (true) since they call their father's brothers "father," their brothers' sons "son," and their father's brothers' sons "brother"; when they wish to designate their actual father or son, they say *xeruba xemonhangara* "my father who engendered me," or, for a son, *xeraira xeremimonhanga* "my son whom I engendered." I never heard an Indian call his wife *xeremireco ete*, but simply *xeremireco* or *xeracig* "mother of my children," and I never heard a woman refer to her husband as *xemenete* "real husband," but simply *xemena* or *xemembira ruba* "father of my children." They use these terms indifferently for their husband or lover. If the husband calls one of his wives *xeremireco ete*, he means the most esteemed or best-loved wife and she is often the last one he took (Anchieta 1846: 259).

This text also shows that the Tupi encountered a difficulty in their kinship system, namely, how to distinguish the classificatory parents or children from the consanguineous ones. This stresses the structural similarity between their kinship system and that of the Nambikuara, since the latter met with the same problem. Apparently the Tupi, like the Nambikuara, felt no need for special terms, but when it was necessary, made comments based on physiological considerations. When the Nambikuara are asked to point out the real status of their consanguineous children, they add to the name for "son" or "daughter" another word, the meaning of which is "child" or "little one." The physiological implication of this new term is perfectly clear, since it is ordinarily used to designate newly born animals, while the former terms are applied only to relationships within the human family. Complementary indications regarding the assimilation of the father's brother to a classificatory father may be found in Soares de Sousa (1851: 316–17).

The old authors give numerous examples of cross-cousin marriage and of marriages between uncles and nieces. Here again Anchieta will be our main source:

> Though many Indians have several nieces, and very attractive indeed, nevertheless they do not use them as wives. However, brothers have such authority over sisters that they consider their nieces as belonging to them and that they are entitled to marry them and to

use them ad libitum if they wish. In the same way they give their sisters to some and refuse them to others. Taragoaj, an important chief of the village of Jaribiatiba in the plain of San Vicente, had two wives one of whom was his niece, his sister's daughter (Soares de Sousa 1851: 259).

Both types of marriage are treated as symmetrical institutions in the same document: ". . . because the fathers give them the daughters and the brothers the sisters. . . ." (Soares de Sousa 1938: 261). Furthermore, cross-cousin marriage is referred to by Staden (1928). "They make presents also of their daughters and sisters . . .", by Soares de Sousa (1938), Claude d'Abbeville (1587), and others. With a sound sociological feeling, Anchieta establishes a link between the custom of a man marrying his sister's daughter and the recognition of the male as the only one responsible for conception, a theory also shared by the Nambikuara. On this matter, Anchieta writes:

> They call the brothers' daughters "daughter" and treat them as such. Therefore they would not have sexual intercourse with them, since they believe that the true kinship link has its origin in the father, whom they consider the only agent, while the mother, according to them, is merely a container in which the children are formed. . . . For that reason too, they use the sisters' daughters "ad copulam" without sin. . . . For the same reason, the father will give his daughters in marriage to their uncles, their mother's brothers, a thing which, until now, was never done with the nephew who is the brother's son. . . ." (Anchieta 1846).

Cross-cousin marriage seems to have a very wide distribution throughout South America.[1] But among the Tupi, avuncular marriage in particular aroused the interest of early travellers. For instance, Léry notices: "As to the uncle, he marries his niece" (Léry 1880); and Thevet: "As soon as they are born, the maternal uncle lifts them from the ground and keeps them for his future wives" (Thevet 1575). Magalhaes de Gandavo expresses himself as follows:

---

[1] For instance, Breton (1665: 11) gives clear evidence of its occurrence among the Antillean Caribs: "First cousins whom we call father's brother's sons call each other 'brothers' and the father's brothers are also called 'fathers.' The children of brothers do not marry, but they may contract marriages with the children of their father's sisters."

> It is their custom to marry the women who are their nieces, the
> daughters of their brothers or sisters; these are considered their
> legitimate and true wives. Fathers of the women cannot refuse them,
> nor can any persons other than their uncles marry them (Magalhaes
> de Gandavo 1922).

But this statement seems to be doubly inaccurate. For other references to the same phenomenon one may turn to Nobrega (1931),
Vasconcellos (1863), and Soares de Sousa (1938).

Regarding polygyny and the sharp differentiation made among
the Nambikuara between the first wife who devotes herself to feminine activities and the younger wives who are their husband's
companions and share his tasks, it may be recalled that Magalhaes
de Gandavo (1922) refers to a special category of women, single
indeed, who shared in masculine activities (Metraux 1928;
Lafone Quevedo 1919: 421–40; Kirchoff 1931: ch. 15).

The preceding similarities may perhaps allow us to establish a
valid comparison between our observations concerning the extension of the "brother-in-law" relationship among the Nambikuara and what seems to have been a very similar institution
among the ancient Tupi. We first quote Yves d'Evreux:

> They scattered part of the French through the villages so that they
> might live according to the custom of the land, which consists in
> having *chetouasap*, that is to say, hosts or god-sibs (*compères*), giv-
> ing them merchandise instead of money. Such hospitality or god-sib
> relationship is very close among them, for they regard you as their
> child as long as you stay with them. They hunt and fish for you and,
> what is more, they used to give their daughters to their god-sibs
> (*compères*) (Yves d'Evreux 1864: 14).

The same author refers later to the "French who were established
in the villages in a god-sib relationship (*compérage*)" (Denis
1864: 109). Evidence of the aboriginal institution may also be
found in Jean de Léry:

> It is worth remarking that the words *atour-assap* and *coton-assap* dif-
> fer, because the first signifies a perfect alliance between them and be-
> tween them and us, so much so that the belongings of the one are
> common to the other. And also that they cannot have the daughter
> or sister of the first named (Léry 1880: 133; Cardim 1925: 169–
> 70).

From this one may infer, conversely, that marriage is authorized
with the sister and the daughter of the *coton-assap*. Therefore,

the *coton-assap* is granted a double privilege: first, marriage with his partner's sister, which makes him a "brother-in-law"; and, secondly, marriage with his partner's daughter, which is equivalent to his assimilation to the rank of "maternal uncle";—then, because he is considered a theoretical brother of his partner's wife, he also becomes a theoretical brother-in-law. Actually, therefore, both privileges have the same result.

One more similarity between the Tupi and Nambikuara brother-in-law relationship remains to be pointed out. All the texts quoted agree that there existed among the Tupi a kind of authority held by young men over their sisters. Cross-cousin marriages seem to have resulted chiefly from a reciprocal exchange of their respective sisters by the male cross-cousins. (The same holds for the giving of a daughter by a father.) The potential or actual brothers-in-law then enter into a relationship of a special nature based upon reciprocal sexual services. We know that the same thing may be said of the Nambikuara brothers-in-law, with the difference that, among the Tupi, the sisters or daughters of the brothers-in-law provided the object of these services, whereas among the Nambikuara the prestations are directly exchanged in the form of homosexual relations.

We may now summarize our observations. The ancient Tupi acknowledged two forms of marriage; namely, cross-cousin marriage and avuncular marriage. The first was usually practised in the form of an exchange of sisters by two male cousins; the second appears to have been a right to the sister's daughter exercised by the mother's brother or granted to him by his sister's husband. In both cases the marriage is the result of an agreement between cross-cousins, actually or potentially brothers-in-law—which is the definition we retained as a suitable translation of the Nambikuara terms *tarúte* and *iópa*. Now, this special "brother-in-law" relationship could be established, under the name of *chetouasap* (Evreux) or *coton-assap* (Léry), between individuals not united previously by any kinship tie, or else only more remotely related, or even between strangers (as was the case of the French and the Indians). The reason for such a step was to ensure intermarriage and by this means to amalgamate familial or social groups, previously heterogeneous, into a new homogeneous unit. One recognizes here the same process described in the analysis of the relations between the newly joined groups, Sabánẹ and Tarúndẹ.[2]

The objection may be raised that the old authors have interpreted inaccurate observations in the light of European data. Since we shall suggest the use of the word *compérage*—borrowed from the French—to identify the institution, which we consider to be an authentic aboriginal one, it will be useful to discuss briefly this aspect of the problem.

Without any doubt there is a striking analogy between the facts related above and the Latin-European institution of compérage. Originally the *compère* and the *commère* were connected with each other, and both with the child's parents, through the mystical link of parrainage. However, the relation was very soon secularized in all small rural communities, or rather, wherever the familial structures were of greater importance than the social ones; it was then used to establish an artificial link of kinship, or, more precisely, as is the case among the Nambikuara, to express in kinship terms a purely external relationship of spatial promiscu-

---

[2] The widespread South American custom of using kinship terms to express social relationships is attested to by Von den Steinen (1897: 286) who was called "elder brother" by the Bakairi and "maternal uncle" by the Mehinaku. We have just established the equivalence of the terms "maternal uncle" and "brother-in-law" in a system of cross-cousin marriage combined with avuncular marriage. Regarding the use of the term "elder brother," two observations should be made. First, in a kinship system such as that of the Bororo, not far distant from the Xingu, each generation is to some extent split into two layers, the elder half being assimilated to the younger half of the generation above and the younger half to the elder half of the generation below. In such a system an "elder brother" may well be a true uncle and a potential brother-in-law.

The use of the term "brother" for social purposes may also be understood in another way. Among the Nambikuara, there is a special term, sometimes used to designate a sibling of the same sex, the meaning of which is "the other one." This term is applied not only to describe a familial relationship, but is also used to name objects belonging to a class which includes several units (for instance, the posts of the huts or the pipes of the whistles). Friendly groups may also consider themselves to be "brothers" and the exclamation, "You are no more my brother!" may often be heard in discussions between angry adversaries.

This suggests that the term "brother" possesses, in addition to its kinship significance, a very wide meaning, both logical and moral. Nevertheless, when the technical problem of establishing new social relationships is put up to the Indians, it is not the vague "brotherhood," which is called upon, but the more complex mechanism of the "brother-in-law" relationship.

ity.[3] The stranger or newcomer was adopted by means of the reciprocal appellation of *compère* or *commère* which he received from—and returned to—his male adult contemporaries. On the other hand, since the stranger usually assimilated himself to the group by marrying within his new community, the terms *compère* and "brother-in-law" soon became synonymous, so that men allied by marriage usually called each other only by the first term. In all small communities of Mediterranean Europe and of Latin America, the *compère*, or *compadre*, is an actual or a potential brother-in-law. No doubt in certain regions of Central and South America the analogy between the European and aboriginal institution has helped the latter to become fixed and modernized. Thus, in Mexico the primitive institution of the *mošte*, that is, of the heads of families bound to exchange gifts at certain periods, now expresses itself by means of the "compadre" relationship, the Spanish term providing an easy translation of the earlier Otomi (Soustelle 1937). The formal analogy between the institutions cannot hide, however, the fact that they are really opposite in character. In Latin-Mediterranean society, the formerly mystical and, actually, social link of compérage may be changed, through marriage, into a real kinship tie. Among the ancient Tupi, as among the Nambikuara, the actual kinship provides the type of link used to establish wider relations.

This being admitted, there are two strong reasons why our authorities cannot have constructed a pseudo-institution based on a European pattern from inconsistent observations. In the first place, men as well acquainted with religious problems as were Yves d'Evreux, Cardim, and Léry could not have assimilated a relationship whose first consequence and probable aim was to permit new forms of marriage to the relationship between godfathers and parents, the main purpose of which, especially since the thirteenth century, had been to impose new and very rigid restrictions upon marriage. At the time they were writing, the matter was of immediate interest and was being discussed by the Council of Trent, where the earlier rules were somewhat mitigated. But there is a much stronger argument: From the moment

---

[3] The same sociological derivation is expressed in English through the etymological origin of the word "gossip" (god-sib).

of the arrival of the European missionaries both institutions, the European and the aboriginal, actually co-existed among the Indians, at least among those who were baptized, and neither they nor their European priests ever interpreted the Christian "god-father" relationship in terms of the native "brother-in-law" institution. On the contrary, and much more logically, since the new relationship placed restrictions on marriage, they considered it as a modality of the relation of paternity; thus, they assimilated the "god-father" to a classificatory "father."

> They [the newly baptized children] regarded their god-fathers as their true fathers and called them *Cherou,* that is to say, "my father," and the French called them *Cheaire,* that is to say, "my son," and the little girls *Cheagire,* "my daughter. . . ." (Yves d'Evreux *in* Denis 1864: 234).

Therefore, it cannot be doubted that the *compérage* is quite distinct from its European parallel.

A sufficient number of convergent indications have been recorded so that we may consider the outstanding character of the "brother-in-law" relationship a specific feature of South American sociology, constituting the core of an original institution of *compérage* which appears clearly among the Nambikuara and which, as suggested by the documents presented in this article, may formerly have had a much wider distribution on the continent.

10 THE STRUCTURE OF PARALLEL
COUSIN MARRIAGE[1]

Robert F. Murphy and Leonard Kasdan

THE PROBLEM

A GREAT DEAL OF ATTENTION has been given within the literature of anthropology to the analysis of cross-cousin marriage and, more generally, exogamy. However, with a few notable exceptions (cf. Ayoub 1957; Barth 1954; Chapple and Coon 1942), comparatively little interest has been devoted to the study of preferential patrilateral parallel cousin marriage and kin group endogamy. This is understandable when one considers that the contemporary occurrence of this practice is limited to the Arabs and their immediate Moslem neighbors, while the reverse phenomena of exogamy and cross-cousin marriage recur throughout the world. The latter is a regularity of such high order that it has demanded functional explanations. Such analyses have been so numerous and so persuasive that one may now wonder how preferential endogamy could possibly be a viable social form. This problem will form the substance of the present paper.

Patrilateral parallel cousin marriage is evidently ancient in the Near East, from whence it spread during the Arab conquests to adjacent peoples through the vehicles of clientship, intermarriage, and religious conversion. Most commentators on the custom have

Reprinted from *American Anthropologist*, Vol. 61, 1959, pp. 17–29, with permission of the authors and of the editor of *American Anthropologist*.

[1] A much-abbreviated version of this paper was read at the annual meeting of the Kroeber Anthropological Society in Berkeley, California, on May 17, 1958. We are much indebted to our colleague, David M. Schneider, for his astute criticisms and contributions. Murphy wishes to acknowledge the support during the writing of this paper of a Faculty Research Fellowship awarded by the Social Science Research Council.

repeated the Arab explanation that it keeps property within the family (cf. Rosenfeld 1957; Granqvist 1931). But, as Barth notes (1954: 170), this explanation is valid only when the Koranic law through which a daughter inherits half the amount received by a son is observed. This is very frequently not the case. In any event, the argument ignores the fact that the daughter of another family could well bring into the husband's group a most welcome inheritance, and we are thus able to use the same motivation to show that exogamy is a potential means of enhancing familial fortunes. Or phrased in another way, if we admit this to be an effective means of preserving the patrimony, why is it not common practice in a wider range of societies?

In a recent article on father's brother's daughter marriage among the Kurds, Barth (1954: 171) offers a variant explanation of the practice in his statement that it ". . . plays a prominent role in solidifying the minimal lineage as a corporate group in factional struggle." His argument runs that the paternal uncle is willing to forego the bride price in the case of the nephew, because he can thereby rely upon the latter's complete political support. We have here another means-end explanation, although this one has the merit of being predicated upon the particular structure of Kurdish society rather than upon a presumably general drive toward economic aggrandizement. Since Barth suggests the applicability of his argument to the Arab Bedouin, there are two points that should be here stressed. First, it is quite clear that at least among the Arabs, the paternal uncle does not give his daughter to the nephew; rather, the nephew has a right to her, whatever may be the uncle's sentiments and motivations (cf. Dickson 1949: 116; Musil 1928: 137–40; Murray 1935: 179). However, the end result of consolidation of the minimal lineage through parallel cousin marriage may be applicable to the Arabs, and we will explore this thesis later in the paper. Barth also emphasizes the process of lineage fission that underlies Kurdish power struggles, and he attributes its peculiar intensity to the lack of those cross-cutting modes of segmentation that dampen conflict among the Nuer and other segmentary, agnatic African groups. In such a setting, he sees parallel cousin marriage as a solidifying factor. We will maintain a converse proposition in this paper—namely, that the Arab evidence indicates that parallel cousin marriage underlies this extreme fission process. Thus, while consolidation of wealth, or of power, may constitute a motivation for those who wish to marry their father's brother's daughter, one structural function of the institution is to promote the segmentation process. From this point of view, feud and fission are not at all dysfunctional factors but are necessary to the persistence and viability of Bedouin society.

BEDOUIN SOCIAL STRUCTURE

The overall outlines of Arab Bedouin[2] society are well known to anthropology, despite the lack of detailed studies in recent years.[3] The Bedouin trace descent and inheritance patrilineally, and they are nominally patrilocal. Historically, they are known to have expanded in numbers and territory, and the social system has accommodated these increases through the fission of agnatic lines. Thus patrilineal units split off from parent units through segmentation of the sibling group. In time, the offspring agnatic line attains considerable size, and it in turn segments. Ideally, accurate genealogies are maintained whereby these ramified and scattered groups may trace common ancestry. W. Robertson Smith (1885: 3–4) has summarized Arab social structure neatly:

> According to the theory of the Arab genealogists the groups were all patriarchal tribes, formed, by subdivision of an original stock, on the system of kinship through male descents. A tribe was but a larger family; the tribal name was the name or nickname of the common ancestor. In process of time it broke up into two or more tribes, each embracing the descendants of one of the great ancestor's sons and taking its name from him. These tribes were again divided and subdivided on the same principle, and so at length that extreme state of division was reached which we find in the peninsula at the time of the prophet. Between a nation, a tribe, a sept or sub-tribe and a family, there is no difference, on this theory, except in size and dis-

---

[2] The structural models employed in this paper were largely derived from the literature on the Arab Bedouin, or camel nomads. Although Arab peasant social structure is quite similar to that of the Bedouin, it does present certain differences which we do not intend to discuss at this time.

[3] Emrys Peters has completed a study of Cyrenaican Bedouin, the published results of which will undoubtedly be a valuable addition to the literature. We have not, however, been able to obtain a copy of his doctoral dissertation (Oxford) for the preparation of this paper.

tance from the common ancestor. As time rolls on the sons of a household become heads of separate families, the families grow into septs, and finally the septs become great tribes or even nations embracing great tribes.

Thus far, the Bedouin social system appears to be of a type quite often described by anthropologists, especially those concerned with Africa. There are, however, certain difficulties in identification of the agnatic units, themselves. This is reflected in the variable application of European terms for kin groups, which sees a unit of essentially the same scope called by different writers a tribe, a confederation, a lineage, or a clan. And there are no generally applicable terms in Arabic. The prefix *bait*, for example, may be encountered in the name of a group numbering in the thousands and can also be correct usage for the inhabitants of a single tent. As Evans-Pritchard (1949: 75) notes, ". . . all these terms are relative and are used in a more or less comprehensive sense according to the context."

Further indications of this lack of rigid boundary nomenclature may be found within the political system, the units of which are identical with those of kinship. A *shaikh* may be merely a family head who in turn acknowledges the leadership of another shaikh, who is the head of the agnatic line, as defined by descent from some common ancestor. The latter shaikh may acknowledge the position of still another chieftain, who bears the same title and is leader of a more comprehensive patrilineal group. Each leader has an active role at a certain level of segmentation as given in the genealogies. But under normal circumstances, he exercises authority and direction only when his unit becomes involved in joint action. That is, his duties lie mainly in the representation and leadership of the unit in relations, usually of conflict, with other units of approximately the same scope. Though an influential and prestigeful figure, he does not exert direct authority over the internal affairs of his unit. For the most part, he is the leader of a family-household group. This can perhaps be illustrated best diagrammatically. In this very simplified model, A is the chief of a patrilineal section of several generations in depth (level IV). All the other letters represent other chieftains owing allegiance to him. Under circumstances of peace, A directs the activities of his own family, on level I. However, if E becomes involved in conflict

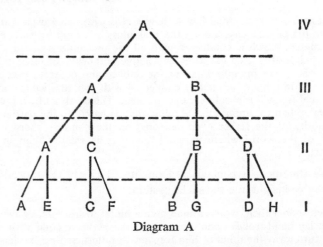

Diagram A

with F, A will side with E, and C with F. A and C will command their respective sections in combat. If on another occasion chief F is attacked by H, then lineal ties will involve people up to level III, and the sections under chiefs A and B will oppose each other. Finally, if another unit of the scope of level IV attacks any one of the sections in the diagram, the whole group under A becomes involved in a joint effort against the antagonist. Evans-Pritchard (1949a: 59) has described the Bedouin political system succinctly: "Authority is distributed at every point of the tribal structure and political leadership is limited to situations in which a tribe or segment of it acts corporately." In its underlying principle, the process of segmentary opposition between patrilineal sections corresponds closely to the Arab proverb: "Myself against my brother; my brother and I against my cousin; my cousin, my brother and I against the outsider."

In this system, it is almost impossible to isolate a solidary ingroup, and groupings are continually being activated or redefined through struggles that may even pit members of the nuclear family against each other. Such fluidity is congruent with the extreme weakness of internally exercised authority in agnatic sections, whatever the level of segmentation in question. W. Robertson Smith (1885: 55–56) had an excellent understanding of this facet of the nomad social system:

And as it was with tribal law so it was also with tribal organisation; up to the present day, among the Bedouins, it is only in war, or on the march, which is conducted with all the precautions of war, that the sheikh of a tribe exercises any active authority. In other words the tribe is not organised except for offence and defence; except in war and in matters ultimately connected with war the licence of individual freewill is absolutely uncontrolled. There cannot be a greater mistake than to suppose that Arab society is based on the patriarchal authority of the father over his sons; on the contrary there is no part of the world where parental authority is weaker than in the desert. . . .

Smith's statement is echoed by Doughty (1955: 73) who adds a remarkable insight into the social system:

Much sooner then, would a man give a buffet to his wife, or twenty, than lay handstrokes upon the back of the perverse child their son, and turn away the mind of him forever. In bitterness of a displeasure he will snib his disobedient son with vehement words, but his anger shall pass no further to break the house-peace; *after years this child shall be better than himself, and therefore he is one whom he durst not now offend* (italics ours).

It should be noted here that this quality of loose authority in Arab kin groups does not correspond with Fortes' (1953: 32) statement on unilineal, corporate groups in Africa: "As a corporate group, a lineage exhibits a structure of authority. . . ." It is obvious that Arab kin groups have only a limited corporate nature in this sense. Internally exercised jural authority is not normative at any level. We will comment further upon this later.

The above described lack of solidarity in the Bedouin family is abetted by the inheritance system, according to which the estate is divided among the sons in equal parts, daughters being commonly disinherited. In its ideal form this should not be a source of conflict, but special provisions for the eldest son and for sons who remain under the paternal roof until the father's death frequently cloud issues and result in dispute within the family. In his discussion of the problems connected with distribution of the wealth, Jaussen (1908: 21) notes that after the settlement is concluded: "Before witnesses, each declares himself to be satisfied, and peace reigns in the family, something that is quite rare, it is to be noted in passing." The harmony of the family is further disturbed by the efforts of the sons to claim their share of the inheritance—and, consequently, independence—from the father before his death. Jaussen (1908: 22) notes of the Arab family in general: "Among the nomads, as among civilized peoples, discord occasionally bursts out within the family." Thus, in a system where every male sibling is a potential point of segmentation, and therefore a significant political role player, even the interests of brothers or of sons and fathers are not necessarily convergent.

The seeming disorganization of the Bedouin family is of course, simply a part of the fundamental structure of Arab society. Just as there is structural opposition between agnatic sections of several generations' depth, so also is there opposition within the family, for the agnatic units differ only in scope and not in organization. That Bedouin society follows fundamentally the same principles at all levels of organization can be seen when one considers the maximal units of the society. Ideally, all Arabs, whether nomadic or sedentary, form a single super-lineage, the member units of which trace common ancestry to the prophet Abraham. Following Abraham, there was a bifurcation of the Arabs into two great maximal lineages. One of these, the descendants of Adnan, constitutes the present-day Northern Arabs. The other, the line of Qahtan, includes the Southern Arabs, or Yemenites, as they are commonly called. Hostility characterized relations between the two branches during the Ummayad dynasty of Islam (Lewis 1954: 75), and opposition between the two great groupings today rationalizes intertribal wars and the commonly encountered split of peasant villages into two antagonistic factions (Patai 1952: 11–12). It is noteworthy that these comprehensive agnatic units are structured in the same way as small groupings of but a few generations in depth, and they are defined and maintained by the same oppositional process.

Arab Bedouin society is characterized by the potentiality for massive aggregation of its agnatic units, on one hand, and atomistic individualism, on the other. Cohesive relations between and within sections do not have an enduring, continuing quality, but are situational and opportunistic. The most stable segment is the tribe, which, as it is usually defined in the literature, consists of those sections tracing common ancestry that possess corporate rights in grazing lands and water holes. By virtue of its tenure of these critical resources, it is also the section most commonly involved in warfare. The tribal territory, it must be stressed, is the only corporately held property among the Bedouin; this mode of tenure is a simple ecological necessity in a pastoral economy. All other forms and sources of wealth are owned by individuals. However, even the seemingly stable tribal unit is subject to shifts of membership and realignment of its sections in accord with the processes of segmentation and the vicissitudes of life in the desert.

Significantly, relations between groups and individuals and alignments in conflict are ordered through genealogy and the reckoning of distance from a common ancestor. This importance of degree of relationship as a principle of Arab social structure may also be seen in the institution of blood responsibility. Although warfare and raiding take place between agnatic sections, the group that shares blood guilt, or is responsible for the exaction of blood revenge or money, consists in most Arab tribes of all persons within five degrees of agnatic relationship to the malefactor or the victim (Jaussen 1908: 220; Kennett 1925: 55–56; Murray 1935: 205; Musil 1928: 48–49). Each group of unmarried siblings therefore has a different group of people with whom it shares blood responsibility; the respective groups of a father and his sons vary slightly in composition, those of the sons and their patrilateral parallel cousins vary somewhat more. By the same logic, a man may belong to the blood responsibility groups of a number of people, depending upon degree of relationship of the kinsman in question. Thus, in one of the more important corporate obligations of Bedouin society, there is no bounded and stable group with which the individual is totally identified and the membership of which is interchangeable, one for another.

PARALLEL COUSIN MARRIAGE

Patrilateral parallel cousin marriage is, we maintain, an essential factor in the structuring of Arab society and is especially related to the above-discussed importance of genealogy and degree of relationship in the social system. Parallel cousin marriage among the Bedouin is ultimately preferential endogamy within the agnatic line.[4] The father's brother's son is considered to pos-

---

[4] Statistical material on the frequency of parallel cousin marriage among the Bedouin is regrettably scant, although it is well known that it is not an

sess marital rights over his cousin, and, in cases in which he does not take her as his bride, his permission is nonetheless necessary for her marriage to another. If there is no patrilateral parallel cousin, reports Musil (1928: 137), the girl falls to the nearest kinsman descended from the brothers of the paternal grandfather or great-grandfather. Ayoub (1957: 86) reports mother's sister's daughter marriage to occur among Lebanese peasants, but it is obvious that insofar as patrilateral parallel cousin marriage is the dominant preference, marriage with the matrilateral parallel cousin is also endogamous to the agnatic section.

Now inasmuch as Arab nomadic society tends toward endogamy, so also does each agnatic unit thereby tend to isolate itself. As patrilineal sections segment, the preference for the closest female relative (barring sisters) in the line deepens the gulf between collateral branches by turning affinal bonds inward. Since Bedouin society is based largely upon ties of kinship, each minimal-sized agnatic unit becomes virtually self-contained and encysted. This can be shown in diagram B, which illustrates the convergence of father's and mother's lines in an ideal system of patrilateral parallel cousin marriage. Even the sporadic occurrence of cross-cousin marriage fails to break the social isolation of the kin group. Diagram C shows a cross-cousin marriage within a system structured primarily by parallel cousin marriage; it can be seen that the cross-cousins indicated are also second degree patrilateral parallel cousins, and we would venture to hypothesize that the Bedouin would interpret the relation in the latter way. This isolating effect of parallel cousin marriage has been noted by Barth (1953: 70–71) for the Kurds: "Lineage segments which have become widely separated in terms of descent will continue as separate endogamous segments, and in such a situation it is difficult for one segment to accept the informally enforced authority of the leader of another segment." Following Barth's gen-

---

invariable practice and generally applies only to first marriages. However, it is the preferred and normative form of union among the Bedouin. We have therefore worked from a mechanical model, oversimplified, of course, in which it is the predominant practice. In this regard, David Schneider has noted that the diffuseness of Bedouin social structure may be partially attributable to the fact that a socially significant number of marriages are non-endogamous. It must be cautioned that rigorously collected census data, especially on marriage and residence, are necessary for a more complete resolution of the problems raised in this paper.

eral thesis, parallel cousin marriage may well contribute to the
temporary unity of minimal segments, but it is also effective in
inhibiting the formation of corporate groups on higher levels of
segmentation.

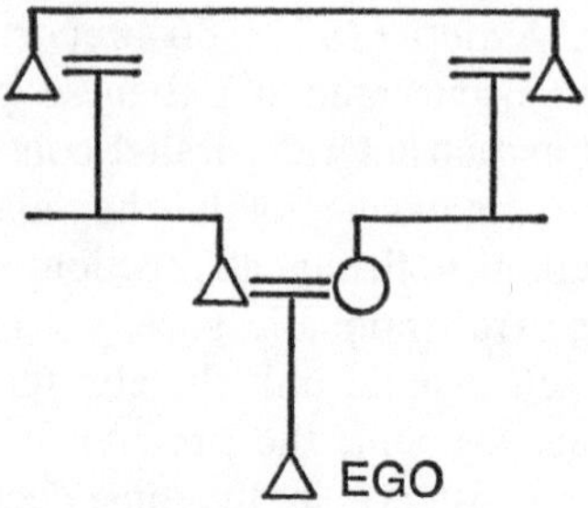

Diagram B

It follows then that parallel cousin marriage has the opposite
effect of cross-cousin marriage, which is generally considered to
be a means by which kin groups interrelate and thus become integrated into the larger society. But there *is* a larger Arab society,
and we might well ask how these insulated agnatic lines join for
certain purposes. The answer, of course, was given earlier in the
paper when we discussed genealogical reckoning as a means of
structuring allegiances and antagonisms. We need only add here

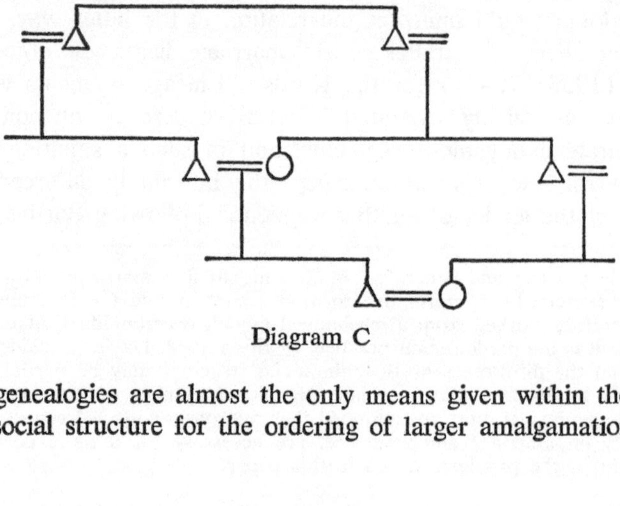

Diagram C

that genealogies are almost the only means given within the formal social structure for the ordering of larger amalgamations. A

certain amount of intertribal marriage between families of shaikhs has had this explicit purpose, although these are not normative unions. Also, the institution of blood-brotherhood has been used to establish, or make closer, bonds between individuals or kin groups (Smith 1885: 44–52). But the means par excellence of ordering relations between and within agnatic sections is genealogy, and the closeness of bonds depends, at least in theory, on the closeness of kinship. Genealogies are not at all strait-jackets within which nomad society is contained. Rather, they can be and are manipulated, added to, and altered as circumstances and tribal fortunes require or allow. Whether only in part or almost wholly false, they are tools. And, as Fortes (1953: 27) suggests, the Arab genealogies are perfectly valid if viewed not as history, but as the social structure projected backward in time and thereby legitimized and rationalized.

CONCLUSION

We have analyzed the structural-function of parallel cousin marriage in terms of three main facts about Bedouin society:

1. It has the potentiality for atomistic fission.
2. Through the use of genealogies, Arab agnatic sections may trace relationships that can ultimately include all Arabs.
3. Degree of relationship is the significant criterion in the determination of allegiances. Distance from a common ancestor in terms of numbers of intervening kinsmen is crucial to the ordering of relations within and between agnatic sections, and the principle of degree of relationship determines the composition of the Ego-centered blood responsibility group.

The third fact tells us a great deal about the patrilineal units of Arab society: except perhaps at the level of the tribe, there are no lineages in the sense of bounded groups having a continuing and cohesive base in corporate rights and duties. Differing degrees of relationship within the named groupings tend to break up their internal homogeneity; they are not solidary units, but become activated only temporarily at the call of political expediency. That this is contradictory to the basic unity of unilineal descent groups was clearly recognized by Smith (1885: 52–53). Members of Arab agnatic sections do not at all occupy a position of "status," as defined by Maine, but neither can relations between them be said to be "contractual." Clearly, the Arabs lie between the two, and we will now define their position more closely.

We have stated that there are no corporate segments in Bedouin society, except for the pasture-owning tribe, which is only weakly so. This position should, of course, be qualified by the note that agnatic segments do indeed have names and leaders and do wage warfare, as distinguished from blood feud, as units. They do not, however, have the qualities of homogeneity of membership, control over productive resources, and a system of authority related to this control that are such important criteria of the "corporation." The primary function of the agnatic segments is to provide organization for offense and defense; they are not multi-functional (cf. Smith 1885: 56). Fission and segmentation are thus promoted by the very fact that the interests of component groups and individuals are not directly contingent upon the integrity and stability of a more comprehensive unit. As for lineages in Bedouin society, it is obvious that descent is traced to common patrilineal ancestors and that there are recognizable agnatic segments. There are thus lineages in a formal sense. But in a system of patrilateral parallel cousin marriage, patrilineality in the usual sense of reckoning of descent in the father's line for certain purposes to the exclusion of that of the mother cannot exist. Exclusion after all is generally accomplished by exogamy, and as reference to diagram B will show, mothers' and fathers' lines merge on ascending generations. The system, then, has no mechanisms for the delineation of the lineage as an exclusive group or for the maintenance of structural balance between consanguineal and affinal relationship. The latter is clearly indicated by the impossibility of complementary filiation, which, as Fortes notes (1953: 33), is a consistent feature of unilineal descent groups. Such a system can work only by making filiation—usually done through recognition of degree of kinship—a general principle which applies to all kinsmen. Given this principle underlying Bedouin social structure, and in light of the composition of the blood responsibility group, the units of Bedouin society correspond more closely to the bilateral kindred than to the patrilineage. In this regard the remarks of Schneider and Roberts (1956: 21) on Zuni are highly pertinent to the Arab nomad:

> In the formal sense in which the terms are used today, however, we must still regard Zuni as matrilineal in descent and not bilateral. Yet the Zuni pattern of integration is "bilateral" or "Ego centered" in type and not unilineal.

This statement is even more true of the Bedouin than of Zuni, for although patrilineal descent does not follow through both mother and father in theory, it does in fact. Steward (1949: 734), in his discussion of the ayllu in ancient Peru, also lends support to our viewpoint: "The ayllu was patrilineal only in that office was so inherited; group affiliation in an endogamous group is necessarily bilateral."

Further confirmation of our thesis that Arab kin alignments are integrated bilaterally can be seen through comparison with Gluckman's (1955: 22) analysis of the Anglo-Saxon bilateral kin group:

> The Anglo-Saxon vengeance group, called the *sib*, which was entitled to claim blood-money for a dead man, was composed of all his kindred, through males and females, up to sixth cousins. But the group which resided and worked together seems to have been some form of patriarchal joint family: again we find that the vengeance group did not coincide with the local group. And if you trace each man's kin up to his sixth cousins, they form a widely scattered grouping which could not mobilize. Each man, with only his full-brothers and full-sisters, was the centre of his own sib; and every individual was a member of the sibs of many other people. Indeed, I venture to suggest that in a long-settled district, where there had been much intermarrying, almost everyone would have been a member of everyone else's sib. Hence where vengeance had to be taken, or redress enforced, some people would have been members of both plaintiff and defendant sibs. They would surely have exerted pressure for just settlement.

It is exactly the presence of a similarly structured blood responsibility group among the Arabs that makes the acceptance of blood money far more common than resort to blood feud. And it is also this kind of potential role conflict that inhibits the development of any internally solidary kin group; the principles underlying lineage unity and Bedouin blood responsibility are antithetical. As Murdock (1949: 60–61) has succinctly stated of systems of like structure:

This intersecting or non-exclusive characteristic is found only with bilateral descent. Every other rule of descent produces only clearly differentiated, isolable, discrete kin groups, which never overlap with others of their kind.

The Bedouin data would seem to suggest that rather than unilineal descent alone being the crucial factor in the production of discrete kin groups, the factor of exogamy is of equal if complementary importance. Thus with unilineal descent present, but in association with endogamy rather than exogamy, no "isolable, discrete kin groups" are found.

Bedouin society does not, of course, have bilateral kindreds in the narrowest definition of the term, for parallel cousin marriage must operate within a somewhat different system. This can be seen by considering Eggan's (1955: 532) summation of Northern Algonkian bilaterality:

> The essence of cross-cousin marriage is that it creates multiple bonds between a limited group of relatives and maintains these from generation to generation, rather than tying nonrelatives together in an expanding system. Thus it intensifies relationships locally but tends to isolate each local group from its neighbors, though never completely, of course.

In a limited sense, cross-cousin marriage in formally bilateral kindreds has the same isolating effect as parallel cousin marriage among the Bedouin,[5] but there are two primary differences. First, parallel cousin marriage with patrilineality allows for agnatic segmentation and structural opposition that extends even to the level of the nuclear family. And second, on higher levels of segmentation, formal patrilineality and patrilineality as an ideology provide the basis for the large-scale integration of which Arab society is capable but which is beyond the reach of societies structured only by bilateral kindreds.

It is, then, our hypothesis that the peculiar nature of agnatic sections among the Arabs is closely related to the practice of parallel cousin marriage. It might also be hypothesized that lack of internal solidarity and homogeneity in Arab kin groups is promoted by the combining of affinal and consanguineal ties. If

---

[5] We are indebted to Melvin Mednick of the University of Chicago for this observation.

we may deduce from our knowledge of affinal relations in other societies, patrilateral parallel cousin marriage could hardly be a cohesive factor but may well underlie the fission and faction that are so important a part of Arab society. Beyond this consideration, we must contemplate the anomaly presented by the existence of patrilateral parallel cousin marriage in a patrilineal system. Homans and Schneider (1955: 51) have argued convincingly that: "Societies in which marriage is allowed or preferred with mother's brother's daughter but forbidden or disapproved with father's sister's daughter will be societies in which jural authority over ego male, before marriage, is vested in his father or father's lineage. . . ." Their argument follows that relations of authority would be in conflict with bonds of sentiment with the father-in-law, and that the direction of unilateral cross-cousin marriage is therefore a means by which balance may be maintained between jural and effective ties. Now accepting their thesis, how much more disturbing to the system it must be for a member of a patrilineage to marry his father's brother's daughter. We believe that this question can be easily resolved by pointing out again that there is minimal potestality within the Arab family, or more comprehensive units, and "lineages" are most weak. Patrilateral parallel cousin marriage could not work if the converse were true. We have thus a further explanation of the previously noted looseness of Bedouin social structure.

Patrilateral parallel cousin marriage has other implications in the structuring of kin groups. As has been stated, in societies having exogamous descent groups the boundaries and membership of the group are clearly set by stipulating marriage outside of it; descent groups among the Bedouin have no such clear-cut means of definition. Rather, the internal logic of the system extends agnatic ties in decreasing degree to all members of Arab society. Thus, from a study of endogamy, we arrive at the general statement that exogamy functions not only to relate kin groups, but to identify their boundaries and define the membership that shares in their corporate rights and duties.

Arab Bedouin society is not simply another case of a simple patrilineal, segmentary society structured along the lines of our African models. In a very real sense, its plasticity, its capacity for fusion and fission, its lack of bounded and stable descent groups has contributed to its enormous persistence in time. Bedouin society has maintained itself for centuries despite the physical and social environment. Since even the nuclear family is a miniature of the larger social system, the population may expand in numbers and area, or become fragmented and dispersed, without any disturbance of the social system itself. Such dispersals may result from warfare with agrarian states or other tribes and, under less violent circumstances, occur annually as part of the ecology of steppe pastoralism. And the beauty of Arab genealogies—and their manipulation—is that larger units may coalesce when necessary. Thus, the Bedouin have frequently had to deal in strength with the states on the borders of the desert. That they have often done so with striking results is amply illustrated by the Moslem conquests. The same historical events show a cyclical process in Arab society, however, for fission usually sets in shortly after the disappearance of the common cause. The Bedouin have never been able to exert stable and unified political power for any length of time. But perhaps we should not look upon this as a weakness, for Bedouin society persists today amid the ruins of empires that once sought to shatter it.

SUMMARY

Most explanations of patrilateral parallel cousin marriage are of a causal-motivational kind, in which the institution is explained through reference to the consciously felt goals of the individual role players. We have not attempted to explain the origin of the custom in this paper but have taken it as a given factor and then proceeded to analyze its function, i.e., its operation within Bedouin social structure. It was found that parallel cousin marriage contributes to the extreme fission of agnatic lines in Arab society, and, through in-marriage, encysts the patrilineal segments. Under these circumstances, integration of larger social units is accomplished vertically, through genealogical reckoning to common ancestors, and not horizontally, through affinal bonds. Common ancestry, whether myth or fact, has been an effective means of obtaining the great coalitions necessary to the persistence of Arab society on the fringes of agrarian states. Conversely, the ability of larger units to fractionate into microsections without disturbing the social structure gives the society a quality of resilience and adaptability in the face of adversity. This may also be taken as evidence that social cohesion and social integration are not necessarily directly related.

Finally, we have analyzed the relation of parallel cousin marriage to the importance of degree of kinship in Arab society. Following Smith's insights, we argued that the heavy emphasis placed upon numbers of intervening kinsmen, or distance from a common ancestor, is antithetical to the homogeneity of the bounded, corporate lineage and that one of the functions of exogamy is the maintenance of the latter type of social unit. Conversely, kin group endogamy is functional to a system in which integration is obtained bilaterally. In conclusion, we would suggest that we re-evaluate some of our notions that equate cohesion, or solidarity, and integration, or structural equilibrium, and that we analyze in greater detail the typological differences between societies based on true corporate lineages and the one under discussion in this paper.

11 THE MARRIAGE ALLIANCE

Louis Dumont

To INTRODUCE AN INSTITUTION which is shared by all groups referred to here and, I believe, by many others, some criticism of current anthropological categories is first necessary.

MARRIAGE REGULATIONS AND AFFINITY

A (positive) marriage regulation like 'a man should marry his mother's brother's daughter' might be a native statement indicating whom a given individual should marry. But, in anthropological thought, it takes on a slightly different meaning. There it appears as a rule for deriving a man's marriage from a relationship excluding any idea of marriage or affinity, i.e. from a relationship of consanguinity. It is implied that consanguinity is pre-existent to the marriage, since I must be born before I marry. The marriage regulation is in fact used as a tool for deducing a secondary category (a certain marriage) from a primary category (a certain relationship of consanguinity). After marriage is so introduced, it brings with it relationships of a secondary kind (affinal relationships) which are never considered as full kinship relationships, because they are individual and above all temporary—they disappear with the married person and are not transmitted to his or her descendants but under the form of a consanguinity relationship.

I submit that all this is wrong and needs revision for the follow-

Reprinted from *Occasional Papers of the Royal Anthropological Institute*, No. 12, 1957, pp. 24–29, by permission of the author and of the Royal Anthropological Institute.

ing reasons: (1) it rests only on undue generalization of our common-sense categories, and does not do justice to the facts because in our societies marriage is an individual affair, not positively regulated; (2) it is contradictory for, as I shall show, the very existence of the marriage regulation implies that affinity is transmitted from one generation to the next just as consanguinity ties are. We have thus to give a proper definition of marriage regulation on the one hand and to widen our concept of affinity on the other.

First, it is almost unnecessary to recall that marriage cannot in general be considered as a secondary product of other institutions such as descent, which are then taken as being primary; there is rather an interrelation in the complete make-up. Still less is it possible to reduce the content of the marriage regulation to the codification of an individual affair, which marriage is not. Consequently, the regulation should not be considered as consisting of a relation between consanguineous ties and affinity, but as a feature of affinity itself. It is possible to do so, by pointing out that the regulation determines one's marriage by reference to one's ascendants' marriages: in a patrilineal, patrilocal society, marrying the matrilateral cross-cousin means reproducing the marriage of one's father, while in the patrilateral formula one reproduces one's grandfather's marriage, and so on. In general, the regulation determines a cycle of repetition of a marriage of a certain sort. If we say that 'one marries one's cross-cousin', we merely state a condition to be observed in order to maintain a certain pattern of intermarriage.

In other words, the regulation causes marriage to be transmitted much as membership in the descent group is transmitted. With it, marriage acquires a diachronic dimension, it becomes an institution enduring from generation to generation, which I therefore call 'marriage alliance', or simply 'alliance'.

In the matter of affinity, we generally admit too readily that, while the relationship between a man and his brother-in-law is affinal, the relationship between their sons (cross-cousins) has no longer any affinal content, but is a mere consanguineous relationship. This is certainly not so in South India, where to call E and A cross-cousins—as in Figure 1 (b)—instead of 'sons of affines'—as in Figure 1 (a)—is quite deceptive. Being sons of affines, they are *ipso facto* affines, at least in a virtual or rather a general sense, before or without becoming so individually, as when E marries A's sister. We are now out of the vicious circle and we can look at it with amusement: 'marrying a cross-cousin'[1] is nothing but marrying an affine, i.e. the person who is the closest affine by virtue of the transmission of affinity ties from one generation to the next.

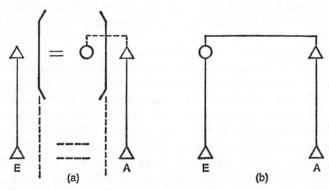

Figure 1.   Cross-cousins or affines. (a) A as an 'affine' of E; (b) A as a 'cross-cousin' of E.

I submit that, in societies where there are (positive) marriage regulations: (1) marriage should be considered as a part of a marriage alliance institution running through generations; (2) the concept of affinity should be extended so as to include not only immediate, individual relationships (affines in the ordinary sense) but also the people who inherit such a relationship from their parents, those who share it as siblings of the individual affines, etc.; (3) there is likely to be an affinal content in terms which are generally considered to connote consanguinity or 'genealogical' relationships (such as 'mother's brother' etc.). This is obviously so when there are no special terms for affines, for otherwise we should have to admit that in such cases affinity is not expressed at all.

---

[1] Briffault (1927, I, pp. 563 ff.) rightly uses the Tamil term for 'cross cousin', *machuna* (for *maccuNaN*) to stress the affinal content of the category; he speaks of a 'marriage agreement between two groups'. Aiyappan (1945, p. 68) classifies the sister's son among the *bandhukkal* or affines, but contradicts it in a footnote.

TERMINOLOGICAL DICHOTOMY: KIN AND AFFINES

Structure of Terminology

All our groups share with many others a structurally identical terminology which in its broad features has been recorded from all four written Dravidian languages. Here I shall summarize a separate study (Dumont 1953a; see also Radcliffe-Brown 1953 and Dumont 1953b).

The two sexes should be taken separately. With certain exceptions there is one term for all males in the grandfather's generation, but two terms in the father's generation. The latter terms, generally translated as 'father' and 'mother's brother', denote two classes, the members of which are respectively brothers-in-law to one another. Or, if we call 'alliance relationship' this relationship between two persons of the same sex, and represent it by $\Delta[=]\Delta$, standing for $\Delta = \overline{\delta \ \Delta}$ as well as for $\overline{\Delta \ \delta} = \Delta$ etc., the relation between the two classes is $\Delta[=]\Delta$. This is true also in Ego's generation (for older and younger relatives), whereas the distinction does not fully operate in Ego's son's generation, where a mere prefix is used, and disappears in the grandson's generation. Terms for males are recapitulated in Figure 2(a).

Among females, the 'mother' and the 'father's sister' may be distinguished exactly as above. Now if we remark (1) that the terms for grandmother and grand-daughter are not distinct, except for the ending, from those for grandfather and grandson, and that the same root is used for all in the son's generation; and (2) that the principle of distinction is the same for males and for females, we can represent the whole by a symmetrical scheme in which the identity of terms is expressed by superpositions of signs —see Figure 2(b). One sees that the distinction of sex and the alliance distinction go together, and that the system might be called 'bifurcate-merging' in a new sense, that is, bifurcate in the central and merging in the extreme generations. One sees also how simple and regular the system looks once one ceases to remove alliance artificially from the content of kinship terms. It consists in distinguishing, in three generations or age groups, two kinds of relatives of each sex: those related to Ego by a link

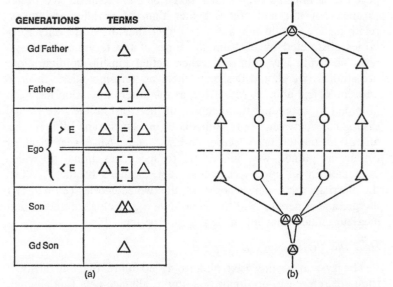

GENERATIONS	TERMS
Gd Father	△
Father	△ [=] △
Ego { > E	△ [=] △
Ego { < E	△ [=] △
Son	△△
Gd Son	△

(a)   (b)

Figure 2. Structure of the system of kinship terms. (a) Terms for males only, five generations; (b) terms for both sexes, five generations. The superposition of signs shows identity of terms, apart from word endings.

excluding alliance, or 'kin link' (on the left), and those related to the first by alliance (on the right). From the basic structure of the system we have on one side the 'fathers', on the other the 'fathers' affines', and on one side the 'mothers', on the other the 'mothers' affines'; and nowhere such beings as mother's brother or father's sister, who are just particular cases of fathers' affines and mothers' affines. Obviously, too, the system implies a marriage regulation, namely that one marries an affine in one's generation, the nearest of these in terms of individual relationship being a cross-cousin.

Definitions

The whole of the kinship terminology is split into two halves, 'kin' terms and 'alliance' or 'affinity' terms. By thus stating that kinship = kin + affinity, we escape an ambiguity found in anthropological writings, where 'kin' or 'kinship' is sometimes op-

posed to affinity and sometimes taken as embracing it. We prefer
to speak of kin and affines rather than of parallel and cross-
relatives. We should not however forget that these are only categories abstracted by us from the form of the terminological system. To avoid any confusion when actual kinship configurations
are studied, we should designate them as 'terminological kin' and
'terminological affines'. Moreover, as the latter expression has been
obtained by extending the meaning of the word 'affine', we should
distinguish between (*a*) immediate or synchronic affines, i.e.
affines in the ordinary sense, in-laws, and (*b*) genealogical or
diachronic affines, who inherit, so to speak, an affinal tie which
originated in an upper generation (e.g. mother's brother). When
the marriage regulation is observed, the two categories (*a*) and (*b*)
merge, and a person is at the same time a genealogical and an immediate affine, what might be called a perfect affine.

How the Terminology is Applied

The system as analysed hitherto is no more than an abstract
frame of reference, no doubt pointing to alliance as a fundamental
institution, but one to which each social group will give a particular concrete form according to its particular institutions. (We may
imagine, for instance, that in a matrilineal matrilocal society the
kin link is with the mother's brother while the father is an affine;
then their ordinary positions in the system would be reversed,
without the structure being altered.) Among our groups, the actual
relationship with the father's sister may vary, but there will always be found as a common background the fact that she is different from a 'mother', first of all in the sense that Ego may marry
her daughter even if she is not the preferred mate, while he may
not marry a 'mother's' daughter.

Again, within one and the same terminological class the distinction of particular relatives, whether expressed or not in the language, may differ from one group to another. The broad opposition
between kin and affines suggested by the terminology will itself
be unequally realized for different relatives: among the terminological kin, a part is singled out as really or fully kin, and
the same happens among terminological affines. The choice
varies, but all the different choices fit into the general terminological frame, no doubt because they fit into a common alliance pat-

tern. Another general difference is found in the degree to which relationships are extended from the groups of siblings to extensive socio-political groups. A comparison will show how the terminological categories are given different shapes by different institutions.

The Pramalai Kallar are patrilineal and patrilocal. In one locality there is as a rule only one or a few patrilineages. Hence:

1   The category of 'brothers' is split into two: on the one hand all my paternal 'brothers' (sons of my father's brothers etc.) are members of my local descent group, on the other hand my maternal 'brothers' (sons of my mother's sisters etc.) are spread over different groups and places. On the paternal side each individual link is made to endure through generations by becoming an element among all other similar elements in the continuous fabric of the local group, clearly defined as against others by the exogamic rule. On the maternal side, each individual relationship, being isolated—see however 2 below—is liable to be rapidly forgotten. While the paternal half is stressed to the point of becoming almost equivalent to the whole, the maternal half appears, except in special cases, as temporary, subsidiary, almost conventional.

2   The opposition between kin and affines takes on a spatial aspect; there are kin places and affinal places, and as one marries mostly in the neighbourhood, this might be represented ideally in the form of concentric circles, a territorial unit made up of kin, A, being surrounded by affinal places, B. As these in their turn intermarry with other places, there arises a third circle, C, made up of people who are affines to B, and hence 'brothers' to A, as the affine of my affine is kin to me. (In these C places will be found some of the maternal brothers mentioned above.) The matter is of course not so simple in fact, but on the whole, when seen from one point, there is a picture of the division of the not-too-far-removed localities into the two fundamental categories. It will be readily grasped that this apparent dichotomy in space results from the working of the organization and has nothing to do with a systematic division or a dual organization of the society. Nevertheless it represents a maximum in the extension to groups of the basic terminological categories.

3   Let us now compare the position of the mother's brother with that of the father's sister. The mother's brother is not only terminologically opposed to the father, who is here kin *par excellence*, but he also lives in an affinal place. He is an affine pure and simple, in fact the closest, at least until one marries. On the contrary, the father's sister, born in one's local descent group, becomes only with her marriage a member of an affinal group, just as the mother, born in an affinal group, has become kin first as mother, at the same time thrusting, so to speak, the father's sister into the affinal category. The terminology here directs us to look at the father's sister as already married and as mother of affinal cousins. Nevertheless she is at the same time to some extent kin, and it follows that she is less clearly and unambiguously an affine than the mother's brother. If we then suppose, as will be confirmed, that affinal relatives are in charge of ceremonial functions, we may expect the mother's brother to precede the father's sister in those functions.

The picture is quite different for the matrilineal, patrilocal Kondaiyam Kottai Maravar. With them descent and locality work in opposite directions, with the result that individual kinship relationships are not backed by corresponding relationships between groups. Here the sons of two brothers on the one hand and of two sisters on the other are recognized as 'brothers' in two different ways and the two kinds of relationship are stressed in quite different conditions, the first in a context of locality and the second in a context of alliance or of special ceremonial circumstances. On one side, a remote relationship between patrilocal brothers does not in general exclude alliance, so that the category in the long run is stripped of any kin content, being mainly a matter of socio-economic neighbourliness. On the other side, it is between sisters (and not brothers) and their descendants that the matrilineal kin relationship endures. The descent group has no tangible reality. What is stressed here is a matriline scattered in different localities, shifting from place to place and from house to house in each generation. In every locality a number of matrilineal exogamous units are represented, and a man may marry into any of them, except his own. In one's own village the terminological categories are fully realized only for three kinds of people: a smaller or larger circle of patrilocal brothers, a number of matrilineal brothers, and the affines of the first two. At the same time, a great number of people are undifferentiated: they may be at the same time brothers in a loose, merely local sense, and virtual affines, and it is only the nexus of individual alliances and their classificatory extensions which decides the question.

The opposition between father and mother's brother is seen here in different ways. From the matrilineal point of view the situation would be reversed, the mother's brother could be considered as kin and the father as an affine, but nevertheless the mother's brother's children will be terminological affines. We see that it is the mother's brother who receives the ambiguous character which attaches to the father's sister among Pramalai Kallar. In contradistinction to them, the foremost affine here is the father's sister, because locality is not exclusive of alliance and because matrilineality stresses the kin link with the mother. This will be confirmed later, when we study the ceremonial functions.

If the two preceding examples are compared, the difference in the affinal value of the mother's brother and of the father's sister can perhaps be summed up by saying that when paternal features (authority, locality) are present, the foremost affinal relative in the upper generation is the affine of the lineally-stressed parent, i.e. the mother's brother in patrilineality and the father's sister in matrilineality. This is only another expression of harmony and disharmony (Figure 3). It is hoped that this brief comparison has shown how we may speak of a common underlying alliance pattern which, when combined with different institutions, assumes different concrete forms.

(a)   (b)

PRAMALAI KALLAR   KONDAIYAM KOTTAI MARAVAR

Figure 3. Stress on one affine in relation to descent: Pramalai Kallar and Kondaiyam Kottai Maravar.

PART IV
THE FAMILY

12 THE FAMILY: SOME COMPARATIVE CONSIDERATIONS[1]

M. J. Levy, Jr., and L. A. Fallers

IN ORDER TO CARRY OUT comparative analysis, one clearly requires concepts on the most general level which are applicable to any society. The concept "family" is commonly used in this way; that is, it is commonly assumed that in every society there is something called "the family." We feel, however, that the concept as it is most often used is ill-adapted to comparative analysis. It is usually assumed, either implicitly or explicitly, that in every society there is a single social unit, which is invariably associated with certain functions. It may even be assumed that this unit is everywhere structurally the same.

Now progress in the field of comparative analysis of societies has regularly involved clearer distinction between structure and function and between concrete social units and analytically distinguishable aspects of such units (Levy 1952). The political field provides a case in point. The term "political system" in its common-sense Western meaning refers to a series of specialized concrete social units (bureaucracies, legislatures, courts, parties) with particular structural forms (hierarchical in the case of bureaucracies, collegial in the case of legislatures, and so on) and having particular functions with regard to the exercise of power and authority (adjudicating disputes, making decisions, securing consent). However, a concept like this is of little use com-

Republished from *American Anthropologist*, Vol. 61, 1959, pp. 647–51, with permission of the authors and of the editor of *American Anthropologist*.
[1] This is a slight revision of a paper presented at the 1957 meeting of the American Anthropological Association in Chicago, in a symposium on "Models for the Study of Kinship" organized by Harry W. Basehart.

paratively. On the one hand, by this definition many societies simply do not have "political systems." In many societies a single social unit—perhaps a unilineal kinship group—may combine the functions of "church," "state," and "firm" and it will very likely differ greatly in structure from any of the specialized political units characteristic of the modern West. On the other hand, the above type of definition of "political system" tends to obscure as much as it reveals even within the systems to which it is indigenous. Even the specialized political units of the modern West have nonpolitical aspects, while other units, not of a specialized political nature, nevertheless have political aspects. It is only when these distinctions are recognized that the political systems of the full-range of human societies become commensurable.

As applied to the political field or to most other fields of comparative interest, distinctions of this kind are commonly made and, indeed, seem obvious, but in comparative studies of the family they seem to be considered unnecessary. Undoubtedly the reason for this is the apparent empirical ubiquity of small, kinship-structured domestic units having reproductive, socialization, and sex-regulation functions. In most other respects human society is empirically so variable that distinction between structure and function, between social units and analytically distinguishable aspects of them, comes quite naturally to the social analyst. But the family, it seems to be felt, is an exception because a particular set of functions is so regularly associated with a particular type of unit. Murdock, in what is certainly the most extensive and influential comparative study yet undertaken, feels able to assert at the outset, on the basis of data from his sample of 250 societies, that "Either as the sole prevailing form or as the basic unit from which more complex familial forms are compounded, [the nuclear family] exists as a distinct and strongly functional group in every society" and that it universally performs ". . . four functions fundamental to human social life—the sexual, the economic, the reproductive and the educational" (Murdock 1949: 2–3). Murdock's position has been widely adopted, perhaps most notably by Parsons and Bales (Parsons 1954; Parsons and Bales 1955).

It is not our purpose here to question the empirical ubiquity of small, kinship-structured domestic units with reproductive, sex-regulation, and socialization functions. That there are striking regularities in this sphere seems clear. Neither do we propose to take a stand on the question of whether or not these regularities are in any sense "biologically based." Rather we propose to argue that, in spite of such considerations—in a sense just *because* of the temptations to conceptual shoddiness to which apparent empirical regularities in the family sphere expose us— it is desirable to preserve in this field the conceptual distinctions, which have proved so necessary in the comparative analysis of other aspects of human society.

Let us assume, then, that small, kinship-structured units are universal—are indeed structural requisites of any society. Functionally, socialization would appear to be the heart of the matter. Parsons and Bales have argued with great cogency that socialization requires small units and that completely non-kinship-structured small units are unlikely to carry out the function effectively (although, of course, human ingenuity may devise alternatives). Of the other "universal functions" attributed by Murdock to the family, reproduction and sexual regulation would appear to be associated with, and probably secondary to, socialization. Parsons' argument here seems to us convincing (Parsons 1954). Murdock's remaining "universal function"—the economic—seems to us to be on an entirely different level. It is not so much that families universally fulfill economic functions vis-à-vis other units and the society at large; clearly, the degree to which and the ways in which they do so are subject to enormous variation. Rather, the point would seem to be that families, like other social units, must make provision for the distribution of goods and services—that, like other units, they have economic aspects. If families are universal, probably because of their usefulness as socialization devices, then indeed in every society they have economic functions. It would appear to be the socialization function, however, which lies at the root of the requisite nature of families.

But, assuming that small, kinship-structured units are structural requisites of any society, and assuming that they are so because socialization requires it, it does not follow either that (a) there is a single such unit in every society (*"the* family") which carries out every aspect of the socialization function and its associated or derivative functions or, still less, that (b) in every society this unit is the nuclear family. We do not believe that either Murdock or Parsons has shown these statements to be true. If they are not true, then it becomes seriously misleading to use the term "family" as a comparative concept on the most general level to refer to a concrete unit, to a particular structural type and to an invariant set of functions taken together. It becomes necessary to distinguish these elements so that the ranges of variation which are thereby admitted, may be discussed.

Let us first consider the universality of the nuclear family as the unit for socialization. Murdock argues that, even where the nuclear family is "enveloped" in more extended domestic units, it is always clearly distinguished as a separate subunit and he rather implies that it is always the more fundamental unit vis-à-vis the "universal functions of the family." We would not deny that in most, if not all, societies persons are typically able to distinguish their own parents and siblings from other kinsmen. We do not believe, however, that extended family households always "consist" of aggregations of nuclear families—that in such households children are always socialized primarily in terms of the nuclear family subunit. This is essentially the point made by Linton in his distinction between "conjugal" and "consanguineal" families (Linton 1936: 159–60). We cannot in this paper undertake to test this notion on a wide range of empirical data, but we would cite data with which we are familiar from societies which are not particularly unusual in the relevant respects. One of us has pointed out that in the traditional Chinese family children are typically socialized in terms of the patrilineal extended family unit and that within this unit the nuclear family was by no means the "strongest" subunit for socialization purposes (Levy 1955). Among the Basoga of East Africa, the typical household is occupied by a nuclear family plus odd individual kinsmen. However, the solidarity of exogamous patrilineages is strong and nuclear families tend to be split by the conflicting loyalties of the spouses. Divorce is consequently very common and hence children are very often socialized in households where only one parent is present. More importantly, even where marriages remain intact, the conflict of lineage loyalties results in a primary orientation on the part of children to the lineages of the two parents rather than to the nuclear family as a unit (Fallers 1957). The Hopi would appear to represent an analogous situation on the matrilineal side, while among the famous Nayar, apparently, the nuclear family disappears altogether in favor of the consanguineal unit (Eggan 1950: 113–14; Gough 1952a, 1952b). (Thus the Nayar seem to us, not an ethnographic oddity, but merely an extreme extension of a quite widespread pattern.)

Secondly, there is the question of whether in every society there is a single small, kinship-structured unit which carries out the socialization function. Again, the traditional Chinese extended family would seem to represent a relatively common contrary case. Young children tend to be socialized almost exclusively by mothers and grandmothers; later the sexes divide, boys associating primarily with adult males and girls with adult females. Thus, at various times and with regard to the two sexes, different sub-units emerge as primary for socialization. Among the matrilineal Ashanti of Ghana, it is quite clear from Fortes' material, the typical child is primarily oriented during one phase of socialization to a consanguineal unit centering upon its mother and her brother, while during another phase it is associated primarily with a conjugal unit based upon father and mother (Fortes 1949b).

We are well aware that this brief discussion is far from doing justice to Parsons' complex psychoanalytic argument concerning socialization and the nuclear family. From a psychogenetic standpoint, the kernel of the problem is whether adequate socialization requires the "Oedipus situation" in its full sexual sense—that is, the regular presence in the domestic unit of a cohabiting pair or "conjugal family"—or whether the mere presence in the domestic unit of adult male and female role models—an adult brother and sister, for example—is sufficient. An attempt to deal more fully with the psychogenetic argument must await another occasion, but we do feel that considerations of the sort put forward here suggest a restatement of the problem along the following lines:

It seems to us untenable to assume that the socialization function is invariably carried out primarily within a single kinship-structured unit—the nuclear family or any other—even though we assume that small, kinship-structured units are structural requisites of any society and that their requisite nature is bound up with the socialization function. This being so, we suggest that the concept "family," to be useful for general comparative purposes, should be used to refer not to a single social unit in each society, but rather to any small, kinship-structured unit which carries out aspects of the relevant functions. We suspect that, using the term in this way, one would find in most societies a series of "family" units. We cannot systematically spell out the possibilities here, but one would want to distinguish, among others, units for socializing each of the two sexes and units associated with distinguishable aspects and temporal phases of socialization. We have noted above that, while the requisite and universal nature of small, kinship-structured units probably rests upon the socialization function, once such units exist other functions come into the picture. Thus, for example, one would have to distinguish units, which fulfill the economic functions arising from the existence of the socialization units; there is no reason to assume that these units would be the same. In Ashanti, a child and its mother may commonly live in the household of the mother's brother, but the mother may nevertheless send food to her husband living in another household.

We suggest that the concept of the family presented here facilitates a more differentiated analysis of small, kinship-structured units and their functions; that it brings the study of such units into more systematic relationship with other kinship studies; and that it facilitates the systematic comparison of such units with non-kinship-structured units. There is clearly something special about "the family"; we argue only that the study of it deserves the same conceptual care that we customarily apply to the study of other aspects of society.

13   IS THE FAMILY UNIVERSAL?

Melford E. Spiro

THE UNIVERSALITY of the family has always been accepted as a sound hypothesis in anthropology; recently, Murdock has been able to confirm this hypothesis on the basis of his important cross-cultural study of kinship. Moreover, Murdock reports that the "nuclear" family is also universal, and that typically it has four functions: sexual, economic, reproductive, and educational. What is more important is his finding that no society "has succeeded in finding an adequate substitute for the nuclear family, to which it might transfer these functions" (1949: 11). In the light of this evidence there would be little reason to question his prediction that "it is highly doubtful whether any society ever will succeed in such an attempt, utopian proposals for the abolition of the family to the contrary notwithstanding" (1949: 11).

The functions served by the nuclear family are, of course, universal prerequisites for the survival of any society; and it is on this basis that Murdock accounts for its universality.

> Without provision for the first and third [sexual and reproductive], society would become extinct; for the second [economic], life itself would cease; for the fourth [educational], culture would come to an end. The immense social utility of the nuclear family and the basic reason for its universality thus begins to emerge in strong relief [1949: 10].

Although sexual, economic, reproductive, and educational ac-

Reprinted from *American Anthropologist*, Vol. 56, 1954, pp. 839–46, with permission of the author and of the editor of *American Anthropologist*. "Addendum" from Norman W. Bell and Ezra F. Vogel, eds., *A Modern Introduction to the Family*. Reprinted with permission of the author and the Free Press.

tivities are the functional prerequisites of any society, it comes as somewhat of a surprise, nevertheless, that all four functions are served by the same social group. One would normally assume, on purely a priori grounds, that within the tremendous variability to be found among human cultures, there would be some cultures in which these four functions were distributed among more than one group. Logically, at least, it is entirely possible for these functions to be divided among various social groups within a society; and it is, indeed, difficult to believe that somewhere man's inventive ingenuity should not have actualized this logical possibility. As a matter of fact this possibility has been actualized in certain utopian communities—and it has succeeded within the narrow confines of these communities. The latter, however, have always constituted subgroups within a larger society, and the basic question remains as to whether such attempts could succeed when applied to the larger society.

Rather than speculate about the answer to this question, however, this paper presents a case study of a community which, like the utopian communities, constitutes a subgroup within a larger society and which, like some utopian communities, has also evolved a social structure which does not include the family. It is hoped that an examination of this community—the Israeli *kibbutz*—can shed some light on this question.

MARRIAGE AND THE FAMILY IN THE *kibbutz*

A *kibbutz* (plural, *kibbutzim*) is an agricultural collective in Israel, whose main features include communal living, collective ownership of all property (and, hence, the absence of "free enterprise" and the "profit motive"), and the communal rearing of children. *Kibbutz* culture is informed by its explicit, guiding principle of: "from each according to his ability, to each according to his needs." The "family," as that term is defined in *Social Structure*, does not exist in the *kibbutz*, in either its nuclear, polygamous, or extended forms. It should be emphasized, however, that the *kibbutzim* are organized into three separate national federations, and though the basic structure of *kibbutz* society is similar in all three, there are important differences among them. Hence, the term *kibbutz*, as used in this paper, refers exclusively to those *kibbutzim* that are members of the federation studied by the author.[1]

As Murdock defines it (1949: 1), the "family":

> is a social group characterized by common residence, economic cooperation, and reproduction. It includes adults of both sexes, at least two of whom maintain a socially approved sexual relationship, and one or more children, own or adopted, of the sexually cohabiting adults.

The social group in the *kibbutz* that includes adults of both sexes and their children, although characterized by reproduction, is not characterized by common residence or by economic co-operation. Before examining this entire social group, however, we shall first analyze the relationship between the two adults in the group who maintain a "socially approved sexual relationship," in order to determine whether their relationship constitutes a "marriage."

Murdock's findings reveal that marriage entails an interaction of persons of opposite sex such that a relatively permanent sexual relationship is maintained and an economic division of labor is practised. Where either of these behavior patterns is absent, there is no marriage. As Murdock puts it (1949: 8):

> Sexual unions without economic cooperation are common, and there are relationships between men and women involving a division of labor without sexual gratification . . . but marriage exists only when the economic and the sexual are united in one relationship, and this combination occurs only in marriage.

In examining the relationship of the couple in the *kibbutz* who share a common marriage, and whose sexual union is socially sanctioned, it is discovered that only one of these two criteria—the sexual—applies. Their relationship does not entail economic co-operation. If this be so—and the facts will be examined in a moment—there is no marriage in the *kibbutz*, if by "marriage" is meant a relationship between adults of opposite sex, characterized by sexual and economic activities. Hence, the generalization that, "marriage, thus defined, exists in every known society" (1949: 8), has found an exception.

---

[1] The field work, on which statements concerning the *kibbutz* are based, was conducted in the year 1951–52, and was made possible by a postdoctoral fellowship awarded by the Social Science Research Council.

A *kibbutz* couple lives in a single room, which serves as a combined bedroom-living room. Their meals are eaten in a communal dining room, and their children are reared in a communal children's dormitory. Both the man and the woman work in the *kibbutz*, and either one may work in one of its agricultural branches or in one of the "service" branches. The latter include clerical work, education, work in the kitchen, laundry, etc. In actual fact, however, men preponderate in the agricultural branches, and women, in the service branches of the economy. There are no men, for example, in that part of the educational system, which extends from infancy to the junior-high level. Nor do women work in those agricultural branches that require the use of heavy machinery, such as trucks, tractors, or combines. It should be noted, however, that some women play major roles in agricultural branches, such as the vegetable garden and the fruit orchards; and some men are indispensable in service branches such as the high school. Nevertheless, it is accurate to state that a division of labor based on sex is characteristic of the *kibbutz* society as a whole. This division of labor, however, does not characterize the relationship that exists between couples. Each mate works in some branch of the *kibbutz* economy and each, as a member (*chaver*) of the *kibbutz* receives his equal share of the goods and services that the *kibbutz* distributes. Neither, however, engages in economic activities that are exclusively directed to the satisfaction of the needs of his mate. Women cook, sew, launder, etc., for the entire *kibbutz*, and not for their mates exclusively. Men produce goods, but the economic returns from their labor go to the *kibbutz*, not to their mates and themselves, although they, like all members of the *kibbutz*, share in these economic returns. Hence, though there is economic co-operation between the sexes within the community as a whole, this co-operation does not take place between mates because the social structure of this society precludes the necessity for such co-operation.

What then is the nature of the relationship of the *kibbutz* couple? What are the motives for their union? What functions, other than sex, does it serve? What distinguishes such a union from an ordinary love affair?

In attempting to answer these questions it should first be noted that premarital sexual relations are not taboo. It is expected, however, that youth of high-school age refrain from sexual activity; sexual intercourse between high-school students is strongly discouraged. After graduation from high school, however, and their election to membership in the *kibbutz*, there are no sanctions against sexual relations among these young people. While still single, *kibbutz* members live in small private rooms, and their sexual activities may take place in the room of either the male or the female, or in any other convenient location. Lovers do not ask the *kibbutz* for permission to move into a (larger) common room, nor, if they did, would this permission be granted if it were assumed that their relationship was merely that of lovers. When a couple asks for permission to share a room, they do so—and the *kibbutz* assumes that they do so—not because they are lovers, but because they are in love. The request for a room, then, is the sign that they wish to become a "couple" (*zug*), the term the *kibbutz* has substituted for the traditional "marriage." This union does not require the sanction of a marriage ceremony, or of any other event. When a couple requests a room, and the *kibbutz* grants the request, their union is *ipso facto* sanctioned by society. It should be noted, however, that all *kibbutz* "couples" eventually "get married" in accordance with the marriage laws of the state— usually just before, or soon after, their first child is born—because children born out of wedlock have no legal rights according to state law.

But becoming a "couple" affects neither the status nor the responsibilities of either the male or the female in the *kibbutz*. Both continue to work in whichever branch of the economy they had worked in before their union. The legal and social status of both the male and the female remain the same. The female retains her maiden name. She not only is viewed as a member of the *kibbutz* in her own right, but her official registration card in the *kibbutz* files remains separate from that of her "friend" (*chaver*)—the term used to designate spouses.[2]

But if sexual satisfaction may be obtained outside of this

---

[2] Other terms, "young man" (*bachur*) and "young woman" (*bachura*), are also used in place of "husband" and "wife." If more than one person in the *kibbutz* has the same proper name, and there is some question as to who is being referred to when the name is mentioned in conversation, the person is identified by adding, "the *bachur* of so-and-so," or "the *bachura* of so-and-so."

union, and if the union does not entail economic co-operation, what motivates people to become "couples"? It seems that the motivation is the desire to satisfy certain needs for intimacy, using that term in both its physical and psychological meanings. In the first place, from the sexual point of view, the average *chaver* is not content to engage in a constant series of casual affairs. After a certain period of sexual experimentation, he desires to establish a relatively permanent relationship with one person. But in addition to the physical intimacy of sex, the union also provides a psychological intimacy that may be expressed by notions such as "comradeship," "security," "dependency," "succorance," etc. And it is this psychological intimacy, primarily, that distinguishes "couples" from lovers. The criterion of the "couple" relationship, then, that which distinguishes it from a relationship between adults of the same sex who enjoy psychological intimacy, or from that of adults of opposite sex who enjoy physical intimacy, is love. A "couple" comes into being when these two kinds of intimacy are united in one relationship.

Since the *kibbutz* "couple" does not constitute a marriage because it does not satisfy the economic criterion of "marriage," it follows that the "couple" and their children do not constitute a family, economic co-operation being part of the definition of the "family." Furthermore, as has already been indicated, this group of adults and children does not satisfy the criterion of "common residence." For though the children visit their parents in the latter's room every day, their residence is in one of the "children's houses" (*bet yeladim*), where they sleep, eat, and spend most of their time.

More important, however, in determining whether or not the family exists in the *kibbutz* is the fact that the "physical care" and the "social rearing" of the children are not the responsibilities of their own parents. But these responsibilities, according to Murdock's findings, are the most important functions that the adults in the "family" have with respect to the children.

Before entering into a discussion of the *kibbutz* system of "collective education" (*chinuch meshutaf*), it should be emphasized that the *kibbutz* is a child-centered society, *par excellence*. The importance of children, characteristic of traditional Jewish culture, has been retained as one of the primary values in this avowedly antitraditional society. "The Parents Crown" is the title given to the chapter on children in an ethnography of the Eastern European Jewish village. The authors of this ethnography write (Zborowski and Herzog 1952: 308):

> Aside from the scriptural and social reasons, children are welcomed for the joy they bring beyond the gratification due to the parents—the pleasure of having a child in the house. A baby is a toy, the treasure, and the pride of the house.

This description, except for the scriptural reference, applies without qualification to the *kibbutz*.

But the *kibbutz* has still another reason for cherishing its children. The *kibbutz* views itself as an attempt to revolutionize the structure of human society and its basic social relations. Its faith in its ability to achieve this end can be vindicated only if it can raise a generation that will choose to live in this communal society, and will, thus, carry on the work that was initiated by the founders of this society—their parents.

For both these reasons the child is king. Children are lavished with attention and with care to the point where many adults admit that the children are "spoiled." Adult housing may be poor, but the children live in good houses; adult food may be meager and monotonous, but the children enjoy a variety of excellent food; there may be a shortage of clothes for adults, but the children's clothing is both good and plentiful.

Despite this emphasis on children, however, it is not their own parents who provide directly for their physical care. Indeed, the latter have no responsibility in this regard. The *kibbutz* as a whole assumes this responsibility for all its children. The latter sleep and eat in special "children's houses"; they obtain their clothes from a communal store; when ill, they are taken care of by their "nurses." This does not mean that parents are not concerned about the physical welfare of their own children. On the contrary, this is one of their primary concerns. But it does mean that the active responsibility for their care has been delegated to a community institution. Nor does it mean that parents do not work for the physical care of their children, for this is one of their strongest drives. But the fruits of their labor are not given directly to their children; they are given instead to the community which, in turn, provides for all the children. A bachelor or a "couple" without children contribute as much to the children's physical care as a "couple" with children of their own.

The family's responsibility for the socialization of children, Murdock reports, is "no less important than the physical care of the children."

> The burden of education and socialization everywhere falls primarily upon the nuclear family. . . . Perhaps more than any other single factor collective responsibility for education and socialization welds the various relationships of the family firmly together (1949: 10).

But the education and socialization of *kibbutz* children are the function of their "nurses" and teachers, and not of their parents. The infant is placed in the "infants' house" upon the mother's return from the hospital, where it remains in the care of nurses. Both parents see the infant there; the mother when she feeds it, the father upon return from work. The infant is not taken to its parents' room until its sixth month, after which it stays with them for an hour. As the child grows older, the amount of time he spends with his parents increases, and he may go to their room whenever he chooses during the day, though he must return to his "children's house" before lights-out. Since the children are in school most of the day, however, and since both parents work during the day, the children—even during their school vacations— are with their parents for a (approximately) two-hour period in the evening—from the time that the parents return from work until they go to eat their evening meal. The children may also be with their parents all day Saturday—the day of rest—if they desire.

As the child grows older he advances through a succession of "children's houses" with children of his own age, where he is supervised by a "nurse." The "nurse" institutes most of the disciplines, teaches the child his basic social skills, and is responsible for the "socialization of the instincts." The child also learns from his parents, to be sure, and they too are agents in the socialization process. But the bulk of his socialization is both entrusted, and deliberately delegated, to the "nurses" and teachers. There is little doubt but that a *kibbutz* child, bereft of the contributions of his parents to his socialization, would know his culture; deprived of the contributions of his "nurses" and teachers, however, he would remain an unsocialized individual.

As they enter the juvenile period, pre-adolescence, and adolescence, the children are gradually inducted into the economic life of the *kibbutz*. They work from an hour (grade-school students) to three hours (high-school seniors) a day in one of the economic branches under the supervision of adults. Thus, their economic skills, like most of their early social skills, are taught them by adults other than their parents. This generalization applies to the learning of values as well. In the early ages, the *kibbutz* values are inculcated by "nurses," and later by teachers. When the children enter junior high, this function, which the *kibbutz* views as paramount in importance, is delegated to the "homeroom teacher," known as the "educator" (*mechanech*), and to a "leader" (*madrich*) of the inter-*kibbutz* youth movement. The parents, of course, are also influential in the teaching of values, but the formal division of labor in the *kibbutz* has delegated this responsibility to other authorities.

Although the parents do not play an outstanding role in the socialization of their children, or in providing for their physical needs, it would be erroneous to conclude that they are unimportant figures in their children's lives. Parents are of crucial importance in the *psychological* development of the child. They serve as the objects of his most important identifications, and they provide him with a certain security and love that he obtains from no one else. If anything, the attachment of the young children to their parents is greater than it is in our own society. But this is irrelevant to the main consideration of this paper. Its purpose is to call attention to the fact that those functions of parents that constitute the *conditio sine qua non* for the existence of the "family"—the physical care and socialization of children—are not the functions of the *kibbutz* parents. It can only be concluded that in the absence of the economic and educational functions of the typical family, as well as of its characteristic of common residence, that the family does not exist in the *kibbutz*.

INTERPRETATION

It is apparent from this brief description of the *kibbutz* that most of the functions characteristic of the typical nuclear family have become the functions of the entire *kibbutz* society. This is so much the case that the *kibbutz* as a whole can almost satisfy the criteria by which Murdock defines the "family." This observation is not meant to imply that the *kibbutz* is a nuclear family. Its structure and that of the nuclear family are dissimilar. This observation does suggest, however, that the *kibbutz* can function without the family because it functions as if it, itself, were a family; and it can so function because its members perceive each other as kin, in the psychological implications of that term. The latter statement requires some explanation.

The members of the *kibbutz* do not view each other merely as fellow citizens, or as co-residents in a village, or as co-operators of an agricultural economy. Rather do they view each other as *chaverim*, or comrades, who comprise a group in which each is intimately related to the other, and in which the welfare of the one is bound up with the welfare of the other. This is a society in which the principle, "from each according to his ability, to each according to his needs," can be practised not because its members are more altruistic than the members of other societies, but because each member views his fellow as a kinsman, psychologically speaking. And just as a father in the family does not complain because he works much harder than his children, and yet he may receive no more, or even less, of the family income than they, so the *kibbutz* member whose economic productivity is high does not complain because he receives no more, and sometimes less, than a member whose productivity is low. This "principle" is taken for granted as the normal way of doing things. Since they are all *chaverim*, "it's all in the family," psychologically speaking.

In short, the *kibbutz* constitutes a *gemeinschaft*. Its patterns of interaction are interpersonal patterns; its ties are kin ties, without the biological tie of kinship. In this one respect it is the "folk society," in almost its pure form. The following quotation from Redfield (1947: 301) could have been written with the *kibbutz* in mind, so accurately does it describe the social-psychological basis of *kibbutz* culture.

> The members of the folk society have a strong sense of belonging together. The group . . . see their own resemblances and feel correspondingly united. Communicating intimately with each other, each has a strong claim on the sympathies of the others [p. 297]. . . .

the personal and intimate life of the child in the family is extended, in the folk society, into the social world of the adults. . . . It is not merely that relations in such a society are personal; it is also that they are familial. . . . the result is a group of people among whom prevail the personal and categorized relationships that characterize families as we know them, and in which the patterns of kinship tend to be extended outward from the group of genealogically connected individuals into the whole society. The kin are the type persons for all experience.

Hence it is that the bachelor and the childless "couple" do not feel that an injustice is being done them when they contribute to the support of the children of others. The children *in* the *kibbutz* are viewed as the children *of* the *kibbutz*. Parents (who are much more attached to their own children than they are to the children of others) and bachelors, alike, refer to all the *kibbutz* children as "our children."

The social perception of one's fellows as kin, psychologically speaking, is reflected in another important aspect of *kibbutz* behavior. It is a striking and significant fact that those individuals who were born and raised in the *kibbutz* tend to practise group exogamy, although there are no rules that either compel or encourage them to do so. Indeed, in the *kibbutz* in which our field work was carried out, all such individuals married outside their own *kibbutz*. When they are asked for an explanation of this behavior, these individuals reply that they cannot marry those persons with whom they have been raised and whom they, consequently, view as siblings. This suggests, as Murdock has pointed out, that "the *kibbutz* to its members *is* viewed psychologically as a family to the extent that it generates the same sort of unconscious incest-avoidance tendencies" (private communication).

What is suggested by this discussion is the following proposition: although the *kibbutz* constitutes an exception to the generalization concerning the universality of the family, structurally viewed, it serves to confirm this generalization, functionally and psychologically viewed. In the absence of a specific social group —the family—to whom society delegates the functions of socialization, reproduction, etc., it has become necessary for the entire society to become a large extended family. But only in a society whose members perceive each other psychologically as kin can it function as a family. And there would seem to be a population limit beyond which point individuals are no longer perceived as kin. That point is probably reached when the interaction of its members is no longer face-to-face; in short, when it ceases to be a primary group. It would seem probable, therefore, that only in a "familial" society, such as the *kibbutz*, is it possible to dispense with the family.

ADDENDUM, 1958

This is, quite obviously, an essay in the interpretation, rather than in the reporting of data. After rereading the paper in 1958, I realized that the suggested interpretation follows from only one conception of the role which definitions play in science. Starting with Murdock's inductive—based on a sample of 250 societies—definitions of marriage and family, I concluded that marriage and the family do not exist in the *kibbutz*, since no single group or relationship satisfies the conditions stipulated in the definitions. If I were writing this essay today, I would wish to explore alternative interpretations as well—interpretations which, despite Murdock's definitions, would affirm the existence of marriage and the family in the *kibbutz*. Hence, I shall here very briefly outline the direction which one alternative interpretation would take.

The *kibbutz*, it should be noted first, does not practice—nor does it sanction—sexual promiscuity. Each adult member is expected to form a more-or-less permanent bisexual union; and this union is socially sanctioned by the granting of a joint room to the couple. The resulting relationship is different from any other adult relationship in the *kibbutz* in a number of significant features. (1) It alone includes common domicile for persons of opposite sex. (2) It entails a higher rate of interaction than is to be found in any other bisexual relationship. (3) It involves a higher degree of emotional intimacy than is to be found in any other relationship. (4) It establishes (ideally) an exclusive sexual relationship. (5) It leads to the deliberate decision to have children. These characteristics which, separately and severally, apply uniquely to this relationship, not only describe its salient features but also comprise the motives for those who enter into

it. The couple, in short, viewed either objectively or phenome-
nologically, constitutes a unique social group in the *kibbutz*.

What, then, are we to make of this group? Since economic
co-operation is not one of its features, we can, using Murdock's
cross-cultural indices, deny that the relationship constitutes marriage. This is the conclusion of the foregoing paper. In retrospect,
however, this conclusion does not leave me entirely satisfied.
First, although we deny that the relationship constitutes a marriage, it nevertheless remains, both structurally and psychologically, a unique relationship within the *kibbutz*. Moreover, it is,
with the exception of the economic variable, similar to those
distinctive relationships in other societies to which the term
marriage is applied. Hence, if I were writing this paper today, I
should want to ask, before concluding that marriage is not universal, whether Murdock's inductive definition of marriage is, in
the light of the *kibbutz* data, the most fruitful, even for his large
sample; and if it were agreed that it is, whether it ought not to be
changed or qualified so as to accommodate the relationship between *kibbutz* "spouses." Here I can only briefly explore the
implications of these questions.

If the stated characteristics of the *kibbutz* relationship are
found in the analogous relationship (marriage) in other societies
—and I do not know that they are—it is surely apposite to ask
whether Murdock's definition could not or should not stipulate
them, as well as those already stipulated. For if they are found
in other societies, on what theoretical grounds do we assign a
higher priority to sex or economics over emotional intimacy, for
example? Hence, if this procedure were adopted (and assuming
that the characteristics of the *kibbutz* relationship were to be
found in the marriage relationship in other societies) we would,
since the *kibbutz* relationship satisfies all but one of the cross-
cultural criteria, term the *kibbutz* relationship "marriage."

Alternatively, we might suggest that Murdock's definition of
marriage, as well as the one suggested here, are unduly specific;
that cross-cultural research is most fruitfully advanced by means
of analytic, rather than substantive or enumerative, definitions.
Thus, for example, we might wish to define marriage as "any
socially sanctioned relationship between non-sanguineally-related

cohabiting adults of opposite sex which satisfied felt needs—mutual, symmetrical, or complementary." A non-enumerative definition of this type would certainly embrace all known cases now termed "marriage" and would, at the same time, include the *kibbutz* case as well.

In the same vein, and employing similar definitional procedures, alternative conclusions can be suggested with respect to the family in the *kibbutz*. Although parents and children do not comprise a family, as Murdock defines family, they nevertheless constitute a unique group within the *kibbutz*, regardless of the term with which we may choose to designate it. (1) Children are not only desired by *kibbutz* parents, but, for the most part, they are planned. (2) These children—and no others—are called by their parents "sons" and "daughters"; conversely, they call their parents—and no other adults—"father" and "mother." (3) Parents and children comprise a social group in both an interactional and an emotional, if not in a spatial, sense. That is, though parents and children do not share a common domicile, they are identified by themselves and by others as a uniquely cohesive unit within the larger *kibbutz* society; this unit is termed a *mishpacha* (literally, "family"). (4) The nature of their interaction is different from that which obtains between the children and any other set of adults. (5) The rate of interaction between parents and children is greater than that between the children and any other set of adults of both sexes. (6) The psychological ties that bind them are more intense than those between the children and any other set of adults of both sexes.

Here, then, we are confronted with the same problem we encountered with respect to the question of *kibbutz* marriage. Because the parent-child relationship in the *kibbutz* does not entail a common domicile, physical care, and social rearing—three of the stipulated conditions in Murdock's definition of family—we concluded that the family does not exist in the *kibbutz*. But, since parents and children comprise a distinct and differentiated social group within the *kibbutz*, I am now not entirely satisfied with a conclusion which seems, at least by implication, to ignore its presence. For, surely, regardless of what else we might do with this group, we cannot simply ignore it. We can either perceive it, in cross-cultural perspective, as a unique group, and invent a new term to refer to it, or we can revise Murdock's definition of family in order to accommodate it.

Should the latter alternative be preferred, it could be effected in the following way. The stipulation of "common residence" could be qualified to refer to a reference, rather than to a membership, residence; and this is what the parental room is, for children as well as for parents. When, for example, they speak of "my room" or "our room," the children almost invariably refer to the parental room, not to their room in the communal children's house. If, moreover, the educational and economic functions of the family were interpreted as responsibilities for which parents were either immediately or ultimately responsible, the *kibbutz* parent-child unit would satisfy these criteria as well. For, though parents do not provide immediately for the physical care of their children, neither do they renounce their responsibility for them. Rather, they seek to achieve this end by working jointly rather than separately for the physical welfare of all the children—including, of course, their own.

Similarly, though the parents have only a minor share in the formal socialization process, they do not simply give their children to others to be raised as the latter see fit. Rather, socialization is entrusted to specially designated representatives, nurses and teachers, who rear the children, not according to their own fancy, but according to rules and procedures established by the parents. In short, though parents do not themselves socialize their children, they assume the ultimate responsibility for their socialization. Interpreted in this way, the relationship between *kibbutz* parents and children satisfies Murdock's definition of family.

To conclude, this addendum represents an alternative method of interpreting the *kibbutz* data concerning the relationship between spouses, and among parents and children. I am not suggesting that this interpretation is necessarily more fruitful than the one adopted in the paper. Certainly, however, I should want to examine it carefully before concluding, as I previously did, that marriage and the family are not universal.

14 INTERGENERATIONAL CONFLICT AMONG THE MOSSI: FATHER AND SON

Elliott P. Skinner

INTERGENERATIONAL CONFLICT is almost universal in human societies; that between father and son is often the most dramatic. Freud sees this conflict as the primeval rivalry between father and son over sexual access to the mother, and uses this basic postulate to delineate the nature of man and his relation to society. The Oedipus complex is a valid explanation for certain conflicts within the family which are ultimately responsible for an individual's maladjustment to his society. But it is questionable whether one is justified in extrapolating from individual psychology to the study of human society and cultural systems. The relations between generations and those between fathers and sons are also social relations and thus conditioned by the social structure and the cultural system within which they take place. Therefore, any serious attempt to understand these relationships must be viewed against the background of particular socio-cultural systems. Only when we know this background can we investigate and understand the individual reaction of father to son. I will attempt to analyze a pattern of conflict between father and son among the Mossi as a function of their socio-cultural system. I will show not only how the social structure of Mossi society builds and maintains these relationships, but how they support rather than impair the socio-cultural continuity of the system.

Before looking at intergenerational conflict among the Mossi as characterized by father-son relations, it will perhaps be well,

Originally published in the *Journal of Conflict Resolution*, Vol. 5, 1961, pp. 55–60. Reprinted with permission of the author and of the editor of the *Journal of Conflict Resolution*.

in order to facilitate an understanding of the problem, to present a brief outline of the structure of Mossi society. The one and one-half million Mossi live in the Voltaic Republic which is just north of Ghana. They have traditionally been governed by rulers called Moro Nabas who once held feudal-like control over the provinces, districts and villages which comprised their kingdoms (Skinner 1957). A rather complex hierarchial administrative apparatus extended the power of the rulers into the smallest village, and funneled taxes and tribute back to them. Most of the taxes were paid in grain and livestock, the basic local commodities. Other economic activities in the society were cotton manufacture and caravan trading between the forest and desert zones of West Africa.

The Mossi are divided into stratified royal, noble, and commoner patrilineages. Characteristic of this segmentary lineage system is a process by which royal sublineages descend serially until they merge with the mass of commoner lineages. Before the French conquered the Mossi in 1896, there were large classes of serfs and slaves of non-Mossi origin, but these persons have now been grouped into lineages and have become Mossi. The basic Mossi settlement pattern consists of virilocal, polygynous households grouped into villages. Marriages are arranged between unrelated persons through the agency of lineage members who establish "friendly" relationships. The two friends may ask their lineage heads for women to exchange as wives, or the "friend" who has received more gifts from his opposite number may give over a wife. Since it is mainly the older men who have women and goods at their disposal and can make friends, they are the ones who receive wives. As a result, young men usually lack wives and must content themselves with occasional lovers until they inherit wives from lineage members, or in lieu of this obtain women from chiefs and later on return the daughters of these women to the chiefs (Skinner 1960a).

The Mossi are strongly patrilineal, and despite the advantages which may accrue to the fathers of girls in the marriage exchange, men desire male children to carry on the lineage. Men are accorded complete control over all of their children, and questions of paternity cannot weaken the patrilineal system because the Mossi emphasize sociological rather than biological parenthood.

Any child born to a man's wife is unquestionably his whether he is at home or has been away for years. This patrilineal principle is further strengthened by the ritual prohibition against a woman giving birth to her child in any but her husband's village. If this happens accidentally, the husband's patrilineage must be propitiated lest harm befall either the child or its mother. Even when the Mossi mother takes the child to be reared in her own patrilineal village during the lactation period, she is not allowed to take it away in the usual manner. She must sneak away with it so that neither her husband nor his lineage brothers will see her.

A woman normally remains away with the child for about two to three years and only returns after the child can take care of himself. If she becomes pregnant shortly after she comes home, she again returns to her parents taking the baby and the young child with her. Ultimately the woman comes home, but if her first child is a boy she is enjoined by custom to leave it with her patrilineage so that she will be able to rear her younger child. The Mossi believe that it is "dangerous for two young brothers to urinate in the same hole" and fathers send their first son to live with the boy's maternal relatives until he is grown. The important point here is that a father has little contact with the one son who is most likely to be his heir and successor. Nevertheless, it is this first son, and not any of the younger ones, with whom a man is most often in conflict.

A first son does not return to his father's compound until he is past puberty, but does visit him from time to time. These visits are quite formal and from very early time the first son is taught to be circumspect with his father. He learns to efface himself before his father and not to seek attention from him even though he sees younger siblings playing with him. When the boy does return home he is made to live with other young men of the extended family either within the compound or in special young men's quarters outside the compound.

Sons normally work for their fathers most of the day and are only permitted to work for themselves in the late afternoon. Their corporate labor is used for the maintenance of the compound and to meet its standard obligations. The heads of households also use some of these resources to maintain the nexus of gift exchanges which are calculated to bring wives to the lineage. A

Mossi boy may never question the use to which his labor is put by his father. His father may send him to help a friend build a hut, dig a well, or even cultivate a field. Mossi fathers believe that since they are responsible for the birth of their sons, they have the right to command all of their sons' goods and services. Implicit here, but not often stated, is the understanding that the sons, in turn, will inherit the father's goods.

The wives who normally devolve to a man either through inheritance or through marriage partners during the development cycle of the extended family are the source of actual or potential conflict between sons and fathers. Young men are required to treat their fathers' wives with the greatest formality, but this strict relationship is constantly undermined by the realization by both the boys and the women that some day they may be married to each other. The problem is further complicated by the fact that women and their future husbands live in the same household and are constantly seeing each other. To avoid unnecessary encounters between them, the Mossi practice a form of avoidance. Mossi fathers do not like their grown sons to visit the inside of the compound for trivial reasons. Furthermore, they do not like to meet their sons in the doorways of the compound. If a son is entering or leaving the compound he usually says something in a loud voice so that a person approaching him will know of his presence; the Mossi father does the same thing.

Mossi fathers of limited means, and even wealthy ones, are loath to procure wives for their sons. They declare that their sons do not want the responsibilities that go with having wives. Today, when many young men migrate to Ghana for work (Skinner 1960b), the old men say that if boys wanted wives they would stay and aid their fathers to obtain them rather than go away to earn money for such trifles as bicycles. Moreover, the fathers point to the pattern of young men's sexual liaisons with married women as evidence of their opinion. The fact is that the Mossi father sees the possession of a wife by his son as representing the economic advantages which the son will gain when he dies. The antagonism between father and son is further heightened by the father's realization that the son's very advancement in the community is dependent on his father's death. Seen in this way, the father's death is imbued with a greater emotional impact than would normally be accounted for. Thus, fathers resist conferring the status of husband on their sons because this would mean that they themselves would have to adopt the status of elder, a status which, while conferring honor upon a man, also suggests his coming demise.

Mossi fathers are so sensitive about being eventually replaced by their sons that they often resent the boys' growth and development. The first son is the target of this fear and hostility because he is the one who will benefit most from his father's death. However, if the first son happens to die, then the son who is next in line becomes the subject of his father's uneasiness. Mossi men have been known to upbraid their sons for growing beards, the significance of which is seen in the fact that men do grow beards as a sign of mourning on the death of their father. Mossi fathers are also very anxious as to whether the "heads" of their eldest sons are "stronger" than their own. If a boy shows by his actions that he is not afraid of his father, then he is said to have a bigger head than his father and is in danger of being killed by sorcery instigated by his progenitor. As a rule, Mossi fathers tend to avoid any situation in which their eldest sons may be compared with them. For example, a man and his grown son do not walk together for fear of the embarrassment which would be created if a stranger, not recognizing the age differential between them, greeted the son before he greeted the father. Once when I asked a chief why his eldest son sat far away from him while his younger sons sat near by, he said, "Since he is going to inherit everything I own when I die, why should he come close to me now?" Some fathers even give their eldest sons separate compounds to see less of them. Mangin (1921: 35–36), writing about the Mossi some fifty years ago, said, ". . . the eldest son seldom remains in his father's household, especially if the father is wealthy or a naba [chief]; he is much too afraid that his son may do away with him, the sooner to come into his inheritance."

Mossi social structure induces opposition between father and son. Yet, owing to the emphasis which they place on patrilineality, the Mossi value sons who can carry on the lineage. A man without sons is considered to have been a failure, and fathers are expected to take an interest in their sons. This is especially true with regard to the first son since he is most often the one who succeeds his father. Thus, while a Mossi father cannot show affection for his eldest son, he is always aware of what this son is doing and very often summons him at night to give him advice and counsel as to how he should behave. According to custom, the Moro Naba of Wagadougou places his son in a district about 50 miles from the capital and almost never sees him in public. Nevertheless, it is common knowledge that they often meet at night and that the father scarcely ever refuses a request from his son. So concerned are Moro Nabas over their sons that when the first son of Moro Naba Wobogo (1890–96) took ill and died, he had all the guardians of the boy executed.

The relationship between a chief and his son shows quite clearly the other side of the traditional opposition between a Mossi and his first son. Owing to a lack of primogeniture within the Mossi political system, any person within the ruling sublineage or even within the lineage is theoretically eligible to rule. A chief who has not angered his political superiors may be relatively certain that his son will succeed him, and fears that the boy will welcome his death. At the same time, the chief is also aware that during the interregnum caused by his death some other relative may inherit the chieftainship (Skinner 1960c). He must therefore spend a great deal of his time establishing the right connections so that he may be relatively sure that his son will succeed him. It is very important for a chief that this should happen. If, by chance, his son should not succeed him, then for all practical purposes his line would lose its nobility and might even be reduced to commoner status. This would mean, among other things, that he himself would lose his position as an ancestor of the ruling chief, that his name would be dropped from the genealogy of the new line of chiefs, and that he would lose the veneration which normally would have come to him if his descendants had succeeded him. The Mossi say that aside from the possible conflict which prevents a chief's son from sitting with his father, there is another element, the fear that if both of them stayed together, they might be harmed by the same natural or supernatural agency. Thus, in a sense, this separation functions to ensure the continuity between father and son, a continuity which is treasured in this patrilineal society.

Although it is considered a sign of filial perfidy for a son to yearn for the death of his father—and no one would openly voice such a desire—the Mossi say that some young men "just wait for their fathers to die." The death of a father, whether wished for or not, does give a man wives and property, and does release him from a few ritual restrictions. The most important of these pertains to various aspects of funeral celebrations, a not unimportant thing since the funeral is the most important ceremony in Mossi society. If his father is still alive, a man may not beat the drums at a funeral, and he may not visit the compound of the dead person with the other celebrants at an important stage of the ceremony. More important, however, is the prohibition against a man taking a bow and arrow and dancing. It is during this dance that young men show their skill by dancing within a ring of people, pantomiming the activities of warriors, stalking, ambushing and killing their enemies. No young man would willingly desire the death of his father so that he could take part in these activities, but his prestige does rise when he can show his skill and finesse at this sport.

However, even after death the antagonism between father and son is not laid to rest. The son continues to reassure his father after death that he, at least, has not taken advantage of him, and attempts to disavow the conflict between them in order to gain his legacy. During the burial ceremony the father's body is carried through a hole made in the wall of the compound. It is then placed on the ground parallel to the wall but a few feet away from it. The first son is then carried through the same hole and made to stand between the wall and the body. Then he attempts twice to step over the body before going over it the third time. This is to show the people that he has been faithful to his father during his lifetime and has not slept with any of his father's wives. A man who had violated this norm would not go through this ritual for fear that his father's shade would kill him. Needless to say, a man who shows his guilt by refusing to perform this act is disinherited by the minimal lineage.

Until the end of the funeral celebration some months or even a year later, the eldest son or other relatives of the dead man are barred from using his property or appropriating it. If the dead man had been a chief, the command of his territory is even turned over to ritual or administrative personnel for the duration of the interregnum, and is not allowed to remain in the hands of his son or heir. It is only during and after the funeral ceremony that a man may fulfill the ritual obligations that will give him the right to utilize his father's property. The most important of these rites is that granting a man the use of his father's granary. This privilege is expressly denied the eldest son in his father's lifetime, while it is granted to the younger brother. During the burial ceremony the undertaker trusses up a living sheep and places it on the granary so that the dead person could take both meat and cereal with him to the land of the ancestors. The sheep is later removed and eaten, but no one is allowed to use the grain for any purpose. During the funeral ceremony the eldest son and the dead man's brother go to the granary where the eldest son is ritually shown his father's grain by his father's brother. Next the father's brother takes three calabash measures of grain from the top of the granary and mixes them with three measures which the eldest son takes from the bottom of the granary. The grain is then given to the eldest daughter of the dead man to be cooked for the evening meal. According to one informant, "this rite is designed to show the people that the eldest son has followed his father's prescription in everything, and those things which were forbidden to him before he can now perform with impunity."

It is not quite true, however, that the son can now do all the things formerly prohibited to him. He must still indicate that he has not usurped his father's property and so must ritually leave his father access to it. For example, if a son decides to take over his father's compound instead of building a new one, he has to close the gate his father used and open one for himself. Similarly, if he takes his father's wives he must close up the doors in their huts which his father used when he went to visit them and open new doors. If he does not do these things, he will be censured by the ancestors who will be angry when they discover that on coming to the compound they are visiting not the father but the son. As one man said, "One must close up the things of the dead and open things for the living." What is true about the doors which the ancestors use when they come to visit the living is also true about the sacrifices which must be made to the ancestors. If the heir inherits the head wife of his father whose task it was to prepare the repast for the ancestors, then she, now as his wife, may continue to do so. But if the heir's mother was the first wife and does not marry one of her husband's relatives, she is still considered the wife of the dead man and is forbidden to prepare the sacrifices. Should she try to do so she would be offering sacrifices to her husband since he would now be one of the ancestors, something a wife is forbidden to do. Any man who violates this rule is said to "have allowed his head" to set him against his father and runs the risks of ritual punishment by the ancestors.

DISCUSSION

The potential conflict between father and son in Mossi society stems from the structure of that society, especially its system of inheritance. In this strongly patrilineal structure, fathers have complete control over their sons and over all goods and services devolving to the family. Sons do not display their resentment of this control, nor do they ordinarily challenge paternal authority, but the possibility of their doing so, particularly in the case of oldest sons (who eventually replace their fathers), is recognized by members of the society. Institutionalized patterns of avoidance and separation between first son and father, while indicative of potential conflict, operate to prevent the hostility between them from disrupting their relationship. To interpret the avoidance between father and son and the ritual following the father's death as signs of a breach in their relationship would be fallacious, for the first averts situations which might arouse open conflict between them, and the second emphasizes paternal dominance. In this sense what appears to be disruptive is positively functional for the maintenance of traditional father-son relations. Thus the institutionalized recognition of potential conflict between father and son tends to preserve the existing norms of patrilineality in Mossi society.

15 THE FAMILY SYSTEM OF JAMAICA

William Davenport

FROM THE PERIOD OF SLAVERY through Emancipation and up to the present, interest in the Jamaican Negro family has been high; there is now a body of literature on the subject greater than that for any other Caribbean island society. This interest has not always been sociological however. Rather it was stimulated by various conditions found in the lower-class family system that offended middle- and upper-class sensibilities. These conditions, obviously, refer to deviations from the prescribed Christian patterns of marriage, sexual relations, and faithful monogamy. As viewed through a screen of Euro-American middle- and upper-class values, these deviant patterns have been interpreted as degenerate or broken-down forms of the accepted norms. Some writers have liberally mixed this view with problems of race, colour, and the legacy of slavery, while others, attempting to avoid these evaluative pitfalls, have approached it from the point of view of a Negro or social class subculture which has different historical origins. The fact remains that Jamaican society is a single society, containing within it family patterns and legal norms which are of English derivation, as well as common-law patterns, which have evolved locally, and these differences are highly correlated with variations in colour and social class. These differing patterns are not mutually exclusive or discrete, but blend into one another by a gradual transition, making typologies both difficult and misleading.

Reprinted from *Social and Economic Studies*, Vol. 10, 1961, pp. 420–54, with the permission of the author and of the editor of *Social and Economic Studies*.

To complicate the situation further, there are in Jamaica large ethnic groups (e.g., Chinese and East Indian) whose family systems are again different; these, however, are outside the scope of this paper.

Although it is acknowledged that an analysis of the Jamaican family system should proceed from a holistic view of the society—a perspective from which variations in the family would be seen in relationship to variations in the total social system—this cannot be done here. This regrettable limitation is enforced by limitations in the descriptive data on Jamaica, for nearly all of the detailed studies concentrate on the lower class alone. This bias will be perpetuated here, and furthermore, it will be assumed that the middle- and upper-class family systems are homogeneous, and indistinguishable from those of comparable class strata in England and the United States. This assumption is supported by Henriques (1953), the only writer to attempt an analysis of the Jamaican family in terms of social class. We must also assume that intuitive judgments of social position are reliable, for no comprehensive study of the indices and determinants of social class has been made. Ellis' work (1956; 1957) is a valuable beginning, but his study of Christiana fails to include the lower range of the stratification hierarchy, which is precisely the segment which has commanded the most attention with regard to the family.

The main body of descriptive data on the Jamaican family comes from Simey's pioneer study (1946) which is based upon a sample of families from seven widely separated rural districts; Henriques' work based upon census data and field observations in the parish of Portland; a community study of a mountain settlement called "Rocky Roads" by Cohen (1954; 1955; 1955a; 1956); brief field studies of two coastal villages called "Mangrove Beach" and "Black Point" in the parishes of Clarendon and Westmoreland; Cumper's meticulous study of sampled census data from Porter's Mountain in Westmoreland and the Caymanas Estate (1958; see also M. Smith 1957); and the most detailed field studies of all, a comparison of three communities called "Sugartown," "Mocca," and "Orange Grove" by Kerr (1952) and Clarke (1953; 1957). Information for the analysis to follow will be taken from all these sources, but

mainly from Clarke (1957) and this writer's own field studies
(1956), and unless otherwise noted, it will be from the latter.

The most tangible aspect of the family is the household, and
being physically discrete, it can be dissected, analyzed, and compared with considerable precision. Yet the household is a complicated group, responding structurally to a number of less
tangible systems, no one of which will account for all the variance
to be found in one society. For this reason, we will proceed with
separate analyses of the systems which have the most immediate
effect on the household, in an effort to expose the principles of
organization. The fundamental feature of the household is its
organization according to the principles of kinship. Of equal significance are the influences which the patterns of sexual behaviour, marriage, and reproduction exert on it. Thirdly, it is a group
within which the labour and skills of its members are interde-
pendently organized for production, for consumption, and for
maintaining itself a relatively independent social unit. Finally, it
is a social group which changes over time, and in some instances
it has direct continuity beyond the life span of its members.

KINSHIP

The Jamaican kinship system is based on what may be called
kindred organization. That is, every individual is surrounded by
a set of consanguines who have some mutual rights, obligations,
and responsibilities toward him. Unlike the lineage, this set of kin
is reckoned bilaterally, and its relationship to this common relative (and his siblings) is the only thing all members have in common with each other. Thus, the kindred is not a corporate kin
group of any kind, and there are as many kindred groups in a
society as there are sets of siblings. Half of an individual's kindred is made up of his mother's kin, and half is made up of his
father's kin, while only full siblings have identical kindreds.

In Jamaica the range of consanguinity is supposed to include
all known kin of either sex, reckoned in any way. This inclusive
span is generally referred to by lower-class persons as "family".
"My family" and "he is some family to me" are phrases which
signify consanguinity. Genealogies will reveal, however, that the
effective range of consanguinity is quite narrow, and people can

rarely trace their collateral kin ties accurately farther than the children of first cousins, i.e., to "second cousins." Beyond this range only the knowledge that there is some relationship is retained, and after a few generations even this is lost. Parents, parents' siblings, first cousins, children, siblings' children (both sexes referred to as "niece"), and grandchildren form a hard core of close kin that is sometimes described as "near family," in order to distinguish it from more distant relatives, called "far family." A person's kindred, then, will be defined as his near family, plus any other kin with whom he may have special relationships.

The behaviour and sentiment that is supposed to exist between an individual and his kindred members should be friendly, co-operative, and "loving". It is always reciprocal, and is generally felt to increase with closeness of relationship and decrease slightly with collateral distance. Although many arguments and disputes arise between kindred members, these are almost always settled or quieted without recourse to the police or the law. This is in sharp contrast to the readiness with which Jamaicans carry these conflicts to these agencies when it involves distant kin or non-kin. When kindred members live close to each other, there will be constant exchanges of assistance and favours of a quite different sort than between unrelated but friendly neighbours. Some persons are so kin-oriented as to believe that close friendship should be maintained only between close relatives, never between unrelated persons.

Sexual relationships between a person and anyone of his kindred are generally considered to be incestuous, but there is some local variation in this. Genealogies of some people living at Mangrove Beach who came from a district in St. Elizabeth parish contained many children of first-cousin unions, and these were considered to be neither incestuous nor particularly close. Other people living in the same village who came from a district in Manchester felt that sexual relations between kin of any degree whatsoever were bad, and their genealogies confirmed their abhorrence of close unions. At Black Point, the feeling was that first cousin mating was too close, but the preferred spouse was a person who was far family, i.e., someone beyond the second-cousin range.

Within the nuclear relationships of parents to children and

sibling to sibling, the most striking is that between the mother and child. Unless they are separated by some unavoidable circumstance, the mother remains the dominant figure in the child's life until adolescence. Even in later life, this long, intense emotional and physical dependence is expressed by an overt adulation and idealization of the mother, although there is a respectable amount of evidence to suggest the presence of an underlying pattern of unconscious ambivalence of high intensity. The father is of equal structural significance in the kinship system, and every child bears the surname of its father—except when there is some reason to hide the identity of the father—regardless of the marital status of the mother and father. This differs from the United States, or Great Britain, where children who are jurally defined as illegitimate do not carry their fathers' names. The affective relationship between father and child, however, is rarely as positive or as intense as between the mother and child. This is partly due to the more direct and more prolonged nature of the services she performs for her children, and partly due to the fact that father and child are frequently separated from each other upon the break-up of the parents' common-law union. It is not uncommon to find persons, for example, who have never seen their fathers or have only the most casual acquaintance with them. Still, one finds fathers and their children who have a very intimate and devoted relationship, revealing that there is nothing in the kinship system, as such, that weakens the father-child dyad. Yet the mother-child relationship is the all-important one as far as the Jamaican household is concerned, for the mother and her children are considered to be almost inseparable; in contrast, the father may be separated from his children if the situation demands it.

Between siblings the overt, affective relationships are both positive and strong. From childhood this feeling intensifies between siblings of the same sex, as they internalize the incest taboo and adopt more restraint toward siblings of the opposite sex, and as they learn their respective sex-typed roles. An elder sister may be idealized in much the same way as the mother, since young girls are charged with much of the care of their younger brothers and sisters just as soon as they are capable of assuming these responsibilities. Perhaps the best way to describe the ideal sibling relationship is by the word "sharing". Youngsters are taught at an early age to share almost everything they receive with their brothers and sisters, and a great deal of this carries over into adult life. This model of sibling affection cuts across half-sibling lines with little diminution, for both half- and full-siblings are usually reared together under the care and supervision of their common mother, and they are held together by their enduring affection and obligation toward her.

The importance of the sibling relationship in habitual thinking is expressed in several ways. Close, non-sexual friendships with non-kins are always described in terms of sibling roles, and the intensity of such friendships is frequently expressed in how close they approximate each other. Genealogical relationships of collateral relatives are always described by their connecting sibling relationship; for example, a distant cousin might be described as "my grandfather and his grandfather were brothers", or a second cousin as "my father and his grandmother were brother and sister".

Structurally, however, half- and full-siblings are not alike, for only full-siblings share identical kindreds, and by this, the same sets of reciprocal kinship ties. This structural difference is further marked in some instances by the fact that some of the sibling group may be legitimate and some illegitimate, or "outside," as it is termed in Jamaica. The differences here will be discussed further in connection with marriage and the household itself.

The structural difference between half- and full-brothers and sisters is both reflected and masked by kinship terminology. Both half- and full-siblings refer to each other as "brother" and "sister" without distinction. If the half relationship is to be expressed, it will be done so by mentioning which parent they share, e.g., "same mother" or "same father". On the other hand, a spouse will never refer to his spouse's children by another person as his children or even as his stepchildren. A stepchild is of no consanguine relationship, and there is no term for him in the lower-class terminology. This failure to recognize affinal or conjugal relationships in the kinship terminology is also to be noted in the terms "aunt" and "uncle", which refer only to siblings of biological parents, and not to their spouses. If these are to be designated, the terms "aunt-in-law" and "uncle-in-law" might be used, but informants disagree as whether or not these are really kinship terms. While there is no term for stepchild, a step-parent may be called "mother-in-law" or "father-in-law." As one informant put it, "in-law" means "coming in." But the point of reference here is usually the household and not the kindred. That is, a father-in-law is a man who is living with one's mother, it being understood that one is usually living in the same house as one's mother. The term "mother-in-law" can be used for the woman one's father is living with, but more commonly, it refers to the mother of one's spouse.

When informants are asked whether they have different feelings toward their mothers' and fathers' kin (i.e., different halves of their kindreds), a preference for the mothers' is usually stated. But most of these same informants are quick to explain that this is because they have had more to do with them and know them better, while those who know both equally well show little such preference. All agree, however, that in sexual restrictions and other jural relationships there is no difference between these kin. This is mentioned only to emphasize the bilaterality of the structure, despite the fact of the mother's dominant role in socialization and the effective importance her kin may possess.

In summary, the strong, positive feeling toward close kin, the bilateral structure of the kindred, the cohesiveness of the mother-child relationship in contrast with the divisibility that may obtain between a father and his child, and the equality and solidarity between siblings are the important parameters of kinship in the organization of the lower-class household.

SEXUAL AND MARITAL RELATIONS

Marriage in Jamaica, duly consummated and fully recognized by Church and state, differs in no essential way from marriage in England and the United States. But, as mentioned above, legally recognized marriage, though characteristic of upper socio-economic strata, is not the only form of conjugal relationship to be found in the lower class. While all groups and strata recognize the institution of legal marriage as desirable, in some ways at least, there are significant differences between the lower and upper classes in the kinds and effectiveness of the social sanctions which reinforce and maintain it. In the middle- and upper-class strata, the norms of sexual behaviour, parenthood, and co-

residence of spouses are such that they channel people into marriage, and Jamaican law assumes that the attractions of these are
sufficiently strong to lead most adults into the accepted forms.
Hence the law prescribes only the conditions under which the
marital contract shall be concluded, upheld, and dissolved, leaving the decision to enter into such a contract up to the decisions
of the individuals concerned. All polygamous forms of marriage
are prohibited by law, but between this specific limitation and
the regular, approved forms of Christian marriage, there is a permissible range of conjugal relationship, which is neither illegal
nor recognized by the law. These variations will be called
common-law and non-legal marriage.

Typologies of lower-class marriages have been offered by
Simey (1946: 18–23), Henriques (1953: 105–6), and Clarke
(1957: 77–80), but these will not be followed too closely, for in
some cases they do not underscore the important social relationships of which they are but a part. The paragraphs to follow are
an attempt to show how these variations in marriage are to be
seen as subcultural responses to different structural relationships
within the Jamaican social system, while at the same time, they
respect the norms and laws that govern legal marriage.

Both middle- and lower-class subcultures apply a "double
standard" of expectancies to sexual behaviour, which allows the
men more freedom in these matters than women. Lower-class
socialization and adult sanctions, however, prove to be quite
ineffectual in maintaining the chastity of young women past sexual
maturity. Kerr (1952: 44) and Clarke (1957: 90–96) both bring
out this point, and data from Mangrove Beach and Black Point
fully corroborate their findings. The lower-class attitude toward
pregnancy and motherhood is that they are more or less inevitable, regardless of marital status; but in the middle-class view,
they are inextricably associated with marriage, and co-residence
of husband and wife. The lower-class mother most frequently has
her first child while still residing in her parental household and
before she has concluded any kind of heterosexual relationship
that will lead to legal marriage. She suffers little more than a
formalized upbraiding from her mother for the trouble and expense it incurs, and there is little or no moral feeling about the
matter. Such an event would be little short of catastrophic in

middle-class society, and when a pregnancy does occur before marriage, all efforts are directed toward getting the couple quickly married so as to prevent an illegitimate birth.

Even though considerable freedom in sexual relations is allowed by lower-class norms, the partners expect each other to be faithful, and persistent infidelity inevitably leads to a break-up of the relationship. Lower-class sexual affairs, beginning as they do in experimentation and graduating into a series of relationships of varying permanence and from which a number of children are born, do not inevitably lead to marriage, as they seem to in the middle class when they occur. They are to be regarded as non-legal unions, with and without the common co-residence of the partners, and they are not the functional or the subcultural equivalent of legal marriage. For this reason, the people do not even call them "marriages", which term is reserved for true legal marriage. There is actually no single term for such unions and they are variously referred to as "living a sweetheart life" or, infrequently, as "common-law marriage". Nor do the partners, even of the most long-lasting non-legal unions, call each other "husband" and "wife", which signify the status of legally married persons. Only the terms "boy friend", "girl friend", and "sweetheart" are used to designate a common-law marital partner.

Married persons, and particularly the wife, are accorded more respectability than are persons living in common-law. Married women are always referred to or addressed as "Mistress So and So", a distinction a common-law wife never receives. Few women, indeed, do not regard legal marriage with a suitable man as superior to any non-legal arrangement, even though men are quite often not so enthusiastic. A few, even, are quite vocal in their condemnation of the whole marriage system, but these same men are generally desirous of seeing their daughters legally married someday. This association of marital respectability with women more than with men is but part of the double standard of sexual behaviour and is related to the general feeling in the Anglo-American tradition that women are the real bearers of the proprieties of the culture.

Just as lower-class values charge marriage with a high degree of respectability, so, too, they assess it primarily as a religious institution. A marriage is really not a proper marriage unless it is concluded in a religious setting. As Clarke (1957: 76) also notes, lower-class persons are not always aware of the fact that by law a marriage can be performed only by an authorized marriage officer, and that many religious sect leaders who perform them are not so authorized. In any case, civil ceremonies are rarely performed in rural districts, even though this is the least troublesome and least expensive of marriage ceremonies.

Legal marriage, in contrast with non-legal, is regarded as practically indissoluble. This is due partly to ignorance of the divorce laws, partly to the costs and legal difficulties in obtaining divorce, and partly to the strong religious associations. When this great respect for the permanence of the marital status is coupled with anxieties over the responsibilities toward a wife and one's legitimate children, the positive attractions of respectability are easily outweighed. And since there is no real stigma attached to common-law marriage, the latter can and does remain both appealing and popular in the lower class.

The genuine respect for legal marriage that is held by lower-class persons, despite the high frequency of non-legal marriage, is revealed by the severity of disdain that is heaped upon persons who violate the norms of regular marriage. A deserter in marriage is just as much a deserter, and an adulterer in marriage is just as much an adulterer by lower-class norms, and perhaps even more so, as he is by middle and upper-class standards. But this applies only to legally married persons, and the same behaviour with respect to non-legal unions is not nearly so negatively viewed, and this is also the way it is regarded by law. Many lower-class persons become very indignant at the seemingly flippant attitudes toward the sanctity of marriage which many persons of higher social status seem to have. On the other hand, unsophisticated middle- and upper-class persons remain in a perpetual state of indignation at what seems to them to be promiscuity and a hypocritical tolerance of common-law marriage in the lower class.

Nearly all aspects of non-legal marriage are more variable than in legal marriage. For instance, in some quite stable common-law unions, to which several children have been born, the spouses do not share a common residence at all. Rather, the man visits his girl friend daily, takes some of his meals with her, and occasionally sleeps in her house, but still participates fully in his own household of which she is no part, while their children may spend part of their time in both households. This somewhat anomalous form of residence is in no way considered either inappropriate or odd, and, in fact, accounted for nearly 20 per cent of the common-law unions at Black Point, where most marital unions of all kinds took place between members of that single community. Such an arrangement would be viewed as somewhat odd, however, if the couple were legally married. The termination of a non-legal union is also quite arbitrary and may be permanent; or it may be only a change from co-residence of the partners to intermittent co-residence or some kind of divided residences as described above. But in all cases these decisions are left up to the partners themselves, with kin and society either indifferent or unable to influence greatly the outcome. With regard to property, a common-law union is regarded as having little or no communal property held jointly between husband and wife, or held in the name of either for both partners. When the relationship is terminated, each person is supposed to take what belongs to him, but there are frequent and bitter disputes as to who actually owns what, and in these situations, relatives and friends are likely to become involved.

As already mentioned, despite the attempts of mothers to keep their daughters chaste, at the onset of sexual maturity nearly all lower-class girls have affairs. These are usually with young men of their same age set, but not infrequently a young girl's introduction to sex is by a considerably older man. The mean age of young women at first intercourse at Mangrove Beach and Black Point is 16.6. years, and for young men, about a year later. Young men of this age who have attended school are beginning to look for work, and their parents, especially when poor, are very anxious to see them working, so that they may begin to contribute something toward their own support. Work, needless to say, is nearly always scarce, and many who could be used on their own family property wish to find something more remunerative and interesting. New interests in young women, strong desires to look and dress well, and the attractiveness of participating in adult recreations all increase the need for money, which their parents cannot usually provide. For these young men, this is the beginning of a period of great ambiguity and instability, for they are physically adult, psychologically ready to become independent from their households of orientation, yet unable to find interesting or steady employment which would enable them to begin adult life. During these years, young men and women make and break their sexual alliances easily in what is really a period of sexual experimentation. Sooner or later the young woman becomes pregnant, and the young man responsible is either unable or unwilling to do much about it. Besides, there are many things he wishes to do for himself, and the last thing he wants in life is to settle down to supporting a woman and child. Sometimes a pregnancy of this sort will precipitate a marriage, legal or common law, but usually the birth is more or less ignored as much as possible by everyone. Neither Jamaican lower-class norms nor the law compel the young father either to marry or to establish a permanent common-law relationship with the mother of his child. It leaves this choice up to the couple, and this is considerably influenced by the degree to which the young man has achieved a measure of economic independence and security. The customary expectations of society, and also the law when it is called upon, do hold the father economically responsible, in part at least, for the cost of the birth and for part of the maintenance of his child, but these are realistically related to the ability of the father to provide such support, and the responsibility is not extended to his kin.

The mean age of women and men at the time of birth of their first child (Mangrove Beach and Black Point) is nineteen and twenty-four years. The difference between this age differential and that at the time of first intercourse (one year) is indicative of the fact that young women very soon cast their attentions in the direction of somewhat older men, mainly because only they have enough independence and money to provide the favours and entertainment expected of a lover. The percentage of mothers who never co-resided with the fathers of their first child is 48 (Mangrove Beach and Black Point), and this figure falls with each successive child. Co-residence, as already mentioned, is not a reliable index of a stable non-legal union, so the number of these either associated with or precipitated by the birth of the first child is probably greater than this figure.

After the initial period of sexual experimentation, and particularly after the birth of the first child, conjugal unions tend to persist for longer periods. This is not to say that early relationships, or even initial affairs, never become permanent or life-long, for occasionally they do. The general tendency, however, is for each successive non-legal union to become more stable than the one before. Table 1 summarizes the length of co-residential, common-law marriages for men at Mangrove Beach who had had more than three such relationships. Again, the bias introduced by using co-residence of spouses as an index of common-law marriage must be taken into account. Common-law marriages

Table 1. Duration of Co-residence with Spouse for Males in Successive Common-Law Marriages (Mangrove Beach).

	Mean duration in months	Range in months
First	36	2 – 156
Second	59	12 – 144
Third	96	12 – 324

will also show increasing stability with the number of previous unions, the number of children born to either partner, and with increasing age of either partner.

When a common-law union appears to have become stable, that is, when both partners are confident that their relationship will endure, they take steps to legalize it by marriage. The optimism and pressure for marriage is nearly always greater with the woman. This is to be expected, in the light of the way women are regarded as the carriers of respectability, but it is also the result of constant pressures put on the women by the clergy, social workers, and judges (if the women have had occasion to go to court)—middle and upper class all—to legitimize their children and their own status by marriage. The most pervasive of these pressures emanates from the local church, and these are most effective, since a great many local activities revolve about them. Churches usually do not permit any woman living in common law to become a full member or to hold any church office, although no one is denied admittance to services for this reason. In the same vein, no Jamaican child is denied the rite of baptism, and all mothers hold this to be an important religious ceremony;

but illegitimate children sometimes must be baptized on different days from legitimate children, and the mothers are there reminded of the sin they are perpetuating by living in common law.

There is a real difference between the domestic statuses and roles of married and unmarried women living in common-law marriages (see Clarke 1957: 77–80, 104–9). In the latter instance, a woman can make no strong claim for support, her partner's property is considered to be his own, and she is usually more or less obliged to seek employment for part of her own support. What is more important, she has no recourse in these matters to the courts of law, and there are no sanctions to prevent her spouse from terminating the arrangement at any time he wishes. The reverse is, of course, also true. In marriage, however, the husband is legally considered to be head of his household of which his wife is a part, and he is expected to provide for household dependents, of which his wife is one, in a satisfactory and selfless manner. The legally married wife may work or perform remunerative services in order to augment her husband's income, but ideally, at least, she should not be compelled to do so. These expectations assume that the husband is economically able to fulfill these obligations, and that society has a secure niche for him, which only needs to be occupied by him. Therefore, while the probability that a stable non-legal union will be legalized by marriage increases with the number of children each parent has and with their age (see Tables 2 and 3), these are not really the crucial factors. Economic security and a willingness to enter into the lifelong obligations of legal marriage are what are important. If a man does not feel secure, or if he thinks the legal hold his wife gains on him through marriage will alter their relationship, then he will, indeed, be unwilling to go through with the wedding. On the other hand, if through the stabilization process, the husband's and wife's roles have become what is expected of legally married couples, then, with a little pressure, the man is usually ready to get married. Thus, the sequence of successive non-legal unions leading up to legal marriage can be looked at in at least two ways: it is a process by which the jural obligations of marriage may be postponed, without foregoing more or less normal procreative activities, until full economic security is achieved; and it is a period during which both men and women are working,

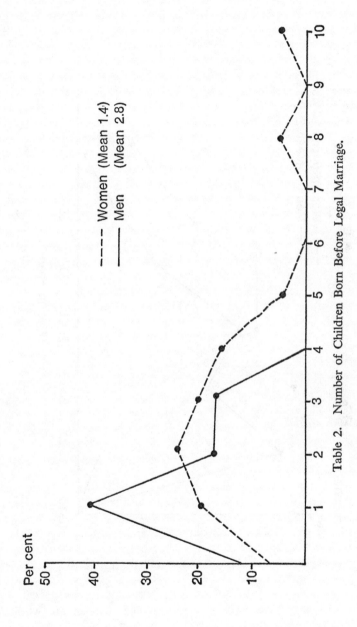

Table 2. Number of Children Born Before Legal Marriage.

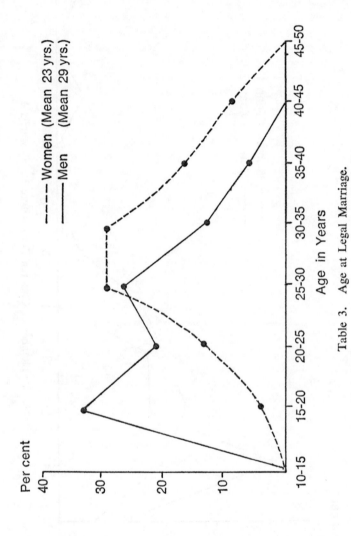

Table 3. Age at Legal Marriage.

through trial and error, toward the perfection of adult marital roles. When both of these are achieved, then the marriage is legalized, and the partners become fully respectable, adult members of the society. In either case, the period immediately following sexual maturity or late adolescence is one of great instability for both sexes. Most lower-class Jamaicans ultimately manage to overcome it and find a secure place in the system, but this is not inevitable. Some go through the remainder of their lives in economic want and without marital stability of any kind. And there are a few who, even though they achieve both economic and marital stability, fail to legalize their marriages ever.

The instability of the post-adolescent period is increased somewhat by the marked difference between men of different age groups. This becomes particularly noticeable after the age of fourteen or fifteen. Before this boys of all ages interact quite freely, far more so than in United States society, where an age difference of even a year or so is very important to preadolescents. After fifteen or so, young men begin to avoid their elders and to be quite deferential to them when they are together. Among these young adult men, there is a strong tendency to associate with each other and to get away from all other age groups. After about age twenty-two years or so, some continue to remain in this detached group of young men, while others return to an ever-increasing equality with the older men. This was quite noticeable among the Black Point fishermen, where some men of eighteen and nineteen were already full-time fishermen with complete economic autonomy. Yet at meetings of the Fishermen's Co-operative Society, some were completely silent before their elders, while some others ventured an independent opinion only once in a while. This variation was found to be correlated with the degree of separation from their parental households. Those who still lived in their household of orientation felt they had no voice in current affairs, while those who were out on their own and managing their own domestic establishment would state an opinion, even though they remained respectful of the older men.

From these and other observations, it is inferred that full adult status is not a factor of age alone, but is achieved through a combination of age, economic security, and independence from the household of orientation. The more significant here are the social and economic factors, for they, unlike age, are not come by automatically. Only socio-economic security enables a man to head his own household group and to achieve a stable marriage. As long as this is thwarted, he will be unwilling to enter into the permanent jural obligations of legal marriage, and he remains in a relatively ambiguous and unstable position in society. And if he remains in this position but still has children, then some of his obligations as husband and head of household must be assumed by other persons. Who these persons are and how this transfer takes place will be discussed below.

All the children born from these successive non-legal unions, though technically illegitimate, are nonetheless considered to be the children of their biological fathers. And although these outside children most often remain with their mothers, their fathers are expected to contribute something toward their support. Most men recognize these obligations and try to give something when they are able. This most often takes the form of intermittent sums of money for clothing, which are given before the major holidays when everybody wants to dress their best. Some men are completely remiss in this, and the full weight of support of their children falls upon the household where the mothers of their children are residing. In some cases these are their own households of orientation. In others, a woman resides in the household headed by her current spouse. In this way a man who brings a woman and her children into his household in common-law marriage does assume some of the responsibility for children that are not his. For this reason, a man may be reluctant to enter into even a common-law marriage with a woman who has a large number of children by other men, and especially if these fathers do not regularly help with their support. Women can and do often go to court in order to get support from the fathers of their children, and the court usually rules in their favour, but these decisions are difficult to enforce if the man insists upon neglecting this obligation. In the last analysis, informal sanctions are the most effective, and if these fail, there is very little that can be done about it.

When, after a series of fruitful non-legal unions, marriage takes place, the legal status of the children is significantly altered.

But only those children of the legalized marriage are legitimized, and the outside children of both the husband and wife remain forever illegitimate. In general, the difference between legitimacy and illegitimacy is not a marked one, but it is great enough to become the source of some conflict for the parents. Men frequently use this as an excuse to postpone marriage, saying that they do not wish to introduce such a distinction between their children, all of whom they insist must be equal. Within a household, too, the outside children of the wife stand in danger of becoming less favoured than the legitimate children of the couple. For these reasons, too, both men and women will sometimes postpone their marriage until all their outside children are old enough to take care of themselves.

Apparently in some cases marriage and its consequent legitimization of the children of the couple introduces a noticeable difference in the attitude of the father toward his outside children, and some men almost completely reject them thereafter. Some cases of this sort were observed at Black Point, and they seemed to be associated with considerable desire for social mobility; hence they are explained in terms of attempts to present an unblemished image of middle-class respectability.

Until marriage occurs, a man's and his non-legal spouse's kindreds are completely independent of each other. This independence permits an easy termination of the common-law unions, for neither set of kin has any particular jural relationship to the other and neither has any particular reason to insist it be held together. This applies almost equally to non-legal unions that have produced children as to those that have not. With legal marriage, however, this independence lessens considerably. The marriage ceremony and the festivities that follow [see Beckwith (1929), Henriques (1953: 96–97), Clarke (1957), Kerr (1952)] bring both close kin into co-operative interaction, probably for the first time, and this serves as the model for their subsequent interaction. Moreover, when a legally married couple has domestic troubles and they are contemplating a separation, these close kin will do everything they can to smooth out the difficulties and bring about a reconciliation.

Only at marriage does godparenthood come into any prominence. In the communities studied by Clarke (1957: 85–87), their roles were limited to making specific contributions to the wedding ceremony. Since the godparents must be legally married, their participation seems to reinforce the respectability of the occasion. At Mangrove Beach and Black Point godparenthood was practically absent, even though in the latter village the people were thoroughgoing churchmen with two long-established Protestant churches and several Fundamentalist sects represented. Godparents here, for those few who had them, were regarded only as favourite relatives who might be called upon from time to time for small favours. The custom of assigning godparents to illegitimate children in order to align them with married relatives, and the bestowal of the honour of godparenthood on some well-to-do persons in hopes of receiving favours from them seems to have been frequent a few generations back, but it is not done at the present time.

Plural unions are to be found, but they are infrequent. The most prevalent kind is where a legally married man keeps a mistress in some other district or village. Even though these are not concealed in any way, there is a certain reticence in discussing them, for many persons strongly disapprove of them. True polygynous unions, in common law of course, also occur occasionally. One notable instance involved a man who for many years had maintained a stable relationship with five women by whom he had over fifty children. What is truly remarkable is that he had managed to provide land and a house for each of the spouses and cultivation land for each of his sons. Even though the community did not condone his pluralistic preferences, they did admire his industry and devotion to the mothers and all the children.

Even common-law polyandrous arrangements can be uncovered if one searches long and hard enough. One such at Mangrove Beach involved a stable union, the man in which had been blinded and permanently maimed in a fishing accident. He is completely unable to work and must be supported by his girl friend. Everyone in the village who can afford to, hires her to do laundry and other chores, just to give her assistance. She has also entered into another non-legal union, cooks all of this man's meals, and spends several nights each week at his house. The two men seem to get along well together and even spend some time with each other. The village chooses to ignore the second common-law relationship and praises the woman for doing everything she can to support her unfortunately crippled boy friend.

Despite these examples, the marital pattern is a monogamous one, but a monogamy which has two jural alternatives—legal and non-legal. While the legal alternative consists of a set of permanent and legally enforceable rights and obligations, the non-legal alternative consists of a set of rights and obligations toward which the legal system is indifferent, and which are terminable at any time by either partner. The modal pattern in the lower class is for one or more non-legal unions to precede a legal marriage, the latter not occurring until the man has achieved some measure of economic security. The period between sexual maturity and permanent marriage is one of great ambiguity and instability, during which a number of illegitimate children are born, as the young adults move in and out of non-legal unions. These children usually remain with their mothers, while their fathers are expected to provide only partially for them. In taking a spouse, either legal or non-legal, a man is expected to help to provide for all the children the woman brings to the union with her, regardless of who their fathers are, or how much maintenance for the children is received from them.

THE ORGANIZATION OF HOUSEHOLD ACTIVITIES

The Jamaican lower-class household, as the term is used here, refers to a co-resident family group, which is spatially separate and usually, but not invariably, consists of more than one person, these being close kin. Economically, it may be a relatively independent unit of production, exploiting its productive capital for its own use and sharing its resources according to the need of each member. But its most important feature is the way in which its members perform a number of essential services for each other, these services being organized according to a division of labour by sex and age.

In physical layout the lower-class household consists of a house, a detached kitchen or cook house, and a yard area. Each of these areas is the location of important activities, which make up the domestic routine. The house is usually used mainly for sleeping and for storing clothing and other articles of personal value. The poorer the household, the more the use of the house is restricted to just these activities, while the houses of the more well-to-do will have space and furnishings for additional activities such as relaxing, entertaining, and eating. Houses vary from simple, one-room structures made of wattle and thatch and with earth floors to multiroom buildings of frame or concrete construction, metal or shingle roofs, and plank or cement floors. The house and its furnishings are one of the best indices of wealth and position among the lower class, for everyone will invest in these all that can be spared. The cook house is usually a temporary structure and has less care lavished upon it than on the living house. It is used for preparing and storing food, and in most poor households, the family eats here in bad weather. It can also serve as a general utility shed and working space when other special structures have not been erected in the yard for these purposes. The yard is the scene of great miscellany of activities. On this swept ground between house and kitchen, the children play, the washing is done, the family relaxes, and friends are entertained. In it and surrounding it a few food-producing trees are grown, the small animals are tethered, and space is given over to a small vegetable garden. The yard is frequently fenced to keep animals in, and friends and neighbours pay respect to this boundary by never entering without being asked. Far more respect, however, is paid to the house, for this cramped space affords the only real sanctum of privacy for the household against the rest of the neighbourhood.

The house, yard, and kitchen are dominated by the adult women of the household, for most of the perennial work which goes on in them is in their charge. Women prepare the food, do the washing and mending, tend the kitchen garden, look after the small animals, and most important, look after the children. Older children lighten the work of the adult women, some by assisting in the easier tasks such as sweeping, watering the animals, collecting kindling, hauling water, picking fruit from the trees, and going to the neighbourhood shop. But even though the youngsters are of considerable economic importance, they must be supervised and directed, and this, again, falls to the adult women. Women, too, see to the weekly marketing, an all-day undertaking which frequently requires a long walk or a ride by bus or truck to the nearest market place. Although this responsibility is not considered to be a particularly onerous one, still many women cannot free themselves for this trip on Saturday, and they have their friends and relatives do it for them.

The adult men and older boys of the household assist in heavier tasks, such as looking after the larger and more valuable animals (if there are any), repairing the house and cook house, chopping logs, spading a new kitchen garden, and even assisting with the processing of food products, which are to be sold. But men's work is not nearly so confined to the round of domestic duties as is the women's. To them falls the major responsibility of the cultivation plot, or "ground," as it is called. In many instances this is removed some distance from the house site, and the men go to and from it daily, leaving the women in charge of the household activities and children. Men, of course, do most of the wage work which takes them away from the domestic scene. They alone congregate in one another's yards or at the local shops to socialize. Women and older children assist the men in the heavy cultivation, and their services are of great value during planting and harvest times. But the women's roles in primary agricultural production are supplemental, just as the men's are in the purely domestic area. To women, however, falls the job of selling the produce, either from house to house or in the system of internal markets (see Mintz 1955: 95–103).

Although the division of adult labour is not rigidly fixed by sex, it is the context of the household group which makes it clear. The rule, as in many European societies, is that women dominate the services of the domestic scene, while the men are concerned with productive working outside. Each sex may assist the other in some of his or her work, but this assistance is supplementary to the major responsibilities of each sphere. With respect to the economic system of the island as a whole, most of the jobs for wages are for men, while the women are limited to the kinds of personal services upon which both sexes of all ages depend. The one major exception to this is the important role the women play in the marketing system, which takes them into a specialized sphere of economic exchange. It is this general but flexible plan which enables the household group to adjust and maintain itself in a variety of situations and with a variety of different compositions. For instance, when the productive potential of men is limited or completely absent in a household, the women are able to take over their economic function by performing domestic services, for pay, in other households (e.g., taking in washing and mending, or cooking for single men). Or the women can expand their marketing activities in order to provide a cash income for their household group. Men may keep a sort of bachelor's household by cooking for themselves, but there are some kinds of services such as washing and mending clothes or caring for children which they never do, and they must get some women to do for them. This dependence upon the household services of women is a major factor of motivation in some temporary non-legal marital unions, which have been called "keeper" and "housekeeper" marriages [Clarke (1957: 100–2), Henriques (1953: 105–11), Roberts (1957: 265–66), Simey (1946: 85)].

Since the household tasks fall so heavily upon the women's shoulders, nothing, except money, is more valued there than extra female hands. An older daughter can look after the younger children, help with the washing, and take over some of the kitchen drudgery. An older woman can do the same things as well as supervise others, and by so doing, relieve a more active woman to go to market or to go to the ground to help her husband there.

Older boys can perform all the tasks that the women leave for the men. In fact, there are some jobs, such as climbing tall fruit trees, which are almost specifically performed by this age and sex group. With an older boy or two in the house, a man can be almost completely free of any household tasks whatsoever, and free to spend all of his time away from the house and yard. Old men have little to do around the house, for they can neither do the strictly feminine tasks nor those requiring agility and strength. Among the fishermen, however, the old men looked after net mending and making bamboo plait for the fish pots. But this limited value of feeble old men is partly the reason so many are reduced to begging and hanging around the younger men for handouts.

This division of labour has an important effect on the interaction patterns between households. Women, saddled as they are with domestic responsibilities, are not always free to leave their yards and to visit each other. Some young mothers hardly leave their homes for weeks on end, because there is no one there to relieve them, even for a few hours. Youngsters are always sent on errands, but if these require going some distance only an older boy can be sent. Men, on the other hand, are working away from the yard most of the time, and when they are free from these duties, they are able to move about as much as they wish. Older women, and particularly those with grown daughters, are free to go to market, and to visit, but they usually restrict their socializing to Saturdays at the weekly market and Sundays at church.

Most of the activities that fall within the framework of the household group—and there are many others not mentioned here (see M. Smith 1957)—relate to the maintenance and support of the dependent members. This becomes clearest when the life history of an individual is traced from his initial to his final dependency on the household. A child is born, literally, in the household of which its mother is a member. During the first years of life, his needs are satisfied there by his mother, older sisters, aunts, and maybe a grandmother. Almost from birth, girls and boys receive different treatment and different behaviour is expected from them. This becomes pronounced during the toddling period as different modesty and toilet habits are learned. By childhood, the domestic tasks which boys and girls are given are almost fully sex-typed. Little girls are with their mothers and older women constantly, imitating and assisting them as they are able. Little boys, although still dependent upon the women for almost everything, are not pressed into occupational roles nearly so strongly, and they are allowed to play more. During the school years, both boys and girls are fairly restricted to the school and home yard, but boys are always allowed more freedom to play and to associate with other boys. The games for boys and girls are different, and when they are playing in mixed games, their roles are clearly sex-typed (Beckwith 1922). It is in these large mixed games supervised by adults where one sees a very wide range of ages among the participants.

Young boys always have fewer and less irksome household chores than girls of the same age. Since they are allowed much more freedom of movement in and out of the yard, many play truant from school from the earliest years there. Many parents care little whether the boys learn anything at school or not, as long as they spend some of their time there. These less motivated boys fall behind the rest of their class and eventually drop out altogether.

By adolescence, most girls are fully capable of performing almost all of their adult domestic tasks, but this is not true of all boys. Adolescent boys seem neither fully competent nor psychologically ready to fill an adult role. By the end of the school years at the age of fifteen or sixteen, the young women are firmly integrated into the adult routine of the household, and they are more restricted to their yards than ever. Part of this restriction consists in their mothers' attempts to keep them away from men. For the young man, late adolescence is the beginning of a time of extremes, depending almost entirely upon the economic circumstances of his household of orientation. If it is extremely poor and without land or other positive resources, the pressures will be strong for him to find a way to provide for himself, and even to leave the house so as to lessen the economic strain of support on others. Or he may be just as strongly enjoined not to leave, but to find work to help support the rest of the group. If the household is not so poor, and land is available, he may be urged to remain and to either assist on it or to take a piece for himself. In this way he can ease considerably the load carried by the aging males of the group. On the other hand, if the household is prosperous, no one will care much what he does, and he can enjoy himself as he pleases for still a few more years. Under these circumstances, and provided that he is bright and interested, he may be sent on to school or apprenticed to a trade. Girls, too, may be sent on to school or into some form of informal apprenticeship such as dressmaking.

In order to alleviate the economic strain, impoverished households may send some of their young children to related households, which can more easily provide for them. When necessary, too, adolescent girls may leave their households to work as domestics in strange middle- and upper-class houses or, sometimes, in the homes of distant relatives. Grown women with children may do the same, leaving their children at their own household to be cared for by the women there. If they become pregnant again while away, and are not living with a man, they need only return to their own household to have the baby.

Much has already been said of the unstable period from adolescence to permanent marriage, and it will be referred to again, for it is a crucial period in the lower-class Jamaican's life. It will be recalled that a woman may move in and out of her natal household several times before she establishes herself permanently with a husband. For the man, the instability of the period is directly related to his economic position, and a measure of security, an early legal marriage, and no illegitimate children allow him to consolidate his resources and obligations within a single household of which he is the head. In this case, it is relatively easy for him to bring in his aging parents or other close relatives as the need arises and, from the point of view of continuity, his household replaces that of his parents. But if he has little security to start with and, through a series of non-legal unions, assumes the responsibility for several outside children who are scattered in different households, and if he has still further obligations to aging parents and grandparents, the conflict of loyalties among them (and to his own well-being) makes his position extremely difficult. The reconciliation of the dilemma lies in one of two directions. The least frequently followed, but one that does occur in many cases, is for the man to cut himself off from all his obligations entirely, and to spend the rest of his life as an unattached individual, working at jobs when and where he is able, and living in periodic non-legal unions as befit his circumstances. From the point of view of the individual life cycle, this means a prolongation of the roles of late adolescence and early manhood throughout life. From the point of view of household continuity, there is none, for such an individual, even though he fathers children, does not establish a complete household within which these children are reared and oriented—all these are done within the context of other households, of which he is not a permanent member.

The more frequent alternative is for a man to move toward a consolidation of all his obligations and potential assets by setting up a household around a permanent marriage. With meagre resources, this is extremely difficult, but it is the only way in which he can fulfill all his obligations of kinship, and at the same time lay the groundwork for security in his own declining years and return to dependency. Choosing the first alternative is a denial of these obligations, and it releases others from their reciprocal duties toward him when he needs them most; choosing the second alternative is the way by which the social system persists.

The achievement of a stable marriage and a consolidated household group does not mean that any measurable degree of social mobility has been gained. For both husband and wife, this is only a repeat performance of what their parents did. But in so doing, the couple provide the fundamental resources with which their children will begin their adult lives. If this is firmly established, then the obligation their children have to them will be strong, and the framework of their own security in old age is also established. Security in old age is ever a concern for lower-class persons, for there is nothing so miserable and degrading as to be forced to live out these years in want and in isolation. The greatest assurance against this threat is to have been successful in establishing a large and prosperous household which contains all one's children and grandchildren.

THE COMPOSITION OF THE HOUSEHOLD

From what has been described already, it can be seen that the Jamaican lower-class household can vary greatly in size and composition. Simey and Henriques attempt to classify these variations according to conjugal relationships around which they are formed. These are: the *Christian family*; *faithful concubinage*; *companionate* or *keeper family*; the *disintegrate, maternal*, or *grandmother family*. Cohen (1956: 670–83) sees two types, *patripotestal* and *matripotestal*, which differ from each other by having or not having a dominant male as head of the household. Clarke (1957: 117) classifies them into *simple, extended, denuded, single person*, and *sibling* types, according to their adult membership, and into *primary, secondary*, and *childless* subtypes, according to the kinds of dependent children present. She goes much farther than this and provides a minute breakdown of each of these types by conjugal status, size, types of kin included, and still more parameters. Cumper (1958) does not attempt a classification by gross type, but presents his data by the variables of conjugal type, categories of kin included, and age and sex of the household head. Out of these excellent data emerge several features which, as Cohen, Clarke, and Cumper have each seen, are best described as organizational patterns, not as a series of discrete or alternative types. The analysis to follow is an attempt to reduce the number of household variables which have already been studied in detail by these and other investigators to what seems to be the most salient few. This, unfortunately, does an injustice to the richness of much of the primary sources, but at the same time it seems to unify many disparate features into a more holistic view of the family.

Let us first consider the size of the lower-class household as separate from other features. Clarke (1953: 196) finds the mean size of household increases from 2.7 persons in Sugartown, to 3.3 in Mocca, to 5.7 in Orange Grove. Correspondingly, she finds the percentages of extended family types (1953: 117–18) increases from 28 in Sugartown, to 42 in Mocca, to 52 in Orange Grove (1953: 191–95). Similar differences are recorded by Cumper (1958) between Caymanas, a sugar estate, and Porter's Mountain, an agricultural community. From the other data included in these reports, the increase in household size in these communities seems to be correlated with the relative stability and amount of productive resources available to the households. Within a single community, Black Point, this same trend is very noticeable, for household size is clearly correlated with the value of the productive capital (land and fishing equipment) controlled by the household.

The relationship between size and economic factors is related to marriage, for it will be recalled that legal marriage usually comes as a consequence of a man gaining and maintaining a measure of economic security and stability. This is brought out by Clarke's (1957: 125) and Roberts' (1957: 297–99) findings that the fertility of married couples is greater than that of common-law unions. It can be summarized, then, that the size of households increases as a function of greater economic wealth and stability, and this also correlates with the rate of frequency of legal marriage.

The size does not increase indefinitely, however, but is distributed around a mode or modes (1.0, in Sugartown, 2.0 and 6.0, in Mocca, 5.0, in Orange Grove) and rarely exceeds ten persons. We expect, too, that central tendencies and standard deviations for household size will vary significantly with the kinds of basic economies they depend upon. For example, a subsistence agricultural household with ample land, because of its need for labour, might accommodate more persons than could a household whose income, though approximately equal, is derived from wages. Hence there should be a decrease in size from country to town.

There is also a reversal of this trend in size when large social class boundaries are traversed. Middle- and upper-class family groups tend to be biological families, consisting only of parents and children, and are not extended by the inclusion of lineal and collateral kin. This is explained by a number of factors which are discussed below, but part of the explanation seems to lie in the fact that within the households in these classes, there is no need to hold and to keep labour within the group.

Given the potentiality to expand, that is, the ability to support and maintain a number of persons collectively in a single household unit, a lower-class household can recruit members in four ways: 1) by the birth of children to the nuclear couple; 2) by the inclusion of children by previous marital unions; 3) by bringing in and supporting dependent children of close, but poorer, relatives; and 4) by incorporating older, dependent relatives of ascending generations. All but the first of these require some explanation, for it is the pattern of each, in connection with the instability of non-legal marriage, which gives to the lower-class households their characteristic structural shapes. We will, for the moment, restrict this discussion to a household which is centred around a stabilized marriage.

As already emphasized, children usually remain with their mother throughout their dependency period, regardless of her marital career. If this culminates in a stable union, then the nucleus of a new and productive household may be established around the married couple. Added to them will be their own children and the dependent children of the wife by previous unions—her husband's stepchildren—who are of no kin to him and who do not have his name. It is not uncommon to find half-siblings with three, four, and even five different surnames together in the same household with their mother and her husband. A legally married husband under these circumstances will rarely bring any of his illegitimate children by other women to live in his home (Clarke 1957: 119).

In addition to these children of the women, and depending upon the ability of the household to support additional dependents, there may be included still other children of the wife's close kin. Most frequently these are children of her daughter or sister, less frequently of her son and her brother. These children are not adopted in the legal sense, but are residing in the household only because their own mothers are unable to provide adequately for them, and they have called upon their kinsmen to help support them. The inclusion of close relatives' children is not motivated solely by kinship obligations, however, for an older couple whose children have left or are about to leave may wish to bring someone in to help with chores around the house. More well-to-do households may bring in a related young woman to be a domestic servant, to whom they may ostentatiously refer as their "maid." Regardless of the underlying motivations and circumstances, the collateral children (sister's and brother's children) may often be treated as second-rate members of the household for, not being adopted, they remain the primary responsibility of their own parents and do not have the rights and privileges of direct descendants.

A man of a household will bring his or his relative's children into his own household only when his spouse (legal or non-legal) has no outside children of hers or her relatives there, and only when there is also a close female relative of his (e.g., his mother or his sister) living there to look after them. The reasons for this are clearly stated by informants; there must be a responsible woman present to care for them, and this woman must be consanguineally close to them and cannot be a stepmother, i.e., mother-in-law. Bringing the wife's or the husband's outside children together under the same roof brings together persons who are not kin to each other in any way, and this sets the stage for favouritism and conflict. Several instances where these rules were violated were closely observed at Black Point, and each revealed that a great amount of tension had developed out of the fact that the father's spouse neither had nor was willing to exert authority over her husband's children, while the husband accused his wife of either showing favouritism and over-concern for her own children or hostility and under-concern for his.

Table 4 summarizes the data from 375 persons at Mangrove Beach and Black Point regarding the principal female agent of socialization in their lives. It is to be noted that, by eliminating the mother and the stepmother, there is no decided preference shown for mother's or father's relatives. Clarke (1957: 129–31) however, finds that out of eighty-eight cases where children were reared by women other than their mothers, mother's kin were selected 67 per cent of the time. It is believed that Clarke's figures, though drawn from a small sample, are more representative of what happens in Jamaica as a whole than the larger samples drawn by Davenport in the two coastal communities. In these latter settings, the

Table 4. Women Performing the Principal Role of Socialization.

Mother's kin	Percent	Father's kin	Percent
"Mother" (Mo)	.76	"Mother in law" (FaWi)	.07
"Grandmother" (MoMo)	.04	"Grandmother" (FaMo)	.04
"Aunt" (MoSi)	.02	"Aunt" (FaSi)	.02
"Aunt in law" (MoBrWi)	.005	"Aunt in law" (FaBrWi)	.005
"Cousins" (MoBrDa)	.002	"Cousins" (FaBrDa)	.002
(MoSiDa)	.002	(FaSiDa)	.002
			.139
Other distant relatives	.02		
Unrelated persons	.01		
	.859		.859
			.998

importance of fishing, a male activity, seemed always to emphasize the male side of the household more than in cases where the productive labour is based on agriculture.

Even though placing a child in a close relative's household for life does not constitute legal adoption, a kind of adoption does occur. One case is recorded at Black Point where a man, by his own reckoning, adopted a boy who was no kin to him by changing his name to his own, but without going through any court formalities. The real father of the child, also a resident of the community, recognized the adoption without complaint. This case is a special one, because the mother of the child was dead; otherwise it is unlikely that adoption would have occurred. Whether or not this would be recognized in a court of law is also open to question.

While the tie between a mother and her dependent children is an especially strong one, there is an almost equally strong reciprocal obligation between an adult man and his mother. This is the economic obligation to support her through old age; it is only slightly less strong between a woman and her mother, and less strong still between a man and his father. The most convenient way for a man to fulfill this obligation is to move his parents into his own household where they may be of some assistance in the domestic round of activity. We thus find a tendency toward skewedness in some three-generation households—kin of ascending generations tend to be those of the husband, while kin of descending generations are either children of both spouses or kin of the wife alone. As noted above, the exceptions to this are where a man has in his household a close female relative of his, e.g., his mother. Then he may bring in some of his own outside children to be taken care of by her. A few exceptions to the rule for ascending generations also occur where a man will have his wife bring her mother into his household to help look after his wife's outside children—but he will never bring in both her mother and father.

These expansional tendencies are illustrated by distributions of households at Black Point, where 89 per cent of all three-generation households with co-residing spouses (married and common-law) contained husband's kin of ascending generations only; none contained wife's kin of ascending generations only; and 11 per cent contained some of both. From the same sample, excluding children of husband and wife together, 74 per cent contained descending kin of the wife only; 2 per cent contained descending kin of the husband only; and 24 per cent contained some of both.

The compositional picture of the lower-class household drawn thus far has overstressed, perhaps, the extended, three-generation (and sometimes, four-generation) group, when in fact, the simple, two-generation, non-extended form is more frequent, and, in some communities at least, single-person households even predominate (Clarke 1957: 196). This was done merely to show in what directions lie the growth potentials of the simple non-extended family, and how these are related to the systems of kinship and marriage. It remains to summarize the way in which new households are formed, and one other way in which households expand.

During the ambiguous period of post-adolescence, and when strong pressures are put on the young man to leave his household of orientation, these are usually strongest for the illegitimate sons of women who are now legally married, and have other legitimate children by their husbands. Not frequently, there is land on their mother's side of the family which may be taken up; or their own fathers may have something to give them; or they may gravitate toward the towns and estates looking for work. Thus the outside sons of legally married women, being the eldest, having no connection with the stepfather in whose houses they have lived, and being separated from their own fathers, are almost sure to detach themselves and set up single-person domiciles.

Often the pressures will be equally strong on the young man to remain part of his household of orientation. This occurs when his labour is needed there to help support the group, for instance when there is no other adult man present, and his own father is failing, has land, and wishes his son to take over the responsibilities. When this is a case of a son replacing another man who is already in the household, it is sure to be this man's son, not his wife's son. If there is no land and no local work, the young man may have to leave the community, as above, in search for employment. However, he leaves not as a detached person, but as a contributing member of his household of orientations, and he probably intends to return to it as soon as possible. Thus the statistics on single-person households which are always reported in high frequency on the estates, contain two types: those men who are completely detached or in the process of becoming so; and those who are living on the estate during the harvest only, and will return to their households when the work is finished.

Men in both these relationships to other households also turn up at fishing communities such as Mangrove Beach. Domiciles there containing two, three, and four men could not be considered as joint male households in the sense that the term is used here, for, unless the men were closely related, they shared nothing. Even after months of living in the same small thatch dwelling, each man cooked his own food, ate it separately, and worked at or shared nothing co-operatively with the other men of his shack. The reason for this is that each man considered this only a temporary state of affairs. Some looked to wives and children in other districts as constituting their households and others were hoping to get enough money and a non-legal spouse in order to set up a household at the beach.

A son who remains in his household of orientation in place of an absent father becomes the male head of that household. He may bring into it a spouse, or a series of non-legal spouses (with and without children by previous unions), and the household assumes the somewhat skewed shape described above. In instances where the father is still resident in the household, but is not able to head that household group fully, the same applies. But where a vigorous and fully competent father is still head of his own household, there is high probability that the son will move out, even though he may be using some of his father's land, when he takes a spouse of his own. In such cases the son may only move to the other side of the yard, where he will build his own living house and a kitchen for his wife, and the two households will share the same yard. This was a frequent occurrence among Black Point households, where it was easy for young men to establish themselves as independent fishermen, but land for house sites was scarce.

When there are several grown brothers, each in turn may remain for a time in the household of orientation, but as long as their father remains fully active, they will move out and establish their own households with their spouses, even though this might only be across the yard. Rarely indeed, do two brothers and their spouses (or two sisters, or a brother and a sister with their spouses) ever set up a joint household, although clusters of closely related households are quite common. The rule of household formation, then, is that no single household will contain more than one active conjugal pair. When this is found, as it certainly is, either the man of the elder couple is partially or wholly dependent upon the younger man, or it is a temporary arrangement, and the younger couple is about to move out and establish its own household. In other words, true patrilocal or matrilocal extended families, which share the same household facilities do not form.

As parents grow old and all their children move out into their own households, even if only across the yard, the independence of the parental household begins to lessen. This decline is marked both by the taking over of many of the activities of the former by the offspring households, and a gradual absorption of the declining household into one or more of the younger ones. With the death of either parent, the process of absorption is hastened, for the surviving parent must eventually be incorporated into one of his children's households.

The social pressures on the post-adolescent woman are very different from those on the man. She is rarely eased out of her household of orientation, although the poverty and drudgery there may make even a temporary non-legal union quite appealing. Unless she has property of her own, both legal and non-legal marriages are virilocal from her point of view; that is, she will join her spouse in his household when he asks her to, but she always has her mother's household to return to, or to send her children to, if she cannot succeed in her marriage or cannot manage to keep her children with her. This strong tie with the mother and with the household of orientation is the basic structural relationship behind the celebrated matricentric (maternal, grandmother, matrifocal, matripotestal) households, which consist of a grandmother without a spouse, her dependent grandchildren (usually her daughter's children) and, not infrequently, one or more of her daughters, who are also without spouses. In other words it is the skewed extended household described above, but without adult men. Such a household can obviously develop only when there is a house, some land, or sufficient income to support the group independently, or else all the members would be absorbed into other, more secure households. But active, mature women can become self-supporting by a number of occupations such as higgling, sewing, washing, and preparing food. This is not too difficult if the house and enough land for a kitchen garden are owned by one of the women. Many of these matricentric households receive some support from the fathers of the young dependent children that are present; from sons who are helping their mothers and sisters; or from some man who is in fact a common-law husband of one of the women, but who is not able to bring her into his own household. At Black Point, for example, in nearly all of the instances of two- and three-generation households without adult men, the house and house site were owned by one of the women, usually having been inherited from her parents, and one of the women had a boy friend who visited regularly and contributed substantially toward the maintenance of the whole household.

Here again we can see why in some non-legal unions the partners do not share the same household. Each is tied to his own household by strong obligatory ties of consanguinity. The non-legal conjugal bond is a weak one and regarded by the society as little different from just a casual sexual affair. The weak positive sanctions of the non-legal marriage are just not strong enough to force the man to either set up a new household into which he might bring his spouse, or to make the necessary adjustments at his own household so that he might move his girl friend there. The result is a split residential arrangement which does not found a new household, but through it children may be born and absorbed into already existing households.

The single male household is to be seen as the complement to the matricentric household. The prevalence of the latter is accentuated, however, by a general excess of marriageable females over males in Jamaica as a whole (Roberts 1957: 70–76). But both are to be seen as unstable structures, which can change into some other form very easily.

CONCLUSIONS

The theoretical orientation of this analysis leans heavily upon ideas taken from the works already cited and liberal borrowings from M. G. Smith (1955; 1957) and R. T. Smith (1955; 1956) as well. But most of all, it has relied upon the ideas of M. Fortes (1958) in his analysis of the phases in the developmental cycle of domestic groups. While Jamaican society as a whole fits his paradigm in most ways, the present writer doubts that a single cycle of domestic development exists. Rather, there are at least three separate but complementary cycles. These are (1) the lower-class household cycle, with its capacity for household expansion and absorption of less stable households; (2) the middle- and upper-class cycle, involving no expansion and absorption, which is not yet fully studied; and (3) the cycle of development of the lower-class, bilocal extended family group. To look at all of these in terms of a single system of development and change would be, it is firmly believed, a misapplied model.

The Jamaican situation brings to the fore still another interesting comparison. As noted above, while human reproduction in the Jamaican lower class is insured through its comparatively unrestricted sexual patterns, marriage and the duration of a woman's fertility do not necessarily limit the phase of household expansion as Fortes (1958: 4–5) suggests. The Jamaican household can go on expanding by absorbing children from other less stable units. A case in point would be where a household incorporates its grandchildren into itself, while the mother of these children goes through a series of unstable non-legal marital unions.

It was also suggested above that not all lower-class households, once established, succeed in replacing themselves, and their children are absorbed into other more durable groups. The same situation probably can be said to apply to the development of the bilocally extended family group. The necessary condition for continuity in both cases is a secure economic foundation, and without it the groups perish. Such a foundation is not guaranteed in the social system, and it can be achieved only by some unknown fraction of groups. Thus to complete Fortes' (1958: 2) analogy from biology, to the "process of social reproduction" we must add a Darwinian footnote: there is selection, and only those units reproduce themselves which achieve the necessary conditions for maintaining their members.

PART V

RESIDENCE AND HOUSEHOLD

16 MARQUESAN POLYANDRY[1]

Keith F. Otterbein

THE MARQUESANS have been famous for several centuries, not only because of their reputed licentiousness, but also because they have been visited by two famous authors: Herman Melville and Robert Louis Stevenson. But for anthropology their fame rests upon the fact that they are reported to have had the only known system of nonfraternal polyandry which prevailed for all levels of their society (Opler 1943). Unfortunately for anthropology, their marriage system was never studied first-hand by an anthropologist. By the time the islands were systematically studied in 1920 by the Bayard Dominick Expedition the old culture had been swept away (Handy 1923).

This paper will review and evaluate (see appendix) seven sources—both historical and ethnographic—which contain information on Marquesan polyandry. The data from these sources will be tabulated and compared in terms of five categories which are relevant for an understanding of their polyandry. This comparison will be followed by a brief description of their polyandrous system as it probably existed at the time of the first white contacts. The purpose of this paper is to demonstrate that if this set of categories are used to analyze Marquesan polyandry, it is possible to construct four household composition types. When these types are examined, their marriage and domestic system no longer appears to be an ethnographic anomaly.

Reprinted from *Marriage and Family Living*, Vol. 25, No. 2, May, 1963, with permission of the author and of the editor of *Marriage and Family Living*.
[1] I am indebted to George P. Murdock and William P. Mitchell of the University of Pittsburgh for their helpful comments and criticisms.

Although there were six inhabited islands in the Marquesans in 1800, all the sources deal with the south coast of Nuku Hiva. Lisiansky estimated the population of this area in 1804 to be 4,000 (Lisiansky 1814); the population of the entire island was probably 10,000. In 1865 a smallpox epidemic reduced the population of 2,000 in two of the south coast valleys to 150 (Dodge 1940). By the time the first actual census of the islands was taken in 1882, the population of Nuku Hiva was 980 (Clavel 1884). In eighty years the population had been cut to one-tenth of its original size. The census gives a sex ratio of 115 males to 100 females. Ten years later there were less than 300 inhabitants living on the south coast (Christian 1895). This rapid population decrease was in part caused by intertribal wars and battles with the explorers (Porter 1823; Dodge 1940; Stewart 1831; Belcher 1843). But perhaps the greatest fatalities were caused by smallpox and famine (Christian 1895; Handy 1923).

Two important points emerge from the above discussion: (1) Because of rapid depopulation, the greatest reliance should be placed on the historical sources. (2) Because the travelers only visited the south coast of Nuku Hiva, their descriptions of poly-

Tabulation of Data by Category and Source

Category	Lisiansky (1814)	Stewart (1831)	Melville (1958)
1. Houses	Houses all of the same type, but varied in size.	People came to feast and helped build.	Many old, empty foundations around which people built on.
2. Authority system	$M_1 > F$ $M_2 < F$	No data. $M \geqq F$?	$M = F$
3. Mating system	Two husbands per wife.	Two husbands per wife.	Mature wife has two husbands.
4. Cross-cutting of social classes	Mainly rich families.	Complete cross-cutting.	Complete cross-cutting.
5. Sex ratio (males to females)	A lot less than 2–1.	2–1.	Less than 2–1.

M_1 = first husband	M_2 = secondary husband	> = authority greater than
F = wife	= = authority equal	< = authority less than.

Tabulation of Data by Category and Source

Category	Tautain (1895)	Handy (1923)	Linton (1939)	Danielsson (1956)
1. Houses	No data.	Feast for outside workmen. Extra husbands a help.	Great competition in house building.	Follows Linton.
2. Authority system	M > F	M > F	F > M	M > F
3. Mating system	Group marriage composed of two couples.	Follows Stewart.	Group marriage.	Many women had three or four husbands.
4. Cross-cutting of social classes	Complete cross-cutting.	All families in all social levels.	Only households on lower social level were monogamous.	Mainly chiefs' families.
5. Sex ratio (males to females)	No data.	Men greatly outnumbered women.	2½–1	120–100

M_1 = first husband M_2 = secondary husband   > = authority greater than
F = wife   = = authority equal   < = authority less than.

andry pertain to this area alone. Therefore, we can not say what regional variations in culture may have existed on the other five inhabited islands.

COMPARISON

Household size, the authority patterns in the household, the mating system, the cross-cutting of social classes and the surplus of males are five important aspects of the Marquesan domestic system. Each of these factors must be considered in order to construct household composition types. A comparison (see table) of the ethnographic data permits the following conclusions to be drawn about the nature of Marquesan polyandry at the time of first white contact.

HOUSES

Since workmen could be gathered together to help in building a house and house platform, it was not necessary to have a large work force living in the household. Hence, the attainment of additional help—by joining together two nuclear families or the attachment of unmarried males to the household—was an asset to a domestic unit, but not a necessity for its continued existence. Thus, a nuclear family could persist as a domestic unit.

(The historical sources indicate very little competition in house building. Apparently Linton and Danielsson inferred great competition because of the many huge boulders used in the construction of the large house platforms.)

AUTHORITY SYSTEM

The head husband had authority over the wife, but the wife had much control over the secondary husband, who may have been her first husband.

MATING SYSTEM

Most women had at least two husbands sometime during their life. Extra husbands and wives might also be added to well-to-do households. A polyandrous household could come into existence in several different ways: (1) A young man might marry a girl by obtaining permission from her parents to move in with them. If the union lasted, they left her home and moved into one of their own. Sometime after this, a wealthy man might marry the girl. She and her first husband moved in with her new husband. If he were already married, she became the secondary wife and her first husband became the secondary husband. (2) Two young men might marry a girl at the same time. The man of higher social class became the household head. (3) An older man of means might marry a young girl who had several lovers. These youths moved into the wealthy man's household along with his new wife. The initial union of two men to one woman can be called marriage, as well as the consecutive marriages of two men to the same women. It is questionable if the unions which resulted when young men attached themselves to households with attractive females can be considered marriages.

CROSS-CUTTING OF SOCIAL CLASSES

Polyandry, in the sense of polyandrous households, cross-cut all social classes. This resulted from one of the two husbands being lower class, from a lower class couple becoming attached to an upper class or chief's household, or from the wife's lovers being lower class.

SEX RATIO

The number of males probably never exceeded a ratio of 6–5. The manner in which households formed and changed over time would not require a ratio any greater than this. In fact, the system could probably have operated if there had been no difference in the number of men and women. The statements by some of the writers that men greatly outnumbered women were probably inferences based upon observations of chiefly households in which the men did outnumber the women.

If a ratio of 6–5 is accepted as being correct, we are left with the problem of explaining the difference. This is especially hard to understand when we consider that tribal wars would have killed off more men than women and produced a surplus of females. However, even though female infanticide is reputed not to have been practiced, it is possible that, since it is a practice in other parts of Polynesia, it was done quietly by the mother without letting others know. The woman retired to a birth house. If infanticide, then, were practiced in seclusion, the early travelers would not have noticed it, and hence they recorded its absence in their accounts (Stewart 1831). Linton states that women refused to bear children because of the adoption practices. "The Marquesan's knowledge of both contraception and abortion made this easy" (Linton 1939; 1936). A request for adoption was made ". . . long before birth, and such a request was never refused, refusal constituting an insult" (Handy 1923). Adopted sons had all the rights of sons born into a family, but adopted girls were practically slaves to their foster brothers. Therefore, if infants were killed because of adoption practices, it would have been females who were selected. In other words, there is no evidence for female infanticide, but all the above factors in combination present a picture in which not only female infanticide would mesh, but would be predicted.

Now that these five categories have been analyzed, it is possible to synthesize the data in such a way that household composition types can be delineated. This is done by considering the manner in which a household grows or develops. In the literature this is known as the developmental or life cycle approach (Otterbein 1963).

CONCLUSIONS

Domestic systems should be analyzed from the point of view of households and not of families. Usually the family is conceived of as a group consisting of an adult male and female and their children. The union existing between the man and woman is termed marriage. The following analysis of household composition will demonstrate the virtual impossibility of delineating families in some social contexts.

A household consists of the relatively permanent members of a dwelling unit. Two kinds of sexual relationships may exist between the adult, opposite sexed members of the household: marital or legal unions and non-legal unions. This raises the question of how to distinguish a marital union. The first step is to define marriage. Over thirty years ago Malinowski suggested that marriage be "conceived as a contract legitimizing offspring" (Malinowski 1930). Recently Kathleen Gough has provided the following definition:

> *Marriage is a relationship established between a woman and one or more other persons, which provides that a child born to the woman under circumstances not prohibited by the rules of the relationship, is accorded full birth status rights common to normal members of his society or social stratum* (Gough 1959).

When such a relationship is established it is symbolized in some manner, however simple, by a ceremony or rite. Thus, the task of the ethnographer is to identify marriage ceremonies and in this manner locate marital unions. Another procedure would be to single out legitimate children. (Native terminology may well distinguish between legitimate and illegitimate children.) The relationships between the children's parents are marital unions.

In many societies in the world one man is married to several women—polygyny. In only a few societies is one woman married to two or more men—polyandry. In no known society is it the norm for several men and women to be married to each other; that is, each man being married to each woman and each woman to each man. This is what nineteenth century anthropologists meant by group marriage. This situation did not prevail for the Marquesans. They had a combination polyandrous-polygynous system. The following types of households can be distinguished on the basis of composition; see diagram.

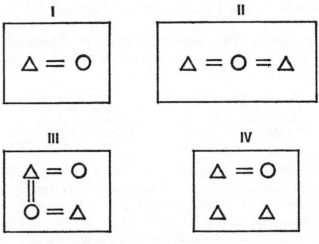

I. Monogamous.

II. Polyandrous. A woman married two men at the same time, or a man married a woman who was already married. She and her first husband went to live in his house.

III. Polyandrous-polygynous. A man, who was already married himself, married a woman who was already married. If her first husband accompanied her, he had sexual rights to the household head's wife, but he did not marry her.

IV. This type resulted when unmarried men attached themselves to any of the other three types of households. They
did not marry the women. Unmarried women did not join
households, but if they wished might live in communal
houses and function as prostitutes (Tautain 1895).

What kind of family or families were living in household type III?
One polygynous and one polyandrous? Three nuclear families? The
inability to make a decision forces one to study households and the
kinds of relationships which exist between members, and not marriage and family systems. Two kinds of unions existed in household types III and IV: legal and non-legal. The differentiating
criteria is the presence or absence of a marriage ceremony. The
legal union is symbolized by a marriage ceremony or by an initial
period of matrilocal residence. The act of the suitor becoming a
member of his wife's parents' household constituted a marriage
rite.

The authority of women varied in each type of household. The
following paradigms are only a guess as to what the authority
rankings were in each household type:

I. $M_1 > F$	M_1 = household head
II. $M_1 > F > M_2$	M_2 = secondary husband
III. $M_1 > F_1 > F_2 > M_2$	F_1 = first wife of M_1
IV. $M_1 > F >$ Lovers	F_2 = wife of M_2
	$>$ = authority greater than

The stratification system was related to household composition
through recruitment of members. Household type I contained lower
class members. The other three types spanned all the social classes.
Undoubtedly the class affiliation of each member was an important
factor in determining his authority in the household.

In conclusion, the Marquesan system of polyandry-polygyny is
not an anomaly if the concept of household types and the categories
used in deriving these types are used to analyze it. Once household
types are delineated on the basis of household composition (various
combinations of persons and relationships), a clearer picture results of the manner in which a household changes into a new type
over time and of the authority system in the different household
types.

APPENDIX

Reliability Estimates for the Seven Sources

1. Lisiansky visited Nuku Hiva in May 1804. He tells us that he got much of his data from Roberts, "a runaway English sailor," who "had long resided on the island" (Lisiansky 1814). His description of the marriage customs seems to be correct.

2. Stewart, a U. S. Navy chaplain, visited Nuku Hiva from 27 July 1829 to 13 August 1829. His book is a diary. It appears to be correct for what little information it contains.

3. Melville was on Nuku Hiva from 9 July 1842 to about 15 August 1842. C. R. Anderson, who has analyzed Melville's works in detail, has this to say about Melville's treatment of Marquesan polyandry:

> Melville, as he wrote, apparently had Stewart's treatise open before him. . . . Wherever Melville got his information—from Stewart, from personal observation, or from a combination of the two—his account of the domestic relations of the Typees is quite accurate, as far as it goes (Anderson 1939).

4. Tautain was the administrator for the Marquesas for three-and-a-half years sometime before 1895. His descriptions should be correct, except that the article is biased by nineteenth century evolutionary theories of group marriage.

5. Handy studied the islands in 1920. He was the ethnographer for the expedition. His discussion of "Secondary Mates" relies almost entirely on Melville and Stewart.

6. Linton was the archaeologist for the same expedition. His major publication on the islands states that he worked in the valley of Tai-pi Vai (Linton 1923) (Melville's Typee Valley). His ethnographic descriptions which were written fifteen to twenty years later are not footnoted to any historical sources. Since his account differs somewhat from the historical sources, and also because the necessary ethnographic information was not available in 1920, it appears that he used his imagination to a great extent in his reconstruction of Marquesan polyandry.

7. Danielsson, who is primarily an ethnographer, spent five months in 1951 in the Marquesas (Danielsson 1954). His account

seems to be essentially correct because he utilizes historical information. He only errs when he follows Linton in regard to competition in building stone platforms. Otherwise, he rejects "Linton,
whose account of Marquesan culture is unfortunately misleading
and unreliable in many other respects" (Danielsson 1924).

17 RESIDENCE RULES[1]

Ward H. Goodenough

DETERMINING A COMMUNITY'S RULE OR RULES of residence in marriage has long been established as a basic requirement for any satisfactory descriptive account of its social system. That residence practices are important determinants of the various forms of family and kinship organization has long been postulated by ethnologists and recently been given impressive statistical documentation by Murdock (1949).

Needless to say, studies such as his are dependent upon the reliability with which ethnographic facts are reported and interpreted. Ethnologists now take it for granted that a reliable report of residence customs is based on a house-by-house census of the community studied. When we read that such a census reveals a given ratio of residence types, I think most of us feel secure in what we regard as reliable information.

It was quite a shock, therefore, when I recently found myself differing considerably with John Fischer about the incidence of residence forms in a community on Truk (Romonum Island) where

Republished from *Southwestern Journal of Anthropology*, Vol. 12, 1955, pp. 22–37, with permission of the author and of the editors of *The Southwestern Journal of Anthropology*.

[1] This is a considerably revised version of a paper originally presented at the annual business meeting of the American Ethnological Society in New York City, January 11, 1955. The author is indebted to Dr. J. L. Fischer for making available his census material from Romonum Island on Truk and for explaining at considerable length in personal correspondence the procedures he followed in interpreting his material. Dr. G. P. Murdock and Dr. D. M. Schneider both offered constructive criticism of the original version of this paper.

we both collected data within the space of three years. Our respective tabulations appear on the following page.[2]

On the basis of my figures we would not hesitate to classify Trukese society as essentially matrilocal, since nearly three-quarters of the married couples are apparently living in matrilocal residence. On the basis of Fischer's figures, with little more than half the married couples in matrilocal residence and almost a third living patrilocally, I would myself be inclined to classify Trukese society as bilocal.

Type of Residence	Goodenough		Fischer	
	Cases	Percent	Cases	Percent
Matrilocal	46	71	36	58
Patrilocal	1	1.5	20	32
Avunculocal	10	15	0	—
Neolocal	4	6	6	10
Other arrangement	3	5	0	—
Ambiguous	1	1.5	0	—
Total	65	100	62	100

In short, two censuses of the same community within three years result in differences of a magnitude sufficient to suggest a different classification of its residence customs. Fischer's and my conclusions were both based on accepted census procedure. Either there were radical changes in residence practice and physical shifts of household accordingly in three years' time or we were honestly interpreting similar census data in very different ways.

As to the first alternative, Fischer's census reveals a move by an entire extended family group from one location to another (a practice for which there is ample past precedent), a shift in residence of several people as a result of the consolidation of two related lineages (a move that was already planned when I was on Romonum), and the residential separation of a segment of

[2] J. L. Fischer, *Native Land Tenure in the Truk District* (Mimeographed, Civil Administration, Truk), p. 23. My own figures, hitherto unpublished, are taken from field notes collected in 1947 by Dr. G. P. Murdock and myself as members of the research team from Yale University in the Coördinated Investigation of Micronesian Anthropology sponsored by the Office of Naval Research and the Pacific Science Board of the National Research Council. Additional financial aid was furnished by Yale University and the Wenner-Gren Foundation for Anthropological Research.

Romonum's largest lineage from its parent body, together with segments of two other lineage groups. Whether these three segments form one extended family is not clear from Fischer's census. His notes also reveal seven marriage dissolutions, three by death and four by divorce, and six new marriages. In order to ascertain whether the difference in our figures was a result of these changes or due to differences of interpretation, I have classified the residences in Fischer's census in accordance with the same principles which I used with my own data. The results for a total of sixty married couples are as follows:[3] 40 cases (67%) in matrilocal residence, 9 cases (15%) in avunculocal, 4 cases (7%) ambiguously in matrilocal or avunculocal, 1 case (1%) in patrilocal, 3 cases (5%) in neolocal, and 3 cases (5%) in some other arrangement. With due allowance for the ambiguous seven percent, the results are virtually identical with those based on my data of three years earlier. Considering the numerous shifts which had taken place, involving sixteen couples in addition to those whose marital status changed as already noted, the consistency of the percentages obtained for the two censuses is remarkable.

Only one interpretation is possible. The differences in Fischer's and my results cannot be attributed to differences in the raw census data. They arise from an honest difference in how to interpret the data.

The most obvious point at which we might differ in our respective interpretations would appear to be on the distinction between patrilocal and avunculocal residence. Indeed, in my own published report on Trukese social organization, I used the term patrilocal where I might better have used avunculocal (Goodenough 1951). But Fischer reports avunculocal residence for another island in the Truk area, and, in any case, confusion of avunculocal with patrilocal residence could not account for the significant difference between his and my reported incidence of matrilocal residence. Here, indeed, is a serious matter. Two trained anthropologists seem unable to agree as to what is and

---

[3] My total of sixty as against Fischer's sixty-two apparently results from the fact that he included some widowed persons in his count. The three men widowed since the time of my census were all still residing as they had been, in each case matrilocally. I am able to use his census material because of the information in my own notes about all of the individuals concerned.

what is not a case of matrilocal residence. Yet few ethnological concepts have been more precisely defined than those pertaining to residence. How, then, is it possible for us to disagree?

One possibility is that we used different kinds of additional information about Trukese society as a basis for interpreting the census data. If this is true, it means that residence forms cannot be reliably determined from the usual type of census information collected by ethnographers. A second possibility is that the established definitions of residence forms are so phrased as to make unclear how they should be applied to the enumeration of individual residences. Thus, without being aware of it, we might actually be using different concepts of residence at the applied level though starting in the abstract with similar ones.

We shall see that both of these factors have been at work. Fischer and I have been using different kinds of additional data to interpret the census material and we have also been working in practice with somewhat different concepts of residence.

Few concepts in ethnology are more clear-cut and seemingly straightforward than are those pertaining to residence. Moreover, we have yet to develop methods which rival in sophistication those already established for empirically determining patterns of family and kin organization. If these concepts and methods are still wanting, we are confronted with a serious challenge. Their reconsideration would appear to be in order.

First, there is the question of the adequacy of census data alone as a basis for determining a society's residence rules. In considering it, I would like to turn from Truk for a moment and use the Nakanai people of New Britain Island in Melanesia for illustrative purposes.[4]

Nakanai communities are made up of several hamlets, which are clustered closely together. Each hamlet's site is said to be the property of the matrilineal descendants of its founder or cofounders, but a census showed no consistent pattern of residence with respect to hamlet. Each hamlet had a group of relatives as its nucleus, but the genealogical relationships between them were

---

[4] The material on the Nakanai is from field notes collected during the spring and summer of 1954 under the joint auspices of the University Museum and Department of Anthropology of the University of Pennsylvania, the American Philosophical Society, and the Tri-Institutional Pacific Program.

of every conceivable kind. Now it ultimately turned out that there is indeed a pattern, that a man regularly brings his wife to live in the hamlet where his father is residing. He and his wife remain there until his father dies. If his father moves elsewhere, they move with him. When the father dies, the couple may continue to reside as before, particularly if the father was without sister's sons or if the husband has no matrilineal association with any hamlet in his father's village. More often, however, the couple removes to the hamlet in which the husband's immediate matrilineage has hereditary land rights, or to one where there is a concentration of his male sibmates.

Several things obscure this pattern. Since many people die before their children marry, a man is likely to start residing with a father-substitute, who may be his father's brother, mother's brother, older brother or parallel cousin on either side, cross-cousin, step-father, or older sister's husband, whoever among them took charge of feeding him as a child and/or negotiating his marriage. The number of cases in which a man and his wife are actually residing in the hamlet of the groom's father or maternal uncle are relatively few. All of the older men and many of the younger have no living fathers or uncles. One man, for example, has taken his two wives to live where no other man of his sib is represented and where his father never resided at any time. His own brother is residing elsewhere, in the hamlet with which their father was associated. The man in question resided there formerly and moved to the present hamlet after a quarrel. On the face of it, his is a case of neolocal residence. But from the genealogies we learn that his mother's brother and mother's mother's brother were associated with this hamlet, though they had died long before he moved there. Thus his apparent neolocal residence actually conforms to the pattern of a move from patrilocal to avunculocal residence, for he is now living where his mother's brothers would be, if he had any.

Furthermore, no amount of census data would reveal that residences with parallel cousins and brothers-in-law were residences with father-substitutes and hence in conformity with patrilocal principles. So frequently is the pattern obscured by the death of close relatives that our census data from Nakanai with its record of sib membership and living close kinsmen proved useless by itself for analyzing residence. The pattern began to emerge only after analysis of the genealogical data, where the dead had equal weight with the living and where questions about where a man lived elicited a list of two or more hamlets rather than just one. When I then redrafted my genealogical charts by hamlet rather than by sib, the essentially patri-avunculocal character of residence in Nakanai became finally apparent. With only census data to work with, the Nakanai must have remained one of those so-called "loosely structured societies" so frequently reported for Melanesia. We are confronted with the unavoidable conclusion, then, that careful census data, though indispensable to ethnographic insight, are not in themselves clear evidence of a society's residence rules, and that reports of residence based directly on such evidence alone are scientifically unreliable.

It is clear, then, that more than census data may be needed for even the semblance of pattern in residence to emerge. It is also clear that after a pattern does emerge, interpretation of particular residences with respect to that pattern requires additional sociological and cultural information. With the Nakanai, for example, it is important to know whether the husband's father is living or dead. If he is dead, did he die before or after the husband got married? If he died before, who acted as father-substitute for the husband? Is the father-substitute living or dead? Are the husband's uncles living or dead? Where do or did they reside? Where does the husband's lineage have land? These are the sociological facts which we must know. Behind them are the cultural facts from which we learn their relevance: the nature of the father-son relationship in Nakanai, the father's responsibility for his son's passage into marriage, which requires paying a bride-price. As long as the father lives he assumes at least nominal responsibility for these things, however much of the burden is, in fact, carried by other kinsmen. When the father dies, these responsibilities are formally assumed by someone else. Just who else depends on a great many considerations, which we need not go into here. Whoever that person is, however, he is likely to become a father-substitute as far as future residence decisions are concerned. Residence with him is, therefore, an expression of the patrilocal principle regardless of what the actual genealogical tie with him may be, or kinship term used for him. Once we understand this, we discover that most Nakanai men who live to marry spend some time in what I regard as patrilocal residence, many ultimately going on to what I regard as avunculocal residence in the hamlets associated with their respective matrilineal lineages.[5]

It should by now be clear that the determination of residence rules poses two different problems. The first problem has to do with recognizing the pattern of residence in a society. We have seen that census data alone may not be sufficient for this. The second problem has to do with classifying the residence of individual couples. We have here seen how essential are sociological and cultural data apart from census and genealogical materials in order to know whether individual cases do or do not conform to the pattern discerned. Such information, moreover, may serve to show how cases which appear to conform to one pattern really conform to another. This brings us back to the problem as it appeared in Truk where Fischer and I, both aware of the presence of patrilocal and matrilocal forms, cannot agree on which is which in specific cases. Even where we agree as to what the patterns are, we cannot agree as to what cases conform to them. In this instance, the same sociological and cultural data were available to both of us. Where we differed was in regard to what aspects of it we considered relevant for classifying a couple's residence. This difference, I believe, may have stemmed in part from a different resolution of ambiguities, which arise when we try to apply our residence concepts. Let me illustrate the problem with an example from Truk.

At the time of my census, I encountered a household in which there resided an elderly man with his second wife and his three sons by his first marriage. The eldest son was married, and his wife resided there too. The composition of this household was typical of that of a patrilocal extended family. The natural thing to do, therefore, would be to count the two married couples as two cases of patrilocal residence. In doing this, we are taking as our criterion for classification the type of extended family which the household presents as indicated by the relationships between

---

[5] This picture of Nakanai residence is based on preliminary analysis of the field data. Further analysis, now in progress, indicates that it will require refinement, without, however, affecting the point illustrated here.

its members. In this instance, both couples are residing in outward conformity with the pattern of a patrilocal extended family and are each, therefore, presumably in patrilocal residence.

Here, of course, we have operationally defined residence forms in terms of conformity with household patterns as defined by genealogical connections between the household members. But if we take as our criterion of patrilocal residence the fact that the bride has removed on marriage "to or near the parental home of the groom," to quote Murdock's (1949) definition, then the pattern of household composition is no longer a reliable basis for classifying individual residence. We must know who moved where at the time of marriage. When we ask about this in relation to the above Trukese household, we learn that both present wives moved into the house from elsewhere, their husbands already residing there, and the patrilocal picture is reinforced. On the basis of this definition of patrilocal residence there is no apparent need to seek further information. Certainly the son's case is clear. He lived here with his parents and when he married he brought his wife to his parents' home.

But let us now look at some additional facts. The father's first wife belonged to a matrilineal lineage, which owns the house and land in which this extended family lives. Nearby is another house in which lives a lineage sister of the dead first wife with her husband and children. We discover that the women of this lineage have lived here together with their husbands in a hamlet cluster and that the father moved here in matrilocal residence with his first wife. His sons belong to the owning lineage. When his first wife died, this lineage allowed him to continue to be with his children. When his son married, he brought his wife not to his father's house but to his own matrilineal lineage's place of localization. The house in which his father was residing was available to him because he had no sisters living there. Had he had sisters there, he would have had to build a separate house, for adult brothers and sisters may not sleep under the same roof. Now, if all the men in a matrilineal lineage brought their wives to live on their lineage land, the result would be an avunculocal extended family. Our seemingly perfect example of a patrilocal extended family turns out to be the result of an initial matrilocal residence by the father (subsequently filiolocal) and an avunculocal residence by the son.[6] But the son's residence is recognizable as avunculocal only when we see what would be the alignments which would result if everyone were residing in the same relationship to their matrilineal kin groups as he.

This example shows that we have a genuine problem when we try to apply our residence concepts to classifying individual marriages for purposes of statistical analysis. Our concepts, which in the abstract appear so precise, become very slippery when we try to use them in this way. If we stop to take into account the context in which these concepts were developed, I think both the reason for the problem and its solution become clear.

Our concepts have been designed for the purpose of classifying prevailing or ideal usages in different societies as a means of grouping these societies for comparative purposes. To do this it is necessary for the usages in question to have been adequately described beforehand. The concepts belong to the same order of abstraction as do such linguistic rubrics as "agglutinating" or "inflecting," which cannot be applied intelligently until the grammatical processes have first been analyzed in other terms. Concepts used for comparative purposes, moreover, must be based on criteria which are independent of any particular culture. That is why we define types of residence in terms of physical alignments of persons differentiated by genealogical (biological) considerations. The criteria are of necessity extra-cultural.

It is, therefore, a procedural fallacy to use these concepts as a basis for classifying the residence choices of individual members of a society. They do not choose on the basis of criteria which are outside their culture, which exist only in the heads of anthropologists. They choose on the basis of the criteria which are provided by their particular culture and which may be quite different —indeed probably are—from those used by the anthropologist in classifying their culture. This means that if I wish to apply the label "patrilocal" to one of the real choices within a culture, I must recognize that it means something different from patrilocal residence in the context of ethnological comparison. I must ex-

---

[6] Fischer's census shows that the father has since moved into matrilocal residence in his present marriage.

plain what I mean by the term in the context of individual choice. But I must do more than this.

Whatever may be the purposes of an ethnographer in describing a culture, he has the duty of describing it in terms which fit the phenomena. If he is going to describe residence, for example, he cannot work with an *a priori* set of residence alternatives, albeit he has defined them with the utmost care. He has to find out what are the actual residence choices which the members of the society studied can make within their particular socio-cultural setting. The only way he can do this is to construct a theory of their residence behavior in accordance with the scientific canons of theory construction. This means that he must try to conceive categories of residence and criteria of choice, which give the simplest and most accurate account of their behavior. He must try to validate them by using them to predict the future residence choices of betrothed persons, or by predicting where pairs of persons would live if they were married to each other and seeing whether his predictions agree with those, which members of the society would also make for such hypothetical marriages. Once he has isolated what are the several residence choices provided by the culture, he is in a position to ascertain their order of precedence and conditions under which the order of precedence changes. Anything less than this cannot claim to be an adequate description of a society's residence rules. Once such a description has been made, one can put whatever labels one wishes on the categories isolated, just as in linguistics once a phoneme has been isolated and described the assignment of an alphabetical symbol to it is a matter of convenience. Working with such descriptions, moreover, the comparativist can see clearly what he is doing when he classifies cultures in accordance with the concepts appropriate to his enquiry.

Let us consider, then, what are the categories of residence choice as I understand them to exist in Truk. Let us see what lies behind the labels which I used without explanation, in the tabulations at the beginning of this paper. Let us dispense with the labels entirely for the time being, and thus avoid any possibility of further nominalistic confusion.

In my published report on Truk (Goodenough 1951), I indicated that the cornerstone of its social structure is the property-owning corporation, which, because it perpetuates its membership by a principle of matrilineal descent and is a segment of the community rather than being widely extended across community lines, I chose to call a lineage. No individual can exist independent of some lineage affiliation. If he goes to another community he must either affiliate with one of its lineages or remain outside the community pale without food, shelter, or protection. If it has enough adult members and access to a suitable site, a lineage has its own dwelling house (or cluster of houses), which is regarded as the place where it is physically located. A large lineage may contain two or even three separately localized sublineages. Lineages may move from one site to another as they gain right of access to different plots of land; house sites are not regarded as permanent. There are several ways in which a lineage may have right of access. It may itself own the ground under full or provisional title (Goodenough 1951); one of its members may hold personal title to the ground; or a sublineage may be the owner. A lineage may also be localized on land which belongs to a man who has married into it. When this happens, the understanding is invariably that the man's children, who are members of the lineage, have received the land in gift from their father, so that in localizing here the lineage has moved, in effect, to land belonging to one of its members. With the tendency nowadays for the lineage to be localized in a cluster of smaller houses instead of a single large one as in former times, the site may consist of several adjacent plots under separate ownership; but each case will conform to the pattern above—three adjacent plots, for example, being held by the lineage, one of its members, and one of its husbands respectively. The need for juggling of this kind has also been increased on Romonum Island with the movement of all house sites to the beach, during the decade before World War II. The point of importance to note, however, is that a man who is living on land which he got from his father is in all probability not living in the extended family associated with his father's lineage, but in that associated with his or his wife's. Let us now see what are the possible choices of residence open to a married couple within this setting.

The first thing to note is that the choice is always between extended family households. Couples do not go off and set up in isolation by themselves. The only exceptions to this are native pastors and catechists whose residence is determined by their occupation. (They find it necessary, however, to try to make some arrangements for domestic coöperation with a neighboring household.) The important question for a married couple, then, is: to what extended families does it have access? It has access by right to the extended family associated with the lineage of either the bride or the groom. A member of a lineage which is not localized becomes a dependent of his or her father's lineage for purposes of shelter. The extended families associated with the wife's father's lineage and husband's father's lineage form, therefore, a pair of secondary possibilities for choice of residence. At any one time, however, a couple has but two alternatives: on the one hand the wife's lineage or, if it is not localized, then her father's lineage, and on the other hand the husband's lineage or, if it is not localized, then his father's. Other things being equal, as long as one party to the marriage belongs to a lineage which is localized, this lineage will be chosen before joining the other's father's lineage. Resort to a father's lineage of either spouse is, therefore, a fairly rare occurrence. Other things being equal, moreover, a couple will regularly choose to live with the extended family associated with the wife's lineage rather than that associated with the husband's. It is regarded as proper for one's children to grow up in the bosom of their own lineage in close association with their lineage "brothers" and "sisters," with whom they are expected to maintain absolute solidarity, no matter what the circumstances, for the rest of their lives. Given matrilineal descent as the principle of lineage membership, regular residence with the extended family associated with the husband's lineage would keep lineage brothers separated from one another until adulthood and lineage sisters would not normally live and work together either as children or adults. Choosing to reside with the wife's localized lineage, therefore, is consistent with the high value placed on lineage solidarity.

But what are the considerations, which make other things unequal? Under what circumstances do people regularly choose in favor of the husband's localized lineage even though the wife's lineage is localized? And under what circumstances do couples prefer to reside with a wife's father's lineage household rather than the household associated directly with the husband's lineage? What are the factors, in short, which favor a husband instead of his wife and a secondary instead of a primary affiliation?

Most instances of residence with the husband's lineage household occur in cases where the wife's lineage is not localized because it does not have enough adult women to run a separate household or lacks access to suitable land. But there are other circumstances favoring such residence. Ultimate responsibility and authority in a lineage is vested in its adult men. If residence with the wife's kin would take the husband too far away from where his own lineage house is located, it may appear advisable for him to bring his wife to live at the latter place. As the physical distance between the husband's and wife's lineage households increases and as the importance of the husband in his lineage affairs increases, the greater the likelihood that residence will be with the husband's kin. Where the husband or his lineage is in a position to provide the children with far more land than the wife's lineage, and at the same time the husband and wife come from communities too widely separated to make it possible to reside in one and maintain the land in the other, residence will be with the husband's kin. If the husband's lineage will soon die out, so that his children will take over its lands, these children may organize as a new lineage temporarily operating jointly with the survivors of their father's lineage. Such of these children as are women may bring their husbands into what may be regarded either as the wife's or wife's father's localized lineage (the former as one looks to the future, the latter as one looks to the past).

Finally, it may happen that a young couple may be requested to reside with elder relatives in a household in which they do not have any *right* to live. In Fischer's census, for example, I note the the case of an elderly man residing with his wife's localized kin group. He and his wife have no children. Nor are there junior kin in his wife's lineage who do not have greater responsibilities to others in the household (judging from my genealogical data). Living with them are this old man's sister's daughter and her newly acquired husband. As head of her lineage, the old man has obviously pulled her into this household with the consent of his wife and her kin (who are thus relieved of undue responsibility). She has no other reason for being there, and the arrangement will terminate when either the old man or his wife dies. Temporary arrangements like this one, made for mutual convenience and with the consent of those concerned, may be on the increase today. I suspect, however, that one hundred years ago they would also have accounted for the residence of up to five percent of the married couples.

The foregoing, then, are the considerations which I believe, the Trukese have in mind when they decide where they are going to live. By postulating them, I am able to give a straightforward accounting of Trukese residence behavior as I experienced it. I find, moreover, that they make the results of the many residential and marital changes revealed in Fischer's census thoroughly intelligible, a fact not without significance for the validity of this view of Trukese residence behavior.

If we accept as valid the formulation of their residence principles presented here, then it is clear that in making their residence decisions the Trukese do not choose between living with the parents of the husband or the parents of the wife. With what parents, if any, a couple resides is a fortuitous by-product of a choice made with other considerations in mind. While there may be specific inquiries for which we might find it desirable to ascertain the frequency with which different parent-child residential alignments occur in Truk, such alignments have nothing directly to do with Trukese residence rules nor are they descriptive of them.[7] Truk is, therefore, in obvious contrast with Nakanai, where couples choose to live in the hamlet where the husband's father resides, regardless of the latter's reason for being there.

It should also be clear that while land-ownership in Truk is a factor which limits the number of sites where a lineage can be localized as an extended family, individual couples are concerned with what extended family they will join, not with whose land they will live on (except in the case of inter-community or inter-island marriages as already noted). To use land ownership as a basis for differentiating types of residence choice, therefore, seems to

---

[7] Their irrelevance for understanding residence possibilities among the Lapps, also, has recently been pointed out by Robert N. Pehrson (1954). He also has difficulty applying the concepts of patrilocality, matrilocality, etc., to the principles governing residence decisions among the Lapps.

me to be artificial.[8] Undoubtedly there are societies, however, where land plays a more direct role in the residence choices of individual couples.

Since it is extended families between which the Trukese choose, we may list the types of residence which are descriptive of the possibilities inherent in their social structure as follows:

1. Residence with the extended family associated with the wife's lineage.
2. Residence with the extended family associated with the husband's lineage.
3. Residence with the extended family associated with the wife's father's lineage.
4. Residence with the extended family associated with the husband's father's lineage.
5. Residence by arrangement with a specific kinsman in an extended family in which one is otherwise without residential right.
6. Residence independent of any extended family—only a hypothetical possibility until recent times, now involving church officials and a few persons seeking to break with traditional ways.

In discussing residence rules in my earlier report on Trukese social structure (Goodenough 1951), I lumped types one and three above under the heading "matrilocal" and referred to types two and four together as "patrilocal," using these terms in a sense equivalent to that for which Adam has coined the expressions "uxorilocal" and "virilocal" (Adam 1947).

This brings us to the problem facing the comparativist. Granting that these are the types of residence inherent in Trukese social structure, by what means are we to equate them with the very different possibilities inherent in Nakanai social structure or that of any other society?

To solve this problem we must have a system of residence classification into which the types belonging to any and every particular culture can be readily fitted. The typology already established, taking as its criteria the several possible alignments of primary and secondary relatives in spatial proximity, is in every

---

[8] Fischer, recognizing that additional sociological information was needed to interpret the residence picture, decided to use information about who now held the land and from whom they had gotten it, collecting this information when he made his census. This *a priori* decision on his part is one of the differences between us in interpreting the residence situation.

respect ideally suited for this purpose. The only thing that has been wrong with it has been the improper use made of it in ethnographic description. But this does not answer the question of how we are in practice to go about fitting the types we get for a specific culture into these types we use for comparative purposes.

Since the comparative system is based on alignments of primary and secondary kin, we must examine each cultural type that emerges in ethnographic description to see what alignments it would logically produce under the ideal conditions in which all couples choose it and everyone has a full complement of living kinsmen. Let us apply this procedure to the first four types we have established for Truk and see what happens.

> *Type 1.* If everyone lived with the extended family associated with the wife's matrilineage, the result would be an alignment of matrilineally related women with their husbands; the mother-daughter link would stand out.
>
> *Type 2.* If everyone lived with the extended family associated with the husband's matrilineage, the result would be an alignment of matrilineally related men with their wives; the link would be between mother's brother and sister's son.
>
> *Type 3.* If everyone lived with the extended family associated with the wife's father's lineage, the result would be an alignment of women whose fathers belonged to the same matrilineage. Strange as this grouping may appear, the Trukese have standard expressions for this kind of relationship; the women would all be *pwiipwi winisam*, "siblings through fathers," or *jëfëkyren eew cëk sööpw*, "heirs (as distinct from members) of the same lineage."
>
> *Type 4.* If everyone lived with the extended family associated with the husband's father's lineage, the result would now be a similar alignment of men who were *pwiipwi winisam*, whose fathers belonged to the same matrilineage. The link would be through father's brother, father's mother's brother, father's mother's mother's brother, etc.

Notably absent from the alignments of kin possible are groupings of patrilineally related men with their wives and of patrilineally related women with their husbands. Such alignments could result only by having everyone in Truk resort to residence type 5, living by special arrangement in an extended family in which they were without residential rights, and doing so in relation to the same set of relatives. It appears, therefore, that as long as extended families based on matrilineal lineages remain the object of residential choice in Truk, no matter what changes occur in the preference given to affiliation through the husband or wife, there cannot develop extended families containing systematic alignments of patrilineally related men or women. Such can only arise through a cultural change of a more profound nature: a change in the object of choice itself, so that, for example, couples no longer see the choice as one between localized lineages but as one between the husband's and wife's parents (wherever they may be residing).

Trukese residence types 1 and 2 are clearly best regarded as equivalent to the matrilocal and avunculocal types of comparative ethnology. By analogy it is possible to regard types 3 and 4 as the logical counterparts of amitalocal and patrilocal residence in a society where localized matrilineal kin groups are the objects of residential choice. The comparable analogues of matrilocal and avunculocal residence will be equally peculiar in a society where the objects of choice are localized patrilineal groups.

These considerations led me to list the incidence of type 4 under the patrilocal heading in the tables at the beginning of this paper. In view of the general association of patrilocal residence with the systematic alignment of patrilineally related men, such practice may lead only to further confusion and for this reason be unwise. The point remains, however, that patrilocal residence in this more usual sense can occur in Truk only following upon a fundamental change in its cultural principles governing the object of residential choice. After such change, Truk would necessarily be a different society for purposes of comparative study, whose residence principles would have to be worked out anew within the framework of its now different social system. The residence types that would fit that system would resemble those which fit its present one no more closely than do those of any other society. While we may balk at calling residence type 4 patrilocal because of the groove in which our thinking about residence has long slid, there is no logical reason for not doing so. Within the framework of Trukese culture as it is presently organized, type 4 is the structural analogue of what in other social systems we would not hesitate to call patrilocal residence.

It has been my immediate purpose in this paper to examine the problem of reliability in ethnographic reporting as it relates to customs of residence in marriage. In doing so, I have necessarily touched on matters which have significance for the study of culture generally. In concluding this discussion, therefore, it may be well to say something directly about them.

We noted first that census data of the usual kind are not sufficient for a reliable formulation of residence customs. We needed additional information. The additional information needed was different for the two societies examined. What was relevant in one was irrelevant in the other. We saw, moreover, that there is no *a priori* way of deciding what of all the possible kinds of information will be relevant; this is a matter to be determined in the light of all the other things an ethnographer is learning about the society he is studying. Every ethnographer knows that as he keeps learning and trying to find order in what he learns, he eventually arrives at a way of viewing his material such that a coherent structure emerges. This is just another way of saying that cultural description is the formulation of theory of a complex sort by which we seek to account for what we observe and what our informants tell us. It is this fact, so much a part of our everyday professional experience, whose significance for ethnographic method I think we have tended to overlook—an oversight, which seems to be responsible for many discrepancies in ethnographic reporting of the sort illustrated here. I think we have tended to regard theory as beginning at the comparative or cross-cultural level and to see the methodology of ethnographic description as largely a matter of accurate recording and truthful reporting. I trust that Fischer's and my experience is sufficient to show that being a careful and honest reporter is only the beginning. One must be a theoretician as well.

But here again our disciplinary bias has done us a disservice. Since we have tended to regard theory as belonging to the domain of comparative study and have looked on ethnography as the means by which we obtain data to support or refute the kinds of propositions which have preoccupied the various schools of comparativists, we have consequently been inclined to try to order our data within the conceptual framework of comparative study. Thus we are inclined to feel that we have made a descriptive ethnographic statement when we say that residence in a society is prevailingly patrilocal, when what we are really saying, of course, is that the society has residence customs of a nature undisclosed but such that we feel they ought to be classified as patrilocal for comparative purposes. Thus we confuse the role of the ethnographer with that of the ethnologist. In view of the problem discussed here, it appears that this can be our undoing.

For this reason I have tried to show that what we do as ethnographers is, and must be kept, independent of what we do as comparative ethnologists. An ethnographer is constructing a theory that will make intelligible what goes on in a particular social universe. A comparativist is trying to find principles common to many different universes. His data are not the direct observations of an ethnographer, but the laws governing the particular universe as the ethnographer formulates them. It is by noting how these laws vary from one universe to another and under what conditions, that the comparativist arrives at a statement of laws governing the separate sets of laws which in turn govern the events in their respective social universes. Although they operate at different levels of abstraction, both ethnographer and comparativist are engaged in theory construction. Each must, therefore, develop concepts appropriate to his own level of abstraction, and in the case of the ethnographer to his particular universe. When we move from one level to the other we must shift our conceptual frameworks in accordance with systematic transformation procedures. Short-cutting in this has, I think, been another major reason for imprecision in our researches.

Despite such imprecisions, comparative study has managed to go forward to a remarkable degree. It is precisely because of the advances there made that we are now having to take serious stock in such matters as ethnographic reliability. I think, in this regard, that we are reaching a point comparable to that reached by linguists a short generation ago. Linguistics, with its already monumental achievements in comparative philology, took a great step forward as a science because linguists recognized that every language presents a new structure unlike any other, and that only by developing rigorous methods for arriving at precise theoretical statements of these structures would it be possible significantly to advance farther the study of language in general. I think we may be coming to a point where substantial progress in cultural anthropology will likewise require concentrating on descriptive ethnography as a legitimate scientific end in itself.

18 AN ALTERNATE RESIDENCE CLASSIFICATION

Paul Bohannan

For some time there has been considerable dissatisfaction among anthropologists about traditional modes of residence classification. It is significant that the Sixth Edition of the Royal Anthropological Institute's *Notes and Queries in Anthropology* reduces the whole problem to a footnote which states that "inquiries should be made as to the residential location, temporary and permanent, of married couples. The definition of marriage as patrilocal when the couple lives in the locality of the husband's parents, and matrilocal when the couple lives in the locality of the wife's parents, is misleading and should be avoided" (1951: 112).

There is similar significance in the fact that Murdock, in *Social Structure*, has gone to the opposite extreme and systematized his own and others' suggestions for the refinement of the categories of residence reckoning, and has found six basic types of residence, based on the initial and subsequent residence of newly married couples (1949: 16 et seq). There have been other attacks on the traditional system, the most noteworthy being Adam's suggestion that the terms patrilocal and matrilocal should be replaced by virilocal and uxorilocal (Adam 1948), and Goodenough's paper stressing quantities and difficulties of classification (Goodenough 1956).

It seems likely that at least part of the dissatisfaction and the attempts to refine notions of residence springs from the fact that we have only a single system of classification: that based on the

Originally published in *American Anthropologist*, Vol. 59, 1957, pp. 126–31. Reprinted with permission of the editor of *American Anthropologist*.

location of the married couple vis-à-vis the kinsmen of one or the other. There are doubtless many other ways in which residence patterns can be classified.

One such classification stems from a distinction—necessary, but often forgotten by anthropologists and especially by sociologists—between families and households.

As Murdock has pointed out (1949: 3–4) there are (logically, but not necessarily terminologically) eight primary relationships which are possible within the nuclear family: (1) husband-wife, (2) father-son, (3) father-daughter, (4) mother-son, (5) mother-daughter, (6) brother-brother, (7) sister-sister, and (8) brother-sister. A family in any society is obviously a small group of people, all of whom stand in one or another of these eight primary relationships, either by marriage, birth, or adoption, to all of the other members of the group. The criterion is kinship or pseudokinship relationship.

A household or domestic group, on the other hand, is made up of people who live in the same house or compound. It is a spatial group, or "local group."

In the past, family and household have often been confused because of the fact that in many—probably most—societies of the world, the two groups are made up more or less of the same people. But households obviously need not be made up of kinsmen; in many societies, many households contain servants, slaves, pawns, boarders, or other members whose tie is not one of kinship. However, because of the fact that kinsmen and family members are so often found in the same household, the idiom for discussing household members is often one of kinship terms. This fact—that one set of relationship terms is made to do double duty—must not blind the analyst; rather, he can use it as one of his tools for classification.

The question becomes, "If two or more different kinship relationships within the household come into conflict, which is the last to be broken in a statistically important number of cases?" That is to say, if a man's father and his wife cannot get on, and he must break one relationship or the other, which one survives? The surviving relationship can be called the basic family relationship for domestic grouping in that society.

In various societies recorded in the literature, I have found households built on five of the eight possible basic relationships. I have not discovered—but see no reason there should not be—a society which stresses the mother-son link in the creation of households. Neither have I found examples of those which stress the brother-brother link or the sister-sister link (although one sometimes hears these values expressed in those societies which more specifically stress the father-son and mother-daughter link respectively).

The five primary relationships on which households are predominantly based are: (1) husband-wife, (2) father-son, (3) mother-daughter, (4) father-daughter and (5) brother-sister.

Households based on the husband-wife relationship. According to our classification, the residence patterns of Western civilization are overwhelmingly based on the husband-wife relationship. In our popular lore and beliefs, we find little but difficulty awaiting the married couple "unfortunate" enough to have to live with the parents of one or the other spouse. We are predominantly "neolocal." Further, it is the norm that, in a dispute which involves a person with spouse and parent, he must take the side of the spouse. Further, parents, in determining modes of action for raising their children, try to work out methods and techniques for presenting a solid front. Among ourselves, the husband-wife relationship forms the basis of household grouping, and in almost all classes we feel that the "normal" mode of living is for the married partners to live together, with no one save their young children.

Yet, not all of the societies whose values incline them to households based on the husband-wife relationship can be classed so decisively as "neolocal." The Hausa of Northern Nigeria are an example. M. Smith (1954: 21) states that "marriage is virilocal, the woman coming to live with the man, usually in his father's compound if it is the man's first marriage." In another place he says that "as marriage is virilocal and usually patrilocal, the core of the co-residential unit is a group of males linked by ties of kinship traced through males" (p. 21). However, Smith points out, and Dry (1950) has explained somewhat more fully, that in middle-class Hausa society a man seeks to set up a house of his own soon after marriage. His reasons are usually expressed in terms of women. "The wives of the household head look on a daughter-in-law as someone who will now do all the work for them. . . . This attitude is resented by the new wife. . . . The husband, who has the unenviable task of composing . . . the quarrels between his wife and his mother is anxious to take the first opportunity of keeping them apart."

Yet, because *purdah* is extreme in this stratum of Hausa society, the young man need move only a very short distance to accomplish his purpose. From the standpoint of the village or the quarter, the marriage can still be regarded as "patrilocal," even though different households have been established. The man and his father still co-operate in agricultural activities, even though each is nominally independent and a new "domestic group" is established.

Households based on the father-son relationship. The Tiv of central Nigeria can also be described as "virilocal and usually patrilocal": all wives move to their husbands' compounds at marriage, and in the case of about 83 percent of males, that compound is in the husband's agnatic lineage area and composed principally of his agnates. In 26 months' field work among the Tiv, we found only three instances of uxorilocal marriage (one of those in official records of murder trials, in which a man killed someone for jeering at him for living uxorilocally). Tiv seldom—almost never—move into compounds of their own while their fathers are still alive. The Tiv compound, spatially based like the Hausa compound on the genealogy of the polygynous family (Bohannan 1954, Appendix A), normally splits a year or so after the death of the compound head, or occasionally following disputes between brothers or other nonlineal kinsmen. The difference from the Hausa becomes apparent when we realize that it never occurs to most Tiv to leave their fathers' compounds should their wives dispute with other members of the compound. In Hausa society, if mother-in-law and daughter-in-law cannot get along, a new household is established; while in Tiv society, if a wife cannot get along with her husband's mother or kinsmen, her marriage is dissolved. Tiv say that you can get a new wife any time but that you have only one set of parents; they hold that the gravest fault a wife can commit is to split agnates. The Tiv father (and, after him, the mother) is always right; a man almost always takes his parents' side against his wife. These facts have a profound effect on the settlement patterns of the two societies.

Households based on the mother-daughter relationship. One of the best-known and best-documented examples of a society whose residence norms stress the mother-daughter relationship is that of the Hopi of Arizona (Eggan 1950; Titiev 1944). Here the houses, or pueblo rooms, are owned by women and handed down from mother to daughter. Although men build houses they do not own them. A man considers his sister's house his real home and he leaves his ritual objects there when he takes his mundane property to the house of his wife. He is peripheral both in his sister's and in his wife's household.

Households based on the father-daughter relationship. This type is the most ephemeral of all, and may be found to depend on some other basic relationship, when more research is done. Like domestic groups based on a mother-daughter relationship, those based on a father-daughter relationship tend to be associated with uxorilocality or matrilocality or both. However, societies, which stress the father-daughter relationship for establishing residence, seem always to be characterized by a strong economic or subsistence relationship between the father-in-law and son-in-law. Opler (1941: 162) notes that among the Apache, "the girl and her female relatives build the house. They put it up near the home of the girl's parents for the young people usually go to live with the girl's relatives. . . . This emphasis upon matrilocal residence calls attention to one of the fundamental themes of the culture, for the organization of economy assumes the presence and closest cooperation of the sons-in-law." Because of a man's economic obligations to his wife's father, it is almost necessary for him to live in the vicinity of his wife's parents. Also, a man's kinsmen sometimes follow him and establish their homes with his affines. Classification of this instance will obviously vary with the definition of "household," and we are not given the Apache definitions.

Households based on a brother-sister relationship. Finally, there are those comparatively rare societies in which the household group tends to be based primarily on a brother-sister relationship. Fortes found an example in Ashanti. When he was working there, he noticed that in Ashanti villages about an hour before dusk, girls were to be seen hurrying in all directions, carrying large pots of cooked food. One child often carried food out of a house, and a few minutes later an equivalent amount of food was carried in by another. Fortes found that the food was being taken from houses where their mothers lived to those where their fathers lived. Husband and wife obviously need not live in the same household group; the children usually divide their time between these two households. Although modern educated Ashanti live in households which differ little from those of Europe and America, the Ashanti of the villages still live in these sibling households. Fortes' analysis of his extensive genealogies shows that the norm in the villages is for the dwelling group to be a single cognatic group with a few affines: most often, a group of brothers and sisters, with perhaps the sons and daughters of the sisters (Fortes, Steel and Ady 1947).

An even more complex example of households formed on the basis of brother-sister groups is provided by the "predominantly matrilocal" Yao of Nyasaland, studied by Clyde Mitchell. Here the women of the matrilineage form a localized group, whereas men are dispersed. "Therefore, within any matrilineage group, groups of uterine sisters are differentiated from each other, *but always in reference to a man who is usually their eldest brother*" (my italics; Mitchell 1951: 316). It is around this relationship of a man to his sisters that domestic groups are organized—the groups which Mitchell calls "sorority groups." Most men (all except those acting as care-takers of their group of sisters) live matrilocally. Yet "only a small portion of a husband's time is spent in the village into which he has married" (ibid: 328). Men caring for sorority groups (composed of their sisters and sisters' husbands and children) take their wives to live with such groups. The domestic group, or hamlet of four or five huts, is thus based primarily on the sibling relationships of sisters and an elder brother. Mitchell says specifically that "The bonds between brother and sister are much stronger than those between husband and wife," and cites a dispute in which a woman took her brother's side against her husband, "though she must have known that this might lead to divorce" (ibid: 330–31).

Households difficult to classify. In the traditional method of classification, it is sometimes necessary to point out that residence norms may vary systematically with different stages of the family cycle: some are matri-patrilocal, and other combinations can be made as needed. It is therefore necessary to make some composite categories when seeking the primary relationships on which households are based. The Nuer form a special and interesting case. They are what Murdock's classification would term matri-patrilocal. In the early stages of a marriage, the father-daughter relationship is stressed, and the bride stays at the home of her father. Then, "when his first born has been weaned, the husband builds his wife a hut in his father's homestead, facing the family kraal" (Evans-Pritchard 1951: 73). It is now the husband-wife relationship which becomes dominant. Husband and wife often live with the husband's father but may move about, living with the kinsmen of either. In other words, the household is established on weaning the first child, not on marriage.

The distinctions to be drawn are clear: the family is a social group, which may or may not be a local, spatial group. If it is, it will almost of necessity choose one or the other relationship as the primary or basic one on which to build households. It is possible to make a supplementary classification of residence patterns by determining the values and norms for residence in this regard, and the proportion of households within the society which conform to it.

Classification of residence patterns by this method cannot be made precisely to correlate with Murdock's classification, nor is it especially desirable that it should. We have two ways of looking at residence classification instead of one. It is noteworthy that both classifications, to be of maximum value, must be supported by quantitative data. As was pointed out in *Notes and Queries*, unless it is so supported, it is not significant to say that a society is patrilocal; neither would it be significant to say merely that it bases its domestic groups on the husband-wife (or some other) relationship.

PART VI

SOME SPECIAL PROBLEMS

19 AN ANALYSIS OF RITUAL
CO-PARENTHOOD (COMPADRAZGO)[1]

Sidney W. Mintz and Eric R. Wolf

As ANTHROPOLOGISTS HAVE BEEN DRAWN into the study of
Latin American cultures, they have gathered increasing
amounts of material on the characteristic cultural mechanisms
of *compadrazgo*. This term designates the particular complex of
relationships set up between individuals primarily, though not
always, through participation in the ritual of Catholic baptism.

This rite involves, among its various aspects, three individuals
or groups of individuals. These are: first, an initiate, usually a
child; secondly, the parents of the initiate; third, the ceremonial
sponsor or sponsors of the initiate. It thus involves three sets
of relationships. The first links parents and child, and is set up
within the confines of the immediate biological family. The
second links the child and his ceremonial sponsor, a person
outside the limits of his immediate biological family. This relation
is familiar to most Americans as the relation between godfather
or godmother and godchild. The third set of relationships links
the parents of the child to the child's ceremonial sponsors. In
Spanish, these call each other *compadres* (Latin *compater-
commater*, Spanish *compadre-comadre*, Italian *compare-commare*,
French *compere-commere*, German *Gevatter-Gevatterin*, Russian

Originally published in the *Southwestern Journal of Anthropology*, Vol. 6,
1950. Reprinted with permission of the authors and of the editor of the
Southwestern Journal of Anthropology.
[1] All translations are by the authors unless otherwise indicated.
The writers wish to thank the University of Puerto Rico and the Rockefeller Foundation for their sponsorship of the Puerto Rico Social Anthropology Project. Field data gathered by the authors and their colleagues on this
Project have been used in the present article.

kum-kuma, etc.), literally co-parents of the same child. The old English form of this term, *godsib*, is so unfamiliar to most English-speaking people today that they even ignore its hidden survival in the noun "gossip" and in the verb "to gossip." In English, as in the Ecuadorian *compadrear*, the meaning of the term has narrowed to encompass just one, if perhaps a notable characteristic of *compadre* relations. Most other aspects of this relationship have, however, fallen by the wayside. In contrast, in Medieval Europe, the *compadre* mechanism was of considerable cultural importance, and in present-day Latin America, its cultural role is attested by its frequent extensions beyond the boundaries of baptismal sponsorship.

> The thing itself is curious, and quite novel to an Englishman of the present day [wrote Edward B. Tylor (1861: 250–51)]. The godfathers and godmothers of a child become, by their participation in the ceremony, relations to one another and to the priest who baptizes the child, and call one another ever afterwards *compadre* and *comadre*. . . . In Mexico, this connexion obliges the *compadres* and *comadres* to hospitality and honesty and all sorts of good offices towards one another; and it is wonderful how conscientiously this obligation is kept to, even by people who have no conscience at all for the rest of the world. A man who will cheat his own father or his own son will keep faith with his *compadre*. To such an extent does this influence become mixed up with all sorts of affairs, and so important is it, that it is necessary to count it among the things that tend to alter the course of justice in the country.

In this article, the writers hope to present some material dealing with the historical antecedents of the *compadre* mechanism, and to discuss some of its present-day functional correlates.

Emphasis in studies of *compadrazgo* to date has largely centered on attempts to identify a European or Indian background for its various component traits (Parsons 1936: 524–25; Redfield and Villa Rojas 1934: 373–74; Foster 1948: 264). Other studies have dealt with the diffusion of the complex in certain parts of Latin America, and the diversity of functions which it has assumed (Paul 1942). A recent trend has been to consider the *compadre* system as a significant feature of a putative Criollo culture (Committee on Latin American Anthropology of the National Research Council 1949: 152).

The present writers hope to deal with the *compadre* system rather in terms of possible functional relationships to other aspects of culture, such as the family, the status system, the system of land ownership, the legal system, the role of the individual in culture, and so forth. We shall especially emphasize its functions in furthering social solidarity. We shall employ the term "horizontal" to designate the direction which the *compadre* mechanism takes when linking together members of the same class. We shall use the term "vertical" to indicate the direction it takes when tying together members of different classes. Finally, we hope to discuss *compadrazgo* not only in terms of the ethnographic present, but also in terms of its past functions, that is, in terms of its historical context.

HISTORICAL ANTECEDENTS

This section will deal with the historical development of *compadrazgo* and its functional implications in the past.

We have seen that in Catholic practice, a sponsor aids in the initiation of a new member into the Church. He must be an established member of the religious community. His presence and ministrations in effect testify that the new candidate is willing and able to receive the prescribed initiatory rite. In Catholic theory, this initiatory rite is regarded as a form of spiritual rebirth, and an analogy is drawn between the role of the biological father in the process of conception on the one hand and the role of the sponsor as a spiritual father on the other. This notion of spiritual affinity has in turn given rise to notions of spiritual kinship, and laid the basis for the formation of ritual kin relationships through the mechanism of sponsorship at baptism.

Each of these three ideas has a separate history. Each is made up in turn of strands derived from different cultural backgrounds. The notion of sponsorship finds no warrant in the New Testament, and Canon Law refers to "custom" as the judicial basis upon which the precept rests (Kearney 1925: 4). It may derive in part from Jewish practice at circumcision where a witness is required to hold the child undergoing the ritual. This witness is called by a term derived from the Greek (Bamberger 1923: 326). In this connection, it is perhaps significant that the Eleusynian Mysteries of the Greeks also made use of sponsors (Drews 1907: 447). The term "sponsor" itself represents an adaptation

of a term current in Roman legal terminology where *sponsio*
signified a contract enforced by religious rather than by legal
sanctions (Kearney 1925: 33–34). Finally, we know that the
primitive Church used sponsors to guard against the admission
of untrustworthy individuals, clearly an important function in
the early days of persecution. Hence the term *fidei iussores*, those
who testified to the good faith of the applicant, by which sponsors
were also known.

The second component, the notion of spiritual rebirth, may
also represent the product of several divergent traditions. However, this aspect of the institution falls outside the province of
the present article.

The aspect of ritual kinship derived from sponsorship at baptism underwent its own special development. During the period
of St Augustine (354–430 AD), parents usually acted as sponsors for their own children. This custom was so widespread that
Bishop Boniface was of the opinion that no one but parents
could act as sponsors for the child's baptism. In a letter to
Bishop Boniface, St Augustine discussed this point, and drew
attention to cases in which the sponsors had not been the parents. Slave owners had acted as sponsors for children borne by
their slaves; orphans had been baptized with the aid of unknown
third persons who had consented to act as sponsors; and exposed
children had been initiated under the sponsorship of religious
women (Kearney 1925: 30–31).

Roughly a hundred years later, the Byzantine emperor Jus-
tinian, who ruled from 527–65 AD, first issued an edict prohibiting marriages between spiritual relatives. The terms *compater*
and *commater* first appeared in 585 and 595 AD, within the
confines of the Western Church. Thus we may note first that
a separate set of sponsors tended to be a later development
from a stage in which parents and sponsors were the same people; and secondly, that this separation must have been effected
within both the Eastern and Western Empires roughly between
the first quarter of the fifth century AD and the end of the sixth
century. Nevertheless, full acceptance of this separation and
consequent exogamy took place only gradually. From the evidence noted by the Byzantine historian Procopius, we may judge
that in the beginning of this period, godparents still actually

adopted their godchildren (Laurin 1866: 220). In 753 AD St Boniface could still write:

> The priests throughout Gaul and France maintain that for them a man who takes to wife a widow, to whose child he has acted as godfather, is guilty of a very serious crime. As to the nature of this sin, if it is a sin, I was entirely ignorant, nor have I ever seen it mentioned by the fathers, in the ancient canons, nor in the decree of the pope, nor by the apostles in their catalogue of sins (Boniface 1940: 61–62).

But the Council of Munich, held in 813 AD, prohibited parents from acting as sponsors for their own children altogether, and in the books of the Council of Metz of the same year, parents and sponsors are clearly referred to by separate sets of terms.

The next two hundred years witnessed a wider and wider extension of the ties of ritual kinship, and a concomitant growth of the exogamous group. A Council of Metz held in 888 AD attempted to restrict the development, but without effect. The incest group, biological as well as ritual, was extended to cover seven degrees of relationship. There was an increase in the number of ceremonials at which sponsors officiated, accompanied by an increase in the number of people executing distinctive roles at any one ceremony who could be included in the circle of kin. Finally, the number of sponsors executing any given function grew as well.

Where baptism and confirmation had originally been one set of rites, they grew apart and became two separate ceremonies, within the area dominated by the Western Church. This separation is documented for the Frankish kingdom in the eighth century, and was accompanied by the development of two different sets of sponsors, for baptism and for confirmation (Laurin 1866: 220). Since confirmation was looked upon as a completion of the baptismal act, confirmation sponsors similarly became ritual kin. In the Eastern Church, however, baptism and confirmation remained one rite, but different sets of sponsors and hence ritual relatives were added for a hair-cutting rite as well as for "wet" baptism (Durham 1928: 304). The Western Church, in turn, added ritual kin relationships with a "catechismal" godfather, who was present at ceremonies and abjurations preceding the

baptismal act. For a long time it was also believed that the
sacrament of confession produced a bond of ritual kinship between the father confessor and the confessant, until Pope Boniface the Seventh abrogated this relationship in 1298 AD.

But as the number of ceremonies productive of ritual kin
relations grew, so grew the number of people who were geared
into kinship arrangements. First, the Western Church extended
spiritual relationships to cover the officiating priest, the sponsors,
the child, the child's parents, and their respective children. Thus
we get spiritual fraternity as well as spiritual co-parenthood. In
this context, we may recall that the final ban against priests'
marriages and concubinage was not issued until the Council of
Trent (1545–63 AD). Finally, the number of sponsors increased,
until general custom admitted between one and thirty baptismal
sponsors (Tuschen 1936: 61). While Pope Boniface abrogated
ritual kin relationships arising from the confessional, he decreed
at the same time that all the sponsors who were present at any
given ceremony entered into valid ritual kin relationships, and
necessarily became part of the widening exogamic circles.

Despite the largely formal nature of the material that deals
with the growth of ritual kin ties during this period, we may
perhaps venture some guesses as to possible functional correlates
of the mechanism, and attempt to delimit some of the factors in
its formation.

Ecclesiastical legislation on the subject tends to center in two
main periods: in the ninth century AD on the one hand, and in
the period from about 1300 AD to the end of the sixteenth century on the other. The interim period witnessed highest development of the feudal order. Its main cultural conditions may briefly
be restated. Ownership of land was vested in the feudal lord. He
also owned a share of the labor of the serfs who lived on his land.
In return he granted the worker rights to use the land, ownership
of certain tools, and the right to consume some of the agricultural
and handicraft goods which he produced. The mutual obligations
and services which made up this system were maintained by
custom, and this complex of custom operated largely through
face-to-face relationships between its carriers. We hope to indicate that the *compadre* mechanism and its ritual kin correlates

were a functioning part of the class system implicit in this basic relationship.

Many writers have suggested that the *compadre* mechanism superseded earlier relationships of a tribal character based on actual or fictitious ties of blood. Thus Kummer feels that "it subordinated the community of blood to the community of faith" (Kummer 1931: 789). Tomasic notes that the *compadre* mechanism maintained itself within Dinaric society while blood brotherhood declined (Tomasic 1948: 80). He sees some relationship between this phenomenon and "the strengthening of the power of the state," and states that the *compadre* mechanism "was transferred from the tribal to the state level." With the growth of the state and its formal institutions, *compadrazgo* thus served to manipulate the increasingly impersonal structure in terms of person-to-person relationships.

In more specific fashion, Dopsch has related some forms of artificial relationships and "brotherhood arrangements" among feudal tenants to changes in the pattern of inheritance (Dopsch 1918–20, 1: 378). When the power of the large landowners was at its peak during the declining phase of the Roman Empire and during the initial period of feudal consolidation, tenants inherited rights of tenure from their neighbors in the absence of descendants in the direct line. With changes away from the predominance of large landowners, and towards increased political centralization, this right of neighbor inheritance gave way to inheritance on the part of other relatives of the deceased, notably on the part of siblings. Blood or ritual brothers then became an asset in the struggle "to lighten the economic and social duties with which the landowners burdened their tenants" (Dopsch 1918–20, 1: 378). During this period, inheritance of tenure on the manor within the same household became more secure, the greater the number of potential heirs and workers. Horizontally phrased mechanisms like the Latin *adfratatio* and the Visigoth *hermandad* kept the land within the group of ritual and blood brothers, and prevented its reversion to the lord's demesne. The Church, anxious to establish itself as an independent landowner in its own right, capitalized on this change in the process of inheritance to press its own claims. It accomplished this through the enforcement of religious rulings regarding exogamy.

The marriages within the kin group and within the group of affinal relatives heavily reinforced the weight of the old Germanic limitations on the right of the individual to dispose of property, and as a result put the Church in a disadvantageous position (Dopsch 1918–20, 2: 227).

These limitations were used against the Church by its main adversaries in the struggle over land, the lay aristocracy and feudal lords. When the Church prohibited marriage within seven degrees of relationship, it prohibited it among all persons who for any legal purpose could claim blood relationship with each other (Maitland and Pollock 1923: 387–88). This struggle was won by the Church, which in the process acquired almost complete control over legislation covering the making and execution of testaments.

Thus we may trace the early increase in exogamy to three different, yet interdependent factors: the attempt of the serfs to maintain their economic status; the attempt of the people to manipulate the growing structure of the state and the growing number of formal institutions through the use of a mechanism with which they were familiar; and the attempt of the Church to establish itself as an independent owner of landed property. In the final analysis, all three factors are but facets of the growing centralization of the feudal structure. This process took place in the main at the expense of the lay aristocracy. In the struggle the Crown attempted to play off Church and serfs against the feudal barons; the Church supported Crown and serfs against its lay competitors; and the serfs looked to both Crown and Church in their effort to increase their rights on the estates of the lay aristocracy.

Just as the increase in ritual brotherhood and in the size of the exogamic group may relate to this early stage of development of feudal tenures, so the great increase in *compadre* relationships and ritual kin prohibitions connected with them appear to relate to later changes in the tenure of serfs in relationship to their feudal lords.

The outstanding characteristic of the *compadre* mechanism is its adaptiveness to different situations. As the structure of the situation changes, so we may expect to see the *compadre* mechanism serve different purposes. As tenure became increasingly fixed within individual households, these units were also drawn into individual vertical relationships to the manorial administration. These different relationships crystallized into different rules for different groups of people on the manor. Far from being homogeneous, manorial custom took clear note of this process of differentiation. Under feudal conditions, then, one of the main functions of the *compadre* relationship was to structure such individual or family relationships vertically between the members of different classes.

In medieval France, "parents attempted to win for the baptismal candidate material advantages through their choice of godparents" (Henninger 1891: 31). In Germany, "poor people invited individuals of higher status to become godparents to their children. . . . The nobles reversed this custom and invited their subjects, or at least their subjects' representatives, as *compadres*" (Boesch 1900: 26–27). Mercenaries asked nobles to serve as godparents; day laborers asked their employers or the service staff of the manor. Officials often asked the city council, and the city budgets of the time show that the outlays arising from these ceremonial duties were often charged to the city treasury (Boesch 1900: 26–27). A "luminous instance" of how the mechanism was manipulated in daily practice is furnished by Coulton (Coulton 1936: 264). Monks were not allowed to stand as godparents, for fear that increased material benefits thus derived might weaken the centralized structure of the Church. But in 1419, the abbot of a French monastery which had suffered grievously under the ravages of war petitioned the Holy See for a dispensation from this ruling. "Seeing that the favor of nobles and of other powerful folk is most necessary and opportune to the said monks for the preservation of their rights; seeing also that, in these parts, close friendships are contracted between those who stand as godparents and the parents of the children," he argued in favor of initiating *compadre* relationships with some forty nobles.

The second function of the mechanism was to solidify social relationships horizontally among members of the same rural neighborhood. It is expressed in linguistic terms in the widening of the meaning of the word *compadre* to include the term "neighbor." In Andalucia, for example, the term *compadre* is easily extended to cover any acquaintance and even strangers (Donadin y Puignan: 863). In the Tyrol, the word *Gevatterschaft* (*com-*

padre group) is used to draw a contrast to the *Freundschaft* (the group of relatives, from the old meaning of the word *Freund*= relative). Hence also the English word, "gossip," derived from *godsib* (Weekly 1921: 654), and the use which Robert Burns makes in his poetry of such Scottish terms as *cummer* and *kimmer* to designate any woman from the neighborhood, a gossip, or a witch (Warrack 1911: 117).

One of the outstanding functions of the neighborhood group during the period of the later Middle Ages was the struggle against prevailing forms of feudal tenure. The eleventh century saw the beginning of the fight to resist labor services on the lord's land "by a sort of passive resistance" (Ganshof 1941: 295). During the twelfth and the thirteenth centuries, tenants consolidated to their own advantage the various rights of tenure which they enjoyed. "Begun in the twelfth century, emancipation was mainly achieved . . . by individual or collective acts of enfranchisement . . . generally brought about through a revolt of the inhabitants of a seignorie" (Ganshof 1941: 319). This struggle was often carried on with the aid of Crown and Church, which supported the claims of serfs and tenants in order to undermine the position of the lay aristocracy. Not the least of these claims was directed against the feudal regulations governing marriage.

One of the most direct consequences of the extension of the exogamic group through ritual kin ties was to put pressure on existing provisions for a stable labor supply. Marriage off the manor meant the loss of property to one of the feudal lords, and he exacted compensation. A serf was not permitted to marry off the manor without payment of an indemnity variously known as *formariage*, *foris*, or *merchet*. Extension of kinship ties through ceremonial sponsorship inevitably brought nearer the day when most of the inhabitants of a village would be ritually related, and yet unable to pay the fee required for marriages outside the estate. Conflicts might for a while be avoided through refusal to marry and baptize in church, through systematic choice of godparents from the group of blood relatives (Boesch 1900: 26) or through systematic choice of sponsors from one family (Sanders 1949: 129). The two last-named techniques are reported for modern Bulgar villages. Yet these devices proved temporary, especially in the smaller communities (Laurin 1866: 262; Handjieff

1931: 36–37). At first, lords tried to meet the situation of increasing migration and marriage off the manor by local agreements (Nabholz 1941: 506), but in the thirteenth and fourteenth centuries, the payment of *merchet* fell into disuse altogether. Serfs acquired the right to marry off the manor when they took over their fathers' land, or bargained with their lords for the privilege of marrying without interference. When a bargain was struck, the serfs had the exemptions written down in the manorial rolls, to be certain of proof when the actual occasion arose (Bennett 1938: 241–42).

The special charters won by the peasantry during these times gave rise to a special kind of neighborhood solidarity, reflected, in terms of the present problem, in attempts to include all the members of the neighborhood within the *compadre* network. Thus we may note a Bosnian practice of including Muslim members of the community by making them sponsors on special occasions, until in 1676 the Holy Office issued a decree against "the admission of heretics as sponsors, even though the strongest reasons of friendship and familiarity prompted the choice of such a person" (Kearney 1925: 58). Also, in some areas neighbors acquired special rights as witnesses in legal proceedings, surviving until recently in the right of the Serb *compadre* to defend his *kum* in court, and to act as witness for him (Ploss 1911: 325).

In passing we may mention that the pattern of sponsorship permitted of easy extension into other spheres of activity. Thus, the organizations of medieval journeymen used both the components of baptism and sponsorship in initiating apprentices to their ranks (Erich 1936: 275; Siemsen 1942: 61, 67) and knights who aided a candidate for initiation into knighthood went by godfather and *compadre* terms (Corblet 1882, 1: 180).

Finally, we must mention the sanctions of the Church in the enforcement of exogamy. In setting new norms for its tenants, it acted in its own self-interest in competition with the lay aristocracy which jealously guarded and reinforced its position of immunity. In extending Canon Law, and at the same time stressing dispensations from it, the Church added a source of income. Canon Law is man-made law, and the Pope has the right, by virtue of his office, to change its stipulations at will. For sixteen groschen a commoner could marry his blood relatives of the fourth degree of relationship, not to speak of ritual kin relations (Flick 1936, 1: 122), and a price list for the years 1492–1513 specifically states that "in spiritual relationships paupers are not dispensed, and the composition is three hundred ducats; nevertheless, one hundred are commonly paid" (Lunt 1934, 2: 525–26). Coulton has pointed out that enforcement to the letter of Canon Law would have meant "papal dispensations . . . in almost every generation of almost every village in Europe" (Coulton 1926: 80), and the law was often honored in the breach. But punishment struck hard, as in the case of one John Howthon of Tonbridge who was whipped three times around market and church for having married a girl to whom his first wife had been godmother (Howard 1904: 365).

As the Middle Ages draw to a close, we find an increasing number of local attempts to restrict the extension of exogamy through ritual kin ties, on the part of both Church and state. A number of synods, held between the years 1310 and 1512, tried to set limits to the number of sponsors at baptismal ceremonies, but failed (Laurin 1866: 263). In 1521 the German Estates petitioned the Pope for redress of a series of wrongs. Their complaint against ritual kinship derived from baptismal sponsorship heads a list of some sixty-odd complaints (Münch 1830, 1: 344). The German Reformation directed its attack against the custom. "This is the work of fools," Luther said (Luther 1539: 301). "Because in this way one Christian could not take another one, because they are brother and sister among themselves. These are the money snares of the Pope." Luther declared that "love needs no laws whatsoever," and that "no man has the right to create such laws." He spoke out sharply against "these stupid barriers due to spiritual fatherhood, motherhood, brotherhood, sisterhood, and childhood. Who but Superstition has created these spiritual relationships? . . . Behold, Christian freedom is suppressed due to the blindness of human superstition" (Luther 1520: 477–78). His collected proverbs stress the purely mundane and neighborly aspects of the *compadre* mechanism, and advocate that just as "good fences make good neighbors," so they also make for good relations among *compadres* (Luther 1500: 348). As early as 1550, Saxony restricted the number of baptismal sponsors to between seven and nine for nobles, and to three for burghers. Under pressures from within and without, the Church also reformed its stand at the Council of Trent (1545–63). It restricted ritual kin relationships to the baptizing priest, the child, the child's parents and the child's sponsors. But it put an end to spiritual fraternity, spiritual relationships between the sponsors themselves, and spiritual relationships arising from catechismal sponsorship. It restricted to one or to a maximum of two the number of sponsors at baptism, and the number of sponsors at confirmation to one. Again, state authorities followed suit, and the rules governing baptism issued by the Duke of Altenburg for the year 1681 are typical for a whole series of German cities. These rulings restricted the number of sponsors according to one's estate. Nobles were permitted more sponsors than burghers and artisans, burghers and artisans more than peasants (Boesch 1900: 32). The Austrian Emperor Joseph II restricted to only two or three the number of sponsors at baptism, although a much larger number had been chosen in earlier times (Ploss 1911: 330).

The rationale for these restrictions emerges perhaps most clearly in rulings prohibiting peasants from seeking their *compadres* in the towns, and "since rich people were often selected as *compadres*," people were prevented from asking unknown persons for the service (Boesch 1900: 32). We may note that the bulk of the restrictions coincide with the period which witnessed the rise of Protestantism and the early beginnings of industrial civilization. The new ethic put a premium on the individual as an effective accumulator of capital and virtue, and was certain to discountenance the drain on individual resources and the restrictions on individual freedom implicit in the wide extension of ritual kin ties. As a result the *compadre* mechanism has disappeared almost completely from areas which witnessed the development of industrial capitalism, the rise of a strong middle class, and the disappearance of feudal or neo-feudal tenures. Within these areas *compadrazgo* has lost its function most completely within the classes in which the family no longer forms the primary unit of production. This would include the economically mobile upper and middle classes on the one hand, and the industrial wage-earning working class on the other. In both these segments, kinship mechanisms became increasingly non-functional, and tended to be replaced by more impersonal, institutionalized forms of organization. Within these same areas, however, kinship mechanisms have been retained most completely where peasants have not yet become farmers. This point of transition comes where production is still largely for immediate consumption rather than for accumulation, and where the familial unit still forms the active basis of economic life. In Europe, as a whole, it has been retained most completely in such areas as Spain, Italy, and the Balkan countries where the development of industrial capitalism, the rise of a middle class, and the disintegration of the feudal order has been less rapid. To this extent Robert Redfield is justified when he called *compadrazgo* a Southern European peasant custom (Redfield 1930: 141). It is from Southern Europe that the complex was transmitted to Latin America, along with the call to baptize the infidels and to bring them into the fold of the Christian community as an addition to the faith through baptism, and as an addition to the riches of the Spanish Empire through labor.

FUNCTIONAL ANALYSIS

The Catholic ceremonial complexes, when carried to the New World, were to develop under conditions very different from those of fifteenth-century Europe. Alienation of Indian lands through such devices as the *repartimiento* and the *encomienda* proceeded concurrently with the wholesale conversion of millions of native peoples to Catholicism. The functioning of such mechanisms as *compadrazgo* in Latin American communities is strongly colored by four hundred years of historical development within this new setting. Yet there is little material on the cultural significance and usages of the *compadre* mechanism during the Colonial period. Certainly considerable research needs to be carried out on the processes of acculturation following early contact. Analysis of the social functioning of *compadrazgo* in its American beginnings is but a minor aspect.

Historical sources attest that baptism of natives had proceeded from the time of first contact. Fray Toribio de Benavente writes that in the fifty-five year period between 1521 and 1576 more than four million souls were brought to the baptismal font (quoted in Rojas Gonzales 1943: 193). The evidence is good that emphasis was not on prior instruction in the catechism, but rather on formal acceptance of the faith. Father Gante and an assistant, proselytizing in Mexico, claims to have baptized up to fourteen thousand Indians in a single day. In all, Gante and his companion stated that they baptized more than two hundred thousand souls in a single Mexican province (Bancroft 1883: 174).

Baptism was a sacrament designed to remove the stigma of original sin. The acquisition of godparents purported to guarantee to the initiate religious guidance during the years following his baptism. Actually, Spaniards who were members of exploring parties frequently served as sponsors for Indian converts, and thus fulfilled but a formal ritual necessity (Espinosa 1942: 70, *passim*). We can assume that most of the social implications of the *compadre* mechanism developed but slowly at first, if for no other reason than this.

Yet the baptismal ceremony established an individual in the Catholic universe, and perhaps by virtue of its symbolic simplicity, it was readily accepted by many native populations. Redfield, Parsons, Foster, and Paul, among others, have sought to differentiate between aboriginal and Catholic elements in the modern Latin American ritual. Parsons, Redfield, and Paul have felt further that certain derivations of the modern godparental ritual have come from the adaptation of this ceremonial form to pre-Columbian ceremonies and social patterns. The Maya of Yucatan possessed a native baptism so like the Catholic ritual that, according to one authority,

> some of our Spaniards have taken occasion to persuade themselves and believe that in times past some of the apostles or successors to them passed over the West Indies and that ultimately those Indians were preached to (Lopez Medel, quoted in Landa 1941: 227).

The Aztecs also had a kind of baptism, and in addition, godparents of sorts were chosen in an indigenous Aztec ear-piercing ceremonial, according to Sahagun (Sahagun 1932: 34–35). Paul feels there may even have been an aboriginal basis for the *compadre* aspect of the complex in the existence of various kinds of formal friendship among native peoples (Paul 1942: 85–87).

But it is impossible to generalize about the ease with which aboriginal ceremonial procedure could be accommodated to the new sacrament, as endorsed by the Church. The most important modern social result of the baptismal ceremony in practice—the creation of a security network of ritual kin folk through ceremonial sponsorship—seems rather to be due to the institution's inherent flexibility and utility, than to any preëxisting pattern with which the new complex might be integrated. Present-day folklore concerning the fate of an unbaptized child (Redfield and Villa Rojas 1934: 169; Parsons 1945: 44; Paul 1942) suggests that a strong emphasis on the moral necessity for baptism was made from the start. In modern practice, however, whether the people in a given culture will feel that baptism requires the official approval and participation of representatives of the Church varies considerably. The evidence is that once the secular utility of this sacred institution was established, the native populations could count on the fulfillment of those reciprocal obligations which godparentage and *compadrazgo* entailed, the Church might not even be consulted. Makeshift ceremonies, consummated without orthodox clerical approval, became so widespread as to be illegalized by ecclesiastical ruling in 1947, except in cases where the child's death seemed imminent before official baptism.

As has been indicated, the mechanism of godparenthood took shape originally as a means for guaranteeing religious education and guidance to the Catholic child. This aim was achieved through the ritual kinship established between the newborn infant, its parents, and its godparents, at the baptismal ceremony. The relationship frequently was reinforced, or extended with new sponsors, at other life crisis ceremonies, including confirmation and marriage.

From the original Catholic life crisis ceremonial sponsorship, godparenthood has been elaborated in various Latin American communities into the ceremonial sponsorship of houses, crosses, altars, or carnivals (Gillin 1945: 105), circumcision (Beals 1946: 102), the future crop (Parsons 1936: 228, n. 96), commercial dealings (Zingg 1938: 717–18), and so on. Gillin lists fourteen forms of *compadrazgo* for a single community (Gillin 1945: 105). In certain cases, it cannot be said with any certainty whether the new adaptation was developed locally, or constitutes a carry over of some kind from some older European elaboration.

In general, ritual ties between contemporaries seem to have become more important than those between godparents and godchildren. This point is elaborated by Gillin in his discussion of the Peruvian community, Moche. He writes:

> The essence of the system in Moche is an "artificial bond," resembling a kinship relationship, which is established between persons by means of a ceremony. The ceremony usually involves a sponsorship of a person or material object by one or more of the persons involved, and the ceremony itself may be rather informal. However in Moche it seems to be placing the wrong emphasis to label the whole system . . . "ceremonial sponsorship." . . . The emphasis in Moche is upon the relations between sponsors of an individual or thing, and between them and other persons—in other words, relations between adults rather than between adults and children or things (Gillin 1945: 104).

While the custom derives primarily from a conception of spiritual parenthood, modern Latin American emphasis seems to be rather on ritual co-parenthood; the *compadre-compadre* relationship outweighs the godparent-godchild relationship.

The ritual complex has been demonstrated to be of so flexible and adaptable a nature that a wide group of individuals can be bound together ceremonially. Paul makes the points that the mechanism of *compadrazgo* may be used either to enlarge numerically and spatially the number of ritually related kin on the one hand, or to reinforce already existing blood or ritual ties on the other. These contrasting motives he calls "extension" and "intensification" (Paul 1942: 57). The authors of the present article feel that whether the *compadre* mechanism will be used prevailingly to extend or to intensify a given set of relationships will be determined in a specific functional-historical context.

In modern Latin American communities, there is clear patterning of choice. *Compadres* may be chosen exclusively from within one's own family, or perhaps blood kin will be preferred to outsiders. In other communities, on the other hand, one pair of godparents may serve for all of one's children, or *compadres* chosen from outside one's own family may be rigidly preferred. The present writers are convinced that the rare usages of *compadrazgo* in inheritance indicate the lack of utility of this mechanism in dynamically affecting prevailing patterns of ownership. It is a mechanism that can be used to strengthen existing patterns, but not to change them. In the two cases in which *compadrazgo* plays any role in determining land inheritance, land is held by the village community, and all that is inherited is temporary right of use (Wisdom 1940; Villa Rojas 1945). Marital impediment under Canon Law, a factor of continuing importance in much of the New World (Herskovits 1937a: 98), and the selection of *compadres* within the kin group or outside it, are also factors bound together functionally and historically. This problem lies beyond the scope of the present article.

Compadrazgo, once accepted by a social grouping, can be moulded into the community way of life by many means. It is a two-way social system which sets up reciprocal relations of variable complexity and solemnity. By imposing automatically, and with a varying degree of sanctity, statuses and obligations of a fixed nature, on the people who participate, it makes the immediate social environment more stable, the participants more interdependent and more secure. In fact, it might be said that the baptismal rite (or corresponding event) may be the original basis for the mechanism, but no longer its sole motivating force. Some brief examples will demonstrate the institution's flexibility.

In Chimaltenango (Wagley 1949: 19), two *compadres*

> will lend each other maize or money ("as much as six dollars").
> . . . Two *comadres* should visit each other often and they may
> borrow small things readily from one another. When one is sick, or
> when one has just had another child, her *comadre* should come
> bringing tortillas for the family, and she should work in her *co-
> madre's* house "like a sister."

In Peguche (Parsons 1945: 45), "white compadres are an asset for anyone who has business in Otovalo or Quito."

In Tzintzuntzan (Foster 1948: 264),

> On the economic level, the *compadrazgo* system forms a kind of so-
> cial insurance. Few are the families which can meet all emergencies
> without outside help. Often this means manual help at the time of a
> fiesta, or the responsibility of a *carguero*. Sometimes it means lend-
> ing money, which near blood relatives do not like to do, because of
> the tendency never to repay a debt. But *compadres* feel obliged to
> lend, and no one would have respect for a man who refused to repay
> a *compadre*.

In San Pedro de Laguna (Paul 1942: 92),

> The practical purpose motivating the selection of Ladinas as *co-madres* is the belief that they can cure infant illnesses and have access to the necessary medicines. The Indians store no medicine. But the Ladinas—by virtue of their cultural tradition and their greater income —customarily have on hand a number of drugstore preparations. The godparent bond imposes on the Ladina the responsibility of coming to the medical aid of her Indian godchild. The first year or two is correctly considered to be the most critical period of the infant's life. Hence the natives sacrifice long-run considerations in favor of providing a measure of medical protection during the infancy of the child . . .

Evidence from studies of two communities in Puerto Rico suggests that the *compadre* relation may be invoked to forestall sexual aggressions (Wolf 1950; Manners 1950). Cases are mentioned where a man concerned about the attentions of a family friend to his wife, sought to avoid trouble by making his friend his *compadre*. Thus a new and more sacred relationship was established.

Among the Huichol (Zingg 1938: 57), the *compadre* relationship

> unquestionably strengthens Huichol social organization outside the family, which is not strong. Though *compadres* are not under economic bonds to each other, the injunction to be kind and friendly prevents drunken fights and brawls, which are the greatest source of weakness in Huichol society.

One form of *compadrazgo* is

> specifically organized to avoid aggression between two *compadres*: "*el compadrazgo de voluntad.*" People say that where there are two bullies in the same *barrio*, they will conclude a "non-aggression pact" and make themselves *compadres de voluntad*, which means that they can no longer fight each other (Wolf 1950).

The persistence of *compadrazgo* in very secularized contexts, and its existence in such cases even without the sponsorship of a person, object, or event, is evidence of its frequently high social and secular plasticity.

The formal basis for selecting godparents for one's children—religious guidance, and if necessary, the adoption of orphaned children—is sometimes carried out. Gamio mentions this tradi-

tional usage in the Valley of Teotihuacan (Gamio 1922, 2: 243),
Redfield and Villa Rojas for Chan Kom (1934: 250), Villa Rojas
for Tusik (1945: 90), Rojas Gonzales for the Mixe and Zoque
(1943: 204–5), and Wisdom for the Chorti (1940: 293–94).
Among the Chorti,

> the godfather often acts in every way as the actual father in the event
> of the latter's death. He gives his ward advice, gets him out of diffi-
> culties, sometimes trains him in a man's work, and may act as his
> parent when he marries. The same is done by the godmother for her
> female godchild. If both parents die, and the godchild is young, the
> godparent may receive the portion of the property which the child
> inherited, and put it to his own use, in return for which he must
> bring up the child as one of his own family. As soon as the young
> man or woman becomes eighteen years of age, his inheritance is
> made up to him by his godfather. Where there is more than one
> minor child, each godfather receives his ward's share out of the total
> property, each child going to live in the home of its own godfather,
> leaving the adult children at home.

This usage is of particular interest because the *compadre*
mechanism can be seen here as a link in the process of inheritance. Yet final property rights in this society are vested in the
village, and not in the individual. A single case of the same kind
of usage is mentioned by Villa Rojas for the Maya Indian community of Tusik (1945: 90). Yet *compadrazgo* cannot override
the emphasis on group land tenure in either of these societies.
The mechanism is flexible and adaptable specifically because it
usually carries with it no legal obligations—particularly regarding
inheritance. Paul makes this point clearly when he writes that,

> Unlike the involuntary ties of kinship those of ritual sponsorship
> are formed on the basis of choice. This enables godparenthood to
> serve as the social link connecting divergent income groups, dis-
> parate social strata, and separated localities. Affinity too may cut
> across class and locality through the practices of hypergamy and
> intermarriage. But the frequency with which such irregular forms of
> marriage occur throughout the world is sharply limited by strong
> social pressures operating to keep the unions within the class or com-
> munity. This is understandable in view of the fact that marriage is
> the means by which the in-group perpetuates itself. Because no
> such considerations of social recruitment impede the formation of
> godparent bonds between persons of different social strata, godpar-
> enthood more readily serves as a mechanism for intergroup inte-
> gration (Paul 1942: 72–73).

It may be fruitful to examine cases of *compadrazgo* as examples of mechanisms crosscutting socio-cultural or class affiliations, or as taking place within the socio-cultural confines of a single class. The authors believe such patternings will prove to be determined, not haphazard in character, nor determined solely along continuums of homogeneity-to-heterogeneity, or greater-to-lesser isolation. Rather they will depend on the amount of socio-cultural and economic mobility, *real and apparent*, available to an individual in a given situation. There is of course no clear-cut device for the measurement of such real or apparent mobility. Yet the utility of *compadrazgo* might profitably be examined in this light. The aim would be to assess whether the individual is seeking to strengthen his position in a homogeneous socio-cultural community with high stability and low mobility, or to strengthen certain crosscutting ties by alignment with persons of a higher socio-cultural stratum, via reciprocal-exploitative relationships manipulated through *compadrazgo*. Some examples may illuminate the problem.

The Maya Indian people to Tusik (Villa Rojas 1945: 90), a community in east central Quintana Roo, Yucatan, are homogeneous in a tribal sense, rather than having a mono-class structure. Says Villa Rojas:

> There are no classes here in the sense that different groups of people have different relations to the production and distribution of economic goods; in the sense that some people own land on which other people work, or that some people are engaged in producing goods while others are engaged in distributing them or in servicing the rest of the population. As we have already pointed out, everyone in the subtribe has the same relation to the land as everyone else; the land is commonly held by the subtribe, and a man's rights to a piece of land rests only on the right that he has put agricultural labor into the land and is entitled to the products of his labor. Every man makes *milpa*—even the sacred professionals earn their living as farmers—and since the secular division of labor is practically nonexistent, there are no merchants or artisans.

The economic life of the group centers about maize, and the people consume all that they produce. Labor for other men is rare, and when done, payment in kind prevails. The only cash commodity is chicle. Says Villa Rojas:

Apparently all the people of the subtribe enjoy the same economic circumstances. Nothing one observes in their ordinary, daily behavior suggests the existence of differences in accumulated wealth. . . . The acquisition of wealth is related directly to the personal ambition of the individual, for there are no differences in opportunity and no important differences in privilege. The principal source of wealth is the extraction of chicle, which is within the reach of all. . . . This equality of opportunity is a recent matter, for some years ago when the chiefs had greater authority, the lands of the bush were distributed by them and the best portion preserved for their own use. In some cases men were thus able to enrich themselves through special advantage.

Regarding *compadrazgo*, the grandparents of the child to be born, preferably the paternal ones, are chosen. If they are not alive, chiefs or *maestros cantores*, as persons of prestige and good character, are selected. It is noteworthy that no mention is made of any choice of travelling merchants as *compadres*, although

the travelling merchants are the natives' main source of contact with the outer world. It is they who bring into the region . . . the most important news from the city. . . . The arrival of the merchant is the occasion for the people to gather together and excitedly discuss the events he relates to them, and in this atmosphere the merchant's own friendly ties with the natives are strengthened.

Chicle is sold, and commodities bought through these travellers, but apparently ritual kinship is not used to bind them with the community.

In marked contrast to the isolated, subsistence crop, tribal culture of Tusik, we may examine two communities which exhibit cultural homogeneity under completely different conditions. They are fully integrated economically, and to a great degree welded culturally into national cultures. The first of these is Poyal (Mintz 1950).

Barrio Poyal is a rural community on the south coast of Puerto Rico, in an area of large-scale sugar cane production, with corporate ownership of land and mills. The lands are devoted exclusively to the production of the single cash crop. While the *barrio* working population forms what is practically a mono-class isolate, *compadres* could be selected among the foremen, administrators, public officials, store owners, and so forth. Instead, there is an overwhelming tendency to pick neighbors and fellow workers as *compadres*. A man who seeks a wealthy *compadre* in Poyal is held in some contempt by his fellows; a wealthy *compadre* would not visit him nor invite him to his house. People remember when the old hacienda owners were chosen as godparents to the workers' children, but this practice is totally outmoded now. A local land-owning group no longer exists in Poyal.

Compadre relationships generally are treated reverentially; *compadres* are addressed with the polite *Usted*, even if they are family members, and the *compadre* relationship is utilized daily in getting help, borrowing money, dividing up available work opportunities, and so forth. However, as more and more Poyal workers migrate to the United States, the utility of many *compadre* ties is weakened.

Another example of the same category is Pascua (Spicer 1940), a community of essentially landless, wage-earning Yaqui Indian immigrants who, with their descendants, form a village on the outskirts of Tucson, Arizona. The economic basis of Pascua life bears certain striking resemblances to *Barrio* Poyal: the almost total lack of subsistence activities, the emphasis on seasonal variation, the emphasis on wage-earning as opposed to payment in kind, and so on. Says Spicer:

> Existence is wholly dependent on the establishment of relationships with individuals outside the village. If for any reason the economic relations of a Pascuan with outside persons are broken off for an extended period, it becomes necessary to depend upon other Pascuans who have maintained such relations.

While the economic linkages are exclusively with external sources of income and employment, the *compadre* structure is described

> as an all-pervasive network of relationships which takes into its web every person in the village. Certain parts of the network, here and there about the village, are composed of strong and well-knit fibers. Here the relationships between *compadres* are functioning constantly and effectively. Elsewhere there are weaker threads representing relationships which have never been strengthened by daily recognition of reciprocal obligations. These threads nevertheless exist and may from time to time be the channels of temporarily re-established *compadre* relationships.

Spicer notes that:

> sometimes in Pascua sponsors are sought outside the village in Libre
> or Marana, or even among the Mexican population of Tucson.

But everything suggests that the ritual kinship system here functions predominantly within the wage-earning, landless mono-class
grouping of the Yaqui themselves. Spicer's description of *compadrazgo* is probably the most complete in the literature today,
and the Pascua system appears to be primarily between contemporaries in emphasis, and as in *Barrio* Poyal horizontal in character.

These three cases, Tusik, *Barrio* Poyal, and Pascua, illustrate the selective character of *compadrazgo* and some of its
functionings, within small "homogeneous" groupings. The mechanism plainly has considerable importance and utility and is
treated reverentially in all three places. Yet while Tusik is isolated and lacks a class-character, *Barrio* Poyal and Pascua are
both involved in wage-earning, cash crop, world market productive arrangements where the homogeneity is one of class membership only, and isolation is not characteristic.

In Tusik, *compadrazgo* is correlated with great internal stability, low economic mobility, ownership of land by the village,
and the lack of a cash economy and class stratification. In *Barrio*
Poyal and Pascua *compadrazgo* correlates with homogeneous
class membership, landlessness, wage-earning, and an apparent
growing identity of class interest.

An interesting contrast is provided by Gillin's study of Moche.
This is a Peruvian coastal community which, according to the
Foreword,

> is in the last stages of losing its identity as an Indian group and of
> being absorbed into Peruvian national life. . . . Surrounded by large,
> modern haciendas, Moche is "Indian" only in that its population
> is largely Indian in a racial sense, that it has retained much of its
> own lands, that it exists in a certain social isolation from surround-
> ing peoples, retaining a community life organized on a modified
> kinship basis, mainly of Spanish derivation. . . . Its lands, however,
> are now owned individually, and they are being alienated through
> sale and litigation. It is on a cash rather than subsistence basis
> economically. . . . Many Mocheros even work outside the commu-
> nity for wages, and some are in professions. . . . Formal aspects
> of native social organization have disappeared, and contacts with
> the outside world are increasing (Gillin 1945).

In Moche, the *compadre* system would expectably be subject to the same stresses as those suffered by any other local social institution. Yet

> the whole idea of this type of relationship has been carried to extremes in Moche. There are more types of *padrinazgo* [i.e. godfatherhood] in this community than in any other concerning which I have seen reports. This fact may be linked with the absence of spontaneous community organization and solidarity.

Gillin finds evidence for fourteen different kinds of *compadre* relations. As to the choice of *compadres*, Gillin says:

> Godparents may be blood relatives, but usually the attempt is made to secure persons who are not relatives of either of the parents. Not only Mocheros, but in these days, trusted *forasteros* [i.e. outsiders] are chosen. From the point of view of the parents it is desirable to choose godparents who are financially responsible, if not rich, and also persons who have "influence" and prestigeful social connections. The real function of godparents is to broaden, and, if possible, increase the social and economic resources of the child and his parents and by the same token to lower the anxieties of the parents on this score.

In a later section, however, Gillin states that he does not feel that socially defined classes as such exist in Moche (Gillin 1945: 107, 113).

It is extremely noteworthy that the mechanism of *compadrazgo* has maintained itself here in the face of what appears to be progressively accelerating social change. We wonder whether the elaborations of the mechanism's forms may be part of the community's unconscious effort to answer new problems. It must increasingly face the insecurity of growing incorporation into the national structure and increasing local wage-based, cash crop competition. This may call forth an increased emphasis on techniques for maintaining and strengthening face-to-face relationships. Eggan's study of Cheyenne kinship terminology (Eggan 1937) suggests that the kinship structure is sensitive to rapid social change if the changing terminology reflects genuine structural modifications. Ritual kinship structures may react to the weakening of certain traditional obligations by spreading out to include new categories of contemporaries, and therefore potential competitors.

Other examples suggest that vertical phrasings of the *compadre* system may take place in situations where change has been slowed at some point, and relationships between two defined socio-cultural strata, or classes, are solidified. San Jose is a highland coffee and minor crop-producing community of Puerto Rico (Wolf 1950). The frequency distribution of land shows a considerable scatter, with fifty-five percent of the landowners holding ten percent of the land at one extreme, and five percent holding forty-five percent of the land at the other. Thus, while Tusik people hold their land communally, *Barrio* Poyal and Pascua people are landless, and Moche people are largely small landowners with no farm over four acres, San Jose people are in large part landowners with great variability in the size of holdings. While a large part of the agricultural population is landless, agricultural laborers in San Jose may be paid partly in kind, and frequently will be given in addition a small plot of land for subsistence farming. Production for wages is largely of the main cash crop, coffee.

In the rural zones of this community, a prevailing number of the *compadre* relations tie agricultural workers to their landholding employers, or small landholders to larger ones. Thus a large landowner may become *compadre* to twenty smaller landowners living around his farm. In isolated areas, where the "community" is defined entirely in familial terms, most *compadre* relationships take place within the family. Yet it must be recognized that members of the same family, and brothers of the same filial generation, may be variously landowners, sharecroppers (*medianeros*), and laborers.

Compadrazgo in San Jose may help in the stabilization of productive relations between large and small landholders, or between landholders and their share-cropping employees and laborers. Interesting in this connection is the fact that the economic basis in San Jose is much less exclusively cash than in Tusik, *Barrio* Poyal, or Pascua. The land tenure pattern in San Jose does not appear to be changing rapidly. *Compadrazgo* relations are phrased vertically, so as to cross-cut class stratification, quite probably serving in this connection to solidify the relationships of people to the land. There is evidence of landowners getting free labor out of their laborer brothers who have been made *compadres*. Contrariwise, laborers bound by *compadrazgo* to their employers are accustomed to rely on this bond to secure them certain small privileges, such as the use of equipment, counsel and help, small loans, and so on.

The authors know of no fully documented study of *compadrazgo* in the context of an "old-style" plantation or hacienda. Siegel's material on the Guatemalan plantation community of San Juan Acatan indicates that the Indians there often invite Ladinos with whom they come in contact to sponsor the baptisms of their children. But Siegel adds that the relationship in this community is "virtually meaningless" (quoted in Paul 1942: 72). The authors of the present article would in general predict that plantation laborers, either bound or very dependent on the plantation, with daily face-to-face contacts with the owner or *hacendado* would seek to establish a reciprocal coparental relationship with the owner. Historical material from old informants in *Barrio* Poyal offer evidence of this tradition, now markedly altered in the pure wage, absentee ownership context.

The mechanism may be contrasted, then, in several distinct contexts. In the first context are Tusik, *Barrio* Poyal, and Pascua. These communities are alike in their "homogeneity," and the horizontal structuring of the *compadre* system; yet they are markedly different in other respects. Tusik is tribal and essentially isolated from the world market, while *Barrio* Poyal and Pascua are incorporated into capitalistic world economies, and are fully formed working class strata.

In the second context is San Jose, with its varied land ownership pattern, its mixed (cash and subsistence) crop production and its several classes. Through the vertical phrasing of its *compadre* system, San Jose demonstrates a relatively stable reciprocity, economic and social, between the landed, large and small, and the sharecroppers and laborers.

In the third context is Moche. Land is held predominantly in small plots; the crops, as in San Jose, are both cash and subsistence, and while Gillin doubts the existence of classes, certainly the *compadre* system is described as a vertical structuring one. Here, too, the elaboration of face-to-face ceremonialism may help to slow the accelerated trend toward land concentration, a cash economy, and incorporation into the world market.

CONCLUSION

In the first section of this article, the writers traced the relationship between land tenure and the functioning of ritual kin ties under conditions of European feudalism. During this period, ritual kin ties gradually changed from bonds of blood brotherhood to those of *compadre* relationships. This accompanied a change from neighbor inheritance to the family inheritance of tenure. As these changes in the pattern of land tenure took place, the ritual ties were shifted correspondingly from a horizontal cementing of relationships to a vertical phrasing of artificial kinship at the height of feudalism.

With the breakdown of feudal land tenures and the increased assertion of peasant rights, such ritual ties were again rephrased horizontally to unite the peasant neighborhoods in their struggle against feudal dues.

Under conditions of advanced industrial development, mechanisms of social control based on biological or ritual kin affiliations tend to give way before more impersonal modes of organization. *Compadrazgo* survives most actively in present-day Europe within the areas of lesser industrial development. From one such area, Spain, *compadrazgo* was carried to the New World, and developed here in a new historical and functional context.

In the second section of this article, five modern communities with Latin American culture were analyzed to show the functional correlates of the *compadre* mechanism. In cases where the community is a self-contained class, or tribally homogeneous, *compadrazgo* is prevailingly horizontal (intra-class) in character. In cases where the community contains several interacting classes, *compadrazgo* will structure such relationships vertically (inter-class). Last, in a situation of rapid social change *compadre* mechanisms may multiply to meet the accelerated rate of change.

20 TEKNONYMY IN BALI: PARENTHOOD, AGE-GRADING AND GENEALOGICAL AMNESIA

Hildred and Clifford Geertz

TEKNONYMY, THE PRACTICE OF DESIGNATING ADULTS according to the names of their children, is not often examined for its functional significance, but more frequently assumed to be a mere ethnological detail, or a minor nomenclatural usage. When social consequences are attributed to it, they tend to be confined to the most personal and domestic spheres of life.[1] Bali, however, provides material for the contrary thesis: there teknonymy becomes a vital social mechanism with important structural impact both on village organization and on the process of corporate kin-group formation. On the one hand, the systematic application of teknonymous names serves to mark out explicit age-grades within each Balinese village. These age-cohorts are unnamed and informal in operation, but they are, nevertheless, highly influential components of the community structure. On the other hand, the custom of teknonymy plays an equally significant role within the Balinese kinship system. It creates, through its progressive suppression of personal names and its regular substitution of what are essentially impersonal status terms, a curtain of genealogical amnesia which steadily descends over each generation in turn. Recognition of common descent becomes a most flexible matter,

Originally published in the *Journal of the Royal Anthropological Institute*, Vol. 94, 1964, pp. 94–108. Reprinted with permission of the authors and of the Royal Anthropological Institute.
[1] Two of the more extended treatments of the functions of teknonymy are Tylor (1889) and Lowie (1920). Tylor suggested an association between teknonymy, matrilocal residence, and son-in-law avoidance. Lowie rejected this theory, and took the view that any explanation of teknonymy should be limited to the particular case.

so that corporate descent groups among Balinese commoners are free to expand or contract their memberships readily in response to changing circumstances, such as shifts in the relative wealth, political power or prestige of their members. Teknonymy thus serves as a potent if indirect agent for creating the elasticity, the adaptability which is one of the most distinctive and fundamental peculiarities of the Balinese kinship system, and in fact, which enables the system to work at all.[2]

Further, there is an interesting countercase which adds support to these assertions regarding the social function of teknonymy in Bali, namely, that one segment of the Balinese population—the gentry—does not employ teknonymy extensively, and correspondingly, their place in village society and the structure of their descent groups as well is different from those of the commoners. Gentry families, who comprise about ten per cent of the total population, are almost identical culturally and economically (with some exceptions) with commoners, and they live scattered among the commoners in nearly every village. The two social groups are closely intermeshed and interdependent in most areas of life. Yet the gentry are often excluded in a legal, civil sense from the local community governing body, and it is in precisely this sphere that age-grading is prominent. Further, the absence of teknonymy is linked with differences in the gentry kinship system: their kin-groups are more strongly corporate, larger, more enduring, and are buttressed by lengthy genealogical traditions, traditions which are absent among the commoners.

In its general outline, the system of teknonymic nomenclature

[2] The field work upon which this analysis is based was conducted in the principalities of Tabanan and Klungkung, Bali, in 1957–58. It was supported by a grant from the Rockefeller Foundation, administered by the Center for International Studies, Massachusetts Institute of Technology, Cambridge, Massachusetts. We are indebted for financial assistance in the writing of this paper to the Center for Advanced Studies in the Behavioral Sciences, Stanford, California, and to the Committee for South Asian Studies of the University of Chicago. We are also grateful for probing critical readings by Fred Eggan, Lloyd A. Fallers, Paul W. Friedrich, and David M. Schneider. A monograph is in preparation giving full description of the Balinese kinship system. Since the main focus of the present paper is on teknonymy, it is possible only to give the briefest, unsubstantiated sketch of the system as a whole. Published material on the Balinese kinship is scarce; some data are found in Belo (1936) and Korn (1936).

is quite simple. At birth each person is given a proper name, by which he is called until he marries and has a child. Soon after this event people begin addressing and referring to him as 'Father-of-So-and-So', employing his child's personal name. The wife, likewise, becomes 'Mother-of-So-and-So', with the result that man and wife now have essentially the same name. It becomes extremely discourteous to use a person's childhood name instead of his teknonymous name, for to do so is to imply that he is still immature, and as a result his original name gradually fades from view. There is, in most cases, a second change of name some years later when the couple have become grandparents. Their children now lose their childhood names in turn, and are referred to as 'Father-of . . .' or 'Mother-of . . .' their own child, while the grandparents' names shift to 'Grandfather-of . . .' and 'Grandmother-of . . .', the inserted name being that of the new grandchild. And finally, when they become great-grandparents, all the names again shift upwards, with the older couple now being called 'Great-grandparent-of . . .' the most recent offspring.[3]

It is immaterial whether the child after whom all these adults are named is male or female. Since adoption of a teknonym occurs not overnight by means of a ceremony, but gradually through the building up of a habit, the name is not firmly acquired until after the child has survived the perilous Balinese infancy. If the eponymous child dies after the name is firmly attached to his parents, they will usually continue to be called by it.

From the point of view of the individual, therefore, his name may shift as many as four times during the course of his life. Since not only a personal name is employed, but also always a status term—'Father-of', 'Grandfather-of', 'Great-grandparent-of' —the name indicates each person's current familial status. From the point of view of the local community, everyone is categorized

---

[3] The terms current in Klungkung area were:
Father-of: *Nang*, or *Pan* (derived from *Nanang*, or *Bapa*, 'Father').
Mother-of: *Mèn* (derived from *Mémé*, 'Mother').
Grandfather-of: *Kaki*, or *Pekak*, or *Ki*, or *Kak*.
Grandmother-of: *Tjutjun*, or *Tjun* (derived from *Tjutju*, 'Grandmother').
Great-grandparent-of: *Kumpi*.

by his teknonym into a set of generational classes, i.e., children, parents, grandparents, and great-grandparents.

The settlement pattern of Bali is determined in large part by its topography and by the cultivation of irrigated rice. Dwellings are clustered tightly together on ridges of higher land with rice paddies descending in terraces round the residential areas. Population densities are very high, and many settlements contain several thousand or more inhabitants. Balinese social organization is intricate, and there is no unitary, multifunctional 'village' community of the type usually found in peasant societies.[4] Instead there is a variety of groupings of different sizes and functions: modern governmental units; spheres of influence of former kings, princes, and lordlings; temple congregations of many kinds; irrigation societies with scattered members from diverse localities; Bali-wide 'caste' organizations; and various others. All these types of affiliation interpenetrate and overlap, so that any one settlement cluster is socially and territorially segmented in a number of non-co-ordinate ways.

One kind of Balinese association does correspond somewhat to a local village community, however, the 'hamlet' or *bandjar*. Although it is not always exclusively territorial in membership, the hamlet council has jurisdiction over most civil and domestic matters, such as marriage, divorce, inheritance and minor criminal acts. While individual hamlet members generally have many social allegiances and responsibilities outside of the hamlet itself —to temples elsewhere, to various political groupings, to agricultural societies, etc.—the hamlet frequently is the extra-domestic primary group with greatest personal significance for its citizens. It is the group within which each person has the most daily interaction, and since it tends to be strongly endogamous most of his kinsmen are also members and he spends his life span within its confines. Many hamlet associations own all the houseland in the vicinity, and have full power to evict members for antisocial behaviour. Since eviction means, essentially, social death,

---

[4] Cf. Geertz, C. 1959.

this is a powerful lever for conformity. Small crimes are punished by fines, levied by unanimous judgment of the hamlet council. Most hamlets are also religious congregations, being responsible for the upkeep and observances at one or two local temples.

The hamlet is kept small, generally below five hundred in all; and in these days of marked population growth, the splitting of oversize hamlets is frequent. Through much of the lowlands of Bali the settlements are quite extensive and those which are subdivided into as many as ten hamlets are not uncommon; in the mountain areas hamlet and settlement may coincide. Each hamlet is entirely separate both from all other forms of association and from all other hamlets. Each one has its own distinctive set of rules and regulations, concerning membership qualifications, responsibilities, sanctions, etc., so that precise ethnographic generalization is very difficult.

Teknonymy makes its contribution to hamlet organization by providing a classificatory frame, a set of categories of like-named people. In the first place, it clearly identifies man and wife, since they both carry the name of the same child. Membership in the hamlet council, the governing body of the hamlet which meets once a month, is open only to men who have a female co-partner. Every male head of a household is automatically a member, but only if he has a woman as his co-member, for she is needed to perform the many hamlet ritual duties and other obligations traditionally carried out by women. While it is permissible under certain circumstances to substitute a sister, mother, or daughter, the normal pattern is that of man and wife. Other Balinese associations, too, such as the temple affiliations and the traditional allegiances to feudal lords, have the same rule of dual man-and-woman membership. The common appellation by a teknonym serves to underline this social identification of man and wife as a single unit.

In the second place, teknonymy distinguishes the main generational strata, the children, parents, grandparents and great-grandparents, strata which in turn are significant components of village society. Practices vary considerably, but generally a young man joins the hamlet council at the time of his marriage. In some hamlets he must wait until he has a child, at which point his parents retire from the council, relinquishing their seat to their son.

In such cases the parallel between the acquisition of a teknonym and of adult citizenship in the hamlet is a formal one. Generally, however, the connexion is much looser, and the name-shifts are often delayed or accelerated to fit the actual social status of the individual. Thus a very young man may continue to be called by his childhood name for some time after he has become a parent, if he is clearly still a dependent and insignificant youth. Likewise, a man of vigour and political weight often continues to be addressed by his 'Father-of . . .' title, long after the birth of a grandchild. In many hamlets, in fact, it is customary for older sons to leave the parental homestead after marriage, with only the youngest son staying with their parents, and in these cases the older parents are not called 'grandparent-of . . .' their first grandchild, but of the child of their youngest son, who may come into the world many years later, when the older parents have in actuality begun to lose their active place in the community. Those called 'Grandfather-of . . .' tend to take more passive advisory roles which can be quite high in prestige and influence. A very old person who is senile or physically weak may more rapidly come to be addressed by a teknonym as 'Great-grandparent-of-So-and-So'.

There is, further, a strong element of relativity in the conferring of a teknonym. A man's peers tend to call him by his 'Father-of' name long after he is a grandfather or even a great-grandfather. The first ones to make the shift are always the children. Thus, for example, in one village studied, there was a very aged man who was a great-grandfather. One of his age-mates, another old man, always referred to him as 'Father-of-Membah'. The majority of the middle-aged villagers called him 'Grandfather-of-Sukana'. But the children called him 'Great-grandfather-of-Puri', for little Puri was their playmate, and the point of reference from which they saw him. It was obvious that the number of those who might call him 'Father-of' was rapidly diminishing, and the centre of political balance in the village had long ago moved from his age-group to the next below, so that his actual status was most nearly specified by the title 'Grandfather-of', and that was indeed the name he most often went by.

In this way the teknonymic generational strata are verbal categories which are adjusted in everyday interaction to coincide roughly with the community's real (but un-named) social organizational layers of minors, active citizens, elders, and senile dependents. From another point of view these are age-grades, for civic activity, power, and influence are closely correlated with age.

The Balinese gentry exhibit in reverse the relationship between teknonymy and community social position. Most nobles are addressed not by teknonyms but by a single honorific title which persists throughout their lives, a title which is unaffected by either age or generation. There are, however, some instructive exceptions to the rule that gentry do not use teknonymy. Some low-ranking, impoverished nobles are, in fact, customarily addressed by teknonyms in place of their titles. These variations in mode of address appear to parallel the kinds of status the gentry may have vis-à-vis the commoner hamlet community. Those of very high rank who also have considerable wealth or regional political position often live in the same settlement with commoners, but they are completely excluded from the hamlet government, or if they are accepted as citizens they have a very special status and certain specified privileges. These are the ones who are never addressed by teknonyms. On the other hand, the gentry of inferior rank who do use teknonymy also generally are accepted as nearly full and equal hamlet citizens. In such cases, the teknonyms employed are specially modified forms, terms which are more elegant than those employed by commoners, and which vary quite precisely with their rank within the gentry group.

This parallel between teknonymous usage and hamlet role is by no means regular. In so far as it holds, however, the co-variation must be related to the importance that Balinese place on titles of address. In general, in Bali, the external forms of social intercourse, the manners of speech and modes of etiquette, are highly valued. In fact their system of social stratification as a whole is best understood neither as an arrangement of bounded social groups (e.g., a 'caste' system) nor as a fluid ordering of persons according to their economic resources (a 'class' system), but rather as several overlapping series of ranked honorific titles. The pivotal distinction between gentry and commoners in Bali is that the former must always be addressed by their title, and the latter, while they do actually have inherited titles, may never be addressed by them. Teknonymy comes, for the commoners, to be a means of addressing one's equals respectfully, and of avoiding the use of either personal names or honorific titles.

The members of the hamlet council are all absolutely equal citizens; decisions are always reached unanimously in full meeting, and their leaders are never more than representatives of the common will. Thus, to be a member of the hamlet council places the gentry in a situation of chronic conflict, for their noble blood is a claim, however weak, to political and social superiority, a claim to membership in an exalted and non-localized aristocratic community above and outside of the hamlet. Mode of address in this situation becomes the weather-vane for their social situation, summing up the various vectors of prestige, and correspondingly, shifting with changes in their social position.

TEKNONYMY AND THE KINSHIP SYSTEM

It is in the area of kinship that teknonymy in Bali plays its most interesting functional role. Here again the contrast between gentry and commoner proves suggestive. The kinship system for both is about the same at the domestic level; it is only in the formation of larger, socially significant corporate kin-groups that the two strata differ.

Descent is patrilineal, residence is virilocal, but in contrast to most lineal systems, marriage is preferentially endogamous. The most favored marital partner is the father's brother's daughter, and contracts of this nature are in fact quite frequent. The dwelling unit is the house-yard, a walled-in complex of open pavilions, kitchen sheds, and closed one-roomed houses, together with a small house-yard temple. Within this compound reside one or more nuclear families, most often those of a father and some of his sons, although house-yards containing but a single nuclear family are common, as are also ones with large extended patri-families of brothers, cousins, and uncles. The main symbol for expression of their social unity is their collective worship at the same house-yard temple, and internal sub-division of the family is always followed by a shift to a separate house-yard temple.

While the house-yard group is largely a domestic unit, the various sorts of larger corporate kin-groups are not domestic in function, but rather political, economic, and ceremonial. Most important of all, they act to establish, confirm and celebrate the social rank of their members. They are associations of house-yards, or more precisely, of their component family head-couples. The house-yards may be contiguous as is the case for high gentry families, or scattered in various parts of the hamlet as is the case for most commoner kin-groups. The key feature distinguishing a corporate kin-group in Bali from an unincorporated, simple network of related families is the presence of a large, separate temple, built outside of any of the member house-yards, on public land, which stands for the group as a whole. While terms vary, the most usual word for a commoner kin-group temple is the *dadia* temple, and the group itself is often referred to as a *dadia*. Gentry use more elevated terms, but we shall use *dadia* here for gentry and commoners alike, to refer to those corporate kin-groups which possess a separate temple and a conviction that they are all descended from one ancestor.

Common descent of *dadia* members is largely presumptive for commoners, since, in contrast to the gentry, they keep no geneal-ogies. For gentry and commoners alike, however, the important cultural concept is not the notion of a descent-line stemming from a personalized ancestral figure, but rather the idea of a single and impersonal genetic source, an origin point symbolized sometimes by a deity, or more often simply by a geographical spot, a certain temple. However, since most of the gentry preserve written genealogical histories, their *dadias* are generally both much larger and more internally differentiated into a main core line and numerous intricately ranked branch and sub-branch cadet lines. Every noble family knows exactly its genealogical position and relative rank in regard to all the others in its *dadia*.

In nineteenth-century Bali, the gentry *dadia* were the units in the supra-local political system. Each one represented a potential or actual small autonomous state, competing with all the others for primacy within its region. There was no all-Bali kingdom, but rather a number of major and minor ones, shifting in numbers and position. At the time of the imposition of Dutch direct rule in 1906–8, there were six major kings and dozens of minor ones, plus scores of lesser gentry *dadia* subordinate to them. The king's immediate kinsmen, especially his brothers and half-brothers, were his ministers and representatives. He would place them, or the heads of allied *dadia*, in various villages strategically located round his realm, and each of these would then establish a branch *dadia* of his own. In consequence, the gentry *dadia* to-day have branches dispersed all over the entire island. Family visits, endogamous marriages, adoption of kinsmen, and yearly worship at the original *dadia* temple serve to keep these sprawling kin-groups together.

Commoner *dadia* on the other hand never extend beyond the boundaries of a single hamlet. This is not because of their smaller membership, but because of the political relationship between hamlet and *dadia*. For commoners, the hamlet is the fundamental political unit; it makes many demands on its citizens—in labour, attendance at rituals and meetings, and in dues. These hamlet demands conflict, often quite directly, with the demands of other associational groupings, most especially the *dadia*. So, for instance, if a man, or even several families move away from their hamlet to a new one, their *dadia* membership gradually dissolves. They find, for instance, that workdays on hamlet projects in their new place of residence conflict with workdays of their old *dadia*, and they are forced to choose between them. There are attempts to maintain the ties to the old *dadia*, especially if it was an influential one, but after two generations at the most, and usually very much sooner, the connexion is lost. Pressure on commoners to keep their marriages within the hamlet are intense. In a situation of choice between a woman of the same hamlet and one from, say the *dadia* of one's mother in another hamlet, the first one is strongly preferred. Likewise, when a hamlet swells beyond a manageable size and decides to split in two, the *dadias* are also forced to split, even though for many *dadias* such segmentation means loss of viability and eventual dissolution.

Thus commoner *dadia* are politically subordinate to the hamlet; they are parts or components of the hamlet first, and kin-groups second. Their very existence as corporate groups is in each case contingent on the relative social prestige and power of the members, rather than, as in many other societies with organized kin-groups, an automatic function of kinship principles alone.

The contingent, variable quality of corporate kin-groups is one of the most fundamental structural features of the Balinese kinship system. Not all commoners need belong to *dadia* and such groupings do not include all members of the community. Many commoner families have no further associations than the bilaterally extending network of relatives, the usual ego-centred kindred. When they exist, however, commoner *dadia* are highly organized, with elected leadership, treasuries, temples, and strong corporate identities. They may have as many as a hundred adult members. Very few hamlets are found in which the entire population is divided into *dadia*; but at the other extreme, there are few hamlets with no *dadia* at all. Most general, probably, is the kind of hamlet in which about half the people are members of from one to six *dadia*, while the remaining portion remain unorganized. For a group of kinsmen to have and maintain a *dadia* requires continued prestige, influence, and wealth. Socially rising families try to join existing *dadia* or to establish one of their own; socially falling families cling to their *dadia* temple for as long as they can, but in the end, through deaths and out-marriages, the *dadia* group itself disintegrates, and its temple passes into the hands of others.

This high degree of elasticity in commoner *dadia* formation is directly related to their attitudes toward descent as a criterion for membership in the *dadia*. While gentry *dadia* are clearly patrilineal in structure, it is more accurate to say of the commoner *dadia* that they are patrifiliative. It is only one's father's *dadia* affiliation which is relevant to a commoner; further generations in the past are unimportant. Actually it is one's father's honorific title that is the significant element. As mentioned previously, almost all commoners have titles which, however, are not employed in ordinary intercourse, either in address or reference; they are merely taken for granted. The title carries with it a mythical history of an illustrious ancestor who, in most of the stories, was once of gentry birth but for some misbehaviour or treachery lost his right to high title. All persons with the same title are considered to be ultimately related, and are usually referred to as 'cousins'. Those who have no *dadia* rarely mention their title to anyone, but any knowledgeable community member knows the title of everyone.[5] If a man's father had no *dadia* affiliation, if for instance he has moved from his original hamlet, or if, through changing circumstances he has become relatively affluent and personally powerful, he can join or establish a new *dadia* simply on the strength of common title ownership. Thus the title-system provides an alternative, non-historical means for establishing the fact of collateral kinship in a group.

However, this odd phenomenon of kin-groups without descent lines is not merely a matter of the absence of genealogical records and the substitution of patrifiliatively inherited titles as a charter. Balinese commoners have always before them the exemplary model of the gentry *dadia*, consciously based on an explicit trunk-and-branch framework of known descent lines. Something remains to be explained: why the commoners neglect genealogies. Causal questions such as this, of course, can lead to a morass of ever-receding explanatory factors; all we presume to suggest here is the mechanism by which the preservation of family history becomes impossible for Balinese commoners. This mechanism is their system of teknonymy.

The striking thing about Balinese commoner families is the almost complete ignorance each generation has about its predecessors. The average man knows virtually nothing about any of his forbears whose lives did not happen to overlap with his. He does not know the personal names of most of those living kinsmen who are older than he, and none of those deceased. And he knows very little about his collateral kinship ties; men living in the same village with a third cousin and at times even a second, are often ignorant of their precise relationship. This absence of information is greater for Balinese than for persons of other societies, societies like ours for instance where the tending of ancestral trees is merely neglected from lack of concern. In Bali, the process is an active one, a regularly enforced amnesia, one which starts cutting off kinship information even at the parental generation.

---

[5] In some regions, most especially in south-west Bali, many family groups are found who claim to have 'forgotten' their titles through disuse. They continue to accept the title system, and feel that they 'should have' one. They may even maintain a *dadia* temple for their group.

Teknonymy brings about systematic genealogical amnesia through its regular replacement of each man's personal name with a series of teknonymous ones.[6] It is extremely bad form for a son to ask anyone what his father's personal name is, unthinkable for him to use it, if by some accident he learns what it is. Each man's living ascendants are, or should be, viewed as having progressed half-way toward a non-individualized divinity. After death, the taboo on personal names is even more stringent, for by that time the ascendants are either potentially malicious spirits or completely nameless but benevolent deities. In any case, the names by which a man knows his father, grandfather, and great-grandfather are all actually the names of his contemporaries and juniors. Since a man does know the personal names of those of his own generation and below, it is theoretically possible for the oldest men in the neighbourhood to identify every living person by an individual, absolute, and fixed designation, but even the oldest men are likely to have forgotten many people's personal names after years of addressing them as 'Father-of' or 'Grandfather-of' someone else. After a man dies he is in a sense inevitably lost to his descendants as a particular individual because none of them know his proper name. Thus a man cannot say to his son 'your great-great-grandfather' was So-and-so and was the brother of Such-and-such, because he doesn't know 'who', in a personal sense, he was even though he may vaguely remember him as an actual living great-grandfather of himself. All he can tell his son is that 'your great-great-grandfather was my great-grandfather', a simple and generalized

---

[6] Balinese never name children after other persons, and in fact, among commoners, there is a conscious effort not to duplicate any names of members of the hamlet. The number of different names is very large, and considerable innovation is permissible. Actually, even children's personal names are seldom employed in direct address. Instead of calling them by their personal names, a system of sibling-position terms or titles are employed. The first child is usually called Wajan, the second Njoman, the third Made, and the fourth Ktut. In most areas the fifth child is named Wajan again, and the series reiterated. These four titles are actually the everyday 'names' of everyone who does not have a teknonym, with the result confusing apparently only to the ethnologist, that everyone seems to have the same name. Personal names are employed only when exact reference is needed. For instance, one will speak of two boys named Wajan Regreg and Wajan Tantra, but will usually address both of them as Wajan.

tautology which contains information about kin-term usage but nothing about people. There is in fact no way older people can communicate to younger people about a dead individual whom the older knew as a man but the younger did not in more than general terms so far as social identity is concerned. Of course, other characteristics about the man can be communicated—that he was wise, handsome, or came from North Bali—but the general loss of personal identity enforced by kin-term usages tends to be part of a general cultural veil which falls over him in all aspects. One should not expect to know much in detail about one's progenitors, living or dead, and to ask too many or too particular questions is to show a lack of breeding and piety.

In terms of kinship reckoning this means that any tie which is based on a collateral relationship between two individuals both of whom were dead when the oldest living member of the kin-group was born is in principle untraceable. Or, to put it the other way round, any tie is intrinsically untraceable which is based on a common ancestor more than four generations ascendant from the oldest living member of the kin-group, assuming the life of a man and his great-great-grandchild rarely if ever overlap.

Chart I depicts in an idealized graphic form how teknonymy operates to erase knowledge of previous generations, and why four ascendant generations is the logically maximal time depth of commoner kinship knowledge. Actually, four generations represents an absolute maximum range under ideal conditions in which the life of every individual overlaps with that of his great-grandchild, and the memory of sibling ties among the kinsmen one has known is perfect. Not only will most Balinese never know their great-grandfathers, and sometimes not even their grandfathers, as living men, but during the course of a long lifetime with many name-changes, they can easily forget facts of relationships they once knew. Thus, for instance, two men who are third or even second cousins could easily forget that their great-grandfathers were brothers, even if they once knew it. Indeed, their own fathers may have forgotten this fact themselves. Consequently the dissolution of traced kin ties typically occurs much more rapidly than in the model. Second cousins are often completely unaware how they are related, so that when their fathers die the specific nature of the tie can no longer be stated.

When one takes genealogies in a Balinese village, one can actually see the curtain of amnesia descending, for informants of older generations know the kinship links of younger men, who when they report their own genealogies, regard themselves as related only in a vague and untraceable way. Thus a man's father may know who his son's second cousin is without the son himself being aware that this individual is his second cousin; and in most cases the father will never feel called upon to impart this information to the son. For older men, the neighbourhood contains a much wider range of specific kin ties than for younger ones, and their knowledge is not, by and large, transferable. When the younger men grow older they will know the ties which have been generated in their time, but not those of their fathers' and grandfathers' times.

The Balinese place a ritual seal on the two ends of the four-generation genealogical span. When an individual dies all his living descendants, including nephews and nieces and cousins younger than he, are obliged, at the funeral ceremony, to make obeisance and pray to him as to a god. However, this obligation extends only to the generation of a man's grandchildren and not to his great-grandchildren. In fact, the members of the third descending generation, and any lower ones if they exist, are expressly *forbidden* to pray to the deceased, on the grounds that they are of equal status. A great-grandparent and a great-grandchild call each other by the same reciprocal term (*kumpi*), emphasizing their identity. For the Balinese, the very old and the very young are near to the world of Gods. When a man has reached the status of great-grandparenthood, he has fulfilled his generational obligations and socially (and, according to some, mystically) reincarnated himself. A set of four generations is thus a complete unit, with a beginning, an end, and a new beginning, with the status of *kumpi* (great-grandparent; great-grandchild) marking the point of juncture between units, the end of one cycle and the beginning of another.

In this way the Balinese version of teknonymy creates an ever-repeating sequence of four impersonal statuses—child, parent, grandparent, and great-grandparent—and systematically erases the knowledge of collateral kinship ties. It is this function of teknonymy which may be unique to Bali. But, unique or not, it is crucial to Balinese social structure. The contrast between the many branched, powerful gentry *dadia*, and the inhibited, weak commoner ones, is in direct response to their differing political positions in the larger society. The gentry derived its strength, in large part, from the cohesiveness and extensiveness of its kin-groups, which enabled the rulers of Bali to spread their influence over wide regions. Among the commoners on the other hand, it is the hamlet association which is the nearest equivalent to an effective polity. In an ecological setting of compact, nucleated settlements, the hamlet council most often represents a terri-torially identified, largely endogamous community, and the domi-nant Balinese sentiment is that hamlet interests should override those of any component groups in certain crucially important local matters. The hamlet is conceived of by them as a collegium in which all members are fully equal, and no internal segments or factions are legally recognized. The members of a commoner *dadia* are considered to be casting their votes strictly as indi-vidual members. 'The hamlet knows no kinship', says a Balinese proverb. In this context, strongly cohesive kin-groups which extend over the bounds of the local community would be dis-ruptive rather than integrative in effect.

CONCLUSION: TEKNONYMY AS A CULTURAL PARADIGM

Any internally coherent arrangement for naming, such as the Balinese system of teknonyms, is a fragment of culture. We consider 'culture' to refer to those ordered systems of symbols, those accepted patterns of meaningful conceptions, in terms of which social interaction takes place. It embraces all those beliefs, theories, expressive images and values which are held in common by a group of people and by means of which they orient them-selves toward each other and their world.

'Social structure', in this view, is not a mere 'reflex', 'part', or 'aspect' of culture, but a partially independent system of another sort. It is the enduring form of social interaction within a par-ticular group, the stable system of regular social relationships. The culture of the actors is only one element among several contributing to the persistence and systematic organization of their social structure. Others include ecological and demographic conditions, the motivational dynamics of the actors, the presence and actions of neighbouring social groups, and, perhaps, certain regularities intrinsic to social interaction as such. The analysis of the functions to teknonymy provides an opportunity to investigate further the manner in which culture and social structure are related in one, particularly instructive, instance.[7]

In these terms, we must think of Balinese teknonymy not merely as an odd social practice, yet one more miscellaneous custom to add to the ethnographic record, but as a set of interconnected concepts which provides the Balinese with a meaningful framework for the perception, and in fact the actualization, of certain aspects of their own social structure. Teknonymy functions in Bali as a 'cultural paradigm' of social roles and relationships which serves the Balinese as an interpretive guide for understanding and manoeuvering within their own institutional system and as a set of instructions, a programme in the computer-theory sense, for maintaining that system. It is cultural because it is, at base, a coherent system of ideas, a consistent set of beliefs, a theory even, about the way in which social life is, and ought to be, organized. It is a paradigm because it is not just a set of beliefs, a mere theory, but is actually used as a template or blueprint in terms of which Balinese may pattern their concrete behaviour. Teknonymy does not merely reflect Balinese institutional structure, nor does it merely 'rationalize' it. By providing a general conception of social order which men are committed to realize, it actively shapes it.

In certain other societies it is kinship terminology in the conventional sense which serves most prominently as such a cultural paradigm. These are the societies where, unlike Bali, kinship is the central organizing force for virtually the whole of the social structure. A classic case in point is the Hopi pueblo, where Crow terminology classifies certain kinsmen together and distinguishes certain others in such a way as to single out the corporate lineage blocks which form the core of Hopi community life, and at the same time indicates the structural relationships of

---

[7] For a more extended discussion of this theoretical standpoint, see Geertz, C. 1957.

these blocks to one another (Eggan 1950).[8] Here the kinship terminology becomes a kind of cognitive map of the society in terms of which individuals scattered variously through the system can form a reasonably veridical image of the whole.

In a more limited way teknonymy also can be a map of certain social locations, a set of culturally agreed-upon indicators of social status.[9] As with kinship terminology, teknonymy has certain formal structural elements which can be analytically compared from culture to culture, and their functions assessed within each society. It need not—in fact, rarely does—have the full elaboration of its systematic possibilities that it exhibits in Bali.

Teknonymy's most rudimentary form is probably its most common.[10] For example, the Penan of central Borneo give teknonyms only to couples with living offspring. They have no grandparental or great-grandparental teknonymic levels, while childless couples, or those who have lost the child after whom they were named, retain their personal names. For the Penan, teknonymy has the function of focusing attention on the marital couple as joint procreators by classifying them together socially under the single name of their child, and setting them apart from the immature, the childless, and the aged, but lacks the two other implications we have traced for Bali (Needham 1954).[11]

---

[8] Leach has dealt with Jinghpaw kinship terminology more explicitly in these terms, speaking of it as giving an 'ideal frame of reference' or 'basic ideology', as a system of 'categories into which the speaker divides the individuals with whom he has social contact' (Leach 1961).

[9] Balinese kinship terminology as such is cognatic and generational, with Hawaiian cousin terms. That is, all cousins are called by the same terms as siblings, and uncles and aunts by the same terms as parents, with no distinction being made between paternal and maternal kin lines. What the significance of such a bilateral and non-lineal, 'generational' paradigm might have for Balinese social relationships would have to be the subject of another complete paper. Here we can only remark that the kin terms themselves are rarely employed outside the nuclear family, and in their place are found teknonyms wherever possible, and sibling-position titles plus personal names for the remainder.

[10] Teknonymy even appears, evanescently, in the United States, where its only users are children of pre-school age for whom the dominant feature of all adult roles is that of parenthood (Schneider and Homans 1955, p. 1206).

[11] The Penan are nomadic hunters and gatherers, with bands of thirty to forty people, bilateral kinship, and no descent groups of any importance. Teknonymy, for the Penan, is an aspect of a larger system of address-titles. Persons who do not have teknonyms, i.e. who are not at the peak of their

Among the Land Dayak, also of central Borneo, teknonymous usage is somewhat more developed. Here teknonyms are applied to nearly every adult member of the society, and the same principle of 'graduation' to grandparental status as is found in Bali appears. Since, however, the Dayak confer teknonyms irrespective of actual parental status (a childless couple may take the name of anyone in the next lower generation, or even the name of a favourite cat or dog), the Dayak system does not draw attention to conjugal fertility (though it does to the marriage bond as such), but rather to the generational levels which cut across the entire community. Also, unlike Bali, the names do not serve to mark off family lines, because one's teknonym need not be that of one's own child. Similarly, on graduation to grandparenthood, the new teknonym need have no relationship to that of one's adult son, but may again be chosen at random from any small child (or pet) in the community. (There is no mention of a Dayak 'great-grandparent' teknonym.) Thus the Land Dayak system of teknonymy has as its main functional consequence the layering of the society into three levels: children, parents, and grandparents (Geddes 1954).[12]

Even so cursory and geographically limited a comparative analysis of teknonymy as this brings out somewhat more clearly the formal features implicit in it as a cultural paradigm. First, there is the identification of man and wife as joint procreators. Second, there is the generational or age-stratification of the community. And third, there is the feature we find only in Bali: the delineation of a four-position chain of filiation, a truncated 'descent' line with all members bearing the same name.

These could be called 'descent' lines, but only in a partial and somewhat Pickwickian sense, for the focus of the naming system

---

child-bearing period, are generally addressed by death-terms, titles preceding the proper name which indicate which of one's nearest of kin has most recently died. Thus for the Penan, teknonymy is part of a wider cultural paradigm concerned with the ultimate human facts of procreation and death.
[12] The Land Dayak are shifting cultivators, with settled communities of several hundred inhabitants, bilateral kinship, no supra-village political structure. The community has no internal class structure, no formal political leadership. Geddes interprets the function of teknonymy not as organizing the community into generational or age strata, as we should, but as creating a network which performs a much needed integrative function.

falls not on the progenitor of the line, but on its most recent addition. The patriline is defined in terms of its lowest (generationally speaking) rather than its highest member, in terms of the present rather than the past. It is not who one's ancestor is, or was, which is stressed, but who one's descendant is, whom one is ancestor to. It is a 'downward looking' rather than an 'upward looking' system, and a man sees himself, so to speak, producing structure below him rather than emerging from it above him. Probably there are other formal directions in which teknonymy can be developed with consequently different implications for social organization, though how many of these are in fact realized in one or another of the world's societies is not known, systematic attention to teknonymous usage being very rare in the literature.

Such a cross-cultural comparison of the possible variations implicit in the idea of teknonymy suggests that there are several analytically distinct aspects of any cultural paradigm. First, there is the paradigm as a cultural object, a more or less integrated set of ideas and images which can be examined by the outsider, and its formal qualities and their logical implications studied irrespective of their social and psychological contexts. Second, there is the paradigm as an internalized guide to behaviour, as an actual part of the cognitive equipment of individual culturebearers. The degree to which any specific cultural paradigm genuinely governs perception, cognition, and motivation is obviously a variable matter, ranging from near irrelevance to central concern. Thirdly, there is the range of different social structural contexts to which it is relevant, that is the degree of specificity or generality of social behaviour that the paradigm is assumed to embrace, the amount of functional significance it has for the society as a whole.

In addition to such positive factors as these, any cultural paradigm has, however, also an obverse aspect: in the very process of suggesting certain modes of social relationship to the culture-bearers, it also, and equally crucially, blocks other possibilities from sight. The acceptance of any particular set of verbal categories and of the concepts embedded in them tends to preclude the awareness of alternative classifications; a way of seeing is also a way of not seeing. Since teknonymy is more than just a system of status-terms, however, but also a system of name-changing, it can go even further in this direction. It can, by the regular discouraging of remembrance of personal names and identities, actively prevent other modes of relationship—in the Balinese case, translocal descent ties—from developing at all.

In many societies with corporate, unilineal kin-groups, characteristic cultural paradigms are found which stress a river-like image of ever-branching lines with explicitly specified personal links between the living and the ancestors. The substance of the kin-group, so to speak, flows through time, braiding out as it goes, each crucial point of separation being marked and to an extent explained by a bit of genealogical knowledge, real or invented, of some sort. But Balinese teknonymy cuts off the present from the past by erasing the genealogical ties which connect them, and in so doing leaves the Balinese free to develop very strong local patrilineal descent groups while at the same time inhibiting the natural tendency for such groups to link up with one another in terms of a many-branched family tree, a development which would be disruptive not only to hamlet political organization but to a wide range of local social groups—irrigation societies, temple congregations, etc. A good deal of attention has been paid in the literature to the forces making for the development and maintenance of various forms of social structure. Perhaps it will prove equally useful to develop methods of analysis of the forces, especially cultural forces, which inhibit the development of structures which would, in all likelihood, prove dysfunctional to the established system. What is absent may be as significant as what is present in a social system; some things which do not happen, do not happen for a reason.

The phenomenon under consideration, the regular disappearance of the knowledge of antecedent kinship ties, is by no means uncommon. P. H. Gulliver, confronting a somewhat similar situation in his study of Jie kinship, uses the term 'structural amnesia', to refer the systematic forgetting of certain genealogical connexions and the simultaneous substitution of fictitious ones (Gulliver 1955, pp. 113 seq. See also Barnes 1947). Jie genealogical information, as the Balinese, stops above the level of the grandparents of the oldest living men. Despite the fact that the Jie assume that the kin-group which Gulliver terms the 'Family' must segment into several independent Families each generation, in actuality most of the existing Families appear not to have actually segmented in the past. To account for this he proposes that there must be a simultaneous process of merging going on, by which second cousins gradually come to consider themselves first cousins and thus to be descended from one single grandfather, consequently preserving the integrity of their family from segmentation. He then suggests that there must be a process of constant forgetting and cognitive re-organization of the actual kinship connexions at the great-grandparental level. However, other than suggesting a psychological process in which the personalities of weak grandparents tend to become confused with those of strong ones until the assertion is made that there had in fact historically been only one grandfather, Gulliver sees no institutional or cultural mechanism which could bring about this structural amnesia.

For the Balinese the structure-inhibiting mechanism is the cultural paradigm inherent in the regular and systematic use of teknonymy. The Jie, and many other such societies with shallow genealogical recall, do not have teknonymy. And there are countless societies, China for one, which have both teknonymy and lengthy genealogies (Feng 1936). No claim is being made for simple, direct, or uni-factoral causation. The concepts and symbols to which men are attached are only one element among many which can and do influence their concrete actions, and consequently there can never be a one-to-one relationship between cultural paradigms and social structure. Nevertheless, if our data and analysis are correct, the presence of teknonymy in the cultural equipment of the Balinese has far-reaching reverberations, both positive and negative, in their domestic and political life.

BIBLIOGRAPHY

d'ABBEVILLE, CLAUDE
   1614 *Histoire de la Mission des Pères Capucins en L'isle de Maragnan et Terres Ciconvoisines* . . . Paris: L'impr. de F. Huby.
ADAM, LEONHARD
   1947 "Virilocal and Uxorilocal," *American Anthropologist* 49: 678.
   1948 "'Virilocal' and 'Uxorilocal,'" *Man* 48, 13: 12.
AIYAPPAN, A.
   1935 "Fraternal Polyandry in Malabar," *Man in India* 14: 108–18.

   1937 "Polyandry and Sexual Jealousy," *Man* 37: 104.

   1945 *Irvas and Culture Change*. Bull. Madras Govt. Mus., N.S., General Section, Vol. 5, No. 1.
AMES, C. G.
   1934 *Gazetteer of Plateau Province, Jos, Nigeria*.
ANCHIETA, JOSÉ DE
   1846 *Informacão dos Casamentos dos Indios do Brasil*. Revista Trimensal del Instituto Historico e Geographico Brasileiro, T. 8, I 2da Seria.
AYOUB, MILLICENT
   1957 "Endogamous Marriage in a Middle Eastern Village." Ph.D. dissertation, Harvard University.
BAMBERGER, M. L.
   1923 "Aus meiner Minhagimsammelmappe," *Jahrbuch für Jüdische Volkskunde* I: 320–32.
BANCROFT, H. H.
   1883 *History of Mexico*. San Francisco: A. L. Bancroft and Co.
BARNES, J. A.
   1947 "The Collection of Genealogies," *Rhodes-Livingstone Journal* 5: 52–53.

   1951 *Marriage in a Changing Society; A Study in Structural Change Among the Fort Jameson Ngoni*. Rhodes-Livingstone Papers 20. London: Oxford University Press.

   1957 "Land Rights and Kinship in Two Bremnes Hamlets," *JRAI* 87: 31–56.

BARTH, FREDRIK
   1953 *Principles of Social Organization in Southern Kurdistan,* Universitetets Etnografiske Museum Bulletin, No. 7, Oslo.

   1954 "Father's Brother's Daughter Marriage in Kurdistan," *Southwestern Journal of Anthropology* 10: 164–71.
BEALS, R. L.
   1946 *Cherán: A Sierra Tarascan Village.* Publication, Institute of Social Anthropology, Smithsonian Institution, No. 2. Washington: Government Printing Office.
BECKWITH, MARTHA WARREN
   1922 *Folk Games in Jamaica.* Publications of the Folklore Foundation, No. 1, Vassar College, Poughkeepsie, New York.

   1929 *Black Roadways: A Study of Jamaican Folk Life.* Chapel Hill: University of North Carolina Press.
BELL, SIR CHARLES
   1928 *The People of Tibet.* Oxford: Clarendon Press.
BELO, J.
   1936 "A Study of the Balinese Family," *American Anthropologist* 38: 12–31.
BENNETT, H. S.
   1938 *Life on the English Manor.* Cambridge: Cambridge University Press.
BERREMAN, G. D.
   1959 "Kin, Caste and Community in a Himalayan Hill-Village." Ph.D. dissertation, Cornell University.

   1960 "Cultural Variability and Drift in the Himalayan hills," *American Anthropologist* 62: 77–94.
BJÖRKVIK, HALVARD
   1956 "The Farm Territories," *Scandinavian Economic History Review* 4: 33–61.
BOESCH, H.
   1900 *Kinderleben in der Deutschen Vergangenheit.* Monographien zur Deutschen Kulturgeschichte, Vol. 5. Leipzig.
BOHANNAN, PAUL
   1954 *Tiv Farm and Settlement.* London: H.M.S.O.

   1957 "An Alternate Residence Classification," *American Anthropologist* 59: 126–31.
BONIFACE, GEORGE WASHINGTON ROBINSON. Trans.
   1940 *The Letters of St. Boniface.* New York: Columbia University Press.
BRETON, RAYMOND
   1665 *Dictionnaire Caraïbe-Français.* Auxerre: G. Bouquet.
BRIFFAULT, ROBERT
   1927 and 1959 *The Mothers.* London: George Allen & Unwin, Ltd.
BROWN, PAULA AND BROOKFIELD, H. C.
   1959 "Chimbu Land and Society," *Oceania* 30: 1–75.
BUCHANAN, FRANCIS (HAMILTON)
   1807 *A Journey from Madras Through Mysore, Canara and Malabar.* 3 vols. London: T. Cadell and W. Davies.

CARDIM, FERNAO
1925 *Tratados da Terra e Gente do Brasil.* Rio de Janeiro: J. Leite and cia.
CARRASCO, PEDRO
1959 *Land and Polity in Tibet.* Seattle: University of Washington Press.
CEYLON, GOVERNMENT OF
1935 *Report of the Kandyan Law Commission, 1935.* Sessional Paper XXIV. Colombo: Government Press.

——
1946 *Census of Ceylon, 1946.* Vol. 1, Part 2, Statistical Digest. Colombo: Government Press.
CHAPPLE, ELIOT D. AND COON, CARLETON S.
1942 *Principles of Anthropology.* New York: H. Holt and Co.
CLARKE, EDITH
1953 "Land Tenure and the Family in Four Jamaican Communities," *Social and Economic Studies* 1, 4: 81–118.

——
1957 *My Mother Who Fathered Me.* London: George Allen and Unwin, Ltd.
COHEN, YEHUDI A.
1954 "The Social Organization of a Selected Community in Jamaica," *Social and Economic Studies* 2, 4: 104–33. Mona, Jamaica, W.I.: University College of the West Indies.

——
1955 "Character Formation and Social Structure in a Jamaican Community," *Psychiatry* 18: 275–96.

——
1955a "A Contribution to the Study of Adolescence: 'Adolescent Conflict' in a Jamaican Community," *Samiska* 9: 139–72.

——
1956 "Structure and Function: Family Organization and Socialization in a Jamaican Community," *American Anthropologist* 58: 664–86.

——
1961 "A Hypothesis for the Genetic Basis of the Universality of the Incest Taboo and Its Relation to Kinship Organization." Paper read at the annual A.A.A.S. Meetings, Section H, Symposium on Cross-Species Incest Behavior, December 30, Denver, Colorado: mimeo.
COLSON, E.
1951 "Residence and Village Stability Among the Plateau Tonga," *Rhodes-Livingstone Journal* 12: 41–67.
COMMITTEE ON LATIN AMERICAN ANTHROPOLOGY, NATIONAL RESEARCH COUNCIL
1949 "Research Needs in the Field of Modern Latin American Culture," *American Anthropologist* 51: 149–54.
COOPER, JOHN M.
1941 *Temporal Sequence and the Marginal Cultures.* The Catholic University of America Anthropological Series, No. 10.
CORBLET, J.
1882 *Histoire Dogmatique, Liturgique et Archéologique du Sacrament de Baptême.* Vol. 1. Geneva.
COULTON, G. G.
1926 *The Medieval Village.* Cambridge: Cambridge University Press.

1936 *Five Centuries of Religion*, Vol. 3. Cambridge: Cambridge University Press.

CUMPER, G. E.
1958 "The Jamaican Family: Village and Estate," *Social and Economic Studies* 7, 1: 76–108. Mona, Jamaica, W.I.: University College of the West Indies.

CZAPLICKA, MARIE ANTOINETTE
1914 *Aboriginal Siberia*. Oxford: Clarendon Press.

DAS-GUPTA, H. C.
1921 "A Short Note on Polyandry in the Jubbal State (Simla)," *The Indian Antiquary* 50: 146–48.

DAVENPORT, WILLIAM
1956 *A Comparative Study of Two Jamaican Fishing Communities*. Unpublished Ph.D. dissertation, Department of Anthropology, Yale University.

DICKSON, H. R. P.
1949 *The Arab of the Desert*. London: G. Allen and Unwin.

DONADIN Y PUIGNAN, D. D.
no date *Diccionario de la Lengua Castellana*, Vol. 1. Barcelona.

DOPSCH, A.
1918–20 *Wirtschaftliche und Soziale Grundlagen der Europäischen Kulturentwicklung*. 2 vols. Vienna: L. W. Seidel and Sons.

DOUGHTY, CHARLES M.
1955 *Travels in Arabia Deserta* (abridgment by Edward Garnett). Garden City, New York: Doubleday.

D'OYLY, JOHN
1929 *A Sketch of the Constitution of the Kandayan Kingdom (Ceylon)*. Colombo.

DREWS, P.
1907 "Taufe, Liturg, Vollzug," *Realenzyklopädie für Protestantische Theologie und Kirche* 19. Leipzig.

DRY, D. P. L.
1950 "The Family Organization of the Hausa of Northern Nigeria." B.Sc. thesis, Oxford University.

DUMONT, LOUIS
1953a "The Dravidian Kinship Terminology as an Expression of Marriage," *Man* 53, 54.

1953b "Dravidian Kinship Terminology," *Man* 53, 224.

DURHAM, M. E.
1928 *Some Tribal Origins, Laws and Customs of the Balkans*. London: G. Allen and Unwin.

DURKHEIM, ÉMILE
1898 "La Prohibition de l'Inceste et Ses Origines," *L'Année sociologique* 1: 1–70.

EGGAN, FRED
1937 "The Cheyenne and Arapaho Kinship System," *Social Anthropology of North American Tribes*, F. Eggan, ed. Chicago: University of Chicago Press.

———
1950 *Social Organization of the Western Pueblos.* Chicago: University of Chicago Press.

———
1955 "Social Anthropology: Methods and Results," in *Social Anthropology of North American Tribes,* revised edition, F. Eggan, ed. Chicago: University of Chicago Press.

ELLIS, ROBERT A.
1956 "Social Status and Social Distance," *Sociology and Social Research* 40: 240–46.

———
1957 "Color and Class in a Jamaican Market Town," *Sociology and Social Research* 41: 354–60.

EMBER, MELVIN
1961 "The Incest Taboo and the Nuclear Family." Paper read at the AAA Annual Meetings, Philadelphia, November 16–19.

ERICH, O.
1936 *Wörterbuch der Deutschen Volkskunde.* Leipzig: A. Kroner.

ESPINOSA, J. M.
1942 *Crusaders of the Rio Grande.* Chicago: Institute of Jesuit History.

EVANS-PRITCHARD, E. E.
1940 *The Nuer.* Oxford: Clarendon Press.

———
1945 *Some Aspects of Marriage and Family Among the Nuer.* Rhodes-Livingstone Papers, No. 11, London: Oxford University Press.

———
1946 "Nuer Bridewealth," *Africa* 16 (4): 247–57.

———
1948 "Nuer Marriage Ceremonies," *Africa* 18 (1): 29–40.

———
1949a *The Sanusi of Cyrenaica.* Oxford: Clarendon Press.

———
1949b "Nuer Rules of Exogamy and Incest," *Social Structure: Studies presented to A. R. Radcliffe-Brown,* Meyer Fortes, ed. London: Oxford University Press.

———
1951 *Kinship and Marriage among the Nuer.* Oxford: Clarendon Press.

FALLERS, LLOYD A.
1957 "Some Determinants of Marriage Stability in Busoga: A Reformulation of Gluckman's Hypothesis," *Africa* 27: 106–23.

FENG, H. Y.
1936 "Teknonymy as a Formative Factor in the Chinese Kinship System," *American Anthropologist* 38: 59–67.

FIRTH, RAYMOND
1936 *We, the Tikopia; a Sociological Study of Kinship in Primitive Polynesia.* London: G. Allen and Unwin.

FISCHER, H. T.
1952 "Polyandry," *International Archives of Ethnography* 46: 106–15.

———
1956 "For a New Definition of Marriage," *Man* 56: 87.

FISCHER, J. L.
   1950 *Native Land Tenure in the Truk District,* Civil Administration,
        Truk: mimeo.
———
   1958 "The Classification of Residence in Censuses," *American An-
        thropologist* 60: 508–17.
———
   1959 "Reply to Raulet," *American Anthropologist* 61: 679–81.
FLICK, A.
   1936 *The Decline of the Medieval Church,* Vol. 1. London: K. Paul,
        Trench, Treubner and Co., Ltd.
FORDE, DARYLL
   1938 "Fission and Accretion in the Patrilineal Clans of a Semi-Bantu
        Community in Southern Nigeria," *JRAI* 68: 311–38.
———
   1950 "Double Descent Among the Yakö," *African Systems of Kinship
        and Marriage,* A. R. Radcliffe-Brown and Daryll Forde, eds. London:
        Oxford University Press.
———
   1952 "Applied Anthropology in Government: British Africa." Unpublished
        Inventory Paper for Wenner-Gren Foundation International Symposium
        on Anthropology, New York City.
FORTES, MEYER
   1936 "Kinship, Incest and Exogamy of the Northern Territories of the
        Gold Coast," in *Custom is King,* L. H. D. Buxton, ed. London: Hutch-
        inson.
———
   1945 *The Dynamics of Clanship Among the Tallensi.* London: Oxford
        University Press.
———
   1949a "Time and Social Structure: An Ashanti Case Study." In *Social
        Structure: Studies Presented to A. R. Radcliffe-Brown,* Meyer Fortes,
        ed. London: Oxford University Press.
———
   1949b *The Web of Kinship Among the Tallensi.* London: Oxford Uni-
        versity Press.
———
   1950 "Kinship and Marriage Among the Ashanti," A. R. Radcliffe-
        Brown and Daryll Forde, eds., *African Systems of Kinship and Mar-
        riage.* London: Oxford University Press.
———
   1953 "The Structure of Unilineal Descent Groups," *American Anthropol-
        ogist* 55: 17–41.
———
   1958 "Introduction," Jack R. Goody, ed., *The Developmental Cycle
        in Domestic Groups.* Cambridge Papers in Social Anthropology, No. 1.
   ———, STEEL, R. W., AND ADY, P.
   1947 "Ashanti Survey, 1945–46: An Experiment in Social Research,"
        Geographical Journal, 110.
FORTUNE, REO
   1932a "Incest," *Encyclopedia of the Social Sciences* 7: 620–22.

—— 1932b *Sorcerers of Dobu; the Social Anthropology of the Dobu Islanders of the Western Pacific*. New York: E. P. Dutton and Co.

FOSTER, G. N.
1948 *Empire's Children: the People of Tzintzuntzan*. Publication, Institute of Social Anthropology, Smithsonian Institution, No. 6. Washington: Government Printing Office.

FREEMAN, J. D.
1955 *Iban Agriculture*. Colonial Research Studies 18. London: HMSO.

—— 1958 *The Family System of the Iban of Borneo*. Cambridge Papers in Social Anthropology 1: 15–52.

FREUD, SIGMUND
1950 *Totem and Taboo*. (James Strachey, trans.) London: Routledge and Kegan Paul.

GAMIO, M.
1922 *La Población del Valle de Teotihuacán*. 3 vols. Mexico: Dirección de talleres gráficos.

GANSHOF, F. L.
1941 "Medieval Agrarian Society in Its Prime: France, the Low Countries and Western Germany," in *Cambridge Economic History of Europe from the Decline of the Roman Empire*, Vol. 1. Cambridge: Cambridge University Press.

GEDDES, W. R.
1954 *The Land Dayaks of Sarawak*. Colonial Research Studies, XIV. London: Colonial Office.

GEERTZ, C.
1957 "Ritual and Social Change: a Javanese Example," *American Anthropologist* 59: 32–54.

—— 1959 "Form and Variation in Balinese Village Structure," *American Anthropologist* 61: 991–1012.

GEERTZ, H.
1959 "The Balinese Village," *Local, Ethnic, and National Loyalties in Village Indonesia:* A Symposium. Yale University Southeast Asia Studies.

GILLIN, J.
1945 *Moche: A Peruvian Coastal Community*. Publication, Institute of Social Anthropology, Smithsonian Institution, No. 3. Washington: Government Printing Office.

GLUCKMAN, MAX
1950 "Kinship and Marriage Among the Lozi of Northern Rhodesia and the Zulu of Natal," in *African Systems of Kinship and Marriage*, A. R. Radcliffe-Brown and Daryll Forde, eds. London: Oxford University Press.

—— 1955 *Custom and Conflict in Africa*. Glencoe: Free Press.

GOODENOUGH, WARD H.
1951 *Property, Kin and Community on Truk*. New Haven: Yale University Publications in Anthropology, No. 46.

1956 "Residence Rules," *Southwestern Journal of Anthropology* 12, 1: 22–37.

GOUGH, KATHLEEN

1952a "Changing Kinship Usages in the Setting of Political and Economic Change Among the Nayars of Malabar," *JRAI* 52: 71–88.

1952b "A Comparison of Incest Prohibitions and Rules of Exogamy in Three Matrilineal Groups of the Malabar Coast," *International Archives of Ethnography* 46: 81–105.

1955a "The Traditional Lineage and Kinship Systems of the Nayar." Unpublished manuscript in the Haddon Library, Cambridge.

1955b "Female Initiation Rites on the Malabar Coast," *JRAI* 85: 45–80.

1959 "The Nayars and the Definition of Marriage," *JRAI* 89: 23–34.

GRANET, MARCEL

1930 *The Chinese Civilization*. New York: Knopf.

1939 "Catégories Matrimoniales et Relations de Proximité dans la Chine Ancienne," *Annales Sociologiques*, Série B, Sociologie Religieuse, Paris.

GRANQVIST, HILMA

1931 "Marriage Conditions in a Palestinian Village," *Commentationes Humanarum*, Societas Scientarium Fennica, Vol. 3, Helsingfors.

GRIERSON, GEORGE A.

1916 *Linguistic Survey of India*, Vol. IX, Part IV. Calcutta: Superintendent of Government Printing.

GULLIVER, P. H.

1955 *The Family Herds*. London: Routledge and Kegan Paul.

HAMILTON, ALEXANDER

1727 *A New Account of the East Indies*. 2 vols. Edinburgh: J. Mosman.

HANDJIEFF, W.

1931 "Zur Soziologie des Bulgaraischen Dorfes." Thesis: Leipzig.

HEATH, DWIGHT B.

1955 "Sexual Division of Labor and Cross-Cultural Research." Paper read at the 54th Annual AAA Meetings, Boston. Reference in *The World of Man* by J. J. Honigmann. New York: Harper and Bros. (1959) p. 374.

HENNINGER, E.

1891 "Sitten und Gebräuche bei der Taufe und Namengebung in der Altfranzösischen Dichtung." Thesis: Halle a. S.

HENRIQUES, FERNANDO

1953 *Family and Colour in Jamaica*. London: Eyre and Spottiswood.

HERSKOVITS, MELVILLE J.

1933 *Outline of Dahomean Religion*. Memoirs of the American Anthropological Association, No. 41. *American Anthropological Association*.

1937a *Life in a Haitian Valley*. New York: A. A. Knopf.

1937b "A Note on 'Woman Marriage' in Dahomey," *Africa* 10, 3: 335–41.

1938 *Dahomey: An Ancient West African Kingdom.* 2 vols. New York: Augustin.

HOBHOUSE, LEONARD T., WHEELER, G. C. AND GINSBERG, M.
1915 *The Material Culture and Social Institutions of the Simpler People.* London: Chapman and Hall, Ltd.

HOGBIN, H. IAN AND WEDGWOOD, CAMILLA H.
1953 "Local Grouping in Melanesia," *Oceania* 23: 241–76; 24: 58–76.

HOLMBERG, A. R.
1950 *Nomads of the Long Bow; the Siriono of Eastern Bolivia.* Institute of Social Anthropology Publication 10. Washington: Smithsonian Institution.

HOMANS, GEORGE AND SCHNEIDER, DAVID M.
1955 *Marriage, Authority and Final Causes.* Glencoe: Free Press.

HOWARD, G. E.
1904 *A History of Matrimonial Institutions,* Vol. 1. Chicago: University of Chicago Press.

HOWELL, P. P.
1954 *A Manual of Nuer Law.* London: Oxford University Press.

HSU, FRANCIS L. K.
1942a "The Myth of Chinese Family Size," *American Journal of Sociology* 48: 555–62.

1942b "The Differential Function of Relationship Terms," *American Anthropologist* 44: 248–56.

1943 *Magic and Science in Western Yunnan.* New York: Institute of Pacific Relations.

HUNTER, MONICA
1936 *Reaction to Conquest.* London: Oxford University Press.

JAUSSEN, ANTONIN
1908 *Coutumes des Arabes au Pays de Moab.* Paris: J. Gabalda.

JOSHI, L. D.
1929 "The Khasa Family Law in the Himalayan Districts of the United Provinces of India." Allahabad: The Superintendent, Government Press.

KAPADIA, K. M.
1955 *Marriage and the Family in India.* London: Oxford University Press.

KEARNEY, R. J.
1925 "Sponsorship at Baptism According to the Code of Canon Law." Thesis: Catholic University of America.

KENNETT, AUSTIN
1925 *Beduin Justice.* Cambridge: Cambridge University Press.

KERR, M.
1952 *Personality and Conflict in Jamaica.* Liverpool: University of Liverpool Press.

KIRCHOFF, PAUL
1931 "Die Verwandschaftsorganisation der Urwaldstämme Südamerikas," *Zeitschrift für Ethnologie* 63: 85–193.

KIRKPATRICK, G. S.
1878 "Marriage and the Family in India," *The Indian Antiquary* 7: 86.
KORN, V. E.
1936 *Het Adatrecht van Bali.* Second revised edition. 's Gravenhage: G. Naeff.
KUMMER, BERNHARD
1931 "Gevatter," *Handwörterbuch des Deutschen Aberglaubens,* Vol. 3. Berlin: Walter de Gruyter and Co.
LAFONE QUEVEDO, SAMUEL A.
1919 "Guarani Kinship Terms as an Index of Social Organization," *American Anthropologist* 21: 421–40.
LANDA, DIEGO DE
1941 *Landa's Relación de las Cosas de Yucatán.* (A. M. Tozzer, trans.) Papers, Peabody Museum of American Archaeology and Ethnology, Harvard University, Vol. 18.
LAURIN, F.
1866 *Die Geistliche Verwandtschaft in ihrer geschichtlichen Entwicklung.* Archiv für Katholisches Kirchenrecht, vol. 15. Mainz.
LEACH, EDMUND R.
1955 "Polyandry, Inheritance and the Definition of Marriage," *Man* 55: 182–86.
——
1961 "Jinghpaw Kinship Terminology," *Rethinking Anthropology.* London: Athlone Press.
LE HÉRISSÉ, A.
1911 *L'Ancien Royaume du Dahomey: Moeurs, Religion, Histoire.* Paris.
LERNER, I. MICHAEL
1958 *The Genetic Basis of Selection.* New York: John Wiley and Sons.
LÉRY, JEAN DE
1880 *Voyage fait en la Terre du Brésil,* Gaffarel, Paris.
LÉVI-STRAUSS, CLAUDE
1949 *Les Structures Élémentaires de la Parenté.* Paris: Presses Universitaires de France.
LEVY, M. J., JR.
1952 *The Structure of Society.* Princeton: Princeton University Press.
——
1955 "Some Questions About Parsons' Treatment of the Incest Problem," *British Journal of Sociology* 6: 101–17.
LEWIS, BERNARD
1954 *The Arabs in History.* London: Hutchinson House.
LI, AN-CHE
1947 "Dege: A Study of Tibetan Population," *Southwestern Journal of Anthropology* 3, No. 4.
LIN, YU-TANG
1936 *My Country and My People.* New York: Reynal and Hitchcock.
LINTON, RALPH
1936 *The Study of Man.* New York: D. Appleton Century.
LOURIÉ, ALISA S.
1957 "Concepts in Family Sociology." Unpublished manuscript.
LOWIE, ROBERT H.
1920 *Primitive Society.* New York: Boni and Liveright.

1934 *An Introduction to Cultural Anthropology.* New York: Farrar and Rinehart, Inc.

LUNT, W. E.

1934 *Papal Revenues in the Middle Ages,* Vol. 2. New York: Columbia University Press.

LUTHER, M.

1520 "Von der Babylonischen Gefangschaft de Kirche: von de Ehe," *Reformatorische Schriften, Luther's Werke,* Vol. 2, 1924. Leipzig.

1539 "Tischreden: Anton Lauterbach's Tagebuch aufs Jahr 1539," in *D. Martin Luther's Werke,* Kritische Gesamtausgabe, Vol. 4, 1916. Weimar: H. Böhlau.

1900 *Sprichtwörtersammlung.* Thiele, ed. Weimar: H. Bölhaus nachfolger.

MC LENNAN, J. F.

1865 *Primitive Marriage.* Edinburgh: A. and C. Black.

MAGALHAES DE GANDAVO, PEDRO DE

1922 *The Histories of Brazil.* New York: The Cortes Society.

MAJUMDAR, D. N.

1944 *The Fortunes of Primitive Tribes.* Lucknow: The Universal Publishers, Ltd.

1953 "Children in a Polyandrous Society," *The Eastern Anthropologist* 6: 177–89.

1955a "Family and Marriage in a Polyandrous Society," *The Eastern Anthropologist* 8: 85–110.

1955b "Demographic Structure in a Polyandrous Village," *The Eastern Anthropologist* 8: 161–72.

MALINOWSKI, BRONISLAW

1927 *Sex and Repression in Savage Society.* London: Routledge and Kegan Paul.

1929 *The Sexual Life of Savages in North-Western Melanesia.* New York: H. Liveright.

1931 "Culture," *Encyclopedia of the Social Sciences,* Vol. 4: 621–46.

1932 *The Sexual Life of Savages in North-Western Melanesia,* 3rd edition with special foreword. London, Routledge.

MANDELBAUM, D. G.

1938 "Polyandry in Kota Society," *American Anthropologist* 40: 574–83.

MANGIN, FR. EUGENE

1921 *The Mossi.* Paris: Augustin Challmel.

MANNERS, R. A.

1950 "A Tobacco and Minor Crop Community in Puerto Rico." Unpublished manuscript.

MEAD, MARGARET
1961 "A Re-examination of the Problem of Incest." Paper read at the AAA Annual Meetings, Philadelphia, November 16–19.
MEEK, C. K.
1925 *Northern Tribes of Nigeria.* London: Oxford University Press.
———
1931 *Tribal Studies in Northern Nigeria.* London: Kegan Paul.
MÉTRAUX, ALFRED
1928 *La Religion des Tupinimbas.* Paris: E. Leroux.
MINTZ, S. W.
1950 "A Sugar-Cane Community in Puerto Rico." Manuscript.
———
1955 "The Jamaican Internal Marketing Pattern," *Social and Economic Studies* 4, 1: 95–103. University College of the West Indies, Jamaica, W.I.
MITCHELL, J. C.
1951 "The Yao of Southern Nyasaland," *Seven Tribes of British Central Africa,* M. Gluckman and E. Colson, eds. London: Oxford University Press.
———
1956 *The Yao Village; A Study in the Social Structure of a Nyasaland Tribe.* Manchester: Manchester University Press.
MORGAN, LEWIS HENRY
1907 *Ancient Society.* New York: Henry Holt and Co.
MORTON, NEWTON E.
1961 "Morbidity of Children from Consanguineous Marriages," Arthur G. Steinberg, ed., *Progress in Medical Genetics,* Vol. 1: 261–91. New York: Grune and Stratton.
MUKHERJI, ANIMA
1950 "The Pattern of Polyandrous Society with Particular Reference to Tribal Crime," *Man in India* 30: 56–65.
MULLER, H. F.
1913 "A Chronological Note on the Physiological Explanation of the Prohibition of Incest," *Journal of Religious Psychology* 6: 294–95.
MÜNCH, E.
1830 *Vollständige Sammlung Aller Älterer und Neueren Konkordate,* Vol. 1. Leipzig.
MUNSHI, K. M.
1955 "Foreword," *Social Economy of a Polyandrous People,* by R. N. Saksena. Agra: Agra University Press.
MURDOCK, GEORGE PETER
1934 *Our Primitive Contemporaries.* New York: Macmillan Company.
———
1949 *Social Structure.* New York: Macmillan.
———
1955 "Changing Emphasis in Social Structure," *Southwestern Journal of Anthropology* 11: 361–70.
———
1957 "World Ethnographic Sample," *American Anthropologist* 59: 664–87.

MURRAY, G. W.
1935 *Sons of Ishmael.* London: G. Routledge and Sons.

MUSIL, ALOIS
1928 *The Manners and Customs of the Rwala Beduins.* New York: American Geographical Society. Oriental Explorations and Studies No. 6.

NABHOLZ, H.
1941 "Medieval Agrarian Society in Transition," *Cambridge Economic History of Europe from the Decline of the Roman Empire,* Vol. 1. Cambridge: Cambridge University Press.

NEEDHAM, R.
1954 "The System of Teknonyms and Death-Names of the Penan," *Southwestern Journal of Anthropology* 10: 416–31.

NOBREGA, MANOEL DE
1931 *Cartas do Brasil, 1549–1560, Cartas Jesuiticas I.* Rio de Janeiro: Publ. da Academia Brasileira.

NOTES AND QUERIES IN ANTHROPOLOGY
1951 Sixth Edition. London: Routledge and Kegan Paul.

OPLER, MORRIS EDWARD
1941 *An Apache Life-Way.* Chicago: University of Chicago Press.

PARSONS, ELSIE C.
1936 *Mitla: Town of the Souls.* Chicago: University of Chicago Press.

—— 1945 *Peguche: A Study of Andean Indians.* Chicago: University of Chicago Press.

PARSONS, TALCOTT
1954 "The Incest Taboo in Relation to Social Structure and the Socialization of the Child," *British Journal of Sociology* 5: 101–17.

PARSONS, TALCOTT AND BALES, ROBERT F.
1955 *Family, Socialization and Interaction Process.* Glencoe: The Free Press.

PATAI, RAFAEL
1952 "The Middle East as a Culture Area," *The Middle East Journal* 6: 1–21.

PAUL, B. D.
1942 "Ritual Kinship: with Special Reference to Godparenthood in Middle America." Ph.D. thesis, University of Chicago.

PEHRSON, ROBERT N.
1954 "Bilateral Kin Grouping as a Structural Type," *Journal of East Asiatic Studies* 3: 199–202.

PLOSS, H.
1911 *Das Kind in Brauch und Sitte der Völker.* Third edition, Vol. 1. Leipzig: T. Grieben (L. Fernau).

PRINCE PETER OF GREECE AND DENMARK
1948 *Tibetan, Toda and Tiya Polyandry: A Report on Field Investigations.* Transactions of the New York Academy of Sciences, Series II, 10: 210–25.

—— 1955a "Polyandry and the Kinship Group," *Man* 55: 179–81.

—— 1955b *The Polyandry of Ceylon and South India.* Actes du IVe Congrès

International des Sciences Anthropologiques et Ethnologiques. Vienne (1952) 2: 167–75.

1955c *The Polyandry of Tibet.* Actes du IVᵉ Congrès des Sciences Anthropologiques et Ethnologiques. Vienne (1952) 2: 176–84.

1956 "For a New Definition of Marriage," *Man* 46: 35.

RADCLIFFE-BROWN, A. R.
1930–31 "Social Organization of Australian Tribes." Part I. *Oceania* 1: 34–64.

1935 "Patrilineal and Matrilineal Succession," *Iowa Law Review* 20, 2.

1941 "The Study of Kinship Systems," *JRAI* 71: 1–18.

1950 "Introduction," *African Systems of Kinship and Marriage,* A. R. Radcliffe-Brown and Daryll Forde, eds. London: Oxford University Press.

1953 "Dravidian Kinship Terminology." *Man* 53, Art. 169.

——, AND FORDE, DARYLL, EDS.
1950 *African Systems of Kinship and Marriage.* London: Oxford University Press.

RAGLAN, F. R. S.
1933 *Jocasta's Crime.* London: Methuen and Co., Ltd.

RANASINHA, A. G.
1950 *Census of Ceylon, 1946.* Vol. 1, Part I, General Report. Colombo: Government Press.

RATTRAY, R. F.
1929 *Ashanti Law and Constitution.* London: Oxford University Press.

RAULET, HARRY M.
1959 "A Note on Fischer's Residence Typology," *American Anthropologist* 61: 102–12.

REDFIELD, ROBERT
1930 *Tepotzlan: A Mexican Village.* Chicago: University of Chicago Press.

1947 "The Folk Society," *The American Journal of Sociology* 52: 293–308.

—— AND VILLA-ROJAS, ALFONSO
1934 *Chan Kom: A Maya Village.* Publications, Carnegie Institution of Washington, No. 448. Washington: Carnegie Institute of Washington.

RIVERS, W. H. R.
1906 *The Todas.* London: Macmillan and Company, Ltd.

ROBERTS, GEORGE W.
1957 *The Population of Jamaica.* Cambridge: Cambridge University Press.

ROJAS GONZALES, F.
1943 *La Institución del compadrazgo entre los Indígenas de México. Revista Méxicana de Sociologica* 5, 1.

ROSENFELD, HENRY
1957 "An Analysis of Marriage Statistics for a Moslem and Christian Arab Village," *International Archives of Ethnography* 48: 32–62.

SAHAGUN, B. DE
   1932 *A History of Ancient Mexico.* Fanny R. Bandelier, Trans. Nashville: Fisk University Press.
SAKSENA, R. N.
   1955 *Social Economy of a Polyandrous People.* Agra: Agra University Press.
SANDERS, I.
   1949 *Balkan Village.* Lexington: University of Kentucky Press.
SCHNEIDER, DAVID M. AND ROBERTS, JOHN M.
   1956 *Zuni Kin Terms.* Laboratory of Anthropology, Notebook 3, Monograph 1, University of Nebraska, Lincoln.
——, AND HOMANS, G. C.
   1955 "Kinship Terminology and the American Kinship System," *American Anthropologist* 57: 1194–1208.
SELIGMAN, BRENDA Z.
   1929 "Incest and Descent," *JRAI* 59: 231–72.

   1950 "The Problem of Incest and Exogamy." *American Anthropologist* 52: 305–16.
SHIROKOGOROFF, S. M.
   1929 *Social Organization of the Northern Tungus.* Shanghai: The Commercial Press, Ltd.
SIEMSEN, R.
   1942 *Germanengut in Zunftbrauch.* Berlin-Dahlem: Ahnenerbe-stiftung verlag.
SIMEY, T. S.
   1946 *Welfare Planning in the West Indies.* Oxford: The Clarendon Press.
SKINNER, ELLIOTT P.
   1957 "An Analysis of the Political System of the Mossi," *Transactions of the New York Academy of Sciences* 19, Ser. 2, 8: 740–50.

   1960a "The Mossi 'Pogsioure,' " *Man* 60: 20–23.

   1960b "Labor Migration and Its Relationship to Socio-Cultural Change in Mossi Society," *Africa* 30: 375–401.

   1960c "Traditional and Modern Patterns of Succession to Political Office Among the Mossi of the Voltaic Republic," *Journal of Human Relations* 8: 394–406.
SLATER, MARIAM KREISELMAN
   1959 "Ecological Factors in the Origin of Incest," *American Anthropologist* 61: 1042–59.
SMITH, M. G.
   1953 "Secondary Marriage in Northern Nigeria." *Africa* 23, 4: 298–323.

   1954 "Introduction," *Baba of Karo,* Smith, M. F. London: Faber and Faber.

   1955 "A Framework for Caribbean Studies." *Caribbean Affairs,* University College of the West Indies, Extra-Mural Department, Mona, Jamaica.

1957 "The African Heritage in the Caribbean," *Caribbean Studies: A Symposium.* Institute of Social and Economic Research, University College of the West Indies, Jamaica.

SMITH, RAYMOND T.
1955 "Jamaican Society Since Emancipation," *The Times British Colonies Review,* London.

1956 *The Negro Family in British Guiana.* London: Routledge and Kegan Paul.

1957a "Family Structure and Plantation Systems in the New World." Paper read at the Seminar on Plantation Systems in the New World, November, 17–23, San Juan, P. R. Mimeo.

1957b "The Family in the Caribbean," *Caribbean Studies: A Symposium.* Institute of Social and Economic Research, University College of the West Indies, Jamaica.

SMITH, W. ROBERTSON
1885 *Kinship and Marriage in Early Arabia.* Cambridge: Cambridge University Press.

SOARES DE SOUSA, GABRIEL
1851 *Roteiro do Brasil.* Revista do Instituto Historico e Geographico Brasileiro, T. 14.

1938 *Tratado Descriptivo do Brasil em 1587.* Nova edição. São Paulo: Campanhia editora nacional.

SOUSTELLE, JACQUES
1937 *La Famille Otomi-Pame de Mexique Central.* Paris: Institut d'Ethnologie.

SPICER, E.
1940 *Pascua: A Yaqui Village in Arizona.* Chicago: University of Chicago Press.

SRINIVAS, M. N.
1952 *Religion and Society Among the Coorgs of South India.* Oxford: Clarendon Press.

STADEN, HANS (1557)
1928 *The True History of His Captivity,* Malcolm Letts, ed. London: G. Routledge and Sons, Ltd.

STEINEN, KARL VON DEN
1894 *Unter der Naturvölkern Zentral Brasiliens.* Berlin: D. Reimer (Hoefer and Vohsen).

STEWARD, JULIAN H.
1949 "South American Cultures: An Interpretive Summary," *Handbook of South American Indians* 5: 669–772, Julian H. Steward, ed. Bureau of American Ethnology Bulletin 143.

STULPNAGEL, C. R.
1878 "Polyandry in the Himalayas," *The Indian Antiquary* 7: 132–35.

TAMBIAH, H. W.
1954 *The Laws and Customs of the Tamils of Ceylon.* Colombo.

TEMPLE, C. L.
1919 *Notes on the Tribes of Northern Nigeria.* Capetown: The Argus Printing and Publishing Co.

THEVET, ANDRÉ
1575 *La Cosmographie Universelle.* Paris: P. Huilier.

THOMAS, NORTHCOTE W.
1906 *Kinship Organizations and Group Marriage in Australia.* Cambridge: University Press.

THOMAS, W. I.
1937 *Primitive Behavior.* New York: McGraw-Hill.

TITIEV, MISCHA
1944 *Old Oraibi.* Papers of the Peabody Museum, Vol. XXII, No. 1.

TOMASIC, D.
1948 *Personality and Culture in Eastern European Politics.* New York: G. W. Stewart.

TREMEARNE, A. J. N.
1912a "Notes on Some Nigerian Head-Hunters," *JRAI,* 42: 136–200.

1912b *The Tailed Head-Hunters of Nigeria.* London: Seeley, Service and Co., Ltd.

TS'AO, CHAN
1929 *Dream of the Red Chamber* (C. C. Wang, trans.), Garden City, N.Y.: Doubleday, Doran and Co.

TUSCHEN, A.
1936 "Die Taufe in der Altfranzösischen Literatur." Thesis: Bonn.

TYLOR, E. B.
1861 *Anahuac.* London: Longman, Green, Longman and Roberts.

1889 "On a Method of Investigating the Development of Institutions; Applied to Laws of Marriage and Descent," *JRAI* 18: 245–69.

VASCONCELLOS, SIMAO DE
1863 *Chronica da Companhia de Jesu do estado do Brasil.* Lisboa: A. J. Fernandes–Lopes.

VILLA ROJAS, ALFONSO
1945 *The Maya of East Central Quintana Roo.* Publication, Carnegie Institution of Washington, No. 559. Washington: Carnegie Institute of Washington.

WAGLEY, CHARLES
1949 *The Social and Religious Life of a Guatemalan Village.* Memoir, American Anthropological Association, No. 71.

WARRACK, A.
1911 *A Scots Dialect Dictionary.* London: W. and R. Chambers, Ltd.

WASHBURN, SHERWOOD L., ED.
1961 *Social Life of Early Man.* Wenner-Gren Foundation Publications in Anthropology, No. 31.

WEEKLY, E.
1921 *An Etymological Dictionary of Modern English.* London: J. Murray.

WESTERMARCK, EDWARD
1894 *The History of Human Marriage.* London: The Macmillan Company.

———
1922 *The History of Human Marriage.* Vol. III. New York: The Allerton Book Company.

———
1929 *Marriage.* New York: Jonathan Cape and Harrison Smith.

WHITE, LESLIE A.
1949 "The Definition and Prohibition of Incest," *The Science of Culture:* 303–29. New York: Farrar, Strauss and Co.

———
1959 *The Evolution of Culture.* New York: McGraw-Hill.

WILSON, PETER J.
1961 "Incest—a case study." Paper read at the AAA Annual Meetings, Philadelphia, November 16–19.

WISDOM, C.
1940 *A Chorti Village in Guatemala.* Chicago: University of Chicago Press.

WISSLER, CLARK
1929 *An Introduction to Social Anthropology.* New York: Henry Holt and Co.

WOLF, E. R.
1950 "A Coffee Growing Community in Puerto Rico." Manuscript.

YOUNG, MICHAEL AND WILLMOTT, PETER
1957 *Family and Kinship in East London.* Reports of the Institute of Community Studies 1. London: Routledge and Kegan Paul.

YVES D'EVREUX
1864 *Voyage dans le Nord du Brésil,* F. Denis, ed. Leipzig et Paris: A. Franck.

ZBOROWSKI, M. AND HERZOG, E.
1952 *Life Is With People.* New York: International Universities Press.

ZINGG, R.
1938 *Primitive Artists: The Huichols.* University of Denver Contributions to Ethnology, Denver.

INDEX